D1083660

WOMEN, SPORT, AND CULTURE

Susan Birrell, PhD
The University of Iowa

Cheryl L. Cole, PhD
University of Illinois at Urbana-Champaign

Editors

Human Kinetics

Library of Congress Cataloging-in-Publication Data

Women, sport, and culture / Susan Birrell, editor, Cheryl L. Cole, editor.
    p. cm.
    Includes bibliographical references and index.
    ISBN 0-87322-650-X
    1. Sports for women--Sociological aspects. 2. Sex discrimination in sports. 3. Feminism. I. Birrell, Susan. II. Cole, Cheryl L.
GV709.W577   1994
796'.0194--dc20   93-38013
                                          CIP

ISBN: 0-87322-650-X

Acquisitions Editor: Richard D. Frey, PhD; **Developmental Editor:** Marni Basic; **Assistant Editors:** Valerie Hall, Ed Giles, and Matt Scholz; **Copyeditor:** Dianna Matlosz; **Proofreader:** Anne Byler; **Indexer:** Barbara E. Cohen; **Production Director:** Ernie Noa; **Production Manager:** Kris Slamans; **Typesetter and Text Layout:** Sandra Meier; **Text Design:** Keith Blomberg; **Cover Design:** Jack Davis; **Printer:** Edwards Brothers

Printed in the United States of America

10 9 8 7 6 5 4 3 2 1

Human Kinetics
P.O. Box 5076, Champaign, IL 61825-5076
1-800-747-4457

Canada: Human Kinetics, Box 24040, Windsor, ON N8Y 4Y9
1-800-465-7301 (in Canada only)

Europe: Human Kinetics, P.O. Box IW14,
Leeds LS16 6TR, England
0532-781708

Australia: Human Kinetics, P.O. Box 80, Kingswood 5062,
South Australia
618-374-0433

New Zealand: Human Kinetics, P.O. Box 105-231, Auckland 1
(09) 309-2259

Contents

PART V Sport and the Politics of Sexuality   323

Preface

This volume is published at a time when gender studies, sport studies, and most other academic disciplines are undergoing significant shifts. Rather than see these disruptions as "crisis" or threat, we see these disciplinary shifts as an attempt to come to terms with a kaleidoscopic interplay of historical conditions and related economic, cultural, and theoretical developments. The expansion of capitalism, multinationalism, and the related rapid forms of production and consumption mark an economic shift that has been called late capitalism, flexible accumulation, and post-Fordism. These shifts intervene in the possibility of a unified, cohesive, and isolated economy just as resistance from marginalized positions troubles and disrupts the dominant modernist narrative of unity, universalism, and transcendence. This combined intervention "structures" a postmodern condition and sensibility marked by notions of diversity, specificity, and the local.

The binary logic central to Western thought—structured around ontological oppositions like nature/culture, mind/body, human/animal, and human-animal/machine—has been destabilized, requiring and allowing for struggle over terms once taken for granted like *identity, body, science, knowledge*, and *sport*. The project of contemporary cultural theorists undertaken in response to these shifts and destabilizations can be understood as one that works to provide conceptual apparatuses that represent and help "us" make sense of the historical-material conditions that structure our lives and constitute our experience.

"Sport" does not stand outside the economic, cultural, political, and theoretical conditions in which it takes form and reform; sport and the bodies that stand at its center are always made and remade within particular histories and places. Theories of and around the field of sport studies have begun to (and we imagine will continue to) change as they develop and respond to conditions of postmodernity. One of the most important signs of this change is the broadening of what is conceptualized as the field and whose work is legitimated "within" and by the field.

Until quite recently, the work of sport studies has been produced, shaped, and confined within the institutional space given to and taken by the fields of physical education, kinesiology, human movement, and sport studies. One of the effects of this territorialization of "sport studies" has been the production of an "imaginary community" of scholars; that is, sport studies actively manufactured its own canon of scholars drawing from one particular disciplinary location and identity, attendance at self-promoted conferences, and publication in a limited number of journals. Although this disciplinary placement developed and legitimated the field within the academy, its once useful boundaries may now be seen as more constraining than enabling.

Feminism and cultural studies have clearly begun an interventionist project, although their influences may have unanticipated consequences. Although the legitimacy of the study of sport is no longer at stake, both of these theoretical traditions place into question exactly what constitutes "sport studies." The concurrent interventions of feminism and cultural studies have disrupted the boundaries historically surrounding the field, yet many of the presuppositions that have traditionally guided it have remained firmly in place. Most prominent among these presuppositions is the unquestioned acceptance of the received notion of "sport" and what counts as sport studies.

Early feminist work in the field of sport studies concentrated on questions around "exclusionary practices" and physiological issues embedded in or enacted through motivation, role conflict, and masculinity and femininity measurement scales. Later scholarship attempted to contextualize these exclusions of women in sports in relation to broader systems of exclusion and mechanisms of control: pornography, abortion, rape, sexual assault, surrogate mothering, and the commercialization of beauty. More recent feminist theory problematizes the very categories at the structural base of "women," "exclusion," and "control"; it interrogates and analyzes the production of sex/gender systems, identity effects, and bodies through practices associated with sport.

Drawing on insights from poststructuralism and postmodernism, feminist cultural studies, for example, problematizes the commonsense notion of "sport" as a seemingly self-evident category. Instead, what we take to be sport, what comes to count as sport, and therefore what is seen to fall properly under the rubric of a field called sport studies is a theoretical effect: a way of seeing (as well as a way of not seeing) produced through the conceptual apparatuses that structure (and limit) our field of vision. In other words, sport is not a given that somehow stands outside of our conceptual frame, but rather "sport" is an "object of knowledge" actively produced through our visual technology (theory). No doubt, then, each of the articles in this volume as well as the structuring frame has a theoretical (not merely empirical) stake.

We see *Women, Sport, and Culture* as a boundary text of sorts, one that begins the project of bringing together work from feminist-informed sport studies (itself an extremely uneven project) and from a feminist cultural studies perspective. To this end, we have included work by several scholars not typically cited or sighted in sport studies literature. We also see this boundary text on women, sport, and culture as part of an ensemble of practices that reflects and contributes to an analysis of the contemporary gendered landscape and the reconceptualization of the cultural significance of "sport."

This collection, like most edited volumes, is uneven but in what we think are important ways. By bringing together articles from varied theoretical positions, written at different points in the generation of feminist theory and sport studies, we have tried to establish a productive tension between traces of traditional scholarship and those theories working to trouble the structural base upon which that traditional work relies. Of course, not all of the traditions that collectively and individually constitute the discursive formation around women/sport are represented in this anthology. For example, those traditions (including role conflict) that theorize masculinity and femininity as properties of individuals and therefore attempt to measure and quantify their presence or absence are not included because the assumptions on which they rely have been heavily critiqued elsewhere.

The sections that comprise *Women, Sport, and Culture* organize the work into five dominant themes. Part I provides theoretical grounding for the volume, examining the politics and issues implicated in the matrix of gender/sport/culture. Part II provides varied analyses of the organizational and structural concerns that have been identified by feminists in sport studies. Part III examines the tensions generated by the reproduction and disruption of sport as a male preserve. Media texts and the representation of women's bodies as they appear in and are structured through and by sport are the topic of Part IV. Finally, the articles in Part V attempt to come to terms with the overlapping issues of gender, sexuality, and the body.

The interplay and intersections of the readings included in *Women, Sport, and Culture* address both multi- and antidisciplinary audiences interested in questions related to gender, the body, and sport. The selections are intended to be useful to teachers, scholars, graduate students, and upper level undergraduates who want to explore new objects, directions, and theories related to gender and sport.

We would like to acknowledge the contributions of the authors whose work is presented here. Many of these articles are reprinted from previous sources, but several have not been previously published. We appreciate the opportunity to bring this original work to print and to reprint our colleagues' other fine articles.

We owe a debt of gratitude to Rick Frey and Marni Basic for their continued patience and for their expertise in the process of publication. We also thank Carol Jasperson for her help in preparing the manuscript; Jay Coakley, the Center for Sport and Leisure, and the Department of Sociology at the University of Colorado, Colorado Springs for their financial support; Jennifer Joslin and Harry Denny for their research assistance; and Jodi Cressman for her comments and suggestions on the final draft of the manuscript.

Cheryl L. Cole
Susan Birrell

PART I

WOMEN, SPORT, AND IDEOLOGY

T he articles in this part serve as an introduction and overview of the diverse debates that have developed over the last two decades as scholars attempt to understand the complex relationships among gender, sport, culture, and power. Scholars who focus on the relationship between sport and gender are making increasingly significant contributions to the study of gender relations that go beyond the boundaries of the field as it has traditionally been conceived. The articles in this section suggest in different ways how attention to sport—and the issues of physicality, sexuality, power, and dominance that are played out in sport—increases our understandings of the dynamics of power that underlie contemporary gender relations. All five articles demonstrate how ideologies enacted through seemingly innocent games work to construct the boundaries and contours of our everyday experiences. Together, these articles map out the developments and debates in feminist theory as they relate to the study and practice of sport.

This anthology opens with Cheryl L. Cole's essay ''Resisting the Canon,'' which marks an intervention into the project of ''sport studies'' while laying out what might be understood as a tenable or viable feminist agenda for those interested in ''sport.'' Cole characterizes the intervention, feminist cultural studies, as an ongoing, counterdisciplinary, theoretical project that constantly revises and reworks the theoretical and political insights of socialist feminism, British cultural studies, and Foucault's work on power/knowledge/body. Reconceptualizing sport as a set of practices, knowledges, and disciplines, Cole argues, provides the theoretical and political space to redefine sport studies and to rethink the matrix of questions that constitute what has come to count as the object of knowledge for the field.

The first half of Cole's essay reviews the central political and conceptual issues addressed by socialist feminist theory and British cultural studies. The second half foregrounds Foucault's conceptualizations of bio-power and surveillance and the contemporary conservative political moment of late, postmodern surveillance-dominated capitalism in which the body is routinely invaded. Using the examples of bodily invasions legitimated by the war on drugs and the new reproductive strategies and debates, Cole suggests the need to consider the relationship among science, technology, and the body, particularly the potential for scientific interventions in an effort to develop bodies designed for sport.

Paul Willis's ''Women in Sport in Ideology'' develops a theoretical framework for understanding the exclusion of women from sport, based on the processes of ideology, hegemony, and the appeal to common sense. Although those in sport science are captivated by sex differences in athletic performance, Willis argues that the apparent performance differentials between the sexes are less interesting than ''the manner in which this gap is understood and taken up in the popular consciousness.'' Willis grounds his analysis in Marxist theory, arguing that sport is a particularly significant arena of gender relations because it is made to appear as though it is outside of real life. The central effect produced through and by sport is that differences between the sexes are natural and that men are naturally superior. In reality, Willis argues, sport is an ideological tool that produces and reproduces images of the domination of men over women in order to naturalize the gendered division of labor upon which the stability of the social order is imagined to depend.

Lois Bryson also shows how masculine hegemony is maintained in and through sport. She argues that the primary dynamics in this process concern the association of men with valued skills and with the sanctioned use of force and aggression. These dynamics are publicly played out in the sports arena through four concrete practices. First, definitions of sport (or what comes to count as sport in a particular culture), which are often male controlled, exclude women by defining their sporting tastes out of existence. Second, because women are excluded from positions of power and responsibility in sport-governing bodies and as coaches and administrators, even in women's sports, men rather than women are positioned to exercise direct control over women's sport. Third, women's sport is largely ignored by the media, thus producing the view that women's sports are not important. And finally, those achievements of women athletes that are reported are often trivialized and framed by patronizing comments. Though Bryson draws on Australian examples, her points are equally valid in the context of North American sport.

Michael Messner shows that gender relations around sport ''change and develop historically'' and must be understood in material context. He identifies the years from 1900 to 1920 and from post-World War II to the present as two periods of ''crisis in masculinity'' when sport served as an arena for struggle between the sexes. Women attempting to gain equality through control of their own bodies and through self-determination were met by masculinist backlashes. Consistent with the arguments of Willis and Bryson, Messner argues that in the present day, ''socially constructed meanings around the physiological differences between the sexes,'' male control of the structures of sport, and trivializing or obscuring media practices work to relegate women athletes and women in general to cultural margins. Messner argues persuasively that sport bolsters ''faltering ideologies of male superiority in the 20th century.''

Finally, the article by Cindy Himes Gissendanner explores the way that race operates alongside and with gender to construct subject positions for athletes, thereby troubling concepts like woman, femininity, and feminism.

Gissendanner exposes the racial and class biases of the Women's Division of the National Amateur Athletic Federation, a group that exercised almost hegemonic control over women's athletics between 1920 and 1960. While the Women's Division was promoting sporting practices for women that deemphasized athletic competition and sought to preserve a particular view of femininity, African-American men and women continued to value high-level competition for black women as an active part of the agenda for civil rights. In part, these differences are explained by the historical construction of black women's bodies and a black femininity that challenges the dominant (white) notion of femininity.

Gissendanner also reveals the class-based ideology of the Women's Division. Pointing out that the Women's Division was controlled by women physical educators from elite eastern colleges, she argues that their vision of sport programs for women often depended on the existence of expensive equipment and a large student body, neither of which was usually available in African-American college communities.

Chapter 1

Resisting the Canon:
Feminist Cultural Studies, Sport, and Technologies of the Body

Cheryl L. Cole
University of Illinois at Urbana-Champaign

The real political task in a society such as ours is to criticize the workings of institutions which appear to be both neutral and independent; violence which has always exercised itself obscurely through them will be unmasked, so that we can fight fear.

Michel Foucault, 1974, p. 171.

There are times in life when the question of knowing if one can think differently than one thinks, and perceive differently than one sees, is absolutely necessary if one is to go on looking and reflecting at all . . .

Michel Foucault, 1985, p. 8.

AN INTRODUCTION TO FEMINIST CULTURAL STUDIES

Contemporary critical theories (post-Marxisms, cultural studies, and feminisms) that take sport as their object of study share an understanding of sport as a site through which questions related to social and political power, domination, ideology, agency, and transformative possibilities must be considered.[1] However, few, if any, of the critics who work from these standpoints have noted or engaged the "crisis" generated by these theoretical interventions. This crisis is marked by the destabilization of the "object of knowledge," the category of sport itself, whose construction has been concealed by its representation as a merely classificatory term describing a discovered object. While this usual understanding of sport has enabled and produced our habits of thinking, knowledges, and truths, it has also shaped the way we see and imposed limits on the questions that structure our work. Stated a bit differently, the understanding one brings to (the organizing category) sport is always already embedded in a theoretical/political position, because any conceptualization of sport presupposes a relationship between power/knowledge and meaning/politics as well as a theory of power, its operations and mechanisms (typically liberal and/or repressive), and corresponding strategies of resistance and change.

This challenge (crisis) necessarily extends to and questions the usefulness of the received division of intellectual labor (the disciplined and imaginary community of sport studies) and disorients intellectual identities invested in and structured around ''sport.'' As such, the effect of critical work is one that challenges ''our'' habitual ways of thinking by problematizing received knowledges and the categories that form and constrain those knowledges (as well as what counts as the study of sport) and ''our'' intellectual identities.

This crisis-condition, of course, is not specific to sport studies; rather, it is one manifestation of the crises faced by all academic disciplines in a poststructuralist, postmodernist, and post-disciplinary era. The extent to which this crisis has remained obscured in sport studies is evidence of the effects of the dominant conceptualization of sport in terms of the isolating boundaries it has placed around the field and the knowledges and canon it has produced. This crisis across disciplines may lead to a broad reorganization in which the lines around various disciplines are redrawn or are at least made increasingly permeable, demonstrating the historical, temporary, and fragile ''nature'' of such alliances. Perhaps traditional disciplinary alliances will remain in place, but, rather than organizing around and legitimating themselves by erasing differences in the name of unity, they may learn to acknowledge and work with differences within, while simultaneously building alliances across fields.

My project is not one that seeks to completely reject or undermine a field of inquiry that calls itself ''sport studies'' but instead calls for a recognition of the crisis of ''sport studies'' and a reflexive relation to the category of sport. By comparison to the openings and possibilities created by the crisis, my goal in this paper is rather modest. The crisis of sport studies serves as the background for a project that attempts to begin rethinking the study of sport from a feminist standpoint that recognizes ''sport'' as a discursive construct that organizes multiple practices (science, medicine, technology, governing institutions, and the media) that intersect with and produce multiple bodies (raced, sexed, classed, heterosexualized, reproductive, prosthetic, cyborg, etc.) embedded in normalizing technologies (classification, hierarchization, identity production) and consumer culture. In addition, this standpoint recognizes that the knowledges and practices produced by sport in advanced capitalism cannot be and are no longer contained by institutional spaces but are dispersed and expressed in the everyday normalizing practices of remaking bodies, identities, and pleasures.

To initiate this project, I propose a conversation among socialist-feminism,[2] British cultural studies, and the work of Michel Foucault: feminist cultural studies.[3] Although each position (each of which is already multiple) contributes significantly to understandings of the relations among cultural practices, the body, and the reproduction of social formations, each offers insights to the others by borrowing from while revising their central organizing concepts. All three critique essentialism, economic reductionism, and the liberal-humanist subject and recognize the need to locate cultural practices within their social-historical specificity.[4] The conceptual apparatus produced at their intersection breaks with classical theories of power by reconceptualizing its location, modalities, and exercise from the state and its repressive effects to its productive effects at the everyday, bodily, local, and state (theorized in dispersion) levels.

Beginning with an introduction to the guiding tenets of socialist-feminism as these concepts have become informed by the theoretical underpinnings of cultural studies, I move to a general discussion of British cultural studies,[5] primarily as it has taken up the work of Louis Althusser. Next I discuss the theorization of the body in feminist cultural studies as it is understood at the crossroads of socialist-feminist theory, Althusser's conceptualization of the state, and Foucault's genealogy of power and technologies of the body/subjectivity. I conclude with a discussion of the relationship between the sport apparatus, culture, and women's bodies in the context of the current political climate in the United States; this discussion is also meant to demonstrate the complex relationships and regularities dispersed across sport and otherwise seemingly unrelated practices.

My position is not one that seeks a stable theoretical position or project. Instead, my intent is to propose a different agenda, one imagined as an ongoing exchange not only about sport and the technologies organized under and that traverse that term, but one that continually includes ''sport studies'' (including sport sciences) as part of its object of knowledge. This agenda seems essential for those whose work currently inhabits the category of ''feminist''—an alliance that itself may prove to be historically specific, temporary, and fragile.

KEY ELEMENTS IN SOCIALIST-FEMINISM

Socialist-feminism can be characterized as an element of feminist studies, the ''counterdisciplinary'' study of gender relations that developed out of the dialogues constituting the 1960s Women's Liberation Movement into a plural signifier for an increasingly uneven and destabilized discursive formation structured around the problematic of gender. Although a detailed overview is not possible here, I want to outline some of the key elements that have constituted socialist-feminist theory.

Socialist-feminism drew from, challenged, and reworked (directly and indirectly) the central organizing concepts of Marxist and radical feminist theory. The political concerns embedded in socialist-feminism have included issues related to domestic labor, child care, reproductive rights, health care, women workers, compulsory heterosexuality, lesbian rights, violence against women, and issues of representation.

The early theoretical work done under the sign of socialist-feminism was structured through two impulses that attempted to conceptualize the interdependence of patriarchy, gender, and capitalism. "Dual systems" theory viewed patriarchy and capitalism as separate but interrelated systems in which women's labor in the family was appropriated under capitalism (Eisenstein, 1979; Mitchell, 1971). A second approach, exemplified by Gayle Rubin's (1976) "The Traffic in Women," theorized patriarchy as a specific instance of a broader structuring sex/gender system, "a neutral term which refers to the domain and indicates that oppression is not inevitable in that domain, but is the product of the specific social relations which organize it" (p. 168).

The "sexual division of labor," viewed as an historical consequence of the separate spheres of work produced by capitalism, was central to the explanation of "women's" subordinate position. This concept drew attention to and emphasized domestic labor (housework and emotional and sexual work) and its role in reproducing labor power, the nuclear family unit, capitalism, and the state (see, for example, Barrett, 1988; Benston, 1969; Phelps, 1975). Familial relations were understood as embedded in economic relations, a division clearly evidenced today through the increasing feminization of poverty, including the structuring and reproduction of an economic-based (hetero)sexuality. This position suggested the state's interest in maintaining the family and its need to regulate women's sexuality and reproduction, specifically in terms of a heterosexuality contained in the home through the institution of marriage. This recognition led to the further recognition of compulsory or obligatory heterosexuality.

Socialist-feminism has examined those practices and ideological fields that organize and reproduce gendered economic relations and regulate women's sexualities, especially medicine, science, law, and the media. These include ideologies that reduce women to their reproductive capacities and naturalize emotional and domestic labor, ideologies of motherhood, ideologies that position and marginalize lesbians and some heterosexual practices as "abnormal," and ideologies that demonize sexually active women, as well as those ideologies that work to regulate child-bearing (e.g., abortion, panic-infertility, and fetal rights).

Although "gender" has remained a central organizing category in feminist thought, its initial framing as a cultural representation depended on a notion of sex/sexual difference grounded in biology, naturalized as a universal bodily property. The logical frame governing socialist-feminist thought was formed and bound by a series of binaries (sex/gender, nature/culture, mind/body, and sex/class), analytic priorities determined by Marxism (labor, class, and exploitation), and a theory of power as repressive and locatable. Three recent and related shifts in socialist-feminist work have challenged this frame: a politics based on difference among women, the increasing centrality of science and technology in everyday life, and a theory of representation that historicizes and destabilizes what comes to count as nature.

Although patriarchy, the sexual division of labor, and gender have remained central but contested concepts, their conceptualizations have become increasingly complex as they have been rethought across articulations of race, class, sexuality, the body, subjectivity, and agency. This (forced) recognition of diversity has brought into question the integrity of the category of ''woman'' while positioning the diversity of women's ''lived experience'' as a central concern (hooks, 1984; Lourde, 1984; Moraga & Anzaldua, 1981).[6] The binaries that structured and constrained the early frame have been disrupted as differences among women have become foregrounded.

Donna Haraway's (1985) ''A Manifesto for Cyborgs: Science, Technology, and Socialist Feminism in the 1980s'' marks an important shift in the socialist-feminist project. Haraway not only calls for an agenda that situates science and technology as important and serious sites of struggle, but she argues for a feminist sensibility structured around the contemporary economic and cultural politics of an info-technic dominated society that has altered the ''nature'' of organic, whole bodies and stable identities. Haraway argues that our condition/being is one organized by cyborg politics, a body-machine relationship that cannot return to natural or organic wholeness and that elides the possibility of or desire for a stable, unified identity. A progressive cyborg politics of resistance is built around fragmentation, partiality, and temporary alliances.

Finally, the early sex/gender distinction that inscribed sex in a dehistoricized nature and biological difference has been challenged (de Lauretis, 1987). Gender has been reframed as the process and a series of practices and effects that produce the possibility of two distinct sexes and whose target is the body/subject. This disruption has drawn attention to the making of the gendered body as a boundary form that marks, contains, and reproduces difference in a sex/gender system (Chapter 24, this volume; Epstein & Straub, 1991).

As Julia Epstein and Kristina Straub (1991) explain, sex/gender systems are ''historically and culturally specific arrogations of the human body for ideological purposes'' in which ''physiology, anatomy, and body codes (clothing, cosmetics, behaviors, miens, affective and sexual object choices) are taken over by institutions that use bodily difference to define and coerce gender identity'' (p. 3). By their view,

> distinctions between male and female bodies are mapped by cultural politics onto an only apparently clear biological foundation. As a consequence, sex/gender systems are always unstable sociocultural constructions. Their very instability explains the cultural importance of these systems: their purpose is to delimit and contain the threatening absence of boundaries between human bodies and among body acts that would otherwise explode the organizational and institutional structures of social ideologies. (p. 2)

The retheorization of the sex/gender system as a semiotics of corporeality and as a symbolic system that constitutes identities and self-representations requires an understanding of ideology and its mechanisms, the technology of gender, the construction of identities, and the politics of everyday lived experiences.

KEY ELEMENTS IN CULTURAL STUDIES

Cultural studies developed as a critical-counterdisciplinary response to the "culture and society" problematic. Just as a complete overview of feminist theory has become an impossible task, a complete codification of cultural studies would be misleading because of the complexity of positions that fall within its framework. As now popularized histories suggest, British cultural studies can be understood, in general, as a materialist theory occupying a space between its first impulse of culturalism that, in its extreme, emphasized creativity and structuralism that, in its extreme, moves to ideological determinism and poststructuralism (theoretical anti-humanism).

Applying the brush with broad strokes, cultural studies, as an intellectual and political tradition, developed in response to the massive cultural changes of postwar Britain (economic shifts, the increasing "Americanization" of mass culture, and the rise of youth and subcultures). Such efforts challenged and broke with the constraints of the disciplines dominant at the time: the elitist and conservative Leavis-inspired literary criticism, the reductionist models of Marxist theory, and the positivist models of social science.

The early works of Richard Hoggart (1957), E.P. Thompson (1963), and Raymond Williams (1958) have been canonized as the most influential texts in the development of cultural studies. Although initially embedded in contradictory discourses that maintained the elitist methodology of Leavis literary criticism (associated with moral-evaluative aesthetic judgment), these texts displaced the privileged position of "high culture" by shifting attention to working-class culture; they challenged a mechanistic Marxism that reduced culture to an epiphenomenon of the economy by shifting attention to the specificity and active role of cultural practices in the reproduction of social relations. In this sense, cultural studies can be understood as an elaboration of an undertheorized superstructure.

The culture-power relationship (each element recognized as complex and historically shifting) constitutes the central problematic of cultural studies. The Birmingham school broke from the elitism and limitations of earlier conceptualizations and moved to a more anthropological theory of culture as "a whole way of life" (or struggle) that included lived practices, belief systems, the ordinary, and high culture.

The category of culture has come to denote the broad arena of dominant and contested symbolic authority within complex and specific socio-historical "fields" and social formations (Brantlinger, 1990; Hall, 1980, 1983; Williams, 1977). Culture has been theorized as the site through which social relations are legitimated and mystified, the site through which the social order is constructed, categorized, experienced, regulated, and made meaningful and pleasurable— raising questions about the active production of identity, agency, and consent. In early cultural studies, culture was understood to exist within an already constituted social formation, theorized almost exclusively in class terms, and as constitutive of those relations.

The key terms and debated concepts influencing the culture/power problematic in British cultural studies have been taken up around a mutually informed constellation of elements drawn from structuralism and poststructuralism, the most influential of those tendencies drawn from Althusserian-informed notions of ideology and the social formation and Gramsci's theory of hegemony. In the United States, British cultural studies has been read alongside feminism, Foucault, and postmodernism. In this section, I focus on Althusser's work because of its tremendous influence on cultural studies and its usefulness for the feminist cultural studies project.

Despite determinist readings of Althusser's work, *For Marx* (1977) has been central in the development of cultural studies. In part, Althusser's project is illuminated in what has become a popular, but typically misread, reading of the essay "Ideology and the Ideological State Apparatuses: Notes Toward an Investigation" (Althusser, 1971), in which Althusser begins to theorize the role of ideology in the reproduction of the relations of material and cultural production and the production of the subject. Althusser's notion of ideology redirects the conception of it as "false consciousness," as an illusion imposed on the masses that ultimately can and will be dissolved in order that real conditions and interests of workers can be known. This conception of ideology marks a move away from a position that sets "the real" apart from systems of meaning. Hall (1985) describes the "false consciousness" thesis as "probably the most ideological conception of all" (p. 105).

Althusser conceptualizes ideology as the "relatively autonomous" web of meanings, categories, and discourse through which human beings become subjects and live out their relation to their world (i.e., ideology produces identities, consciousness, and subjectivities). Such a conceptualization displaces the autonomous, self-formed humanist/Cartesian subject as an ideological effect (the elementary ideological effect) and shifts to the decentered subject, a move necessary to avoid determinism and to rethink agency.

Althusser's concept of "relative autonomy" jars loose a notion of ideology as a simple effect of a more primary level, suggesting the interdependency of structure, ideology, and subjectivity. By Althusser's view, ideology is "a 'Representation' of the imaginary relationship of individuals to their real conditions of existence" (1971, p. 162). Ideology, as the "lived" relation between people and material conditions, works in the sphere of culture to naturalize ideas so that their origins are suppressed and the ideas become taken for granted, thereby validating and mystifying social relations.

The structural effect of ideology is to "interpellate" individuals as subjects. Althusser argues that "all ideology has the function (which defines it) of 'constituting' concrete individuals as subjects" (1971, p. 171). In this sense, ideology is not simply about domination through webs of representation; it is about the active construction of our "selves" as social beings through historically specific subject positions made available through the images we actively consume (and from which we derive pleasure). This notion of the subject accents Althusser's account of all reality as a construction. It is in this sense that Althusser discusses the interpellation of the individual and illuminates the need to theorize individual consciousness and the relationship between the individual, ideology, and power relations.

Teresa de Lauretis (1987) offers a concrete example of Althusser's notion of interpellation:

> Most of us—those of us who are women . . . probably check the F box rather than the M box when filling out an application form. It would hardly occur to us to mark M. It would be cheating or, worse, not existing, like erasing ourselves from the world. . . . For since the very first time we put a check mark on the little square next to the F on the form, we have officially entered the sex-gender system, the social relations of gender, and have become en-gendered as women; that is to say, not only do other people consider us females, but from that moment on *we* have been representing ourselves as women. Now, I ask, isn't that the same thing as saying that the F next to the little box, which we marked in filling out the form, has stuck to us like a wet silk dress? Or that while we thought that we were marking the F on the form, in fact the F was marking itself on us? (pp. 11-12)

De Lauretis's point demonstrates how ideology works to produce "a social representation [that] is accepted and absorbed by an individual as her (or his) own representation, and so becomes, for that individual, real, when it is in fact imaginary" (1987, p. 12). By this view, the belief that an individual is the author of her or his "own" thoughts and actions is an ideological effect; instead, people are "authored" through the interrelations of ideology, subjectivity, and power relations. At the same time, subject positions can never be fixed or guaranteed but are articulated within available historically specific positions. In this sense, power can be thought of as a struggle over individuals, experience, and subjectivity.

In the "ISA" essay (1971), Althusser explains the reproduction of the state by drawing a distinction between two interrelated groups of regulatory institutions based on their primary strategy of reproducing the relations of production. Those that Althusser characterized as Repressive State Apparatuses (RSAs) are primarily public and maintain a threat of physical force, although they are also ideological; those he characterized as Ideological State Apparatuses (ISAs) are primarily private and tend to extend and reproduce dominant ideology with the backing of the RSAs. Although a common critique of Althusser is related to functionalism, by his view the determining function of the ISAs is never completely fixed; they are the site of competing ideologies. Again, because individuals are the target of ideology, they, too, constitute a site of struggle.

Given the recognized significance of popular culture within cultural studies, the neglect of sport, especially given its immense popularity, constitutes a significant absence in this work. In the case where sport is conceptualized as a cultural practice, "sport" is taken to be only the tip of the iceberg and must instead be understood in its historical specificity, in relation to other technologies with which it intersects, and in relation to the reproduction of the social formation, meaning, and subjectivity. I consider these questions in relation to the body and women in the following section by introducing the work of Michel Foucault, who has opened different theoretical and political spaces that help us understand how the body is subjected by and embedded in a complex cultural politics.

THE BODY AS THE SITE OF CULTURAL POLITICS

Foucault's studies can be understood as an attempt to describe modern operations of power in which knowledge and the body are central. By his view (1979), the body is always already "in the grip":

> The body is directly involved in a political field; power relations have an immediate hold on it: they invest it, train it, torture it, force it to carry out tasks, to perform ceremonies and to emit signs. The political investment of the body is bound up, in accordance with complex, reciprocal relations, with its economic use; it is largely as a force of production that the body is invested with power and domination; but, on the other hand, its constitution as labour power is possible only if it is caught up in a system of subjection. (pp. 25-26)

Although feminist critiques produced in the 1970s and 1980s located the body as a site of power, many of the critiques, despite the diverse projects engaged, remained embedded in a politics of "violation" and a corresponding demand for "control over" women's bodies. Such projects locate the body in an unproblematized realm of the private, assume an individual that stands outside of cultural production, and theorize power as easily locatable. The move to "theorize the body" and the series of questions and studies it has generated mark an important moment in feminist cultural studies.

Although the general tendency in social theory has been to repress or erase the body, the recent surge of work on the body might be explained by a combination of the work done by Michel Foucault, the disruption of a series of binaries that have dominated and structured Western thought (nature/culture; mind/body; sex-biological/gender-cultural; organic/machine), and a political climate in which bodies occupy pivotal positions in political struggles. The current juncture, marked by AIDS, the so-called "war on drugs," reproductive politics, new technologies, the Human Genome Project, and the like, has foregrounded the body/power relation, illuminating the role of the body as a central ideological resource, especially its position of management in a raced/sex-gender system in advanced capitalism. In other words, the contemporary political situation has amplified the need to (re)theorize the body as the site of cultural politics struggle.

Elizabeth Grosz (1987) defines corporeal feminism as challenging the body as a prediscursive, stable materiality by taking the body as "the primary object of social production and inscription, located within a network of socio-historical relations" (p. 1). This position makes clear the intersection of the concerns articulated by feminist theory, especially its attempt to recognize the politics of the personal, and Michel Foucault's concern with the body and power.

Much of Foucault's work, especially *Discipline and Punish* (1979) and *The History of Sexuality* (1980), attempts to explicate modern operations of power in which knowledge and the body are central. Although Foucault challenges the reduction of power to repression or to a single effect as inadequate and misleading, his notion of power, especially as he articulates the body/power/knowledge relationship, can be understood as an elaboration of Althusser's discussion of the reproduction of the state in terms of the processes, strategies, and mechanisms of power associated with RSAs and ISAs.

Foucault's account of power in *Discipline and Punish* (1979) is concerned with the relationship between the changing conditions and needs of an emerging industrial society and its power techniques of discipline and punishment that permeate a wide range of institutions, including prisons, the army, schools, and factories. In its modern forms, power is not possessed by or located in individuals or a particular space; it does not function simply through exclusion or repression. Instead, power works as a microphysics, as capillary-like strategies and tactics that operate on a microlevel in and through everyday practices. As a result, Foucault was concerned with power in terms of local and daily practices and struggles, struggles located in the network and web of power.

Foucault used the architectural effect of the Panopticon, a prison designed by Jeremy Bentham, to demonstrate how modern power works to produce docile bodies, that is, the manipulation, subjection, and regulation of bodies in time and space. The effect of the Panopticon was one of self-regulation generated through a "presence of control" and a dissymmetry of vision: A tower light at the center of the circular structure continuously lit each cell, producing an illusory unending ubiquitous surveillance. This illusion produced the convict-in-isolation who could (apparently) always be seen but who could not locate or see the observer and produced a new form of consciousness marked by self-policing (i.e., the efficient and automatic exercise of power in a disciplinary society). Such a model "dissociates power from particular people, investing it in a topographical configuration of light, bodies, gaze and architecture" (Boyne, 1990, p. 112).

Following from Foucault's notion of technologies of bodily production, sport can be understood as an institution whose central feature is one of discipline and surveillance.[7]

SPORT TECHNOLOGIES, BODIES, AND CULTURE

Sport remains a particularly powerful ideological mechanism because it is centered on the body, a site of semiotic condensation whose manifest meaning is intimately bound to the biological. The biologistic knowledges (Foucault's truth-effects) and their appeal to the natural (the body-narratives) work to dissolve the traces of cultural and productive labor on and the training of the body and its movements. The "logic" of the sport/body combination, the seemingly free display of bodies in motion, contributes to an illusion that sport and its bodies are transparent, set apart from politics, culture, and the economy, and extends beyond popular discourses into the critical scholarship of culture, power, and sport. As discussed in the introduction, a frame that limits the study of "sport" to its relationship to broader social inequalities constrains the possibility of intertextual interpretation and analysis (a shift necessary to understand the tensions and effects produced by the multiple categories that traverse the category of sport).

In this section, I want to consider the re/makings of the gendered body, specifically women's bodies, primarily within the contemporary cultural context of late, postmodern capitalism.[8] This section is interested in those cultural practices/discourses that, despite their apparent separateness, remain bound within and to the ensemble of practices that dominate conservative politics in the U.S. and tend to work to reproduce the state. Sport, in this context, is most usefully understood as a technology in the Foucauldian sense: an ensemble of knowledges and practices that disciplines, conditions, reshapes, and inscribes the body through the terms and needs of a patriarchal, racist capitalism (Cole, 1990, 1991).

WOMEN: THE RE/MAKINGS OF THE FEMININE BODY

Numerous feminist critics have argued that women's physicality and participation in sport offer the space for potentially oppositional or transgressive practices and a site for progressive body politics because they challenge the passivity inscribed on "women's bodies." However, most of these arguments have obscured the politics of late, surveillance-dominated capitalism, a context in which the body and exercise have become commodified in ways that manage gender relations. As Willis (1990) has argued, the gender-perfect "hard-bodies" that saturate the culture of the Reagan/Bush era "may represent the most highly evolved commodity form yet to appear in late-twentieth-century-consumer capitalism" (p. 6).

Although Foucault neglected the gendered forms of body technologies, his explanation of the body/power relationship has served as an important background for understanding the making of the feminine body. For example, Sandra Bartky (1988) and Susan Bordo (1988) have demystified and emphasized the everyday technologies of femininity that produce a gendered-docile body. Technologies of femininity refer to those knowledges, practices, and strategies that manufacture and normalize the feminine body; to those techniques, actions, and structures deployed to sculpt, fashion, and secure bodily shapes, gestures, and adornments that are recognizably female, especially as they are taken up within dominant lifestyle politics and disciplinary practices embedded in a discourse of "democratic bodies" permeating contemporary culture.

In this case, the female body can be understood as more docile, malleable, and impressionable than the masculine body and as subject to regimes of everyday bodybuilding in order to produce a normalized self-presentation and feminine identity. Such rituals are aimed at developing a feminine body; a body that is slim, tight, and small-breasted; a body that signifies deference through its posture, movements, and gestures; and a bodily surface disciplined for adornment (Bartky, 1988; Bordo, 1991).

The ongoing body management required to produce and maintain the feminine body within its narrow boundaries is a reminder that the body is always in the process of "becoming," albeit within certain historical and cultural constraints (the availability of technologies and body codifications traversed by broader configurations of gender, race, class, and sexuality). As such, the making of the feminine body requires individual labor (desire and time) and is dependent on various industries (workout clubs, video programs, diet industry, active wear, and science). The continual need for body work simultaneously indicates the instability and duplicity of the naturalized body and thus the possibilities of intervening in dominant bodily codifications.

Although historical fictions of naturally weak and passive female bodies are called into question through women's participation in popular forms of bodybuilding, exercise, and aerobics, women's physical culture is embedded in and structured through a gendered panoptic—the exercise of power. Rather than working as technologies of transgression, exercise and aerobics tend to be normalizing technologies that produce fashionable "dress for success" bodies embedded in promises of material gains; in other words, they are practices invested in the status quo (Schulze, 1990).

This new feminine aesthetic—versatile, athletic, hard, and slick—represents a new dimension in the historical-cultural map of gender body-styles, the health/beauty/exercise complex, and commodity production. This is the culture where beauty, fashion, and style meet Richard Simmons, Jane Fonda, Crystal Light (after all, it believes in us—why shouldn't we believe in it?), *Cosmopolitan*, body by and body *buy* Nautilus, spandex, and cosmetic surgeries of every stripe—now familiar images that punctuate the popular and economic landscape. This aesthetic might be most completely characterized as the "aerobicized-nautilized-Jane Fonda-SlimFast-subject" hailed into the demands and profit-enhancing practices of capitalism. In this cultural logic, women produce themselves as commodities: identities, exchange value, and self-worth are embedded in body management. The potential gender/body transgressions sought by feminist critics have been recuperated to a great extent through body-marketing practices in consumer culture.[9]

Linda Singer (1989) refers to this body-politics as the "new sobriety [that] constructs a body well-designed for the complexities of life in late capitalism, which requires a worker's body and a body of workers that are well-managed in the way a portfolio is well-managed" (p. 56). Singer's depiction aptly summarizes the current state of women's bodies:

> Given that women's place is often constructed in self-effacing service, it is not surprising that female disciplinary strategies often take the form of radical self-denial, as in the case of bodily practices such as anorexia and bulimia. But the well-managed female body of the 80s is constructed so as to be even more multi-functional than its predecessors. It is a body that can be used for wage labor, sex, reproduction, mothering, spectacle, exercise, or even invisibility, as the situation demands. It is also a body that is constructed to accommodate the variable whims of fashion, and a postmodern aesthetic which demands the capacity to project a multiplicity of looks and attitudes with apparent effortlessness. (p. 57)

Susan Bordo (1991) refers to these obsessions with self-representation as a "plastic paradigm"—a Taylorism of the body manufactured within an ideology of limitless improvement, an ideology supported by science and its technologies. Although Bordo's article reads more like William Gibson's cyberpunk novels, which depict surgical boutiques and multiple plastic surgeries as everyday elements of the cultural landscape, she familiarizes and concretizes her description as she talks about "Knifestyles of the Rich and Famous" (a monthly feature of *Details* magazine) and as she describes the new postmodern body aesthetic embellished in a rhetoric of self-determination and choice (democratic bodies). But, of course, not *any* body will do for oneself or other women.

The "surface effects" of bodily practices and micro-powers erase the labor, time, and conditions that make those bodies possible and desirable. The new feminine body, the woman intertwined with a Nautilus machine, is the expression of the postmodern-embodied gendered-panoptic subjectivity, the "woman" whose scrutiny extends beyond her own body to other feminine bodies. This gendered surveillance produces contempt for gender ambiguity and "bodies of excess" as the power relations and the conditions that produce those bodies are effaced (Schulze, 1990; Willis, 1990).

RETHINKING WOMEN'S BODYBUILDING, COMMUNITY, AND SURVEILLANCE

To a great extent, feminist interest in the semi-documentary "Pumping Iron II: The Women" is linked to the transgressive potential of the gender ambiguity of women bodybuilders. (The film is concerned with the relationship between women's muscular development and practices of cooptation and recuperation.)

Such interest is demonstrated by the concern with the cultural significance of the muscularity developed through bodybuilding and the conflict posed between muscularity and femininity (cf. Balsamo in this volume; Kuhn, 1988; and Holmlund in this volume). Such accounts suggest that bodybuilding at least potentially challenges the naturalized order by calling into question the natural-body and undermining the truth of the passive-female body.

In addition to raising questions posed by feminist critics like Balsamo and Holmlund, "Pumping Iron II" provides an opportunity to consider how, in the complex dynamic of recuperation, the technologies of gender work to distance women from one another and contribute to an isolation-effect that interferes with the development of community and the recognition of common interests. For example, the multiplication of privatized workout spaces for women through private clubs, television exercise programs, and video exercise has the effect of isolating women from one another (Willis, 1990). As Willis explains,

> The private spa, then, offers escape from the job or domestic space, but it severely limits the possibility for conversation and community. This is because the woman who participates in aerobics at a spa is made to see herself as an isolated individual. The atmosphere of the spa promotes an aura of body rivalry. Mirrors are everywhere. Women compare but do not share themselves with others. . . . They scrutinize their lines and curves to check out who's wearing the hottest leotard. (p. 7)

This isolation-effect can also be seen in "Pumping Iron II." A duplicitous "community" is structured around a solidarity against the gender-ambiguous and potentially transgressive bodies of Bev and Carla, both positioned as the Other in the film. Although Bev and Carla express their love for strength and their admiration of the strong and powerful, Rachel McLish wants to be every *woman's* ideal, a strong Barbie doll by her view. Like Rachel, the other women competitors stress their desire for the perfect body (the object of male desire), the expression of the internalized gaze, a desire that undermines the possibility of community. The effect produced is both dystopic and recuperative—men negotiate the relationships among the women while women are distanced from one another.

This feminine aesthetic is inscribed in heterosexual desire and compulsory heterosexuality (Schulze, 1990, p. 62). In "Pumping Iron II," the central competitors, with the exception of the one African-American contestant, are positioned in relation to a male (read: heterosexuality). The heterosexualization of these bodies marks the inscription of the now familiar familial ideology and, by extension, the production of the new "reproductive body."

WOMEN AS SUSPECTS:
TECHNOSCIENCE, BOUNDARIES, AND REPRODUCTION

The production of bodies, the regulation of bodies, and our relation to bodies have been modified in advanced capitalism. The body/sport relationship is now part of a social formation dominated by perfect-bodies, moral panics, the "logic of epidemic" incited and legitimated around AIDS, drug use, the regulation of sexual practices and representation, and reproductive struggles. The logic of epidemic is central to a discursive formation of "pure body" politics that has increasingly legitimated and in fact requires state intervention (surveillance/control) into the social and individual bodies. Throughout the 1980s, it was made clear that this regulated order works to maximize productivity and to reproduce the compulsory heterosexuality required in a politics of so-called traditional family values.

The practices that constitute the sport-apparatus contribute to the illusory pure, uncontaminated body that dominates a popular landscape characterized by Kroker and Kroker (1987) as "body McCarthyism": the era of the body under siege, body invasion practices, and, most disturbing, the increasing public consent to such invasive practices. The history of the multiple sites that constitute sport is one in which routine surveillance practices have been legitimated, including the *overall* increased scrutiny of pure bodily fluids, especially as increased surveillance has been legitimated through a "war on drugs" rhetoric. In this case, we might consider the now familiar arguments about drugs invading the "pure space" of sport that remind us that sport serves as society's uncontaminated immune system; the arguments proposed in the name of "fair competition" that normalize and make clear "the need" to subject athletes to increased surveillance; and the media hype around Len Bias's death that produced heightened hysteria and racism in the name of the "war on drugs."

The relationship(s) between surveillance practices in sport and the body-invasions by the state were made clear in 1990 by Gerold Wolf, the superintendent of Melvindale Northern Allen Park School, when he explained his support for the school board's decision to test all 7th- to 12th-grade cheerleaders and athletes for drugs. Wolf argued that this testing was legitimate because "drug testing will reflect the values and opinions of this community" and that it would be in the best interests of the students because "drug testing will be part of their [the students'] life" (Hentoff, 1990, p. 6). In other words, the practice of drug testing, an invasion of bodies and surveillance of bodily fluids in violation of the Fourth Amendment, is legitimated by appeals to the students' involvement with sport, community values, and the manufacture of consent.[10] This bodily invasion is part of a broader pattern of surveillance—a "general regulatory scheme" whose forms are gender-, race-, and class-specific, a point I will discuss.

As demonstrated by the apparatus of and rationale for "drug testing" in sport, the athletic body is always already a suspicious body (because sport participation is sufficient cause to suspect tamperings with the "biological-body") and therefore is a body subject to routine monitoring and invasions designed to detect "illegal" substances and abnormalities. This suspicion, or the athlete as suspect, is to a great extent produced at the intersection of the myth of sport, the myth of the pure/natural body, and the significance of sport in the production of national identities. However, "suspicion" and its corresponding technologies of normalization take explicitly gendered forms whose manifestation is amplified by and legitimated through what have been called "sex tests," "gender verification," and "femininity controls" (Sport Canada, 1991).

The histories of women in general and the athletic female body more specifically are embedded in suspicion, bodily/biological examination, and bodily probes and invasions (Cahn, 1992; Cole, 1991; Patton, 1992; Terry, 1989, 1990). The suspicion inscribed on the athletic woman can be traced to early theories of homosexuality in which "homosexuality" was a symptom of or caused by gender inversion. Such theories led to attempts to locate homosexuality (gender deviance) in the body through bodily examinations aimed at detecting evidence of gender inversion (bodily deviance), which at least initially for lesbians meant a bodily search for masculinity (Chauncey, 1982/83; Terry, 1990). The female athletic body was and remains suspicious because of both its apparent masculinization and its position as a border case that challenges the normalized feminine and masculine body. This suspicion of gender deviance inscribed on women in sport is intertwined with and has been used to produce nationalism and anti-communist sentiment (Patton, 1992).

Although official stories of biological surveillance situate sex testing in sport in the 1960s, there are accounts of sex testing (physical inspections) as early as 1936 (Cahn, 1992). Technologies of gender verification, institutionalized during the 1960s when women participating in the Olympic Games were subjected to routine bodily examinations, have shifted from external physical inspection to buccal smears and chromatin screening to determine chromosomal "normality" and deviance: Deviation from the female karyotype disqualifies a competitor from competing as a female. Although the validity of these examinations has been repeatedly challenged by various medical and sport organizations, the tests remain part of the regulatory regime to which high-level female athletes are subjected. Additionally, gender verification tests constitute one element in a matrix of surveillance and policing practices of the boundaries around gendered bodies.

Keeping this in mind, I want to conclude with a discussion of the relations among the new "reproductive body" (another form of women as suspect), scientific panopticism, and its potential links to exercise and sport. In *The History of Sexuality*, Foucault (1980) elaborates the modern character of power in terms of biopolitics. As Foucault explained, biopolitics as a technology

> focused on the species body, the body imbued with the mechanics of life and serving as the basis of the biological processes: propagation, births and mortality, the level of health, life expectancy and longevity, with all the conditions that can cause those to vary. Their supervision was affected through an entire series of interventions and regulatory controls: a biopolitics of the population. (p. 139)

Given this, it is clear that contemporary "views" of the body, health, exercise, and reproduction are embedded in biopolitics.

In "The Body Invaded: Medical Surveillance of Women as Reproducers," Jennifer Terry (1989) discusses the relations among new scientific/surveillance technologies, the reproductive body, and fetal politics in relation to the "climate of suspicion" generated in an historical moment dominated by what has been discussed in this paper as a logic of epidemic. In an age of moral panic related to AIDS and drug use and the reterritorialization of the ideological-private, a "climate of suspicion" has been generated in which pregnant women or, more generally, women of childbearing age have become positioned as "suspects." Terry's project considers how the logic of biopolitics works in contemporary U.S. culture to legitimate routine invasions of women's bodies through various technologies (e.g., sonograms, X–rays, genetic fingerprinting) that constitute the "new scientific panopticon." Building on Foucault's discussion of vision and Haraway's (1985) arguments about the body/technology relationship, Terry discusses the new scientific panopticon as one that

> moves into a different logic of visual power by its literal penetration of the body. The individual subject is penetrated and disaggregated into various component parts whose codes must be read and interpreted, not merely seen. Her blood, sweat and tears—and DNA—are collected and decoded. She literally cannot claim the status of individual or coherent liberal subject, but is instead an aggregate or network of coded sequences. These coded sequences provide evidence of any 'risks' the subject embodies. . . . [I]t creates a crisis in asserting the language or political rhetoric of right to (bodily) privacy and protection against bodily invasions. (p. 17)

Scientific technology has produced fetal images that work to establish the fetus as an entity independent of the mother's body (Petchesky, 1987; Terry, 1989). Such images are then taken up to produce the fetus as "individual" and to set in place the appearance of an adversarial mother-fetus relationship in which the pregnant woman's body is viewed as a threat to the fetus. Given the state's obligation to "protect" the rights of its citizens, the state appoints itself surrogate for the fetus, the citizen who cannot speak for itself, but whose rights, in terms of life, and its right to a healthy life, the state is obligated to protect. The fetus becomes a surveillance mechanism and state interests are pursued through surrogacy politics and a logic of neo-eugenics.

The series of practices and politics initiated and legitimated through claims of protecting the rights of the fetus to be born healthy suggest that potentially pregnant and pregnant women may eventually be required to participate in particular "health" practices designed to ensure the health of the fetus, including mandatory exercise programs.

On the other hand, suspected pregnancy and fetal rights issues may become grounds for mandatory pregnancy testing of female athletes. For example, although Guideline 3-B in the *National Collegiate Athletic Association Sports Medicine Handbook* (1992) indicates that there is no evidence that suggests that "exercise at submaximal levels" has any adverse effects on pregnancy, it also suggests that pregnant women should not participate in sports that require "sustained maximum performance" because such performance levels "may be harmful to mother and fetus" and fetal growth may be adversely affected by body temperatures in excess of teratogenic threshold (p. 32).

Mandatory pregnancy testing became the topic of debate during the spring of 1992, when Gary Torgeson, the coach of the women's softball team at California State University at Northridge, suspected that a player was pregnant, despite her insistence to the contrary. Torgeson argued that he was concerned about her pregnancy because "harm could come to her and her baby" because the woman was a pitcher (a high-risk behavior by Torgeson's view). Torgeson appealed to the NCAA's mandatory and routine drug-testing policy in an effort to legitimate his call for mandatory pregnancy testing (Torgeson, 1992). Elizabeth Arendt, MD (1992), a University of Minnesota team physician, also argued that the incident at Northridge "raised concerns about the protection of the school's rights and the rights of the unborn child" (p. C14). Given this, Arendt argued, team physicians and trainers should have complete access to lists of medications that athletes are taking, and athletes suspected of being pregnant should be required to take physical examinations. Arendt also appealed to a drug-testing-like model to identify pregnancy among those female athletes who might be compelled to lie about their pregnancy status.[11]

Related to the current debates around reproduction is the Human Genome Project, the international project to map and sequence the 3 billion pairs of DNA that makes a possibility what once appeared to be a science fiction fantasy of bodies designed for enhanced sport performance. The Human Genome Project, developments in molecular genetics, and attempts to determine genetic links to sport performance have clear implications for the sport world, including reproductive and racial issues. According to Claude Bouchard (1991), the developments of the Human Genome Project will extend research that has probed bodies in search of genetic links to sport performance and may lead to the "in vitro fertilization of gametes" from donors selected on the basis of some phenotypical criteria or "the presence of desired genetic polymorphisms" (p. 460).[12]

Not only do women have clear stakes in this project, but given the racist history of eugenics and the racist research that has probed African-American bodies in an attempt to identify traits that lead to enhanced sport performance, we might imagine that the Human Genome Project will intensify such racist projects.

Featherstone (1991) argues a related point in his discussion of sport and contemporary medical efforts in the areas of genetics and neo-eugenics:

> The potential consequences here for, to take an example, sport are tremendous. Not only is there the capacity to enhance performance and repair, or replace body parts to produce cyberbodies. There is also the potential to genetically design optimum types of bodies best suited for particular sports. Once the social restrictions of genetic engineering become weakened there will be little to stop the progressive realization

of these capacities. Genetic engineering is already practiced and it ceases to be a figment of the science fiction writer's imagination that we will one day have the capacity to produce human beings who have the capacities of birds or fishes and can be designed to function in a range of possible environments. (p. 11)

CONCLUDING "OBSERVATIONS"

As the "cultural production of bodies" is situated as a problematic central to the sport studies agenda, we need to engage with and simultaneously depart from understandings that limit "sport" and what counts as sport to its institutional forms. Such a supposedly fixed conceptualization constrains the possibility of understanding how the sport apparatus works in relation to and at the intersection of multiple technologies and in ways that always exceed institutional boundaries. Along with a variety of other cultural (including scientific/technological) and economic shifts, change has occurred in sport, the multiple forms that it takes, and the ways and means through which we experience it in our everyday lives. The dispersion of sport technologies represents only one manifestation of the contemporary political situation. The new agenda developed under the sign of feminist cultural studies requires rethinking the categories of and relations among sport, gender, sexuality, nature, the body, race, class, difference, science, power, representation, subjectivity, and opposition. The contemporary conditions in which we live also suggest a new agenda that addresses the Human Genome Project, AIDS, drug-testing, sex-testing, new reproductive technologies, technologies of gender, technologies of race, sport sciences—and this is only the beginning of the list of possibilities.

In the age of cyborgs, pure-body politics, plastic bodies, scientific panoptics, and increasing state interventions, we need to reconsider how sport, exercise, and the politics of fitness (knowledges, discourses, and technologies) are deployed in our everyday lives. In the age of body McCarthyism, we might ask: What sorts of practices and technologies are being produced through the medicine-sport combination to legitimate state interventions in our everyday lives? What sorts of medicalized exercise are being produced around pregnant women in an age where they have become "suspect"? Given the long history of medical interventions in women's reproduction, how will the new reproductive technologies be used in the so-called sport world? Will we see a future of genetically designed sport-bodies? How will women be affected by such a project? What sort of racist implications are embedded in such a project? How will the new surveillance technologies take up the sport-body as an increasing number of athletes are found to be HIV-positive?

While my focus has been on what appears to be a dystopic present and I have projected a similar dystopic, technological, science fiction–like future (similar to that of Margaret Atwood's *The Handmaid's Tale*, 1985), Haraway (1985) reminds us that not only do we always have to work from within the conditions that we find ourselves, but we must learn to always "see" with "double vision" in an effort to locate the struggles and possibilities. Given these conditions and the new technologies of power, we will also have to generate a different set of questions related to resistance, struggle, and oppositional politics.

REFERENCES

Althusser, L. (1971). *Lenin and philosophy and other essays*. (B. Brewster, Trans.) New York: Monthly Review Press.

Althusser, L. (1977). *For Marx*. London: Verso.

Andrews, D. (1993). Desperately seeking Michel: Foucault's genealogy, the body, and critical sport sociology. *Sociology of Sport Journal, 10*, 148-167.

Arendt, E. (1992, October 13). Teams have a right to know players' physical status. *USA Today*, p. C14.

Atwood, M. (1985). *The handmaid's tale*. New York: Fawcett Crest.

Balsamo, A. (1991). Feminist cultural studies: An overview. *Journal of the Midwest Modern Language Association, 24*, 50-73.

Barrett, M. (1988). *Women's oppression today: The Marxist/feminist encounter* (rev. ed.). London: Verso.

Bartky, S. (1988). Foucault, femininity and patriarchal power. In I. Diamond and L. Quinby (Eds.), *Feminism & Foucault: Reflections on resistance* (pp. 61-86). Boston: Northeastern University Press.

Benston, M. (1969). *The political economy of women's liberation*. Bay Area Radical Education Project.

Birrell, S. (1989). Racial relations and sport: Suggestions for a more critical analysis. *Sociology of Sport Journal, 6*, 212-227.

Birrell, S. (1990). Women of color, critical autobiography, and sport. In M.A. Messner & D.F. Sabo (Eds.), *Sport, men and the gender order: Critical feminist perspectives* (pp. 185-199).

Bordo, S. (1988). Anorexia nervosa: Psychopathology as the crystallization of culture. In I. Diamond & L. Quinby, (Eds.), *Feminism & Foucault: Reflections on resistance* (pp. 87-108). Boston: Northeastern University Press.

Bordo, S. (1991). "Material girl": The effacements of postmodern culture. In L. Goldstein (Ed.), *The female body: Figures, styles, and speculation* (pp. 106-130). Ann Arbor: University of Michigan Press.

Bouchard, C. (1991). Quelques réflexions sur l'avènement des biotechnologies en sport. In F. Landry, M. Landry & M. Yerles (Eds.), *Sport: The third millennium—Proceeding of the International Symposium* (pp. 455-464). Québec City: Presses de l'Université Laval.

Boyne, R. (1990). *Foucault and Derrida: The other side of reason*. Boston: Unwin Hyman.

Brantlinger, P. (1990). *Crusoe's footprints: Cultural studies in Britain and America*. New York: Routledge.

Cahn, S. (1992, November). *Silence as surveillance: The open secret of lesbianism in women's sport*. Paper presented at the annual meetings of the North American Society for the Sociology of Sport, Toledo.

Chauncey, G. (1982/83). From sexual inversion to homosexuality: The changing medical conceptualization of female deviance. *Salmagundi*, **58/9**, 114-146.

Cole, C.L. (1990, November). *Warning: This is not a sport studies advertisement*. Paper presented at the annual meetings of the North American Society for the Sociology of Sport, Denver.

Cole, C.L. (1991, November). *Dialogues "on" the body: Feminist cultural studies and Foucault*. Paper presented at the annual meetings of the North American Society for the Sociology of Sport, Milwaukee.

Cole, C.L. & Birrell, S. (1986, October). Resisting the canon: feminist cultural studies. Paper presented at the annual meetings of the North American Society for the Sociology of Sport, Las Vegas.

de Lauretis, T. (1987). *Technologies of gender: Essays on theory, film, and practice*. Bloomington: Indiana University Press.

Eisenstein, Z. (Ed.) (1979). *Capitalist patriarchy and the case for socialist feminism*. New York: Monthly Review Press.

Epstein, J., & Straub, K. (1991). Introduction: The guarded body. In J. Epstein & K. Straub (Eds.), *Body guards: The cultural politics of gender ambiguity* (pp. 1-28). New York: Routledge.

Featherstone, M. (1982). The body in consumer culture. *Theory, Culture and Society*, **1**, 18-33.

Featherstone, M. (1991, November). *The body, culture and sport*. Keynote paper presented at the annual meetings of the North American Society for the Sociology of Sport, Milwaukee.

Foucault, M. (1974). *The archaeology of knowledge*. London: Tavistock.

Foucault, M. (1979). *Discipline and punish: The birth of a prison*. New York: Random House. (French original published 1975).

Foucault, M. (1980). *The history of sexuality: (Volume I: An introduction)*. New York: Vintage Books. (French original published 1976).

Foucault, M. (1985). *The uses of pleasure: (Volume 2 of the history of sexuality)*. New York: Random House-Vintage.

Gibson, W. (1988). *Mona lisa overdrive*. New York: Bantam Books.

Grosz, E. (1987). Notes towards a corporeal feminism. *Australian Feminist Studies*, **5**, 1-16.

Hall, M.A. (1993). Gender and sport in the 1990s: Feminism, culture, and politics. *Social Science Review*, **2**, 48-68.

Hall, S. (1980). Cultural studies and the centre: Some problematics and problems. In S. Hall, D. Hobson, A. Lowe, & P. Willis (Eds.), *Culture, media, language* (pp. 15-47). London: Hutchinson & Co.

Hall, S. (1983). Cultural studies: Two paradigms. In T. Bennett, G. Martin, C. Mercer, & J. Woolacott (Eds.), *Culture, ideology and social process* (pp. 19-37). London: Open University.

Hall, S. (1985). Signification, representation, ideology: Althusser and the post-structuralist debates. *Critical Studies in Mass Communication, 2,* 91-114.

Haraway, D. (1985). A manifesto for cyborgs: Science, technology, and socialist feminism in the 1980s. *Socialist Review, 80,* 65-107.

Hargreaves, J. (1986). Schooling the body. In J. Hargreaves (Ed.), *Sport, power, and culture* (pp. 161-181). Cambridge, England: Polity Press.

Hargreaves, J. (1987). The body, sport, and power relations. In J. Horne, D. Jary, & A. Tomlinson (Eds.), *Sport, leisure, and social relations* (pp. 139-159). London: Routledge & Kegan Paul.

Harvey, D. (1989). *The condition of postmodernity: An enquiry into the origins of cultural change.* Oxford: Basil Blackwell.

Harvey, J., & Sparks, R. (1991). The politics of the body in the context of modernity. *Quest, 43,* 164-189.

Hentoff, N. (1990, July 16). Teens are resigned to loss of rights. *Des Moines Register,* p. 6.

Hoggart, R. (1957). *The uses of literacy.* London: Chatto and Windus.

hooks, b. (1984). *Feminist theory: From margin to center.* Boston: South End Press.

Jagger, A. (1984). *Feminist politics and human nature.* Chicago: University of Chicago Press.

Kroker, A., & Kroker, M. (1987). Panic sex in America. In A. Kroker & M. Kroker (Eds.), *Body invaders: Panic sex in America* (pp. 10-19). New York: St. Martin's Press.

Kuhn, A. (1988). The body and cinema: Some problems for feminism. In S. Sheridan (Ed.), *Grafts: Feminist cultural criticism* (pp. 22-23). New York: Verso.

Lourde, A. (1984). *Sister-outsider: Essays and speeches.* Trumansburg, NY: The Crossing Press.

Mitchell, J. (1971). *Women's estate.* New York: Vintage Books.

Moraga, C., & Anzaldua, G. (Eds.) (1981). *This bridge called my back: Writings by radical women of color.* New York: Kitchen Table Press.

National Collegiate Athletic Association sports medicine handbook (1992). Overland Park, KS: National Collegiate Athletic Association Publications.

Patton, C. (1992, November). *Steroids, voice, and surveillance.* Paper presented at the annual meetings for the North American Society for the Sociology of Sport, Toledo.

Petchesky, R. (1987). Foetal images: The power of visual culture in the politics of reproduction. *Feminist Studies, 13,* 263-292.

Phelps, L. (1975). Patriarchy and capitalism. *Quest, 2,* 39.

Rubin, G. (1976). The traffic in women: Notes on the "political economy" of sex. In R. Rapp (Ed.), *Toward an anthropology of women* (pp. 157-210). New York: Monthly Review Press.

Sandoval, C. (1991). U.S. Third-World feminism: The theory and method of oppositional consciousness in the postmodern world. *Genders, 10,* 1-24.

Schulze, L. (1990). On the muscle. In J. Gaines & C. Herzog (Eds.), *Fabrications: Costume and the female body* (pp. 59-78). New York: Routledge.

Singer, L. (1989). bodies-pleasures-power. *differences*, **1**, 45-65.

Sport Canada (1991). *International relations background briefing: Gender verification*. Ottawa, ON: International Relations Secretariate, Sport Canada, Government of Canada.

Terry, J. (1989). The body invaded: Medical surveillance of women as reproducers. *Socialist Review,* **19**, 13-45.

Terry, J. (1990). Lesbians under the medical gaze: Scientists search for remarkable differences. *Journal of Sex Research*, **27**, 317-339.

Theberge, N. (1991). Reflections on the body in the sociology of sport. *Quest,* **43**, 123-134.

Thompson, E.P. (1963). *The making of the English working class.* New York: Vintage.

Torgeson, G. (1992, October 13). NCAA must rule on pregnancy. *USA Today*, p. C14.

Whitson, D.J. (1989). Discourse of critique in sport sociology. *Sociology of Sport Journal*, **6**, 60-65.

Williams, R. (1958). *Culture and society, 1780-1950.* London: Chatto and Windus.

Williams, R. (1977). *Marxism and literature.* New York: Oxford University Press.

Willis, S. (1990). Work(ing) out. *Cultural Studies*, **4**, 1-18.

NOTES

1. It is in this sense that the "object of knowledge" ceases to be sport per se and instead becomes a series of questions related to the intersection of meaning and power, the generation of subjectivity and agency, and the reproduction of power relations (Cole, 1990).

2. Despite changes in feminist theory, Jagger's (1984) early feminist typology is still useful for marking differences in feminist theory. In general, my reference to socialist-feminism is consistent with Jagger's explanation. Sandoval (1991) does, however, raise important questions about how this now-dominant feminist typology has been used to marginalize feminist work by women of color. The questions raised by Sandoval work to destabilize what has become the major discourse of feminist theory. Sandoval defines her project as one that moves toward a theory of oppositional consciousness and an affinity politics based on U.S. Third World feminism.

3. Although "feminist cultural studies" was not necessarily discussed as a theoretical position in 1986 when this project was established, much work has since been produced under the sign of that category. See Balsamo (1991) for an historical account of feminist cultural studies. Balsamo traces feminist cultural studies from its development in Britain through its contemporary

and diverse international forms. See Hall (1993) for a discussion of feminist cultural studies and sport.

4. "Decentering the humanist subject" refers to an important theoretical break in the conceptualization of the more familiar notion of the individual. Although the individual of humanist thought is presumed to be free, authentic, fully coherent, and self-authorial, the "subject" of anti-humanist thought assumes that the individual is constructed and that consciousness is actively generated through cultural processes and practices. The term *subject* signifies that break.

5. I have arranged these theoretical positions into separate sections for heuristic purposes; this strategy is not meant to suggest that these theories remain distinct.

6. See Birrell (1989, 1990) for an overview of what these debates might mean for researchers interested in sport.

7. See Andrews (1993), Hargreaves (1986, 1987), Harvey & Sparks (1991), Theberge (1991), and Whitson (1989) for discussions related to the usefulness of Foucault's work for sport studies. Andrews's essay provides an especially good overview of Foucault's work and Foucauldian-informed work on sport.

8. For an accessible explanation of late, postmodern capitalism, see Harvey's (1989), *The Condition of Postmodernity*. In part, late capitalism or flexible accumulation entails a compression in time and space, multi-nationals, new technologies, and an accelerated pace of labor. As Harvey explains, it includes "flexible system production with [an] emphasis upon problem solving, rapid and often highly specialized responses, and adaptability of skills to special purposes [as well as] an increasing capacity to manufacture a variety of goods cheaply in small batches" (p. 156).

9. See Featherstone's (1982) "The Body in Consumer Culture" for an excellent discussion on the making of the contemporary body in late capitalism.

10. The ideas discussed in this section were inspired by Terry's discussion of the new scientific panopticism in "The Body Invaded: Medical Surveillance of Women as Reproducers." I might also note that consent to drug testing and new mechanisms of surveillance are also produced through "drug education" programs like DARE.

11. I would like to thank Jay Coakley for bringing these articles to my attention.

12. Thanks to Geneviève Rail for sharing this article and for her help in translating key sections.

ACKNOWLEDGMENTS

I would like to thank three anonymous reviewers and Larry Wenner for their helpful comments on an earlier draft of this paper. I thank especially Susan

Birrell for her suggestions on several early projects (Cole, 1990, 1991; Cole & Birrell, 1986) on which this paper is based and for her ongoing encouragement and support. I also thank Jenny Terry, whose work inspired many of the arguments in this paper, for her generous sharing of ideas.

Chapter 2

Women in Sport in Ideology

Paul Willis
Wolverhampton University
Dudley, England

What follows is an essay in ideas. It is only a fragment towards the final critical mapping of sport within the social totality. It provides no proper empirical basis for analysis, provides no history of women in sport and does not develop an inclusive theory of ideology. In a way it may be seen as a long footnote to John Hargreaves's general survey of the area. My limited aim is to explore one of the crucial questions within the larger operation of ideological processes in the specific area of women in sport: how a set of ideas which bear a particular 'guilty' relation of support and formation to dominant groups and dominant ideas nevertheless appear 'freely' on the market place of ideas: unbiased, neutral and the property of any independent mind prepared to use 'common sense' and 'work things out for itself'. This is the now classic area defined for us in John Hargreaves's opening article of where 'cultural hegemony' meets the realm of 'common sense', or where more precisely the potential 'good sense' of 'common sense' is displaced and makes room for what are 'dominant' views—but 'freely' taken on.[1] Approaching our chosen area with such an open and apparently simple question may throw some light on women in sport as well as perhaps illuminating some of the ways in which ideology colours 'the natural'.

Sport and biological beliefs about gender difference combine into one of the few privileged areas where we seem to be dealing with unmediated 'reality', where we know 'what's what' without having to listen to the involved self-serving analyses of theorists, analysts, political groups, etc. Running faster, jumping higher, throwing further can be *seen*—not interpreted. 'The natural' is one

---

From "Women in Sport in Ideology" by P. Willis. In *Sport, Culture and Ideology* (pp. 117-135) by Jennifer Hargreaves (Ed.), 1982, London: Routledge and Kegan Paul. Reprinted by permission.

31

of the grounds of ideology because of its apparent autonomy from 'biased' interpretation.

Obvious domination or even insidious infiltration of such areas would, it seems, be spotted very easily: after all Jesse Owens did win X number of gold medals in the 1936 Olympics and Fascism could not dominate sport to show its 'superiority'. Nor should we rush to our socio-cultural cynicism here. John Hargreaves is surely right to insist that sport isn't simply 'the front' for other kinds of social domination. It is wrong to ransack the variety of experience and practice in the area to come up with simple social fits and reflections: sport helps the rulers rule. There is an enjoyment in activity, there are pleasures in competition that cannot be reduced to capitalist competition. Much sport is undoubtedly organised in commercial ways for profit and it is timed and measured like activity in the factory,[2] but people of both sexes do enjoy watching and/or participating in activity, dexterity, co-operation and movement. Most importantly, there are different meanings at play, contested meanings over the same event, the same happening. It is precisely here, I shall be arguing, in the real separation of sport from other areas of society, its differences, its autonomy, wherein lies its power for legitimation—it would not be believed if it did not show this independence and apparent capacity to carry social meaning separately from what the powerful say. This is exactly the freedom, rest and release, that non-political joy in sport, which participants experience as its particular quality and defend precisely against 'political interference'. It is how this complexity is actually nevertheless taken up into ideology that is the focus of this paper—in the concrete example of comparative sports performance of women in sport.

Women in sport and the ideological effect I want to outline are also important in providing us with one of the few examples of the 'circuit of the media' and especially with how the experience of a phenomenon and its communicated meaning relate or differ. Too many media accounts deal with the communications of the powerful or with the adaption of received views, or add on the 'amplification effect'[3] as an internal media process. It is important always in my view to place the *situated generation* of meaning as well as to outline the process whereby it is disseminated, and also to suggest some notion of the structured articulation between them. The area of women in sport and its relation to ideology provide a very revealing case study also of the media's operation in our society.

At any rate sport has attracted more and more attention over recent years as perhaps the central constituency of the burgeoning area of 'leisure'. It is central to *active* notions of 'leisure' and to passive reception. It raises questions both about the event and its media meanings. Though in no way directly related, during the same period there has also been a greatly revived interest in, and opposition to, the oppression of women in society. The intersection of these two important themes, therefore, in the area of women in sport may offer us an unlikely and revealing, concrete manifestation of crucially modern concerns and feelings. We may find that the particular *conjunction* of the two lines helps us to understand better each line even as they lead away from women in sport to more central and abstract concerns.

It may be noted, perhaps unexpectedly, that there is also methodological importance here to a student of social thought, because so many of the approaches to women in sport exhibit the clearest aspects of positivism in contemporary social research. They share an assumed deterministic model, isolated from the general culture, composed of dependent and independent variables. The usual project is to identify and measure the variables in the system, so that causal relations may be uncovered. The system invoked is often the female body, and the aim is to isolate the crucial variables involved in its ability to achieve in sport. Where the system invoked is the body *plus* its social and cultural location, the uneasy aim is simply to add another few variables on to the chain, and identify, with scientific rigour, that such and such cultural factors are ultimately responsible for particular levels of sports performance.

However, this linear determinism will not do if we are interested in the social meaning of a phenomenon. I mean, for instance, that to know, more exactly, why it is that women can muster only 90 per cent of a man's strength cannot help us to comprehend, explain, or change the massive feeling in our society that a woman has no business flexing her muscles anyway.

Even if one could identify all the 'variables' at play in a national culture one would end up with such a vast number that it would be quite impossible to plot co-variation and determination. Secondly, in dealing with cultural meaning we are crucially concerned with the *nature* of symbolic systems, social attitudes and cultural values, and there is no way to qualify this. Thirdly, and perhaps most importantly, it is impossible to think of cultural processes in a linear way. It is not the case that there is a culture over here that affects sport over there, in a simple one-way relationship. The understanding of interrelationship and inter-connection is of the essence if we are even to set the right questions. Sport is influenced by the state of the general society, and reflects that society. Sport, in its turn, influences, and for the most part reinforces, that society. Furthermore, we cannot conceptualise society as a great monolithic entity, with a protuber-ance—sport—stuck on the outside. The society, itself, is nothing but a layered complex of elements all intricately and dialectically interrelated with each other.

I should like to propose a very different approach to women in sport: that of analytic cultural criticism. This approach is different because it is concerned with meaning, and values, and social explanation, without attempting positivistic rigour. It accepts differences in sports performance between men and women, accepts that cultural factors may well enlarge this gap, but is *most* interested in the manner in which this gap is understood and taken up into the popular con-sciousness of our society. In this perspective the fact of biological difference is incontrovertible,[4] but it is an 'inert' fact, socially speaking, until we have explained the colossal social interest in it. After all there are many factual differences facing us in the social world, some people are short, others tall, some fat, some thin, some have blue eyes, others brown, some have black skins, some white, some people speak with deep voices, others with high. The analytic socio-cultural task is not to measure these differences precisely and explain them physically, but to ask *why* some differences, and not others, are taken as so important, become so exaggerated, are used to buttress social attitudes or prejudice. What activates these 'inert' facts, then, is the business of critical qualitative analysis—why do people *think* a particular difference is important, how do they *use* the difference, is this use related at all to a general system of attitudes and beliefs: to ideology?

The course of this article is briefly to identify some of the basic characteristics of how sport is seen in our society, and then to take a preliminary and necessarily perhaps impressionistic view of how the area is inflected through 'patriarchal' ideology in our popular views of the specific area of women in sport. After a 'theoretical detour'—a general abstract view of how ideology 'invades' common-sense understanding—some of the specific mechanisms will be analysed of how this *general* ideological view of the physical inferiority and 'femaleness' of gender is implanted in 'commonsense' views of women in sport, thereby reinforc-ing particular notions of women in sport as well as more general notions concern-ing female genderedness.

THE SOCIAL AND PATRIARCHAL CHARACTER OF SPORT

Sport in general seems to be freer and more voluntary than other activities. It is away from the productive process and away from the family. Though participation and interest is, of course, deeply structured by age, class, gender and race, the fact that its site of operation is structurally separate from the main domains of 'necessity' (waged work for men, domestic *and* waged work for women) seem to confer upon it (and in some ways really does) a freedom not enjoyed in those areas.

And in one very simple straightforward way sport's basis in physical activity and movement does provide a real materialism of expression and freedom because the body and its movement are prescribed by quite freely humanly made rules and methods—not by the 'dull compulsion' of the workplace or the cloying blackmail of the home (which bears, though unequally, on both sexes). It seems to be, one might paraphrase, activity for activity's sake. It is also a field of relative simplicity, where right and wrong, good and bad, are taken to be easily identified. One expects greater strength, or skill, to bring commensurate rewards in sport. It is the area where the apparently unpredictable chance of normal living intervenes least between ability and achievement. The regulation enquiries between sportscasters turn on 'Was it a fair result?' The very fact that so much sports commentary is concerned with who 'deserved' to win, goes to demonstrate the overwhelming expectation of simple physical justice. In some ways sport provides the morality drama of our electronic age: the ideal expression of un-fettered social relations—not worker against manager but player against player.

But this apparent freedom and separate internal life of sport evaporate when we come to women in sport. We realise at once that our ideal description above is a *male* description concerning males. Where women become at all visible, then the terms of reference change. There is a very important thread in popular consciousness which sees the very presence of women in sport as bizarre. Frequently, reporting of women's sport takes its fundamental bearings, not on sport, but on humour, or the unusual. The tone is easy to recognise, it's a version of the irony, the humour, the superiority, of the sophisticated towards the cranks—the UFO believers, the end-of-the-world disciples on the mountain top. Dr. Johnson's hackneyed old phrase cries out to be released in new ways again and again, 'It's like a dog standing on its hind legs. It is not well done—rather one is surprised to see it attempted at all.'

The fundamental anxiety seems to be that men and women have to be continuously differentiated; male preserves continuously guaranteed. One way of emphasising this is to promote laughter or cynicism when females take to the field, another way is (cf. Bobby Riggs) to set out to prove incontrovertibly that women are inferior through direct challenge. Another way is to draw attention to unarguable physical differences out of context. In a 'Daily Mirror' article[5] there is an excellent example of this. In the photograph accompanying the text the female athlete is actually shown with her baby in the background. Even in the case of a successful athlete you see at a glance that she is different from men, defined essentially by sex rather than athletics, and perhaps even a freak for being able to have a baby and be successful in sport.

Games and sports played by women could be judged purely for themselves, without reference, all the time, to what are taken as the absolute values, the only yardstick, of achievement—*male* achievement. And furthermore, the wide spread of characteristics through both sexes, the considerable overlap of the spectrum of physical characteristics between men and women, and the greater salience of fitness rather than gender[6] to performance means that a team of high-ability women will be better, even in so-called masculine qualities, than a low-ability men's team. And yet, the meanest local 5th division, male works' team gets more respect, in popular consciousness, than a women's national team.

Another powerful way in which the sexual identity is given precedence over the sport's identity of female athletes is the vein of sexual innuendo running through much sports commentary. The male may comfortably suppose that even if the sports woman affronts him on the field of play, at least she likes 'a bit of the other' in another field of play. Sometimes the women themselves are guilty parties to this, and collude with being 'sexy' and 'attractive' at the same time as being sportswomen. In such ways the female athlete is rendered a sex *object*—a body which may excel in sport, but which is primarily an object of pleasure for man. A useful technique, for if a woman seems to be encroaching too far, and too threateningly, into male sanctuaries, she can be symbolically vapourised and reconstituted as an object, a butt for smutty jokes and complacent elbow nudging.

It is also clear that sport is strongly associated with the male identity, with being popular and having friends. Rugby and football are archetypal here. We imagine men to be at their most gregarious, expansive and relaxed in the pub after the match. It's not hard to see that the stereotype, 'I'd like-to-be-with-them' males of the beer adverts, 'if you can't beat them join them', are really rugby or football players. Achievement particularly strengthens male identity; it is assumed that sports success *is* success at being masculine. Physical achievement, and masculine activity, are taken to be the same.

When we think of women in sport, the situation is entirely contrary. One thinks of female athletes as alone—there is no popular image of back-slapping in the pub afterwards. Indeed there is an important element in the popular response to the female athlete, of uncertainty before the deviant, distrust of the strange, dislike of the marginal. As the athlete becomes even more outstanding, she marks herself out as even more deviant. Instead of confirming her identity, success can threaten her with a foreign male identity. In so far as she is affected by popular consciousness—and she can hardly ignore it—the female athlete lives through a severe contradiction. To succeed as an athlete can be to fail as a woman, because she has, in certain profound symbolic ways, become a man. Indeed, in certain areas it is not only a symbolic power she faces. The demand for sex tests on female athletes shows us the power of the suspicion—'if she's successful, she's a man'. A moment's reflection that no male athlete lives this painful contradiction of success-being-failure-really, to say nothing of this failure being physically tested, throws up for us once again the severe interest which sport manifests in differentiating the sexes.

Ironically, even in those sports like ice skating and gymnastics, in which girls and young women excel and are publicly acclaimed, sex-role differences are further clarified. Success is to do with fitting the youthful, lithe, nubile, stereotypically 'perfect' popular image of femininity.

I want to suggest that what we have been considering is an ideological inflection of our basic social characterisation of sport. How does ideology gain an entrance here?[7]

IDEOLOGY AND COMMON SENSE

Ideology for our purposes here can be understood as the process of legitimation, in its different forms, within all existing societies, whereby a certain social organisation—most pertinent for us the patriarchal relations of the family and society—system of order and power, and access to reward is constituted as the only possible, or the only fair, pattern of human relations. Crucially it can only achieve this by dissembling its own nature. If it does not succeed in this it may be transparently seen as a dominating interest and may be obeyed only through physical coercion. Unless ideology, in its deepest character, can induce assent to itself, it is only the manifesto of a group that has power over others.

We can only understand this 'dissembling' nature of ideology if we realise that the general notion of ideology is an abstraction, and that ideology proper exists only through its manifestations at the level of apparently concrete circumstance within the zone of common sense, within what is taken to be reality. In order to find a starting point, it is necessary to posit the abstraction of ideology and to indicate its essential parameters, but unless we can show how this abstraction is taken up as the real in the social world, we shall have done nothing more than point to a manifesto.

I should like to represent the operation of ideology in three stages. Though I can only describe them sequentially and separately, they should be thought of as simultaneous, mutually dependent and reinforcing elements of continuing process. These three stages are: (a) the ideological force of definition, (b) the reinterpretation of discrepancies in social sub-regions, (c) the located rebirth of ideology.

In the first instance I posit an ideological content, a general account of what the ideology 'says', as if indeed it were a manifesto. In our own society this would be something like the importance of work, the justice of meritocratic advancement as well as, of course, the natural superiority and aggressiveness of men coupled with the weakness and caring/emotional nature of women. Essentially these 'contents' are beliefs about the nature of reality, and can only be upheld if reality seems to comply with them. We must of course be extremely sceptical of 'reality's' ability to speak for itself, to confirm beliefs held about it. Rather we must recognise that belief seeks to define reality, to find in reality what will satisfy itself, and to neutralise or change what seems to contradict itself. The content of our general notion (abstraction) of ideology, then, is basically a powerful force of definition seeking its own reflection from reality in order to confirm itself.

Now there are competing forces of definition in all the sub-regions that make up society, and the individuals and groups inhabiting every area of the culture have their own at least partially independent forms of understanding and living their own immediate environments that won't immediately yield to an outside version of what is happening to them.

To follow up some of our previous examples: factory workers do not always believe in the 'work ethic' and may seek ways to control and limit production;[8] working class students often realise that success does not seem to depend on merit but more on class, accent and wealth;[9] women know that in many situations they can be more dominant, able and hard-headed than men. But I have argued that ideology can only exist precisely if it can embody itself in the concrete common sense of the actors in such sub-regions. This embodiment, I suggest, is likely to take place in areas of discrepancy within these sub-regions, that is in areas which the immediate forms of understanding have not already been taken up into their own definitional field of force. One way of conceiving this was mentioned at the beginning—the 'inert' fact, an aspect of reality which is visible but not yet taken up into a system of belief. Another way is to regard it as a mismatch felt within particular experiential sub-systems, felt *discrepancies* which the actors involved are puzzled by and cannot adequately account for. In such areas the countervailing local forces of definition are not strong enough to resist ideological forces, and the 'unknown quantity' can be interpreted globally by ideology for its own purposes—can be used to embody general beliefs in a located social example.

To resume our examples: factory workers may not like work but they know that some form of production is necessary to support human life, resistance to work does not account for this and so the capitalist logic and organisation of production can be 'naturalised' as the only possible one so that the capital can proclaim on its own behalf 'if you don't work, you don't eat'. Working-class students might know the importance of class, wealth and accent to success, but they also confusingly recognise that the 'successful' seem also to have those 'qualifications' which they find it so hard to obtain. This is difficult for them to explain, but meritocracy can proclaim 'advance through merit for all in our education system'. Women may know their own real competence and power in some situations but they are also the ones who must leave work to bear children. They can also be physically beaten up or raped by men. Patriarchy strides in to this physical territory to claim superiority in general in all social and cultural fields.

There has been another simplification of course in suggesting that 'inert' facts or social discrepancies are just lying idly by waiting for a more powerful mistress than their local ones. In fact they have always been in a state of having been interpreted, since to have remained uninterpreted is to have remained invisible to social meanings. However, to separate them artificially for a moment from the manner of their cultural investment at least shows the theoretical potential for the incursion of ideological meaning into located social sub-regions.

An important consequence of this incursion is that apparently concrete instances can be used for general legitimations that are quite distinct from the inherent logic of the particular social sub-regions from which they came. Examples can be quoted out of context to support more global versions of reality which may even contradict the organising perspective of the system from which the example is taken. In the modern era of telecommunications, and a central societal consensus based on information provided by the mass media, such out-of-context citations are commonplace and the most important mechanism for allowing the illusion of a central and agreed normative value system. The media could never succeed in presenting their unifying consensual vision of social reality unless it can be continually embodied in a wealth of concrete news items. Television, as the purveyor of the ultimate concrete image, has greatly augmented this process. The contextual disengagement practised by the media certainly gives news reporting a reassuring continuity and feeling of straightforward reasonableness, but for those involved in the real events which are being reported there is a characteristic, if muted, sense of colossal misinterpretation. The continuity of real events has been sacrificed in the media to the continuity of much larger myths about the real. The profound needs of society to embed its ideology in empirical reality totally overrides the participants of particular scenarios, even renders their own reality unintelligible to them, in the interests of a larger coherency, a larger version of social reality.

The distribution of this ideological penetration is most uneven, and a further cause for the rage of the participant actors. There are a number of factors accounting for the degree of penetration of a certain area. The relative powers of definition are always changing within a particular sub-region, and a particular definition of an element of social reality is never won outright. There is always uncertainty and the sway of real events may transform the ability of the various actors to reclaim areas of meanings. Furthermore the various social sub-regions vary greatly in their capacity to be usefully invaded by ideology. An area that seems to exhibit great apparent autonomy is a prime candidate: for instance the areas of the 'natural' or the biological are enormously important to ideology, they seem quite free from human manipulation, and apparently self-determined, the most basic form of external reality. If an example can be won here it offers the ideal opportunity for the embodiment of ideology in the real. The plea to common sense is 'why, even in that separate area the same things are true!'

Even though a particular social sub-region may not offer the advantage of being apparently autonomous it may still be a frequent ideological target if its values and norms in some way impinge on an important principle of ideology. If the particular area throws up values or definitions which challenge ideological beliefs, the field clearly has to be contested. Even if ideology cannot totally submerge itself as common sense, it can at least forward plausible suggestions for the reinterpretation of events. Ideology can never afford to let contradictory interpretations of reality go free from at least a crippling ambiguity. At the other extreme, sub-systems that produce definitions of the real which run parallel to ideological definitions are clear candidates for insurgency. Again, though the meanings derived from such areas may not always have the unquestioned hallmark of the real, or the undetermined, they may all add to a gathering weight of a certain version of reality. It's all cash in the bank of a growing deposit of the 'obvious'.

This investment with ideological meaning of disputed elements in local social systems does not however, fully account for the ideological process. The real dynamic is supplied to the system in our third stage, where the concrete social elements invested with ideology take on an ideological life of their own, and give a genuine rebirth to those beliefs with which they have been invested. This rebirth comes about because the local social actors surrounding an element that has been 'ideologised' do not remain neutral to it—social life is of course continuous and always monitoring and adapting its meanings and actions to its social and cultural environment. Within this reaction lies the basis for the rebirth of ideology (in fact the only real manifestation) in concrete reality. It does not matter whether this reaction is positive or negative so long as the underlying definition of the situation is accepted. Within this response any reaction short of a wholesale counter-redefinition accepts the incursive ideological meaning and inducts elements of that meaning into the system as a whole. Frequently the immediate response of the actors involved will be one of opposition, but the opposition, unless it is extremely self-aware, can only take up the issue in the terms within which it has been offered, the terms which render the phenomenon apparently concrete and real. The reaction of the local actors, then, though hostile to the surface forms of the penetration, in fact gives completely new life to the underlying definitional power of the ideology. To take certain questions up is already to have given up the right to challenge the epistemological foundations of those questions. The 'battle' so to speak, is conceded as soon as it is started, *by* starting it. If the local cultural participants do not attempt to challenge the immediate apparent issue, and have no other account of reality, then they have no choice but to collude in the ideological definition of what confronts them. They may well be puzzled and uncertain as to quite why they are behaving in such and such a way but they have in fact given a mute rebirth to the ideology. They are living the ideology in that social area because they have no other voice to speak with, they act in the only mode that is open. They have conceded the battle without even realising that there was a 'battle'. These points may become clearer by example, one of a 'battle' apparently fought, and another of no 'battle' at all. In both cases I will point to what would have been successful grounds for repelling ideological 'invasion'.

Trade union opposition to employers which is couched in the form of a demand for more money accepts the legitimacy, and gives new life to the legitimacy, of wage labour in general. Even the most vociferous and militant demands for more money, which seem on the surface to challenge the functioning of the capitalist economy, at a deeper level underwrite more forcefully the legitimacy of the market economy and its exchange values. Union activity could only directly challenge the capitalist system if it challenged the terms on which workers are rewarded at all, and offered an alternative account of how the workers could be related to their product.[10]

To take the very different area of crime and deviance, so long as the miscreant herself makes excuses for her misdeeds, she is powerfully supporting the normative structure of the main society. For to make excuses for her conduct (perhaps for no other reason than to attract a more lenient sentence) accepts the whole definition, recreates the definition, which first defined her behaviour as antisocial. The criminals or deviants who are truly a threat to the 'fabric of society' are the ones who place their own definitions across their acts and find them just. It is no accident that such defendants frequently claim the status of political prisoners; the belief system which is strong enough to counter the ideological definition of their actions must be well supported by a complex political analysis of society and its internecine unequal struggle to define reality.

It is not the case, then, that located actors are doomed carriers of ideology. A sufficiently strong repossession of the definition of the situation can reverse the process. But by and large we can see that particular actors in local social areas who are not armed with an analysis, will always struggle in the obvious way. If they are told they are asking for too much money they will reply that they deserve what they get, if they are told that they are evil, they will reply, 'please forgive me'. By not challenging the basic terms of the exchange, they will have given rebirth to the legitimacy of defining the whole situation in terms of money or evil.

The argument at this third stage is that the ideologically imbued concrete elements of particular social sub-regions take on a life of their own, and produce spontaneously the essential elements of ideology. This is the manner of the continuing life of ideology in the commonsense realm of the concrete. If we can accept the continuous complex functioning of this process in all the diverse areas of our social life, we can see that what we take to be the general force of ideology is only ever a set of continually reconstituted beliefs and definitions occurring in empirical circumstances.

PATRIARCHAL IDEOLOGY AND SPORT

If we trace our three processes of ideology through women in sport we shall see just what a fertile and unsuspecting field there is here for the legitimation of a certain dominant version of social reality. Taking as our starting point the general belief that the sexes are innately different, and males superior, we can posit a powerful force of definition seeking confirmation in social sub-regions. The area of sport generally offers itself as an important target because of its apparent autonomy. Sport is just itself and part of the ideologically important area of the 'natural'. If evidence can be found here for ideological belief, then it will have the cache of the real, it will be admirably suited to citation out of context. But within this already privileged zone there is the further sub-region of women in sport which can offer the bonus of biological, and apparently incontrovertible differences between the sexes once the question of sexual comparison arises. Now within the local terms of reference—those women involved in sports performance—this biological difference is noted as discrepancy, but is not necessarily mobilised as the main definition of their social reality in that region. Their main social reality is presumably connected with sport for its own sake, and the frustrations and hopes of that world: for its own enjoyment and meaning. But ideology can claim biological discrepancy fully for its own: to present cultural legitimations as biological factors. There is the tailormade opportunity for transforming ideological belief into an aspect of concrete reality at the plane of common sense. The fact that no one can deny female difference becomes the fact of female sports inferiority, becomes the fact that females are innately different from men, becomes the fact that women who stray across the defining boundary are in a parlous state. An ideological view comes to be deposited in our culture as a commonsense assumption—'of course women are different and inferior'.

   Looking at the third stage of the ideological process, the situation of women in sport offers even more to ideological development. For local cultural participants, the sportswomen, unarmed with a counter-definitional force of their own, either immediately collude with the ideological definitions (the female athlete conspiring to be sexy with the news reporter) or take up the challenge totally within the terms of the preferred ideological definition (the angered sportswoman setting out to prove male equivalence in her sport's performance). In many cases the latter is even preferable to collusion, since it makes the case so much more visible, and so eminently suited to citation out of context. One can think of many examples: Billie Jean King's response to Bobby Riggs is an archetypical example here—not least because she won.

The popular press abounds with examples of how ideological definitions can seek to take over and highlight apparent biological differences to thus render the meaning of women in sport in a specific way—as a commentary on, and therefore reinforcement and reproduction of, gender differences in our society. The clearest move here is when 'sports stories' leave their home at the back of the tabloids and find their way into the centre spread and the general 'human interest', titillating or unusual category. A story concerning female weight-lifting in the 'Sun'[11] is headed 'Building up a Body Beautiful' and 'Muscle Misses' and most of the copy concerns not their sports identity but their gender identity. The male trainer is reported as saying that most women take up weight-lifting to improve their figures and to achieve 'that Raquel Welch look—wide shoulders, slim waist and hips and firm, high breasts'. The story concludes with the vignette of how one woman's weight-lifting career had repaired her marriage—now she could train alongside her re-united weight-lifting husband. No male weight-lifter could face this confusion of his sport and his personal sexual life. The only alternative reading given is that in so far as the sport is taken seriously for itself, then the women become masculinised 'swinging weights which most men could scarcely lift', and give up much that is normal in a female life. Furthermore, the motivation for this apparently, again, concerns the archetypal negation of supposed female qualities and the inflation of supposed male qualities—'I took up body-building because I didn't want to be a passive, weak, dependent female'. Clearly, it's the unspoken 'good' to be aggressive and strong. Guess of which sex that is the general social specification! These are the basic news value of the story: (a) the unusualness, the dog on its hind-legs-ness, of women lifting weights and becoming 'muscly' (hence the liberal use of photographs), (b) through this strangeness, either the lengths to which women will go to *attract* men, or the lengths to which they will go to *emulate* men. Either way, men, and what they stand for, reign supreme. An original ideological definition has framed ' the experience' of female weight-lifting in a certain fashion and the (at least reported) responses of the women—given no doubt the immediate framing of the interview to which they're subjected—either collude in the sexualisation of the topic or reinforce the standards of male comparison used in the original definition.

Researchers and positivist enquiry also bear some responsibility here, since they so often take it as their task to *explain* differences in performance—thereby dignifying that difference. Sometimes they offer a base for closing the gap between male and female sports performance. To accept that it is a worthwhile endeavour to push female performance closer to that of a male, even surpass it, admits at a stroke the stigma of femininity and the legitimacy of that male eminence which coined the standards. So no matter how the actual physical gap is closed, there is an equal and opposite reaction which expands the cultural and ideological resonance of that gap. It creates anew the frame of reference in which, and by which, the gap was measured in the first place. By accepting the terms of the ideological definition, the attempt to approach male performance levels, in fact strengthens popular prejudice about femininity. It creates an expanding bank of the obvious examples of female 'inferiority', which in their turn aid the ideological imbuement of other areas of society, as well as the discrediting of values associated with femininity. Meanwhile male values are firmly established at the natural 'centre-stage' of life and judgment.

The response of the participants in the area of women in sport and of the researchers of positivist academics may, therefore, produce profound and un-intended consequences, and actually exacerbate the processes which in the first place brought unwelcome attention.

Some recent work seems to be at odds, somewhat, with the drift of this analysis.[12] The 'biological gap' or the 'inert fact' of female inferiority in sports performance may be much less than is popularly suggested. The 'fitness' factor far outweighs the sex factor and it is now suggested that in some sports, namely swimming and long-distance running, women could actually outperform men— even in the traditional 'hard' male qualities of performance and time. The addition of such success to an accepted female capacity for greater skilfulness and artistry, say in things like dancing and gymnastics, could offer the prospect of a direct physical challenge to ideologies of male ascendancy.

It should be noted still, however, that the biological arguments continue to indicate greater male powers in direct strength and high-oxygen-needing 'explosive' activity.

Such suggestions perhaps make it necessary to specify and differentiate this analysis more. It may well be that a strong sporting or feminist frame of definitions could focus on certain kinds of female sports performance and argue for success or superiority here as a *general* claim to defeat simplistic, across-the-board notions about male superiority. This is, in a way, precisely strengthening the countervailing local force of definition of 'inert items' to struggle against the trivialisation and ideological incorporation of more general views about gender. There does seem scope for serious and dignified mobilisation here.

On the other hand we should not forget the massive and important area of popular culture and consciousness and its relation to sports reporting and activity. On the one hand we may expect the relative downgrading of sports in which women do excel with a further inflation of speed and strength in sport. On the other hand we should not underestimate the sense in which even success in some areas of sport may be *popularly* presented as the success of male standards in which, now, some women 'happen' to be represented. This would reinforce those notions of competition, effort and measurement which, for instance, are likely massively to turn young women off sport[13] in general, and to make the 'ideological choices' of successful but non-radicalised athletes and performers still more wretched: either they conspire to be 'feminine' under the even bigger contradic-tions of their now superior performance, or they accept an even stronger cultural definition of their inbuilt masculinity.

So much depends again on definition, and the relation between a cultural and biological definition of gender. If for sports women and feminists, physical performance can be properly posed not simply as a challenge to biological definitions but to a wholesale cultural definition, specifically to invalidate the basis of a cultural definition, then excellence in sport may be an important antidote to popular culture. But it must be remembered that this culture/biology relationship is anyway a variable and constructed one—a relationship of relative autonomy. Definitions are not tied to individuals—only to stereotypes. The cultural definition can give up, even thrive on, many individual exceptions: the 'exceptions that prove the rule'. These general specifications of 'maleness' might be strengthened by a few well-publicised examples of a few women *meeting* them. A concession, or a little more commonality between the physical attributes of the sexes, can easily be met anyway by the power of other aspects of the cultural definition—that to behave in that 'masculine' way denies what is most valuable about the other intrinsic aspects of being female. Heroic sports success amongst a few women—without a massive, corresponding ideological battle to change the field of force of meaning—will not lead to greater participation regularly in schools and sports centres by girls and women, nor to a liberation in their sense of gender. A particular notion of masculine standards may, paradoxically, be reproduced and further 'negative' examples of femininity made regularly available.

CONCLUSION

In the general terms of my analysis I would like tentatively to suggest that the culturally effective way for sports women (and others) to counter their role as the unwilling victims in a larger legitimation of belief about the nature of sexes is to offer much more strongly their own version of sports reality which undercuts altogether the issues of male supremacy and the standards which measure it. In some ways such a view would be rooted in part, not in the *negation* of popular images about women, but in a selective reinforcement of some of their strengths. I mean that sport could be presented as a form of activity which emphasises human similarity and not dissimilarity, a form of activity which isn't competitive and measured, a form of activity which expresses values which are indeed unmeasurable, a form of activity which is concerned with individual well-being and satisfaction rather than with comparison. In such a view of sport, differences between the sexes would be unimportant, unnoticed. We wouldn't have the measures to realise that there was difference, or to be able to base conferences, or research projects, on measured differences—there would not be the fuel to supply popular consciousness with its prejudices about femininity.

If such a counter-definition of sport could be mounted, and it's here that research might play a more helpful role, then there would be the possibility of influencing society in the positive direction of challenging received ideas about the nature of men and women. As it is we must pessimistically conclude that, for the most part and for the moment, the responses of women involved in sport, sports reporting and most of the research done on sport, have been a force for reaction. They have been trapped in ideology.

NOTES

1. For the classic reference on hegemony and common sense, see A. Gramsci, 'Prison Notebooks', Lawrence & Wishart, London, 1973.
2. See J. Brohm, 'Sport: A Prison of Measured Time', Ink Links, London, 1978.
3. See S. Cohen and J. Young (eds), 'The Manufacture of News: Deviance, Social Problems and the Mass Media', Constable, London, 1973; and J. Ditton, 'Controlology: Beyond the New Criminology', Macmillan, London, 1979.
4. It is clear that one cannot propose an absolute 'gap' here. It is changeable subject to effort/training, and can in some sports operate to the advantage of women. I deal with the 'cultural' implications of this at the end of the article. See A. White, Sportswomen and society, in 'Report of the Langham Life 1st International Conference on Women in Sport', published by the Central Council of Physical Recreation, 1978.
5. 'Daily Mirror', 20 July 1973.
6. See A. White, op.cit.
7. The focus here is necessarily limited to the operation of ideology as lived experience in particular concrete areas, and does not attempt to outline a general theory of ideology and its connections with social and material relations.
8. See P. Willis, Shop floor culture, masculinity and the wage form, in C. Critcher et al. (eds), 'Working Class Culture', London, Hutchinson, 1979.
9. See P. Willis, 'Learning to Labour', Farnborough, Gower Press, 1977.
10. This is, of course, a very limited and foreshortened view of trade union activity which misses very important elements of opposition and struggle in the whole, complex relation of trade unions to the working class. The purpose here is one of exemplification. This central case is used not to show the total incorporation of trade unions, but to show generally the deep, 'obvious' and organic structure of ideology.
11. 'Sun' 'centre spread', 18 March 1980.
12. See note 4.
13. For a lively indication of just how far adolescent girls turn off from organised competitive sport, see M. Talbot, Girls' games—are they really worthwhile?, 'ILEA P.E. Journal', Summer 1974.

Chapter 3

Sport and the Maintenance of Masculine Hegemony

Lois Bryson
University of Newcastle
New South Wales, Australia

This Special issue of *Women's Studies International Forum* is one more demonstration that sport is at last coming into its own as a topic for mainstream theoretical analysis, and more pertinently for our purposes, for feminist analysis. Organized sport as we know it is historically a recent development (see Eric Dunning and Kenneth Sheard, 1979; Jan Graydon, 1983; Stephanie Twin, 1979) and much more so for women than for men (see Dyer, 1982; Jennifer Hargreaves, 1984; Reet Howell, 1983; King, 1978). This, together with the fact that sport has often been identified as play, has meant that it has generally not appealed to serious analysts as worthy of attention. Sports writing has been largely left to news reporters and commentators, an enterprise of extensive proportions and, as is only now being fully recognised, considerable social significance.

For many feminists, sport has, quite rightly, been identified as a supremely male activity and therefore eschewed, both in practice and as a topic of interest. However such an attitude cannot be sustained, since if we are to understand the processes of our domination, we ignore sport at our peril. Sport is a powerful institution through which male hegemony is constructed and reconstructed and it is only through understanding and confronting these processes that we can hope to break this domination.

On top of this, sport is of great personal importance to many women. It may provide not only a source of enjoyment but also contribute to a sense of identity

From ''Sport and the Maintenance of Masculine Hegemony'' by L. Bryson, 1987, *Women's Studies International Forum*, **10**(4), pp. 349-360. Copyright 1987 by Pergamon Journals Ltd. Reprinted by permission.

and competence (see Susan Mitchell and Ken Dyer, 1985; Stephanie Twin, 1979). For a relatively few women it also provides a source of income. For feminists there is the desire to reclaim, in some revamped form, sporting activities so that the enjoyment, sense of achievement, and physical benefits are maintained but in a manner that does not contribute to the oppression of non-dominant groups.

Male theorists with a critical perspective and progressive ideals are also likely to find themselves in a dilemma. Although some feel that sport is a trivial topic and therefore not worthy of serious consideration, others are concerned about its social implications. They criticize various aspects, such as its contribution to capitalism, racism, or nationalism (eg., Gruneau, 1983; David Rowe and Geoffrey Lawrence, 1984; Colin Tatz, 1984) and some are even concerned to reform its sexism (eg., Dyer, 1982; Paul Willis, 1982). However they often also have a strong emotional attachment to competitive sport, no doubt developed from an early age, which makes them loath, to give it too bad a press.

Some male socialists do however take a position similar to some feminists, that in a genuinely equal society, competitive sport must disappear (Jean-Marie Brohm, 1978: 52; Colin Sparks, 1980). This conclusion is too strong medicine for most, though, and reform is much more likely to be the chosen path. Another reason for radicals and Marxists taking a fairly soft line with sport is because of the 'working class's evident enjoyment' (Brohm, 1976: vii).

For feminists the dilemma is even greater. Sport is so thoroughly masculinized that it seems unlikely that it can be reclaimed to serve women's interests. However there is also a sense in which women cannot afford to allow its effects to continue unchallenged. Negative evaluations of women's capacities are implicit in the masculine hegemony in which sport is embedded. This has the effect of promoting male solidarity through the exclusion process which provides support and fuel for negative male attitudes towards women. Women themselves finish up accepting that men are more capable than they are. Attitudes about the relative gender capability are not confined, in their effects, to the sporting arena. They are basic to maintaining masculine hegemony: sport crucially privileges males and inferiorizes women. As Twin expresses it:

> The way sports are encouraged and organized for boys is perhaps the most impressionable way girls observe that males are to be active while females are not. Psychological theories, custom, and popular prejudice combine to measure women negatively against men. (Stephanie Twin, 1979: xv)

There are two fundamental dimensions to the support sport provides for masculine hegemony. First it links maleness with highly valued and visible skills and second it links maleness with the positively sanctioned use of aggression/force/ violence. The process of coopting sport for males has the effect of inferiorizing femaleness and female activities. By implication it seems that females are unable to do things that are skillful and valued highly. This is of course only one aspect of a very general process, but sport is an area charged with very significant, and frequent, emotive experiences which make its effects potent.

In her book *Towards a Psychology of Women*, Baker Miller (1976) discusses the broad issue of the way emphasis in society on psychological characteristics regarded as masculine has an inferiorizing effect on those considered feminine, for example, skills in interpersonal relationships, nurturing and responsiveness. She suggests that lots of the things that women do are seen as 'not doing anything' (Baker Miller, 1976: 57). Sport is a very significant domain for the perpetuation of this ideology. As Ann Hall expresses it, sport is 'an ideological institution with enormous symbolic significance that contributes to and perpetuates cultural hegemony' (Hall, 1985: 38).

Sporting activities in which women are predominant such as ice skating and gymnastics are treated as different from the 'real' sports, as defined in male interests. Ballet dancing, while recognised as an art form and for its grace, is not recognised for the strength, skill, and endurance of the performers. Apart from a very few stars, it certainly does not provide the same cachet as involvement in the major male sports. Consideration of ballet illustrates that the hegemony is a selective one which while it excludes women also excludes many men as well and certainly gay men. As Tim Carrigan, Bob Connell, and John Lee put it there are 'hegemonic masculinity and various subordinated masculinities' (1985: 590).

A series of social processes is implicated in the way in which sport is coopted by males as their territory and women are effectively excluded, not necessarily from sport itself, but certainly from sport which encroaches on the male domain. Basically women are prevented from competing, often completely, but if they are able to get a toe in, they compete on unequal terms and are unequally recognised for their achievements. The political processes can be peeled off to reveal a sequence of Catch 22 situations. Each layer ensnares a certain number of female participants, or would be participants. If the first layer does not get you then it is very likely that one of the subsequent ones will.

I want to tease out these processes through which women are effectively marginalized in their participation in sport, using examples from the sports scene in Australia to demonstrate these points. The examples are excruciatingly predictable and tally with experiences in most other advanced industrial societies. Despite this familiarity, there remains a need to very carefully analyze what is going on in sport because it is only through understanding the 'actual concrete conditions of women's experience' (Hall, 1985) that we can plan effective strategies to counteract the effects of male dominance.

This is a fortunate time to be writing because the federal government last year published the report of an inquiry into aspects of women's sport in Australia. The report is entitled *Women, Sport and the Media* and was prepared by the Working Group on Women in Sport (WGWS). The group has assembled a very useful array of data, though their conclusions are far more conciliatory than this material would seem to warrant. The reports provide much of the empirical data to demonstrate the concrete processes I have identified as ones through which sport contributes to the maintenance of hegemonic masculinity. Four of these processes are chosen for fairly extensive discussion. These are: definition, direct control, ignoring, and trivialization.

DEFINITIONS OF SPORT

Perhaps the most basic process is one of definition. Sport is largely defined as something in which men, and children participate, though boys far more than girls. As Libby Darlison points out 'if women want to play the game, they are going to have to play it by male rules' (Darlison, 1983: 38). This defining process is effective and shows up in the fact that far fewer women than men participate in sporting activities. This has been observed in virtually all countries for which we have information (see Ann Hall and Dorothy Richardson, 1982; Jennifer Hargreaves, 1982: chap 4; National Advisory Council on Women's Education Programs, 1981; James Riordan, 1980), even in East Germany where a concerted effort has been made to develop women's sport and where women's performances are closer to men's than in any other country (Dyer, 1982: 216).

In Australia a large proportion of women drop out of sport at the end of their school years (WGWS, 1985: 28). A survey by the Capital Territory Health Commission found that up to the age of fifteen years, boys and girls were equally likely to exercise. By seventeen years, fifteen percent fewer girls exercised three times a week or more. The gap widens with increasing age. An extensive 1983 survey by the National Heart Foundation found that only half as many women as men, aged between twenty-five and sixty-four met the minimum exercise requirement for heart and lung fitness in the survey period (WGWS, 1985: 58). This lower rate of involvement in exercise may change as women respond to a general trend to seek increased levels of fitness. Although we do not have longitudinal studies of participation, greater involvement in jogging, aerobics, and other forms of exercise and sport are observable. Nonetheless, any statistical effect may be counterbalanced by an increase in male participation as well.

There is however a vast store of evidence which provides illustration that sport is traditionally defined in such a way as to engage men rather than women. A survey conducted by the Australian Broadcasting Tribunal's Research Branch in 1980 found that thirteen percent of the men interviewed said that if they could only watch one television program per week they would choose a sport. Only one percent of women choose similarly (WGWS, 1985: 125). School children learn very early the message about the masculinity of sport. A recent survey of 2500 school students found that most girls as well as boys acknowledged a sports hero. None of the boys chose a female, though half the girls had male heroes (WGWS, 1985).

Those trying to step outside the traditional definitions are likely to meet with difficulty. The Korfball Association of Australia in answering a questionnaire distributed by the Working Group on Women in Sport, made two comments that are pertinent here. They pointed out that school students who are interested in participating are 'often frustrated' because schools are organized around a traditional division of sport into single sex groupings (WGWS, 1985: 122). Problems also arise with media coverage because commentators find it 'difficult having a non-sexist (non-male?) approach to commentary' (WGWS, 1985: 122).

Probably the most potent ingredient of the hegemonic definitions is the biological element. As Paul Willis points out, this is something that is identified as 'natural.' Thus it can be "seen—not interpreted . . . it is one of the grounds of ideology because of its apparent autonomy from 'biased' interpretation" (Willis, 1982: 117). Yet it is evident that the 'facts' do not speak for themselves. Biological arguments about the relationship between intelligence and sex (and race), have been well rehearsed over this century and, if not entirely won, then substantially so. We are just moving into the phase of contesting the biological issue in relation to sex and sport. Works such as Dyer's *Challenging the Men* (1982) explicitly address this aspect of ideology.

DIRECT CONTROL OF WOMEN'S SPORT

A second level of effect comes from the organization of sport, which is largely in the hands of men even when the sport has a largely female following. For example the Australian National Ice Skating Association with only six percent of its members male, had an all male executive in the 1984-5 period, except for the vice president. Basketball which claimed an equal membership of men and women during the same period had an all male executive at the national level and at the state levels as well. It also has four bodies that are responsible for policy matters, a Women's Commission, Junior Commission (boys and girls), Referees Commission and Referees Committee. Only the Women's Commission had women members and there they occupied three of four positions (WGWS, 1985: 120-1). This is a constantly recurring pattern. The Australian Sports Directory, 1985, contains a list of those occupying official positions in the key national sporting bodies in the country. Fifty-eight positions were held by women and 256 by men (WGWS, 1985: 43). This is equivalent to an 18 percent women's representation whereas even taking the Sports Directory's own figures for the major sports, 28 percent of members are women. This figure is likely to underrepresent women's participation because the list covers only eight sports, including the male bastions of soccer, football, and cricket.

The more the available kudos, the greater the masculinity rate among those in power. Those responsible for sport's policy at the international level are overwhelmingly male. The 1984 International Olympic Committee consisted of eighty-six men and three women and even this representation is a recent thing. The first women were elected in 1981, after a long campaign to break the total male domination. At the same time, however, the Federation of International

Gymnastics which represents the major Olympic sport for women is almost exclusively male (Hargreaves, 1984: 18).

The importance of this male control is clearly demonstrated by a consideration of the unequal involvement of women in Olympic competition. The number of events in which women can compete has been gradually increasing, but while 1984 was the first year there was a women's marathon, there remain for example no 5,000 and 10,000 metre events. Perhaps even more significant is the fact that until 1984, when one event was included, there were no cycling events for women though as Dyer points out this is one of the few sports in which women have held a record 'superior' to the equivalent men's record (Dyer, 1982: 185).

On top of the direct control of the sports' organizations themselves, we have an overwhelming maleness of commentators, politicians who are responsible for decisions of direct relevance to sport, and business people who are responsible for decisions about sponsorship. Thus with few exceptions men are making critical decisions that frame the environment in which women's sport exists.

In netball, in some states, women have made the decision to exclude men from administrative positions, though not always from coaching and officiating. More recently, positions at the national level have been reserved for women. This caused a predictable reaction from some men. A recent letter, which in fact remained unpublished, was received by the editor of the *Bulletin*, probably Australia's leading weekly magazine, in response to an article on discrimination against women in sport. It pointed to the netball situation of 'discrimination' and suggested that "It is unfortunate that the administrators of this sport have failed to understand the advantages of equality in sport."

Recent two inch headlines in the Northern Territory's *Sunday Territorian* announced this as a 'Sex Ban' and reported that one of the Territory's women officials is to take the matter to the local anti-discrimination tribunal, saying 'it's just blatant sex discrimination' (Atkinson, 1986: 21). Such reactions demonstrate what is at stake and the threat involved in such attempts to reclaim control. They also show the depth of acceptance by men of the current system, and because of the strength of the hegemony, by many women as well. Paul Willis (1982) has analyzed in some detail the pressures which lead to collusion by women in the hegemony.

The number of female sport reporters is so few that the recent report on *Women Sport and the Media* had no trouble in listing for Australia all the major newspaper and radio reporters. On radio there are three women (only two at the time of the inquiry), and newspapers have about fifteen women reporters across the whole country.

The effects of direct control, which is basically in men's interests, are too extensive to document, but range from poor funding, through inferior access to grounds, equipment, times for matches and for practice, poor access to the media, sponsorship, training facilities, coaches, and on and on. In calling for submissions the federal government inquiry elicited extensive lists of the discrimination that women suffer in sport.

The list of ways in which women are affected are usually modest in their claims because most women do not thoroughly analyze the extent of the discrimination. The differential provision of facilities is rarely costed, yet the more costly sports are almost invariably those where males predominate. Motor car and motor cycling racing circuits, yachting marinas, horse racing tracks, are but a few of the facilities that are provided for the mostly male participants. Crowd and safety controls are additional costs to the community and these are undoubtedly shared by women even though very few have the benefits of direct participation. Even when costs are paid by sponsors, women pay their share in the increased cost of products to cover the outlays on sponsorship. Where there are tax savings for the company, women suffer at least equally from the loss of government revenue and probably more because they are more likely to be poor and to be reliant on government support and services (Hilda Scott, 1984).

When we consider medical services and the call on these for ministering to sport's injuries there are very clear gender biases. A survey of sporting injuries carried out in New South Wales in one suburb in 1980, found that four sports account for most injuries. Three are men's sports, two codes of rugby and soccer. The fourth is a women's sport, netball. Netball and soccer had about the same injury rate but the injuries from netball were far less serious. The rugby codes between them had an injury rate three times as high and these were also far more serious than the injuries sustained by the netball players (Lawrence Lai, 1982).

Thus it must be recognised that women, although they participate less in sport, and usually in sports requiring fewer expensive accoutrements, are in fact subsidizing male sporting activities. If we took into account the private expenditures within families and between couples the discrimination would be further magnified.

When contemplating the political control that regularly occurs, I will present only one example. This was a quite dramatic case in 1984 which demonstrates a paternalism of extraordinarily, anachronistic proportions. This occurred in New South Wales when the Premier stepped in to ban a bout of kick boxing that had been planned between women contestants. A clause relating to 'the preservation of good manners and decorum,' from The Theatre and Balls Act of 1908, was invoked. It became apparent that women's boxing, with its explicit focus on violence is far too threatening to masculine hegemony to be permitted, let alone encouraged. Such protection of male territory must be recognised as purely ideological since one cannot but agree with one of the organizers, who retorted to the horrified Premier, 'It's no more disgraceful or demeaning for women to fight than it is for men' (Macken, 1984: 3).

IGNORING WOMEN'S SPORT

Ignoring women's sport is the next strategy in the line of exclusionist processes. If women do make it through the masculine definitions and male control then they are largely ignored. The federal report presents yet another set of figures that demonstrate that the media is almost solely concerned with men's sport. A survey of media coverage, over one week in May 1980 was repeated for a comparable week in 1984. Some differences did emerge, though they were not in respect of greater coverage. Rather, in 1984, there was somewhat less trivialization and this seemed to be directly related to the increased number of women involved in the reporting.

The 1980 week's survey revealed that 2 percent of sport reportage in the major capital city newspapers, was devoted to women's sport, in 1984 the comparable figure was 1.3 percent. In 1980, on average, four times as many male sports as female had their results reported. In 1984 the figure was five times as many. The picture is consistent over time for photographs as well. In 1980, pictures of men's sport appeared thirteen times more often than of women's, the figure for 1984 was twelve times. Though somewhat fewer in number in 1984 the shots were, however, 'more serious and less gratuitous.' Tennis, which provides the greatest degree of immediate comparability between men and women, had the same number of photographs in both years and the same male/female ratio, ten to three. In 1980, 200 hours and 39 minutes of television time on Australian capital city channels was devoted to sport during the survey period. Of this, five minutes was devoted to women's sport. Comparable figures are not provided for 1984 (WGWS, 1985).

One area where the examples of ignoring women's sporting achievements are very striking is the case of endurance events where women's performances are often equal to men's or surpass them. Despite women's extensive achievements in those sporting activities requiring endurance, the stereotype of the frail female has not been dislodged. Dyer in his book, *Challenging the Men* summarized the impressive record of women swimmers:

> two of the fastest times in Lake Windemere are held by women, eight of the ten fastest English Channel swims in either direction and the non-stop record each way are held by women; and the each way and both way records for Catalina Channel Swims are held by women. (Dyer, 1982: 184).

Over the last four years in Australia a long distance race from Sydney in Melbourne has been staged. In 1986 this ultra marathon was a distance of 1000 kilometres though in previous years it was marginally shorter. In 1985 a field of twenty-seven started the race, nine finished. All three women contestants finished, coming in at seventh, eight, and ninth position. In 1986, twenty-eight contestants started, and ten finished. Once again three women entered the race but this time only two finished, coming in at fourth and ninth positions. Eleanor Smith was the first woman home on both occasions, thus she demonstrated a significant improvement over the twelve month period and a performance in 1986 better than eighty-eight percent of the men. In both years the newspaper reportage of the women's efforts was minimal. On some days there was a small paragraph at the end of a much larger spread about the male contestants.

Given that the women only achieved minor placings it might be argued that they could not expect more coverage than they received. However, looked at from a different perspective one must ask why their performance was not the highlight of both events. What these women were doing was challenging the 'weak woman' stereotype. Not that this has not been done by many other women and similarly met with silence. Such persistent reactions can only be explained with reference to their ideological basis.

This ignoring of women's achievements is by no means confined to situations in which they fail to win, it extends to situations in which they do win. In 1983 the Australian netball team won the world championships. There was virtually no media recognition of this fact until months after the event when there was a replay on television. The fact that the Australian women's water polo team currently holds the world title and that Sue Cook in 1984, with several women's walking records, was the only Australian to hold a world athletics record, were also unrecognised. These sports are however minor sports and the public may be relatively, though doubtless not equally, ignorant of men's achievements in similar events. Netball, however, is *not* a minor sport. In 1985 the official national registrations for netball, as listed in the Australian Sports Directory were the fourth highest of any sport. They were not far short of the sports occupying the first three places, which were men's cricket, men's Australian rules football, and men's soccer (WGWS, 1985: 100).

It is only recently that Australian women have been allowed to compete as jockeys in major horse races and it seems that they do this exceptionally well. In fact it seems likely that this is one activity in which women would generally outperform men if they were to receive encouragement or at least equal opportunity. While a great deal of effort has been put into explaining why women will never be able to compete with men in sports that require power and speed, very little seems to have been written about the sports in which women are likely to excel, such as the endurance events already discussed. Given that light weight is an advantage for horse racing, there is an obvious case here for superiority. Again the silence that surrounds such matters underlines the ideological nature of the debate about sporting prowess. Horse racing involves the additional facet of, more explicitly than most events, objectifying a 'feminine' image of women. The Melbourne Cup, Australia's most popular and famous event, in similar vein to Ascot, is an explicit fashion show, with almost as much media space devoted to what the women wear as to the race itself.

Most analytic attention devoted to horse racing in Australia has focused on the gambling component (Haig, 1985; McCoy, n.d.; O'Hara, n.d.). It certainly has not provided a locus for feminist analysis. Yet it is the leading 'sport' in Australia as far as media coverage is concerned (WGWS, 1985:116) thus this lack of attention is to be deplored. Though this paper is not the place to try to rectify this omission it is worth pointing out that in Tasmania, Australia's least populous, smallest, and only island state, women jockeys are gaining a significant foothold. Out of ten or twelve apprentice riders in the state half are girls and they are doing extremely well. Bev Buckingham has recently made world herstory by taking out the state annual jockey premiership. At seventeen years and in the second year of a five year apprenticeship, she was not only the first woman to achieve this but also the first apprentice. Her success has not been greeted with enthusiasm by her male opponents. She comments that

> I know that the male jockeys don't like being beaten by girls. They would prefer that girls didn't ride really. I suppose that's normal, because it's been a male territory for so long. (Susan Mitchell and Ken Dyer, 1985: 143)

In another mixed sport, shooting, we find an active response to recent demonstrations by women that they possess equal skill. Australia's Sylvia Muehlberg's achievements provide an example of the pressure being exerted by women. In 1982 she received a gold medal for the prone team event at Caracas, Venezuela (Mitchell and Dyer, 1985: 130). Despite a long history of integrated competition, this sort of success has encountered a backlash from men at the international level. All Olympic events were mixed until 1984 when they were effectively segregated. Sylvia Muehlberg believes this was because of the

> recognition by many men on the International Shooting Union that the days of their supremacy in a traditional male sport were numbered. (Mitchell and Dyer, 1985: 128)

Australian women's cricket has also suffered an interesting fate and one which it would be informative to scrutinize in some detail. There are periodic test matches played against Britain and one such occasion was the summer of 1984-5. There was some publicity and with the federal working party looking into matters of discrimination in sport at that time, even some comparisons between the relatively lavish support provided for men's test teams and the appalling little support received by the women, who incidentally won their series while the men lost theirs.

Reminiscences were also the order of the day and it became apparent that women's cricket at other times had quite a following and that men and women played together on festive occasions, or to raise money. What seems to have happened is that the women did on occasions play superior cricket. Examples were given by retired women players of clean bowling male test players on the first ball. This apparently caused considerable resentment. Gradually the women players were frozen out and have been largely ignored by men's cricket since the forties. This analysis has been pieced together from scrappy pieces of information. At present it really has the status of an hypothesis which requires systematic testing. Nonetheless from this example, the international shooting experience and others reported in the literature, it does become clear that where women do achieve what men see as significant performances these are likely to be ignored and forgotten. If threat is too great they may be excluded from the arena entirely. Only in this way can men maintain their power and sustain the view, as Sattler, an Australian sports commentator expressed it recently, that virtually all 'women's sport is second rate' (Clancy, 1985: 2).

Thus we must recognise the ignoring of women's sport as not merely a passive and inadvertent act. It is a dynamic process and one which is invoked to protect hegemonic masculinity.

The federal inquiry laid some of the blame for the lack of coverage of women's sport at the door of the women's sporting associations themselves. It was suggested that they were not well organized to deal with the media. Be that as it may, and with little funding and experience this may understandably be the case, it is highly unlikely that this is a particularly significant factor in the long run. This can be demonstrated by media reportage, this time of the Australian Surf Life Saving Championships in March 1985. The *Sydney Morning Herald* was clearly in touch with the events, as is evidenced by their story that Grant Kenny, a famous male sports hero, only achieved tenth position in the iron man competition. What they failed to report was that Jodie Larsen won the women's surf racing championship, and did so despite illness. This was the first time that a women's race had been included, or so it is generally believed. The occasion did however elicit a response from an 84 year old Sydney man who claims that his sister, Violet Grover, won the first open surf championship in Australia before World War I against all male competitors. This appears to be another example of amnesia about women's activities and achievements (Grover, 1985: 15).

To return to the judgment that women's sports are intrinsically less interesting than men's, a point that is usually linked to the biological argument that women are less able to produce impressive feats of strength and skill, Norman May, one of Australia's best known sports commentators and a member of the federal inquiry into women and sport, pointed out that sporting events are not intrinsically interesting but are made so. He uses the example of the America's cup which was turned into a popular event over a brief period of its history, and examples of the television hype which has been given in Australia to snooker and lawn bowls, hardly spectacular power sports.

TRIVIALIZATION OF WOMEN IN SPORT

If women do scramble through all the obstacles and lack of support and make it into the media then they are very likely to find their efforts trivialized. The methods by which this is done vary greatly and range from prohibitions on coaching men to the very familiar ploy of treatment as a sex object and mother thus implying that women's real role is in a subordinate relationship to men not acting as a competent individual.

Kathryn Spurling, Australia's first woman to become a qualified Grade 1 Track and Field coach, found that she was prevented from coaching males over 15 years of age. This, she was told would be 'unnatural' (WGWS, 1985: 75). Men of course actually find it unnatural to be excluded from women's sport, as the example of netball administration demonstrates.

References to appearance and to relational, marital, and family situations abound in Australia, as they do in other countries (Graydon, 1983; Hall, 1981; Twin, 1979). So many examples present themselves, the choice is difficult to make. Among some chosen from recent newspaper articles, almost at random we find a picture of Rosemary Longstaff, a marathon runner training behind a stroller, with the caption 'Marathon mum is pushing off to London,' while Vicki Cardwell, a leading world squash player is described as having 'a larrikin laugh and a Ginger Meggs cheekiness written all over her face.' Lisa Harris, a successful jockey, was the subject of the headline 'Lady jockey grounded after lover's tiff.' A similar selection of headlines about men's sport reads 'Thompson hits front,' 'Lewis coasts to 100m defeat,' or more sensationally 'Screaming kick for the big time' (taekwondo graphic), 'Battling Blues trample Saints' (Australian rules).

Female body builders come in for some of the most blatantly patronizing comment with strong sexual innuendos. A recent newspaper article about one of the contestants in the United Bodybuilders Association Australian Titles was by lined 'Michelle's certainly got a great . . . smile.' In the text we are told that 'she is a lithe, personable, blue-eyed blonde, who would not be out of place in a Farrah Fawcett look alike contest' (Romel, 1986: 59). Bev Francis, a power lifter and holder of numerous world records, reports that even judges in women's body building competitions have a definition of muscles for women that is restricted by their definition of femininity. At the Women's World Cup in 1983, in which she came eighth, one of the judges confessed to her after the event that:

> As a body builder you were the best, but in a women's body building competition I just felt that I couldn't vote for you. (Mitchell and Dyer, 1985: 97)

Even women spectators are treated differently. Of the crowd at a boxing match one report reads 'Festival Hall was filled with 2000 people—mainly men but with a sprinkling of dumb blondes' (Clancy, 1982: 2).

Where women do try to change attitudes and mount a successful argument this is likely to be denigrated as well. On a Melbourne television current affairs program, anchored by Michael Willesee, in November 1984, the issues surrounding integrated sporting activities in primary school were debated. Strong views were expressed on both sides and in conclusion the woman journalist hit on the dramatically engaging idea of arranging a swimming race between girls and boys. There were six eleven year olds and the three girls were interviewed individually before the race. All expressed the view that the boys would win but despite these misgivings the girls came in first, second and third. The anchor man could not resist the comment that the race must have been rigged.

MEN'S SPORT AND
MAINTENANCE OF HEGEMONIC MASCULINITY

So far the paper has concentrated on the processes by which women's sport is negated and controlled by men, thus effectively excluding them from direct competition within the territory. I have discussed a series of processes that mesh together to form an extraordinarily resilient, though not totally unassailable, combination in support of male dominance and women's subordination. We need to turn to the reciprocal of this ideological construction of femininity, the masculinity that sport directly promotes and how this is achieved.

As was raised earlier, key features of sport are the linking of maleness with highly valued and visible skills and with the positively sanctioned use of aggression/force/violence. Apart from the processes directed at women, this linking is made through the types of sport men play and through the celebration of men's sport in the public arena. Sporting events have a ritual element which continually strengthens the hegemony and the dimension of male solidarity, not just for the teams, but for men in general. The potential of the effect of the ritual element has been magnified by recent developments in the media. Certain sports are more centrally implicated in hegemonic maintenance than others. In Australia key sports are football and cricket, though different sports may occupy this position in other countries.

The media surveys of 1980 and 1984 not only show the lack of recognition of women's sport, they clearly show just what it is to which people are exposed. In the two surveys the three codes of football ranked second, third and fourth to horse racing. In horse racing, the honours tend to be shared between the horse, the trainer and small men and so this is not a sport of pivotal concern in the construction of hegemonic masculinity, though it undoubtedly plays a solid supporting role here and has other important effects. Racing and football were followed by cricket (even though the survey period was outside the cricket season), car racing, golf, and tennis, though the rank order of these varied marginally over the four years. In 1980 the top sixteen sports were men's, but in 1984 this had dropped to eleven. Women's sports are unstable in the order in which they receive coverage, which suggests that the reasons for inclusion in the media are relatively haphazard. Attendance at the sports seem to broadly follow the media coverage. If we exclude horse racing, the codes of football, together with cricket, provide for the most regular and extensive spectating opportunities.

The same stability of coverage for men's sports is seen in the newspaper photographs and the same instability of women's sport. Horse racing ranked second each time, with codes of football in first, third, and fourth positions. These four provided the overwhelming proportion of all the photographs, accounting for seventy-three percent in 1980 and seventy-four percent in 1984. The top women's sport each time accounted for less than one percent (WGWS, 1985: 117).

In these events, to which the public is massively exposed, maleness is repeatedly linked with skill, strength, aggression, and often violence. Codes of football throughout the world are very much associated with violence, though other sports can also be important, for example, ice hockey in Canada. Much has been written by feminists on the importance of physical threat to the subjugation of women and clearly the annexation of physical force cannot be accounted for by differential strength alone. Small men learn to be tough and aggressive, while even large women rarely do. Sport needs to be analyzed along with rape, pornography, and domestic violence as one of the means through which men monopolize physical force.

The importance of the ritualistic element of any activity is largely dependent on the frequency and the setting in which people are confronted by 'objects of thought and feeling which they hold to be of special significance' (Stephen Lukes, 1975: 291). The reinforcement provided by the sheer volume of male sport that confronts us makes the messages especially potent. Thus we find boys from a very early age being schooled in the appropriate behaviour and sentiments at the same time as girls are learning that they are excluded.

In 1983 in Sydney we witnessed an unusually vivid elucidation of the values embedded in the key male sports. This took the form of a television commercial to promote rugby. It is certainly clear that it is promoting male dominance at the same time. It is presented as a heroic arrangement involving choir and orchestra. The words are as follows:

> See that boy growing up over there,
> They say he's the image of you,
> What would he say if you ruffled his hair,
> And said, 'Son, here's what we'll do:
> Chorus (choir): Show him the game,
> Feel the roar of the crowd,
> This is men against men, doing it proud,
> Show him the courage, show him the skill,
> What it means to be part of a team, someday he will,
> It's never the same, unless you're there at the game (repeat),
> This weekend show your kid the greatest game of all.

The visuals are almost entirely masculine, apart from some indistinguishable women in the large crowd. The excited boy of about ten years watches the tough game with his father. There is much clashing of bodies and finally the jubilation of players and spectators as a try is scored, by a suitably battered 'rough diamond' player.

This popular advertisement was played over and over during that season. However at a certain stage, the blatancy of its masculinity was apparently recognised as not in the advertiser's best interests and a mother and daughter were added to the visuals. This is, of course, only one specific example of the continuing process of differential gender exposure to actual sporting events and information about sport. Nor is the association that is established between maleness, skill, and strength limited to the sporting field. Cynthia Cockburn outlines quite similar effects in the workplace though the concrete form of the political process varies. In an analysis of the basis of the power of male compositors in the British printing industry, Cockburn points out that "the appropriation of muscle, capability, tools and machinery by men is an important source of women's subordination, indeed it is part of this process by which females are constructed as women" (Cockburn, 1981: 44).

We must interpret the tools and machinery of sport to include the organizational machinery and indeed Cockburn's own analysis heads us in this direction. She is in fact interested in the 'material of male power,' choosing the term material rather than economic because of its broader connotations, which include the physical and the socio-political. What we have then are three 'material' areas in which to consider practice, the physical, the socio-political and the economic. Because Cockburn's use of the term material is much more encompassing than that of many other theorists (eg., Rob Beamish, 1984) it is therefore more incisive for feminist analysis.

CONCLUSION

What I have been considering are the concrete methods by which, through the medium of sport, women are maintained in their subordinate position. At this stage it is easy to feel as Graydon says she did, like throwing up our

> hands in horror and say(ing) that women should have nothing further to do with such a self-indulgent festival of masculinity. (Graydon, 1983: 8)

Involvement in sport raises for women similar issues to those raised by involvement in the world of business and employment. Are we to take up places within the current system on men's terms, when it is clear that it has been created by men and they control it. Since women have different interests would these not be better served by a changed or a separate system rather than squeezing into the existing one. This of course is the crux of the argument of radical feminist separatists.

These are issues that are of critical relevance in both arenas. If we contemplate a separate system we must recognize that it is difficult to work out the details of the system we would prefer, and the fact that bringing this about has proved an elusive task. People with power do not give it up easily, and change raises problems and reactions which people, including women, often prefer to avoid. With sport, feminists are in an acute Catch 22 situation, as they are in the management field. To compete almost of itself seems to promote dominant male values, because sport is currently defined in these terms. Yet to not compete tends to confirm the stereotype of women as lacking in those attributes of skill and power that the stereotype conveys.

Closer inspection however, of the way men protect their dominant positions makes it obvious that male domination is in fact continually being constructed and reconstructed as it is constantly under challenge. Greater understanding of the political techniques of the patriarchal order (Tim Carrigan, Bob Connell and John Lee, 1985) will assist in the intensification of this challenge.

An understanding of the processes discussed here, should assist us to mount resistance on many fronts. We need to challenge the definitions of sport; take control of women's sports and a share of men's since at the very least women subsidize these and are spectators; persistently provide information and reject attempts to ignore; and attack trivialization. The means must be chosen imaginatively but these actions can be approached through formal channels, such as anti-discrimination provisions, through encouraging women in sport not only as competitors but as commentators, reporters, administrators, and coaches and through demanding our political rights to equality. In addition, we need to promote the development of counter hegemonic sporting activities, not only for their intrinsic value, but also because of their capacity to highlight the contradictions.

Over recent years much effort has gone into developing women's sport and reclaiming it. I have changed my position somewhat over that time from being unconvinced about the wisdom of becoming enbroiled at all to being convinced that if we vacate the scene, we merely support masculine hegemony. What we must do is encourage the development of reflective and critical understanding and practice.

REFERENCES

Atkinson, Geoff. 1986, April 13. Sex ban. *Sunday Territorian*, p. 21.

Baker Miller, Jean. 1976. *Towards a Psychology of Women*. Harmonsworth, Penguin.

Beamish, Rob. 1984. Materialism and the comprehension of gender-related issues in sport. In Theberge, N. and Donnelly, P., eds, *Sport and the Sociological Imagination*. Texas Christian University Press, Fort Worth.

Brohm, Jean-Marie. 1976. *Sport: A Prison of Measured Time*. Ink Links, London.

Carrigan, Tim, Connell, Bob, and Lee, John. 1985. Toward a new sociology of masculinity. *Theory and Society* **14**(5): 551-604.

Clancy. 1982, October 10-16. Women's role. *The National Times*, p. 2.

Clancy. 1985, February 5-12. *The National Times*, p. 2.

Cockburn, Cynthia. 1981. The material of male power. *Feminist Review* **9**: 41-59.

Darlison, Libby. 1983. The games and the place of women in Australian sport and society. In *The 1982 Commonwealth Games: A Retrospect*. Australian Studies Centre, University of Queensland.

Dunning, Eric and Sheard, Kenneth. 1979. *Barbarians, Gentlemen and Players: A Sociological Study of the Development of Football.* Martin Robertson, Oxford.

Dyer, K. F. 1982. *Challenging the Men.* University of Queensland Press, St. Lucia.

Graydon, Jan. 1983. But it's more than a game. It's an institution. *Feminist Review* **13**: 5-16.

Grover, Harry. 1985. The first iron maiden who broke the surfing barriers. *The Age*, p. 15.

Gruneau, R. 1983. *Class, Sports, and Social Development.* The University of Massachusetts Press, Amherst.

Haig, B. D. 1985. A debate in sports history: Illegal betting 1920/21 to 1970/71. *Sporting Traditions* **2**(1): 69-74.

Hall, M. Ann. 1981. *Sport, Sex Roles and Sex Identity.* Canadian Research Institute for the Advancement of Women, Ottawa.

Hall, M. Ann and Richardson, Dorothy A. 1982. *Fair Ball: Towards Sexual Equality in Canadian Sport.* The Canadian Advisory Council on the Status of Women, Ottawa.

Hall, M. Ann. 1985. Knowledge and gender: Epistemological questions in the social analysis of sport. *Sociology of Sport Journal* **2**: 25-42.

Hargreaves, Jennifer, ed. 1982. *Sport, Culture and Ideology.* Routledge and Kegan Paul, London.

Hargreaves, Jennifer. 1984. Taking men on at their games. *Marxism Today* **28**(8): 17-21.

Howell, Reet. 1983. Women at the Commonwealth games: An historical perspective. In *Seminar Paper: The Commonwealth Games: A Retrospect.* Australian Studies Centre, University of Queensland.

King, H. 1978. The sexual politics of sport; an Australian perspective. In Cashman, R. and McKernan, Michael, eds, *Sport in History.* University of Queensland Press, St. Lucia.

Lai, Lawrence. 1982. Sport injuries, a social burden. *Uniken* **161** : 6.

Lukes, Stephen. 1975. Political ritual and social integration. *Sociology* **9**: 283-308.

Macken, Deidre. 1984, September 14. Wran won't permit women's puch and bootee show. *The Age*, p. 3.

McCoy, Al. n.d. Sport as modern mythology: SP bookmaking in New South Wales 1920-1979. In Cashman, Richard and McKernan, Michael, eds, *Sport: Money, Morality and the Media.* University of New South Wales Press, Kensington.

Mitchell, Susan and Dyer, Ken. 1985. *Winning Women: Challenging the Norms in Australian Sport.* Penguin, Ringwood.

National Advisory Council on Women's Educational Programs. 1981. *Title IX: The Half Full, Half Empty Glass.* U.S. Department of Education, Washington, DC.

O'Hara, John. n.d. The Australian gambling tradition. In Cashman, Richard and McKernan, Michael, eds, *Sport: Money, Morality and the Media.* University of New South Wales Press, Kensington.

Riordan, James. 1980. *Soviet Sport*. Basil Blackwell, Oxford.

Romel, S. 1986, August 24-25. Michelle's certainly got a great . . . smile. *The Weekend Australian*, p. 59.

Rowe, David and Lawrence, Geoffrey. 1984. Saluting the state: nationalism and the olympics. *Australian Left Review* **90**: 28-32.

Scott, Hilda. 1984. *Working Your Way to the Bottom: The Feminization of Poverty*. Pandora, London.

Sparks, Colin. 1980. The opium of our time. *Socialist Review* **14**(7): 23-25.

Tatz, Colin. 1984. Race, politics, and sport. *Sporting Traditions* **1**(1): 2-36.

Twin, Stephanie L. 1979. *Out of the Bleachers*. Feminist Press, New York.

Willis, Paul. 1982. Women in sport in ideology. In Hargreaves, Jennifer, ed, *Sport, Culture and Ideology*. Routledge and Kegan Paul, London.

Working Group on Women in Sport. 1985. *Women Sport and the Media*. Australian Government Printing Service, Canberra.

Chapter 4

Sports and Male Domination:
The Female Athlete as Contested Ideological Terrain

Michael A. Messner
University of Southern California

Women's quest for equality in society has had its counterpart in the sports world. Since the 1972 passage of Title IX, women in the U.S. have had a legal basis from which to push for greater equity in high school and college athletics. Although equality is still a distant goal in terms of funding, programs, facilities, and media coverage of women's sports, substantial gains have been made by female athletes in the past 10 to 15 years, indicated by increasing numerical participation as well as by expanding peer and self-acceptance of female athleticism (Hogan, 1982; Sabo, 1985; Woodward, 1985). A number of commentators have recently pointed out that the degree of difference between male and female athletic performance—the "muscle gap"—has closed considerably in recent years as female athletes have gained greater access to coaching and training facilities (Crittenden, 1979; Dyer, 1983; Ferris, 1978).

However, optimistic predictions that women's movement into sport signals an imminent demise of inequalities between the sexes are premature. As Willis (1982, p. 120) argues, what matters most is not simply how and why the gap between male and female athletic performance is created, enlarged, or constricted; what is of more fundamental concern is "the manner in which this gap is understood and taken into the popular consciousness of our society." This paper is

Note. An earlier version of this paper was delivered at the North American Society for the Sociology of Sport Meetings in Las Vegas, Nevada, October 31, 1986.

thus concerned with exploring the historical and ideological meaning of organized sports for the politics of gender relations. After outlining a theory for building a historically grounded understanding of sport, culture, and ideology, I will demonstrate how and why organized sports have come to serve as a primary institutional means for bolstering a challenged and faltering ideology of male superiority in the 20th century.

It will be argued that women's movement into sport represents a genuine quest by women for equality, control of their own bodies, and self-definition, and as such it represents a challenge to the ideological basis of male domination. Yet it will also be demonstrated that this quest for equality is not without contradictions and ambiguities. The social meanings surrounding the physiological differences between the sexes in the male-defined institution of organized sports and the framing of the female athlete by the sports media threaten to subvert any counter-hegemonic potential posed by women athletes. In short, the female athlete—and her body—has become a contested ideological terrain.

SPORT, CULTURE, AND IDEOLOGY

Most theoretical work on sport has fallen into either of two traps: an idealist notion of sport as a realm of freedom divorced from material and historical constraints, or a materialist analysis that posits sport as a cultural mechanism through which the dominant classes control the unwitting masses. Marxists have correctly criticized idealists and functionalists for failing to understand how sport tends to reflect capitalist relations, thus serving to promote and ideologically legitimize competition, meritocracy, consumerism, militarism, and instrumental rationality, while at the same time providing spectators with escape and compensatory mechanisms for an alienated existence (Brohm, 1978; Hoch, 1972). But Marxist structuralists, with their view of sport as a superstructural expression of ideological control by the capitalist class, have themselves fallen into a simplistic and nondialectical functionalism (Gruneau, 1983; Hargreaves, 1982). Within the deterministic Marxian framework, there is no room for viewing people (athletes, spectators) as anything other than passive objects who are duped into meeting the needs of capitalism.

Neo-Marxists of the 1980s have argued for the necessity of placing an analysis of sport within a more reflexive framework, wherein culture is seen as relatively autonomous from the economy and wherein human subjectivity occurs within historical and structural limits and constraints. This theory puts people back at the center stage of history without falling into an idealistic voluntarism that ignores the importance of historically formed structural conditions, class inequalities, and unequal power relations. Further, it allows for the existence of critical thought, resistance to dominant ideologies, and change. Within a reflexive historical frame-work, we can begin to understand how sport (and culture in general) is a dynamic social space where dominant (class, ethnic, etc.) ideologies are perpetuated as well as challenged and contested.

Recent critics have called for a recasting of this reflexive theory to include gender as a centrally important process rather than as a simple effect of class dynamics (Critcher, 1986; McKay, 1986). Indeed, sport as an arena of ideological battles over gender relations has been given short shrift throughout the sociology of sport literature. This is due in part to the marginalization of feminist theory within sociology as a discipline (Stacey & Throne, 1985) and within sport sociology in particular (Birrell, 1984; Hall, 1984). When gender has been examined by sport sociologists, it has usually been within the framework of a sex role paradigm that concerns itself largely with the effects of sport participation on an individual's sex role identity, values, and so on (Lever, 1976; Sabo & Runfola, 1980; Schafer, 1975).[1] Although social-psychological examinations of the sport-gender relationship are important, the sex role paradigm often used by these studies too often

> ignores the extent to which our conceptions of masculinity and feminin-ity—the content of either the male or female sex role—is relational, that is, the product of gender relations which are historically and socially conditioned. . . . The sex role paradigm also minimizes the extent to which gender relations are based on power. Not only do men as a group exert power over women as a group, but the historically derived definitions of masculinity and femininity reproduce those power relations. (Kimmel, 1986, pp. 520-521)

The 20th century has seen two periods of crisis for masculinity—each marked by drastic changes in work and family and accompanied by significant feminist movements (Kimmel, 1987). The first crisis of masculinity stretched from the turn of the century into the 1920s, and the second from the post-World War II years to the present. I will argue here, using a historical/relational conception of gender within a reflexive theory of sport, culture, and ideology, that during these two periods of crisis for masculinity, organized sport has been a crucial arena of struggle over basic social conceptions of masculinity and femininity, and as such has become a fundamental arena of ideological contest in terms of power relations between men and women.

CRISES OF MASCULINITY
AND THE RISE OF ORGANIZED SPORTS

Reynaud (1981, p. 9) has stated that "The ABC of any patriarchal ideology is precisely to present that division [between the sexes] as being of biological, natural, or divine essence." And, as Clarke and Clarke (1982, p. 63) have argued, because sport "appears as a sphere of activity outside society, and particularly as it appears to involve natural, physical skills and capacities, [it] presents these ideological images *as if they were natural.*" Thus, organized sport is clearly a potentially powerful cultural arena for the perpetuation of the ideology of male superiority and dominance. Yet, it has not always been of such importance.

The First Crisis of Masculinity: 1890s Through the 1920s

Sport historians have pointed out that the rapid expansion of organized sport after the turn of the century into widespread "recreation for the masses" represented a cultural means of integrating immigrants and a growing industrial working class into an expanding capitalist order where work was becoming rationalized and leisure time was expanding (Brohm, 1978; Goldman, 1983/1984; Gruneau, 1983; Rigauer, 1981). However, few scholars of sport have examined how this expanding industrial capitalist order was interacting with a relatively autonomous system of gender stratification, and this severely limits their ability to understand the cultural meaning of orgnaized sport. In fact, industrial capitalism both bolstered and undermined traditional forms of male domination.

The creation of separate (public/domestic) and unequal spheres of life for men and women created a new basis for male power and privilege (Hartmann, 1976; Zaretsky, 1973). But in an era of wage labor and increasingly concentrated ownership of productive property, fewer males owned their own businesses and farms or controlled their own labor. The breadwinner role was a more shaky foundation upon which to base male privilege than was the patriarchal legacy of property-ownership passed on from father to son (Tolson, 1977). These changes in work and family, along with the rise of female dominated public schools, urbanization, and the closing of the frontier all led to widespread fears of "social feminization" and a turn-of-the-century crisis of masculinity. Many men compensated with a defensive insecurity that manifested itself in increased preoccupation with physicality and toughness (Wilkenson, 1984), warfare (Filene, 1975), and even the creation of new organizations such as the Boy Scouts of America as a separate cultural sphere of life where "true manliness" could be instilled in boys by men (Hantover, 1978).

Within this context, organized sports became increasingly important as a "primary masculinity-validating experience" (Dubbert, 1979, p. 164). Sport was a male-created homosocial cultural sphere that provided men with psychological separation from the perceived feminization of society while also providing dramatic symbolic proof of the "natural superiority" of men over women.[2]

This era was also characterized by an active and visible feminist movement, which eventually focused itself on the achievement of female suffrage. These feminists challenged entrenched Victorian assumptions and prescriptions concerning femininity, and this was reflected in a first wave of athletic feminism which blossomed in the 1920s, mostly in women's colleges (Twin, 1979). Whereas sports participation for young males tended to confirm masculinity, female athleticism was viewed as conflicting with the conventional ethos of femininity, thus leading to virulent opposition to women's growing athleticism (Lefkowitz-Horowitz, 1986). A survey of physical education instructors in 1923 indicated that 93% were opposed to intercollegiate play for women (Smith, 1970). And the Women's Division of the National Amateur Athletic Foundation, led by Mrs. Herbert Hoover, opposed women's participation in the 1928 Olympics (Lefkowitz-Horowitz, 1986). Those involved in women's athletics responded to this opposition defensively (and perhaps out of a different feminine aesthetic or morality) with the establishment of an anticompetitive "feminine philosophy of sport" (Beck, 1980). This philosophy was at once responsible for the continued survival of women's athletics, as it was successfully marginalized and thus easily "ghettoized" and ignored, and it also ensured that, for the time being, the image of the female athlete would not become a major threat to the hegemonic ideology of male athleticism, virility, strength, and power.

The breakdown of Victorianism in the 1920s had a contradictory effect on the social deployment and uses of women's bodies. On the one hand, the female body became "a marketable item, used to sell numerous products and services" (Twin, 1979, p. xxix). This obviously reflected women's social subordination, but ironically,

> The commercialization of women's bodies provided a cultural opening for competitive athletics, as industry and ambitious individuals used women to sell sports. Leo Seltzer included women in his 1935 invention, roller derby, "with one eye to beauty and the other on gate receipts," according to one writer. While women's physical marketability profited industry, it also allowed females to do more with their bodies than before. (Twin, 1979, p. xxix)

Despite its limits, then, the first wave of athletic feminism, even in its more commercialized manifestations, did provide an initial challenge to men's creation of sport as an uncontested arena of ideological legitimation for male dominance. In forcing an acknowledgment of women's physicality, albeit in a limited way, this first wave of female athletes laid the groundwork for more fundamental challenges. While some cracks had clearly appeared in the patriarchal edifice, it would not be until the 1970s that female athletes would present a more basic challenge to predominant cultural images of women.

The Post-World War II Masculinity Crisis and the Rise of Mass Spectator Sports

Today, according to Naison (1980, p. 36), "The American male spends a far greater portion of his time with sports than he did 40 years ago, but the greatest proportion of that time is spent in front of a television set observing games that he will hardly ever play." How and why have organized sports increasingly become an object of mass spectatorship? Lasch (1979) has argued that the historical transformation from entrepreneurial capitalism to corporate capitalism has seen a concomitant shift from the protestant work ethic (and industrial production) to the construction of the "docile consumer." Within this context, sport has degenerated into a spectacle, an object of mass consumption. Similarly, Alt (1983) states that the major function of mass-produced sports is to channel the alienated emotional needs of consumers in instrumental ways. Although Lasch and Alt are partly correct in stating that the sport spectacle is largely a manipulation of aliented emotional needs toward the goal of consumption, this explanation fails to account fully for the emotional resonance of the sports spectacle for a largely male audience. I would argue, along with Sabo and Runfola (1980, p. xv) that sports in the postwar era have become increasingly important to males precisely because they link men to a more patriarchal past.

The development of capitalism after World War II saw a continued erosion of traditional means of male expression and identity, due to the continued rationalization and bureaucratization of work, the shift from industrial production and physical labor to a more service-oriented economy, and increasing levels of structural unemployment. These changes, along with women's continued movement into public life, undermined and weakened the already shaky breadwinner role as a major basis for male power in the family (Ehrenreich, 1983; Tolson, 1977). And the declining relevance of physical strength in work and in warfare was not accompanied by a declining psychological need for an ideology of gender difference. Symbolic representations of the male body as a symbol of strength, virility, and power have become increasingly important in popular culture as actual inequalities between the sexes are contested in all arenas of public life (Mishkind et al., 1986). The marriage of television and organized sport—especially the televised spectacle of football—has increasingly played this important ideological role. As Oriard (1981) has stated,

> What football is for the athletes themselves actually has little direct impact on what it means to the rest of America . . . Football projects a *myth* that speaks meaningfully to a large number of Americans far beneath the level of conscious perception . . . Football does not create a myth for all Americans; it excludes women in many highly significant ways. (pp. 33-34)

Football's mythology and symbolism are probably meaningful and salient on a number of ideological levels: Patriotism, militarism, violence, and meritocracy are all dominant themes. But I would argue that football's primary ideological salience lies in its ability, in the face of women's challenges to male dominance, to symbolically link men of diverse ages and socioeconomic backgrounds. Consider the words of a 32-year-old white professional male whom I was interviewing:[3] "A woman can do the same job I can do—maybe even be my boss. But I'll be *damned* if she can go out on the field and take a hit from Ronnie Lott."

The fact that this man (and perhaps 99% of all U.S. males) probably could not take a hit from the likes of pro football player Ronnie Lott and live to tell about it is really irrelevant, because football as a televised spectacle is meaningful on a more symbolic level. Here individual males are given the opportunity to identify—generically and abstractly—with all men as a superior and separate caste. Football, based as it is upon the most extreme possibilities of the male body (muscular bulk, explosive power and aggression) is a world apart from women, who are relegated to the role of cheerleader/sex objects on the sidelines rooting their men on. In contrast to the bare and vulnerable bodies of the cheerleaders, the armored male bodies of football players are elevated to mythical status, and as such give testimony to the undeniable "fact" that there is at least one place where men are clearly superior to women.

WOMEN'S RECENT MOVEMENT INTO SPORT

By the 1970s, just when symbolic representations of the athletic male body had taken on increasing ideological importance, a second wave of athletic feminism had emerged (Twin, 1979). With women's rapid postwar movement into the labor force and a revived feminist movement, what had been an easily ignorable undercurrent of female athleticism from the 1930s through the 1960s suddenly swelled into a torrent of female sports participation—and demands for equity. In the U.S., Title IX became the legal benchmark for women's push for equity with males. But due to efforts by the athletic establishment to limit the scope of Title IX, the quest for equity remained decentralized and continued to take place in the gymnasiums, athletic departments, and school boards of the nation (Beck, 1980; Hogan, 1979, 1982).

Brownmiller (1984, p. 195) has stated that the modern female athlete has placed herself "on the cutting edge of some of the most perplexing problems of gender-related biology and the feminine ideal," often resulting in the female athlete becoming ambivalent about her own image: *Can* a woman be strong, aggressive, competitive, and still be considered feminine? Rohrbaugh (1979) suggests that female athletes often develop an "apologetic" as a strategy for bridging the gap between cultural expectations of femininity and the very unfeminine requisites for athletic excellence. There has been some disagreement over whether a widespread apologetic actually exists among female athletes. Hart (1979) argues that there has never been an apologetic for black women athletes, suggesting that there are cultural differences in the construction of femininities. And a recent nationwide study indicated that 94% of the 1,682 female athletes surveyed do not regard athletic participation to be threatening to their femininity (Woodward, 1985). Yet, 57% of these same athletes did agree that society still forces a choice between being an athlete and being feminine, suggesting that there is still a dynamic tension between traditional prescriptions for femininity and the image presented by active, strong, even muscular women.

Femininity as Ideologically Contested Terrain

Cultural conceptions of femininity and female beauty have more than aesthetic meanings; these images, and the meanings ascribed to them, inform and legitimize unequal power relations between the sexes (Banner, 1983; Brownmiller, 1984; Lakoff & Scherr, 1984). Attempting to be viewed as feminine involves accepting behavioral and physical restrictions that make it difficult to view one's self, much less to be viewed by others, as equal with man. But if traditional images of femininity have solidified male privilege through constructing and then naturalizing the passivity, weakness, helplessness, and dependency of women, what are we to make of the current fit, athletic, even muscular looks that are increasingly in vogue with many women? Is there a new, counter-hegemonic image of women afoot that challenges traditional conceptions of femininity? A brief examination of female bodybuilding sheds light on these questions.

Lakoff and Scherr (1984, p. 110) state that "Female bodybuilding has become the first female-identified standard of beauty." Certainly the image of a muscular—even toned—woman runs counter to traditional prescriptions for female passivity and weakness. But it's not that simple. In the film "Pumping Iron II: The Women," the tension between traditional prescriptions for femininity and the new muscularity of female bodybuilders is the major story line. It is obvious that the new image of women being forged by female bodybuilders is itself fraught with contradiction and ambiguity as women contestants and judges constantly discuss and argue emotionally over the meaning of femininity. Should contestants be judged simply according to how well-muscled they are (as male bodybuilders are judged), or also by a separate and traditionally feminine aesthetic? The consensus among the female bodybuilders, and especially among the predominantly male judges, appears to be the latter. In the words of one judge, "If they go to extremes and start looking like men, that's not what we're looking for in a woman. It's the winner of the contest who will set the standard of femininity." And of course, since this official is judging the contestants according to his own (traditional) standard of femininity, it should come as no surprise that the eventual winners are not the most well-muscled women.

Women's bodybuilding magazines also reflect this ambiguity: "Strong is Sexy," reads the cover of the August 1986 issue of *Shape* magazine, and this caption accompanies a photo of a slightly muscled young bathing-suited woman wielding a seductive smile and a not-too-heavy dumbell. And the lead editorial in the September 1986 *Muscle and Beauty* magazine reminds readers that "in this post-feminist age of enlightenment . . . each woman must select the degree of muscularity she wants to achieve" (p. 6). The editor skirts the issue of defining femininity by stressing individual choice and self-definition, but she also emphasizes the fact that muscular women can indeed be beautiful and can also "make babies." Clearly, this emergent tendency of women attempting to control and define their own lives and bodies is being shaped within the existing hegemonic definitions of femininity.

And these magazines, full as they are with advertisements for a huge assortment of products for fat reduction, muscle building (e.g., ''Anabolic Mega-Paks''), tanning formulas, and so on suggest that even if bodybuilding does represent an attempt by some women to control and define their own bodies, it is also being expressed in a distorted manner that threatens to replicate many of the more commercialized, narcissistic, and physically unhealthy aspects of men's athletics. Hargreaves (1986, p. 117) explains the contradictory meaning of women's movement into athletic activities such as bodybuilding, boxing, rugby, and soccer:

> This trend represents an active threat to popular assumptions about sport and its unifying principle appears as a shift in male hegemony. However, it also shows up the contradiction that women are being incorporated into models of male sports which are characterized by fierce competition and aggression and should, therefore, be resisted. Instead of a redefinition of masculinity occurring, this trend highlights the complex ways male hegemony works in sport and ways in which women actively collude in its reproduction.

It is crucial to examine the role that the mass sports media play in contributing to this shift in male hegemony, and it is to this topic that I will turn my attention next.

Female Athletes and the Sports Media

A person viewing an athletic event on television has the illusory impression of immediacy—of being there as it is happening. But as Clarke and Clarke (1982, p. 73) point out,

> The immediacy is, in fact, *mediated*—between us and the event stand the cameras, camera angles, producers' choice of shots, and commentators' interpretations—the whole invisible apparatus of media presentation. We can never see the whole event, we see those parts which are filtered through this process to us. . . . Rather than immediacy, our real relation to sports on television is one of distance—we are observers, recipients of a media event.

The choices, the filtering, the entire mediation of the sporting event, is based upon invisible, taken-for-granted assumptions and values of dominant social groups, and as such the presentation of the event tends to support corporate, white, and male-dominant ideologies. But as Gitlin (1980) has demonstrated, the media is more than a simple conduit for the transmission of dominant ideologies. If it were simply that, then the propaganda function of television would be transparent for all to see, stripping the medium of its veneer of objectivity and thus reducing its legitimacy. Rather, T.V. provides frameworks of meaning which, in effect, selectively interpret not only the athletic events themselves but also the controversies and problems surrounding the events. Since sport has been a primary arena of ideological legitimation for male superiority, it is crucial to examine the frameworks of meaning that the sports media have employed to portray the emergence of the female athlete.

A potentially counter-hegemonic image can be dealt with in a number of ways by the media. An initial strategy is to marginalize something that is too big to simply ignore. The 1986 Gay Games in the San Francisco Bay Area are a good example of this. The Games explicitly advocate a value system (equality between women and men, for instance) which runs counter to that of the existing sports establishment (Messner, 1984). Despite the fact that the Games were arguably the Bay Area's largest athletic event of the summer, and that several events in the Games were internationally sanctioned, the paltry amount of coverage given to the Games did *not*, for the most part, appear on the sports pages or during the sports segment of the T.V. news. The event was presented in the media not as a legitimate sports event but as a cultural or lifestyle event. The media's framing of the Games invalidated its claim as a sporting event, thus marginalizing any ideological threat that the Games might have posed to the dominant value system.

Until fairly recently, marginalization was the predominant media strategy in portraying female athletes. Graydon (1983) states that 90% of sports reporting still covers male sports. And when female athletes are covered—by a predominantly male media—they are described either in terms of their physical desirability to men ("pert and pretty") or in their domestic roles as wives and mothers. Patronizing or trivializing female athletes is sometimes not enough to marginalize them ideologically: Top-notch female athletes have often been subjected to overt hostility intended to cast doubts upon their true sex. To say "she plays like a man" is a double-edged sword—it is, on the surface, a compliment to an individual woman's skills, but it also suggests that since she is so good, she must not be a true woman after all. The outstanding female athlete is portrayed as an exception that proves the rule, thus reinforcing traditional stereotypes about femininity. Hormonal and chromosomal femininity tests for female (but no masculinity tests for male) athletes are a logical result of these ideological assumptions about male-female biology (Leskyj, 1986).

I would speculate that we are now moving into an era in which female athletes have worked hard enough to attain a certain level of legitimacy that makes simple media marginalization and trivialization of female athletes appear transparently unfair and prejudicial. The framing of female athletes as sex objects or as sexual deviants is no longer a tenable strategy if the media are to maintain their own legitimacy. As Gitlin (1980) pointed out in reference to the media's treatment of the student antiwar movement in the late 1960s, when a movement's values become entrenched in a large enough proportion of the population, the media maintains its veneer of objectivity and fairness by incorporating a watered-down version of the values of the oppositional group. In so doing, the ideological hegemony of the dominant group shifts but is essentially maintained. I would argue that this is precisely what is happening today with women and sport in the media. Women athletes are increasingly being covered by "objective" reports that do not trivialize their performances, make references to a woman's attractiveness, or posit the superior female athlete as a sex deviant. The attitude now seems to be, "They want to be treated equally with men? Well, let's see what they can do."

What is conveniently ignored by today's sportscasters—and liberal feminists, intent on gaining equal opportunities for female athletes, sometimes collude in this—is that male and female bodies do differ in terms of their potential for physical strength, endurance, agility, and grace. Despite considerable overlap, the average adult male is about 5 inches taller than the average female. Can women really hope to compete at the highest levels with men in basketball or volleyball? The average male has a larger and more powerful body. Males average 40% muscle and 15% body fat, while females average 23% muscle and 25% body fat. Can women possibly compete at the highest levels with men in football, track and field, hockey, or baseball? Women do have some physical differences from men that could be translated into athletic superiority. Different skeletal structures and greater flexibility make for superior performances on a balance beam, for instance. And women's higher body fat ratio gives them greater buoyancy in water and greater insulation from heat loss, which has translated into women's best time in swimming the English Channel both ways being considerably faster than the best times recorded by men. But the fact is, the major sports (especially the "money" sports) are defined largely according to the most extreme possibilities of the male body. If cross-sex competition is truly on the agenda, women are going to be competing at a decided disadvantage, "fighting biology all the way" (Brownmiller, 1984, p. 32), on male-defined turf.

Given these physiological differences between the sexes and the fact that major sports are organized around the most extreme potentialities of the male body, "equal opportunity" as the sports media's dominant framework of meaning for presenting the athletic performances of women athletes is likely to become a new means of solidifying the ideological hegemony of male superiority. With women competing in male-defined sports, the sports media can employ statistics as objective measures of performance. Equal opportunity within this system provides support for the ideology of meritocracy while at the same time offering incontrovertible evidence of the "natural" differences between males and females. And male reporters can simply smile and shrug: "We just call 'em as we see 'em."

Male Responses to Female Athleticism

How people receive and interpret the complex and sometimes contradictory ideological messages they receive through the media is an important issue that deserves more analytic attention than can be offered here (Dunn, 1986). I would like to make a tentative speculation here that the emerging images of femininity being forged by women athletes and framed by the media are grudgingly becoming accepted by the majority of males. Although there is clearly some resistance—even outright hostility—toward female athleticism expressed by a small minority of the men I have interviewed, the following statement by a 33-year-old blue collar man is typical of the majority:

> I really enjoy the progress they [female athletes] are making now, having bobby-sox baseball and flag football for little girls. And in high school they have whole leagues now like for the boys. I think that's great. You used to watch women's games in the 60s and in the the 70s even, and you could watch all these mistakes—errors on routine grounders, things like that. But now they're really sharp—I mean, they can play a man's game as far as mental sharpness. But I think physically they're limited to their own sex. There is still the male part of the game. That is, males have better physical equipment for sports, as for what they can do and what they can't do.

This man's statement expresses many of the basic ambiguities of male consciousness under liberal capitalism in the "postfeminist" 1980s: Imbedded in the liberal ideal of equal opportunity is a strong belief that inequality is part of the natural order. Thus, it's only fair that women get an equal shot to compete, but it's really such a relief to find that, once given the opportunity, they just don't have the "physical equipment" to measure up with men. "They're [still] limited to their own sex."

CONCLUSION

I have discounted the simplistic notion that women's increasing athleticism unambiguously signals increased freedom and equality for women with the argument that "equal opportunity" for female athletes may actually mark a shift in the ideological hegemony of male dominance and superiority. But it would be a mistake to conclude from this that women's movement into sport is simply having a reactionary effect in terms of the politics of gender relations. It should not be lost on us that the statement made by the above-mentioned man, even as it expresses a continued need to stress the ways that women are different and inferior to men, also involves a historically unprecedented acknowledgment of women's physicality and "mental sharpness."

It has been argued here that gender relations, along with their concomitant images of masculinity and femininity, change and develop historically as a result of interactions between men and women within socially structured limits and constraints. We can see how the first wave of athletic feminism in the 1920s signaled an active challenge to Victorian constraints on women, and we can see that the way this challenge was resisted and eventually marginalized reflected the limits imposed upon women's quest for equality by an emerging industrial capitalism and a crumbling, but still resilient, patriarchy. Similarly, the current wave of women's athleticism expresses a genuine quest by women for equality, control of their own bodies, and self-definition, but within historical limits and constraints imposed by a consumption-oriented corporate capitalism and men's continued attempts to retain power and privilege over women. As Connell (1987, p. 251) has pointed out, "In sexual ideology generally, ascendant definitions of reality must be seen as accomplishments that are always partial and always to some extent contested. Indeed we must see them as partly defined by the alternatives against which they are asserted."

Organized sport, as a cultural sphere defined largely by patriarchal priorities, will continue to be an important arena in which emerging images of active, fit, and muscular women are forged, interpreted, contested, and incorporated. The larger socioeconomic and political context will continue to shape and constrain the extent to which women can wage fundamental challenges to the ways that organized sports continue providing ideological legitimation for male dominance. And the media's framing of male and female athletes will continue to present major obstacles for any fundamental challenge to the present commercialized and male-dominant structure of organized athletics. It remains for a critical feminist theory to recognize the emergent contradictions in this system in order to inform a liberating social practice.

REFERENCES

Alt, J. (1983). Sport and cultural reification: From ritual to mass consumption. *Theory Culture & Society*, **1**(3), 93-107.

Banner, L.W. (1983). *American beauty*. Chicago: University of Chicago Press.

Beck, B.A. (1980). The future of women's sport: Issues, insights, and struggle. In D. Sabo & R. Runfola (Eds.), *Jock: Sports and male identity* (pp. 299-314). Englewood Cliffs, NJ: Prentice-Hall.

Birrell, S. (1984). Studying gender in sport: A feminist perspective. In N. Theberge & P. Donnelly (Eds.), *Sport and the sociological imagination* (pp. 125-135). Fort Worth: Texas Christian University Press.

Brohm, J.M. (1978). *Sport: A prison of measured time*. London: Ink Links.

Brownmiller, S. (1984). *Femininity*. New York: Fawcett Columbine.

Clarke, A., & Clarke, J. (1982). "Highlights and action replays"--Ideology, sport, and the media. In J. Hargreaves (Ed.), *Sport, culture, and ideology* (pp. 62-87). London: Routledge & Kegan Paul.

Connell, R.W. (1987). *Gender and power*. Stanford, CA: Stanford University Press.

Critcher, C. (1986). Radical theorists of sport: The state of play. *Sociology of Sport Journal*, **3**, 333-343.

Crittenden, A. (1979). Closing the muscle gap. In S.L. Twin (Ed.), *Out of the bleachers: Writings on women and sport* (pp. 5-10). Old Westbury, NY: The Feminist Press.

Dubbert, J.L. (1979). *A man's place: Masculinity in transition.* Englewood Cliffs, NJ: Prentice-Hall.

Dunn, R. (1986). Television, consumption, and the commodity form. *Theory Culture and Society*, **3**(1), pp. 49-64.

Duquin, M. (1984). Power and authority: Moral consensus and conformity in sport. *International Review for Sociology of Sport*, **19**(3/4), 295-304.

Dyer, K. (1983). *Challenging the men: The social biology of female sport achievement.* St. Lucia: University of Queensland Press.

"Editorial." (1986, September). *Muscle and Beauty*, pp. 5-6.

Ehrenreich, B. (1983). *The hearts of men.* Garden City, NY: Anchor Press/ Doubleday.

Ferris, E. (1978). *Sportswomen and medicine.* Report of the First International Conference on Women and Sport.

Filene, P. (1975). *Him/her/self: Sex roles in modern America.* New York: Harcourt Brace Jovanovich.

Gitlin, T. (1980). *The whole world is watching: Mass media in the making and unmaking of the new left.* Berkeley: University of California Press.

Goldman, R. (1983/1984, Winter). We make weekends: Leisure and the commodity form. *Social Text*, **8**, 84-103.

Graydon, J. (1983, February). "But it's more than a game. It's an institution." Feminist perspectives on sport. *Feminist Review*, **13**, 5-16.

Gruneau, R. (1983). *Class, sports, and social development.* Amherst: University of Massachusetts Press.

Hall, M.A. (1984). Toward a feminist analysis of gender inequality in sport. In N. Theberge & P. Donnelly (Eds.), *Sport and the sociological imagination* (pp. 82-103). Fort Worth: Texas Christian University Press.

Hall, M.A. (Ed.). (1987). The gendering of sport, leisure, and physical education. *Women's Studies International Forum*, **10**(4).

Hantover, J. (1978). The Boy Scouts and the validation of masculinity. *Journal of Social Issues*, **34**, 184-195.

Hargreaves, J. (Ed.). (1982). *Sport, culture, and ideology.* London: Routledge & Kegan Paul.

Hargreaves, J. (1986). Where's the virtue? Where's the grace? A discussion of the social production of gender through sport. *Theory Culture and Society*, **3**(1), 109-122.

Hart, M.M. (1979). On being female in sport. In S.L. Twin (Ed.), *Out of the bleachers: Writings on women and sport* (pp. 24-34). Old Westbury, NY: The Feminist Press.

Hartmann, H. (1976). Capitalism, patriarchy, and job segregation. *Signs*, **1**(3), 366-394.

Hoch, P. (1972). *Rip off the big game.* Garden City, NY: Doubleday.

Hogan, C.L. (1979). Shedding light on Title IX. In S.L. Twin (Ed.), *Out of the bleachers: Writings on women and sport* (pp. 173-181). Old Westbury, NY: The Feminist Press.

Hogan, C.L. (1982, May). Revolutionizing school and sports: Ten years of Title IX. *Ms.*, pp. 25-29.

Kimmel, M.S. (1986). Toward Men's Studies. *American Behavioral Scientist*, **29**(5), 517-530.

Kimmel, M.S. (1987). Men's responses to feminism at the turn of the century. *Gender and Society*, **1**(3), 261-283.

Lakoff, R.T., & Scherr, R.L. (1984). *Face value: The politics of beauty*. Boston: Routledge & Kegan Paul.

Lasch, C. (1979). *The culture of narcissism*. New York: Warner.

Lefkowitz-Horowitz, H. (1986, April). *Before Title IX*. Presented at Stanford Humanities Center Sport and Culture Meetings.

Lenskyj, H. (1986). *Out of bounds: Women, sport, and sexuality*. Toronto: The Women's Press.

Lever, J. (1976). Sex differences in the games children play. *Social Problems*, **23**, 478-487.

McKay, J. (1986). Marxism as a way of seeing: Beyond the limits of current "critical" approaches to sport. *Sociology of Sport Journal*, **3**, 261-272.

Messner, M. (1984). Gay Athletes and the Gay Games: An Interview With Tom Waddell. *M: Gentle Men for Gender Justice*, **13**, 22-23.

Messner, M. (1985). The changing meaning of male identity in the lifecourse of the athlete. *Arena Review*, **9**(2), 31-60.

Messner, M. (1987). The meaning of success: The athletic experience and the development of male identity. In Harry Brod (Ed.), *The making of masculinities: The new men's studies* (pp. 193-209). Boston: Allen & Unwin.

Mishkind, M.E., Rodin, J., Silberstein, L.R., & Striegel-Moore, R.H. (1986, May/June). The embodiment of masculinity: Cultural, psychological, and behavioral dimensions. *American Behavioral Scientist*, **29**(5), 531-540.

Naison, M. (1980). Sports, women, and the ideology of domination. In D. Sabo & R. Runfola (Eds.), *Jock: Sports and male identity* (pp. 30-36). Englewood Cliffs, NJ: Prentice-Hall.

Oriard, M. (1981). Professional football as cultural myth. *Journal of American Culture*, **4**(3), 27-41.

Reynaud, E. (1981). *Holy virility: The social construction of masculinity*. London: Pluto Press.

Rigauer, B. (1981). *Sport and work*. New York: Columbia University Press.

Rohrbaugh, J.B. (1979, August). Femininity on the line. *Psychology Today*, pp. 31-33.

Sabo, D. (1985). Sport, patriarchy, and male identity: New questions about men and sport. *Arena Review*, **9**(2), 1-30.

Sabo, D., & Runfola, R. (Eds.). (1980). *Jock: Sports and male identity*. Englewood Cliffs, NJ: Prentice-Hall.

Schafer, W.E. (1975, Fall). Sport and male sex role socialization. *Sport Sociology Bulletin*, **4**, 47-54.

Smith, R.A. (1970). The rise of basketball for women in colleges. *Canadian Journal of History of Sport and Physical Education*, **1**, 21-23.

Stacey, J., & Thorne, B. (1985, April). The missing feminist revolution in sociology. *Social Problems*, **32**(4), 301-316.

Tolson, A. (1977). *The limits of masculinity: Male identity and women's liberation*. New York: Harper & Row.

Twin, S.L. (1979). *Out of the bleachers: Writings on women and sport*. Old Westbury, NY: The Feminist Press.

Wilkenson, R. (1984). *American tough: The tough guy tradition in American character*. New York: Harper & Row.

Willis, P. (1982). Women in sport in ideology. In J. Hargreaves (Ed.), *Sport, culture, and ideology* (pp. 117-135). London: Routledge & Kegan Paul.

Woodward, S. (1985, November 5). "Women alter outlook on sports: Attitude is positive in survey." *USA Today*, p. 1A.

Zaretsky, E. (1973). *Capitalism, the family, and personal life*. New York: Harper Colophon Books.

NOTES

1. While this criticism is generally true of U.S. sport sociology, an international group of scholars has recently made important strides toward the development of a more critical and reflexive feminist analysis of sport. For an excellent collection of articles, see Hall (1987).

2. The discussion here is concerned mainly with sports and the ideology of gender relations. It is also important to employ a social-psychological perspective to examine the meaning of sports participation in the development of gender identity among female athletes (Duquin, 1984) and male athletes (Messner, 1985, 1987).

3. Interviews referred to here were conducted in 1983-84 with 30 male former athletes of diverse socioeconomic backgrounds and ages. Since the sample does not include nonathletes, the data should be considered suggestive, but not representative of a more general male population.

ACKNOWLEDGMENTS

The author would like to thank the following people for helpful comments and suggestions on earlier drafts of this paper: Maxine Baca-Zinn, Robert Dunn, Mary Duquin, Juan Gonzales, Pierrette Hondagneu-Sotelo, Michael Kimmel, Don Sabo, Barrie Thorne, and the anonymous reviewers of the *Sociology of Sport Journal*.

Chapter 5

African-American Women and Competitive Sport, 1920-1960

Cindy Himes Gissendanner
Towson State University

Between 1920 and 1960, a public debate over the appropriate structure for women's sports programs in the United States pitted female physical educators and their allies against amateur and professional female athletes, their coaches, and their promoters. While many women in the physical education profession worked in these years to eliminate interscholastic, intercollegiate, and other competitive forms of sport, the Amateur Athletic Union (AAU), industrial athletic leagues, and independent athletic clubs provided female athletes with opportunities in competitive events at the local, regional, national, and international levels.

This paper examines the participation of African-American women in sport in order to explore the impact of race and class differences on the views of those involved in this debate. I argue that racial segregation, relatively low-class status, and the ideal of a more active femininity predisposed African-American women as a group to reject the athletic model promoted by most white female physical educators.[1]

HISTORICAL BACKGROUND

Between the World Wars, feminists in the United States diverged into two ideological camps, one emphasizing sex differences and the need for protective legislation for women, and the other demanding nothing short of full equality for women in the world of business and politics and the passage of the Equal

Rights Amendment.[2] A similar split guided all discussion in the arena of women's sports as well, with female physical educators taking the protectionist stance. This stance drew as much, if not more, scorn from working-class women involved in sport as it did from women workers, who often viewed protectionism as a barrier to opportunity and equality in the workplace.[3] Not surprisingly, working-class female athletes, seeing an opportunity for recognition and economic betterment in competitive sport, cast their lot with male promoters and the AAU.

In 1923, the newly founded Women's Division of the National Amateur Athletic Federation launched a campaign to reform girls' and women's sports. With strong support and leadership from women in the physical education profession, this coalition of Progressive reformers, community recreation workers, public health officials, and representatives of girls' and women's clubs mapped out an alternative to the highly competitive, commercialized athletic model. Throughout its existence, the division's arena of greatest influence remained the colleges, reflecting the predominance of collegiate physical educators in its leadership.[4]

The division's ideas led to a steady decline in intercollegiate competition in the late 1920s that did not begin to turn around until the late 1950s. Likewise, in high schools, the division was directly responsible for the discontinuation of state championships for girls in many states. By the time of its merger with the National Section of Women's Athletics of the American Physical Education Association in 1940, a wide array of high schools, social welfare organizations, YWCAs, settlement houses, and municipal recreation and playground systems had proclaimed allegiance to the division's principles.[5]

What were some of these principles? Above all else, division members wanted to rid women's sports of male control and what they perceived to be male values. They believed that male coaches and administrators should be replaced by qualified women, that is, women who adhered to division principles, and that women's sports should promote good health, fair play, cooperative endeavor, mass participation in a variety of sports, and "sport for sport's sake." In place of varsity teams, league play, championship contests, and Olympic competition, female physical educators pushed less competitive athletic forms, such as intramural sports programs, community and school play-days, and telegraphic competition.[6]

Underlying these recommendations was the desire to protect female athletes from the exploitation that division members believed would result from the adoption of the male athletic model in girls' and women's sports. The division's platform decried such practices as the collection of gate receipts, frequent and distant travel, long schedules, large expenditures on uniforms and equipment for varsity teams, and the promotion of star performers. They feared such practices would allow or encourage female athletes to compete when injured, exhausted, or menstruating. Furthermore, the division feared for the morality of the scantily clad sportswoman surrounded by male coaches, leering male spectators, male sponsors, and the locker-room masseuse.[7]

HISTORICAL TRADITIONS OF AFRICAN-AMERICANS

The gender separatism of the women's division plan was not in tune with the historical traditions of African-American communities. Slavery and racial segregation drove a wedge between black and white women while forging between black men and black women strong bonds born of a common oppression. In *When and Where I Enter*, Paula Giddings has documented the historical need for autonomous black women's organizations as a response to the racism of white women and the sexism of black men; this need was equally pressing in political movements and in athletic programs.[8] But though black women often formed independent political organizations, united under umbrella groups such as the National Association of Colored Women and, later, the National Council of Negro Women, African-American women athletes remained much more dependent upon their brothers.

Many of the new athletic opportunities open to black women, in the period 1920 to 1960, could not have been won without the cooperation of black male leaders in national organizations, educational institutions, and local athletic clubs. Regardless of what African-American men thought of female athletes at the personal and social levels, they seemed to recognize that the integration of national and international athletic competition for both males and females was an effective way of creating visibility and support for the larger agenda of the civil rights movement.[9] The regular opportunities for competition provided by African-American organizations and institutions, athletic and otherwise, allowed outstanding individual women and women's teams to challenge and occasionally to eliminate the color barrier in a variety of sports.

Basketball

Women's basketball in African-American communities displayed many characteristics that the Women's Division abhorred. Spectators were frequently charged admission, a practice that provided teams with funds for travel, meals, uniforms, and other essential operating costs. Teams were usually coached by men who laid some claim to athletic prominence. Probably because of their limited financial resources, schools and organizations focused their sponsorship on basketball to the exclusion of other sports, reinforcing what Women's Division members saw as a dangerous trend toward athletic specialization.[10] Many black women's teams played by men's rules, shunning the specially formulated six-player rules for women that the Women's Division promoted, with the notable exception of college teams in South Carolina and Alabama.[11]

The organization of women's basketball demonstrates the close ties between community organizations and black schools and colleges. Women's teams from black colleges played teams sponsored by black YWCAs, high schools, community centers, and male athletic clubs as well as independent black women's teams.

It was not uncommon for a women's or girls' basketball game to be the first game in a double-header featuring black men's or boys' teams from similar insitutions, especially in the 1920s. Occasionally, the women's game might even be the featured contest. Games were often played in YMCAs, Boys' Clubs, and local armories.[12]

The relative economic poverty of African-American communities in general and of women in particular often mandated the sharing of institutional resources between the sexes. This probably accounts for the relative scarcity of single-sex colleges for African-Americans. Two notable exceptions for women were Spelman College, the product of philanthropic efforts by whites, and Bennett College.[13] Black women's teams frequently had male coaches. For example, the director of the YMCA, Allen Watty, coached the Baltimore YWCA basketball team in 1922; in 1938, Ezra Murdock, the athletic instructor of the YMCA, supervised "rigid training" for the Apex Beauty School girls' basketball team as its members prepared to take on the Maryland Training School. The Downingtown Industrial School team in Pennsylvania, champions of the Middle Atlantic Athletic Association in 1933, was coached by J.N. Waring, the male principal of the school.[14]

In some instances, black schools were willing to concede that the best "man" for the job might be a woman. In 1930, Miss Anne Bowers, a graduate of Douglass High School and the Fannie Coppin Normal School, coached boys' soccer, boys' basketball, and girls' basketball at School 129 in Baltimore. Likewise, Miss S.A. Young, a graduate of Tuskegee Institute, coached both men's and women's basketball at the Elizabeth City Normal School in Whiteville, North Carolina.[15] That educators often played multiple roles and transcended the traditional sexual division of labor in black schools and colleges attests to the limited financial resources of these institutions as well as the strong commitment of teachers and administrators.

Throughout the 1920s and the 1930s, African-American women showed more enthusiasm for basketball than for any other team sport. Leagues flourished in the Carolinas; Washington, DC; Maryland; Virginia; Pennsylvania; New York; New Jersey; Delaware; Alabama; and Illinois. (In North Carolina in the late '30s, black girls' teams could contend for a state championship title though no parallel opportunity had ever been offered a white girls' team.)[16] After playing in competitive high school or college programs, women in these states could choose from a wide variety of independent teams, some of the most prominent being the Blue Belts of New York City, the Orioles of Baltimore, the Philadelphia Tribune team, the Pittsburgh Pirates, and the Chicago Romas. The Blue Belts and the Tribune team gained enough notoriety in the 1920s and 1930s, respectively, to draw challenges from white teams wishing to establish firmer claims to state, regional, and national championship status.[17]

Tennis

Some of the black female stars of the basketball court also excelled on the tennis court. Isadore Channels of the Chicago Romas and Ora Washington of the

Philadelphia Tribune team both claimed multiple national black women's singles titles in tennis. In basketball, both were initially coached by men but later tried to start teams of their own.[18] In tennis, their opportunities were the result of the efforts of the American Tennis Association, founded in 1916 as the black equivalent of the all-white United States Lawn Tennis Association.

From the beginning, the annual tournaments of the American Tennis Association included women's singles competition. In 1928, women's doubles and mixed doubles were added. To stimulate the development of more and better women players, girls' singles were introduced in 1935, 2 years *before* boys' singles appeared on the slate.[19]

By 1949, the American Tennis Association consisted of 134 local clubs organized into 15 regional associations. In most instances, the local clubs included black women in their membership either as regular members or as members of ladies' auxiliaries. After 1917, local and regional tournaments regularly included women's singles, mixed doubles, and, less frequently, women's doubles.[20] In seeking adequate representation at the annual national tournaments, the local and regional associations served their own interest by running competition for women and girls.

As early as the mid-1920s, sportswriters for the newspaper, *Afro-American*, suggested that a black female challenger should be given a shot at beating Helen Wills, the premier white American player of the era. The author of an article about the efforts of Colonel Little of New York to develop a black player capable of winning the USLTA championship suggested that this player might already exist. "Why should not Miss Isadore Channels, of Chicago, and Miss Helen Wills, of Oakland, settle the world's championship for women's singles' title and leave Mademoiselle Lenglen out of it? Why should we be inferior in tennis?" queried this vexed sportswriter.[21] This question, of course, went unanswered until the appearance of Althea Gibson in USLTA-sponsored tournaments in 1950, a direct result of negotiations between *male* officials of the ATA and the USLTA.

Track and Field

By the time Althea Gibson was able to break into the elite circles of American championship tennis, African-American women had been dominating track and field at the national level for well over a decade. In 1937, the Tuskegee Institute women's track team won the first of its 14 National Senior Outdoor Women's Track and Field Championships of the Amateur Athletic Union. In the mid-1950s, the Tennessee State University Tigerbelles began following in the footsteps of their sisters to the south.[22] The evolution of these two college teams seems all the more remarkable if we consider that their rise to prominence came in an era when no other college, white or black, sent a track-and-field team to the national AAU championships.

At Tuskegee Institute, the existence and ongoing success of the women's track team owed much to Cleveland Abbott, a former college athlete of some prominence who became director of physical education and athletics at Tuskegee in 1923. Abbott instituted the Tuskegee Relays Carnival in 1927 to provide opportunities for men's teams from black schools and colleges to compete in track and field, tennis, and golf. At the third annual meeting in 1929, Abbott added a 100-yard dash and a 1/4-mile relay for girls and women to the line of events. This spurred the formation of a women's track team at Tuskegee under the supervision of Amelia Roberts, the coach of the women's basketball team.[23]

As director of physical education and athletics, Abbott remained active in the financing, recruiting, and coaching of female tracksters. In the summer of 1936, Abbott invited a number of female standouts from the spring Relays to stay on during the summer for a track-and-field training camp, an experiment that became an annual institution and permitted Tuskegee to recruit most of the track-and-field talent available in the rural areas of Alabama and Georgia.[24] In the late 1930s and 1940s, female track stars were often given first chance at part-time jobs in the physical education department to help finance their education. And, most interestingly, the women's track team practiced *with* the men's track team, following similar training routines and regularly testing their abilities against male athletes. Throughout Tuskegee's heyday in women's track and field, the women coaches took their cues from the male athletic staff, serving primarily as assistants during practices and chaperones at meets.[25]

The mandate for a women's track-and-field program at Tennessee State came from the top, the University's president Walter S. Davis. Davis recruited Jessie Abbott, the daughter of Cleveland Abbott and a recent graduate of Tuskegee, where she had excelled in basketball and track. Jessie Abbott formed the first track-and-field team for women at Tennessee State in 1943, but the full development of the program awaited the arrival of Thomas Harris in 1947. Harris's successor, Edward S. Temple, established a program based on the Tuskegee model, which included year-round training, summer track institutes, recruiting efforts, financial backing for trips to the national AAU meets, and work-study packages for members of his teams. As a result, Tennessee State, like Tuskegee, produced a number of female athletes who became national and Olympic champions.[26]

THE WOMEN'S DIVISION PLATFORM AS CLASS-BOUND

The existence of successful programs at Tuskegee and Tennessee State might lead to the conclusion that the message of the Women's Division fell on deaf ears in African-American communities, which is certainly not the case. Some black women physical educators cast their lot with their white sisters in defining physical education and athletics for their female charges.

But in general, the Women's Division and its allies exercised little influence in the small rural high schools of the south and midwest. The class-bound nature of the Women's Division platform was impractical, if not odious, to working-class and rural women and to non-elite institutions.

In educational settings, the division's platform assumed the existence of a well-established, adequately staffed, financially sound, and gender-segregated physical education department. In order to run adequate intramural programs in a variety of sports, a college needed expensive equipment and a large student body. Thus, the Women's Division found its most solid support in elite women's colleges, which were not as dependent upon the benefits of competitive sports programs (i.e., community involvement, recruitment of students, and national publicity) for survival and the building of institutional reputations.[27]

By the early 1930s, Howard University, Morgan College, Spelman College, and Hampton Institute had abandoned their earlier devotion to competitive basketball teams, replacing them with intramural class competitions in a variety of sports, athletic festivals, and play-days with each other.[28] At Howard University, Maryrose Reeves Allen headed the women's physical education program from 1923 through the 1950s. Under her leadership, women at Howard were required to take courses in health and personal development, body aesthetics, and swimming. Apparently there were no varsity teams, only instruction in sports such as archery, badminton, fencing, golf, swimming, and tennis. Maryrose Allen's influence probably extended well beyond the walls of Howard University, for in 1953, 80% of the female physical educators in the black schools of Washington, DC were graduates of Howard.[29]

Public high schools, industrial training schools, some normal schools, and small rural colleges continued to support competitive teams, especially in basketball, throughout the 1930s and 1940s, when the more elite private colleges began to adopt the noncompetitive approach. Ivora King, a proponent of competitive athletics for women and an occasional sportswriter for the *Afro-American* in the early 1930s, noted that many college officials simply would not permit college women to engage in varsity competition. Because of the widespread adoption of intramurals over intercollegiate sports for women in colleges belonging to the Colored Intercollegiate Athletic Association, King stated, "I don't believe I can picture a basketball team from Hampton, garbed in shorts, playing a preliminary game in the New Albert (the gymnasium at Morgan College)."[30] This observation indicates that among college-educated African-Americans, female participation in competitive sport was commonly perceived as a barrier to the attainment of a class-based feminine ideal.

However, middle-class status did not always result in withdrawal from competition; in fact, it sometimes intensified it. The *Afro-American* reported in 1922 that the high school team in Baltimore was looking forward to defeating the Training School women who had "looked down upon them much as a Rolls Royce looks down on a Ford."[31]

Furthermore, certain sports were perceived as more compatible with black middle-class ideals of femininity than others. Several years after the discontinuation of varsity sports for women at Howard, Morgan, and other elite schools, those schools still sent tennis teams to the Colored Intercollegiate Athletic

Association Tennis Tournament. Edgar Brown, an ATA multiple-title winner in the 1920s, reported that mothers often wrote to him with requests such as " 'Will you be kind enough to teach my daughter? She is extremely interested in tennis. Will tennis reduce one? . . . How can I keep from being sunburned?' (Evidently a High 'Y' girl.)"[32] This mother saw participation in tennis as a means of attaining the middle-class ideal of feminine beauty, on the one hand, and as a potential threat to the maintenance of class and color distinction on the other. This ambivalence was no doubt typical.

THE ACTIVE IDEAL OF FEMININITY

Historians of African-American women agree that African-Americans generally adhered to a much more active ideal of femininity than did their white counterparts. The roots of this different ideal lay in the widely divergent conceptions and realities of black and white women's socioeconomic roles. Black women's lives, especially in the rural south, mandated hard physical labor at all stages of the life cycle and through all parts of the menstrual cycle. Employers did not excuse black women from work for a week out of every month, much less for their entire lives, because of their femininity. The African-American woman's experience flew in the face of medical arguments linking physical exertion during menstruation with reproductive malfunction, one of the basic components of the Women's Division argument against scheduled competitive events for girls and women. For African-American women, participation in the labor force, community activities, and political movements symbolized a woman's deep concern and commitment to her family rather than an unwillingness or inability to fulfill her responsibilities as a wife and mother.[33]

The attitude of students at Tuskegee toward female athletes provides an interesting case study. Students at Tuskegee did not view female athletes as ugly, masculine, or socially maladjusted. In fact, the honor of "Miss Tuskegee" was regularly given to physical education majors and female athletic stars. Mabel Smith, the national women's broad-jump champion in 1937, not only received the "Miss Tuskegee" honor but also was voted the most popular woman on campus 2 consecutive years.[34] Beauty, personality, and athleticism were not considered to be mutually exclusive qualities in this African-American student community whose members were drawn primarily from the surrounding rural communities.

Furthermore, the female faculty and faculty wives provided role models for female students interested in athletics. Individuals from both groups often entered tournaments sponsored by Tuskegee and other black organizations. In the 1920s, the faculty women formed their own club, the Diana Athletic Club, and the highlight of the 1929 season was a thrilling game with the female faculty of the Alabama State Normal College. Faculty also played the role of enthusiastic spectators at student athletic events.[35]

Such clubs indicate an acceptance in the African-American community of athletic roles for women in later stages of the life cycle. The embodiment of this attitude is "Mother" Seames of Chicago, a lifelong supporter of black tennis who continued to compete in women's doubles at ATA tournaments even after she passed the age of 60 and the weight of 200 pounds. Seames gained as much respect and affection within the black community as did Lucy Slowe, principal of the first black junior high school in Washington, DC, dean of women at Howard University in the 1920s, and holder of the 1917 and 1921 women's-singles titles of the ATA.[36]

Although Lucy Slowe remained unmarried, many of the most prominent black female physical educators, unlike their white counterparts, were married.[37] This difference may have stemmed, at least partially, from a more positive attitude within the African-American culture towards work-force participation for married women. Whereas African-American women, when comparing themselves to their mothers and grandmothers, probably saw a physical education career as a superior economic opportunity fully compatible with marriage, their white counterparts appear to have used this avenue to economic independence and self-esteem as a means of escaping the oppressive white middle-class ideal of heterosexual marriage.

One of the most striking examples of the greater flexibility of the African-American feminine ideal is found in a 1953 edition of the *Afro-American*, which carried an article on an upcoming set of six wrestling matches, two of which would feature black *women* wrestlers at the Baltimore Frontiers Club. Coverage of such an event in the white press in the early 1950s would probably have been ridden with innuendos about the femininity and sexuality of the participants. The *Afro*, on the other hand, simply presented short, straightforward biographies of the four women. Most interesting is the description of Mary Horton: "Mary is 22 years old, 5 ft 5 inches tall, and tips the scales at 150 pounds. She's well versed in many subjects having studied science, poetry, politics, and criminology in college. Her original plans were to become a college instructor, but upon learning of the financial success of girl wrestlers, she changed her mind."[38] This view of women wrestlers mirrors the more general tendency in the African-American community to alter or ignore restrictive feminine ideals in the face of economic realities.

CONCLUDING REMARKS

Not surprisingly, African-American women in sports found the ideals of the Women's Division largely unworkable. The racially segregated, male-dominated nature of athletics and the institutions that governed them tied the fate of black female athletes tightly to the progress of black male athletes. Although some members of the middle-class African-American community may have held doubts about the compatability of competitive athletics and feminine charm, working-class and rural African-American women enthusiastically embraced the possibilities for racial uplift and individual advancement in highly visible, competitive, and commercialized sports.

NOTES

1. This is a preliminary study based on only a small fraction of the available primary source material. The analysis offered here, rather than being definitive, is intended to stimulate further research and inquiry into a largely unexplored facet of American history. Secondary historical literature on African-American women in sports is sparse, but two valuable sources are Marianna Davis, ed., *The Contributions of Black Women to America*, vol. 1 (Columbia, SC: Kenday Press, Inc., 1982), pp. 493-586; and Arthur R. Ashe, *A Hard Road to Glory: A History of the African-American Athlete*, 3 vols. (New York: Warner Books, 1988).
2. On protective legislation vs. the Equal Rights Amendment, see Stanley J. Lemons, *The Woman Citizen: Social Feminism in the 1920s* (Urbana, IL: University of Illinois Press, 1973), pp. 181-196; William Chafe, *The American Woman: Her Changing Social, Economic and Political Roles, 1920-1970* (London: Oxford University Press, 1972), pp. 116-119; and Rosalind Rosenberg, *Beyond Separate Spheres* (New Haven, CT: Yale University Press, 1982), pp. 110-111.
3. See Alice Kessler-Harris, *Out to Work: A History of Wage-Earning Women in the United States* (New York: Oxford University Press, 1982), pp. 185-194. Kessler-Harris makes the point that many working-class women ultimately joined the fight for protective legislation when it became apparent that male-dominated unions and middle-class female reformers would not support demands for full equality.
4. Alice Allene Sefton, *The Women's Division National Amateur Athletic Federation* (Stanford, CA: Stanford University Press, 1941), p. 32.
5. Ibid.; see also Joan S. Hult, "The Governance of Athletics for Girls and Women: Leadership by Women Physical Educators, 1899-1949," *Research Quarterly for Sport and Exercise* (Centennial Issue, 1985): 66-67.
6. The 1923 platform of the Women's Division appears in Agnes R. Wayman, *Education Through Physical Education*, 2nd ed., rev. (Philadelphia: Lea and Febiger, 1928), pp. 203-209. Mabel Lee, "The Case For and Against Intercollegiate Athletics for Women and the Situation as It Stands Today," *American Physical Education Review* 29 (January 1924): 13-19, also promotes the Division's principles concerning women's sports.
7. A sympathetic view of the Division's plan can be found in Nancy Theriot, "Towards a New Sporting Ideal: The Women's Division of the National Amateur Athletic Federation," *Frontiers* 3 (1978): 1-7.

8. Paula Giddings, *When and Where I Enter* (New York: Bantam Books, 1984), p. 349.

9. Ashe, Vol. 2, p. 6.

10. On the Division's general complaints about the persistence of interscholastic and intercollegiate basketball, see Paula Welch, "Interscholastic Basketball: Bane of Collegiate Physical Educators," in *Her Story in Sport*, ed. Reet Howell (West Point, NY: Leisure Press, 1982), pp. 424-431. Also see *Afro-American*, December 17, 1920, p. 7; "Girls and Ex-Soldiers to Play This Friday," January 28, 1921, p. 7; "Girls' Basketball Game," December 30, 1921, p. 8; and "Livingstone Co-Ed Cagers Eye Title," January 7, 1933, n.p.

11. *Afro-American*, "Claflin Loses First Game to A. and T.," February 6, 1926, p. 8; "South Carolina State Girls to Encounter Tuskegee," February 9, 1935, p. 21; "Both Shaw Teams Take Easy Games," February 1, 1936, p. 23.

12. *Afro-American*, "Girls' Basketball Game," December 17, 1920, p. 7; "Triple Bill at 'Y' Gym," February 4, 1921, p. 7; "Athenians Rout Morgan Varsity," February 10, 1922, p. 9; "Morgan and 'Y' Quints Stage Hot Contest," March 10, 1922, p. 9.

13. Barbara Solomon, *In the Company of Educated Women* (New Haven, CT: Yale University Press, 1985), p. 152.

14. *Afro-American*, "Baltimore Y.W. Wins Over Germantown," March 31, 1922, p. 9; "Downingtown Wins, Loses," January 14, 1933, p. 16; "Nobody Has Licked Them for Two Years," April 13, 1935, p. 20; and "Apex Beauty Team Ready for Battle," February 26, 1938, p. 18.

15. *Afro-American*, "Woman is Coach for Six-Foot Basketball Players," April 15, 1930, p. 15; "Baltimore Has Girl Coach of Boys' Crack Soccer Team," December 27, 1930, p. 14; and "Female Coach Guides Boys at P.S. 112 to 3 City Titles," June 29, 1940, p. 23.

16. *Afro-American*, "Out to Capture N.C. Title," January 27, 1940, p. 21.

17. *Afro-American*, "Blue Belts Win Two," March 16, 1923, p. 14; "Blue Belt Girls of N.Y. in D.C. February 14," February 1, 1925, p. 15; "Stop Those Girls," December 10, 1932, p. 17; "Tribune Girls Lose to Whites," February 4, 1933, p. 16.

18. *Afro-American*, "Tribune Girls Double Score," December 3, 1932, p. 16.

19. Edwin Bancroft Henderson, *The Negro in Sports*, rev. ed. (Washington, DC: Associated Publishers, Inc., 1949), p. 208.

20. *Afro-American*, "Locals Plan Junior Tennis Club," August 8, 1924, p. 15; "1937 Leaders in the World of Sports," January 1, 1938, p. 18.

21. *Afro-American*, Edgar, Brown, "Col. Little to Promote Tennis," December 27, 1924, p. 5.; and Edgar Brown, "Miss Ballard Touted to Beat Woman's Tennis Champion," April 4, 1925, p. 9.

22. For an in-depth study of these women's track and field programs at Tuskegee and Tennessee State University, see Nolan Thaxton, "A Documentary Analysis of Competitive Track and Field for Women at Tuskegee Institute and Tennessee State University," (PhD dissertation, Springfield College, Springfield, MA, 1970).

23. *Tuskegee Messenger*, ''Girls to Have a Track Team,'' March 9, 1929, vol. 5, p. 7. See also Ross C. Owen, *History of Athletics at Tuskegee Institute*, Manuscript collection, Archives of Tuskegee University, Tuskegee, Alabama.

24. Thaxton, pp. 74-75.

25. *Afro-American*, Levi Jolley, ''Tigerettes Owe Success to Dr. Carver's Peanut Oil,'' July 13, 1940, p. 21. Thaxton, p. 77.

26. *Afro-American*, July 11, 1936, p. 6. Thaxton, pp. 124-140, 212-217, 223-224.

27. Not all predominantly white colleges and universities supported Women's Division policies. Sefton, pp. 48-49; Hult, pp. 71-73.

28. *Afro-American*, Ike King, ''Women in Sports,'' August 22, 1931, p. 13; Ollie Stewart, ''Bitters and Sweets,'' January 19, 1935, p. 20; ''Hampton's No. 1 Athlete,'' April 15, 1950, p. 28.

29. Ted Chambers, *The History of Athletics and Physical Education at Howard University* (New York: Vantage Press, 1986), pp. 23-27.

30. *Afro-American*, Ollie Stewart, ''Bitters and Sweets,'' February 2, 1935, p. 20.

31. *Afro-American*, ''H.S. Girls' Quint Stampede T.S. Girls,'' March 3, 1922, p. 9.

32. *Afro-American*, Edgar Brown, ''Our Women Tennis Players Rank High,'' May 18, 1923, p. 13.

33. Jacqueline Jones, *Labor of Love, Labor of Sorrow* (New York: Vintage Books, 1985), pp. 3-5. Also Giddings, p. 349.

34. *Tuskegee Messenger*, ''Girl of High Scholastic Attainment Chosen 'Miss Tuskegee,' '' vol. 2, p. 1. *Campus Digest*, ''Miss Virginia Campbell Elected Miss Tuskegee,'' September 19, 1936, vol. 11, p. 1; ''Popularity Contest Decided by Extremely Narrow Margin,'' February 6, 1937, vol. 11, p. 1; ''Mabel Smith Elected 'Miss Tuskegee,' '' October 1, 1938, vol. 13, p. 1. Above found in Archives of Tuskegee University, Tuskegee, Alabama.

35. *Tuskegee Messenger*, ''Diana Athletic Club Honors President,'' November 10-24, 1928, vol. 4, p. 7. *Campus Digest*, ''Dianas Lose in Exciting Contest,'' March 1, 1929, vol. 4, p. 1; *Afro-American*, ''Bordentown Teachers Defeat Seashore Quint,'' February 6, 1926, p. 9. See also Ross C. Owen, ''History of Tennis at Tuskegee Institute,'' in *History of Athletics at Tuskegee Institute*, Manuscript collection, Archives of Tuskegee University, Tuskegee, Alabama.

36. *Afro-American*, ''Lucy Slowe is Dean of Women,'' June 16, 1922, p. 6; Edgar Brown, ''Our Women Tennis Players Rank High,'' May 18, 1923, p. 13; '' 'Mother' Seames Is Tennis Champion,'' January 17, 1925, p. 6.

37. Hult claims that approximately 90 percent of the female physical educators that she studied were unmarried. Although no such statistical study of black female physical educators exists, my admittedly random and less thorough observations leave me with the impression that the percentage of married women among black physical educators and athletes was much higher.

38. *Afro-American*, ''Girl Wrestlers to Perform for Balto. Frontier's Club,'' November 21, 1953, p. 23.

PART II

GENDER AND THE ORGANIZATION OF SPORT

ne of the most salient characteristics of sport in North America is its high level of organization, bureaucratization, and rationalization. Competition at every level, even in recreational spheres, is structured by dominant organizational practices and policies. Ideological effects can be recognized in terms of performance goals—faster, higher, further—making heightened performance the only legitimate telos in sport; additionally, ideological effects of class, race, and gender insidiously direct sport practices and objectives. The authors in this section address the gendered organizational order of sport, exploring the various levels on which such gendering is accomplished.

Bringing several feminist frameworks to bear on the analysis of gender in sport, Mary Boutilier and Cindy SanGiovanni discuss the effect of legislation on the practice of sport. Focusing on Title IX of the Education Amendments Act of 1972, which legislated gender equality in athletic programs at schools that receive federal funding, they argue that the liberal limitations of that legislation provided the means of equal access to athletic programs for girls and women, but did nothing to change dominant sporting practices to make them more resonant with women's experiences. Boutilier and SanGiovanni advocate more radical solutions to the historical gender inequities of sport, that is, a fundamental restructuring of both the systems and the values of sport. They argue that Title IX forestalled radical change in sport by incorporating women into the prevalent, male-dominated models of sport.

One of the unforeseen consequences of Title IX has been the precipitous decline in the number of women in coaching and administrative positions in women's intercollegiate athletic programs. Vivian Acosta and Linda Carpenter have kept track of this decline for 20 years. Among other things, their data document a decrease in the number of women holding head administrative positions, and a decline in the percentage of women coaching women's teams. They offer a summary of perceived causes for these patterns.

Annelies Knoppers formally engages the issue of women's decline in the coaching profession. She argues that person-centered explanations for women's exclusion from coaching positions in women's athletics are a form of "blaming the victim" and imply that women are faulty workers who must be "repaired" before they can assume leadership responsibilities in sport. Drawing on Rosabeth Moss Kanter's work on women in organizations, Knoppers endorses the theory that "the structure of the workplace shapes the worker." She suggests that future researchers turn away from individualistic approaches to the decline of women coaches and focus instead on the three structural determinants discovered by Kanter: opportunity, power, and proportion. Knoppers argues that we can understand career patterns of female coaches with reference to their lack of opportunity to enter coaching, their exclusion from the positions of power that control resources and the networks that consolidate power, and the burdens of tokenism imposed on them as a result of their underrepresentation in the workplace.

Elaine Blinde addresses the effects of these changes on women athletes themselves. Specifically, Blinde focuses on the increasing professionalization of women's intercollegiate athletics in the post-Title IX era. Within the context of a "fair exchange" model, which considers whether athletes gain as much from their involvement in athletics as the athletic program or the coach does, she documents patterns of exploitation of student athletes. She argues that women are subjected to traditional forms of athletic exploitation that include a sacrifice of both time and attention to academic work as well as the development of friendships and a typical undergraduate social life. In addition, Blinde suggests that a significant dynamic in the exploitation of the female athlete is the male coach-female athlete relationship, which "parallels dominant-subordinate roles of males and females in patriarchal society." Quoting from interviews with student athletes, Blinde describes the coaches' tendency to treat female athletes as nonadults through condescension and coddling, and through intimidation, manipulation, and other controlling behaviors. Finally, she discusses physical exploitation and the endangering of one's health through unwise training techniques and inattention to serious injury. Of particular concern to Blinde is the preoccupation with the body image of female athletes, resulting from male coaches' imposition of unrealistic demands for weight control that lead to bulimia and other eating disorders.

Finally, Laurel Davis explores the gendered meanings that surround athletes and cheerleaders in U.S. culture and what happens when these conventions are challenged or rearranged. Davis shows how dominant ideological practices are naturalized and dehistoricized by uncovering a history of cheerleading, revealing that the first cheerleaders were men and that women's entrance into the activity was vigorously resisted. Cheerleading has thus become constructed as a natural female role only in the past few decades. Davis is particularly interested in understanding why the advent of male and female cheerleaders at women's athletic events has gone virtually unnoticed by the public. Drawing from Lyotard, she argues that the fans' unreflective posture betokens a comfort with ambiguity and inconsistency that is characteristic of the postmodern world. She characterizes the explanations offered by those directly involved in women's sport— cheerleaders, athletes, and fans—as inherently contradictory as well, noting that their simultaneously conservative and liberal rhetoric (if the men have cheerleaders, the women should) in effect ensures that a more profound "criticism of contemporary gender relations is temporarily silenced."

Taken together these articles indicate that the dramatic gains in participation for girls and women since Title IX are only one aspect of what most consider progress. Behind the "progress" of women's athletics lies struggle over the meanings, and thus the future directions, for women's sport.

Chapter 6

Politics, Public Policy, and Title IX:
Some Limitations of Liberal Feminism

Mary A. Boutilier
Seton Hall University

Lucinda F. SanGiovanni
Seton Hall University

Women. Sport. Public policy. It has been only since the early 1970s that these words could be combined to form a theme that elicits passionate, if not fierce, debate. Our goal here is to examine the socially constructed worlds of both ''women'' and ''sport'' and to indicate how their intersections have influenced the development of public policy in the United States regarding women's sport. Specifically, we will examine the varied path of Title IX of the Education Amendments Act of 1972 as a case study of a public policy directed by unexplored assumptions about women, about sport, and about the public policy process itself.

ALTERNATIVE MODELS OF FEMINISM

Recognizing sexism, both in the public realm and in private worlds, has been the joy and the burden of the women's movement in the United States since its

This is a revised and updated version of ''Women, Sport, and Public Policy'' by Mary A. Boutilier and Lucinda F. SanGiovanni. In *Sociology of Sport: Diverse Perspectives* (pp. 181-191) by S.L. Greendorfer and A. Yiannakis (Eds.), 1981, Champaign, IL: Leisure Press. Copyright 1981 by Leisure Press. Adapted by permission.

reemergence in the late 1960s. Recalling the successes and failures of their sisters at Seneca Falls, feminists in the second wave have taken on various forms and strategies to counteract the sexism of their time. The women's movement has members who hold to different models of feminism, each with a unique image of woman, explanations for the source of her oppression as a personal and social being, and a vision of her participation in society that will enhance her potential for self-fulfillment and autonomy.

This second wave of feminism has yielded an unprecedented critique of the subjugation of women in all areas of society. Action (political, legal, economic, sexual) and insight (literary, scientific, theological, philosophical) have flowed back and forth from the pens and mouths of feminists as they discover, document, and denounce the tragically profound and simply irritating ways in which women have been denied, and have denied themselves, access to whatever it has meant to be full human participants in the worlds that men have created.

But feminism as an overarching ideological tree has many branches, each with a special origin, leading in a different direction, with divergent policy implications for the liberation of women, and bearing a message for revamping all sexist institutions and cultural dynamics—including those found in sport.

One of the earliest formulations of the alternative branches of feminism is provided by philosophers Jaggar and Struhl in *Feminist Frameworks* (1978). They identify four feminist frameworks, each with a dual function: to offer both a description of women's oppression and a prescription for eliminating it. What the frameworks hold in common is a rejection of the conservative orientation. Conservatism denies the existence of women's oppression, arguing that their place in society is determined by biological facts and that "for women, freedom is something like the knowledge and acceptance of biological necessity" (p. xii). Each framework thus carries within it "different diagnoses of what is wrong with the present [that] necessarily generate different proposals for the future" (p. xi). We will briefly summarize for each feminist framework or paradigm the cause or roots of women's oppression and the implied solution to overcome this oppression.

Liberal Feminism

Liberal feminism, espoused by women including Gloria Steinem, by *Ms.* magazine, and by NOW (the National Organization for Women), sees the root of women's oppression as the lack of equal civil rights and educational opportunities for women. Liberals do not attack per se social inequities of wealth, power, and prestige; rather they attack their distribution on the grounds of ascribed qualities, such as gender, race, or age. They believe that when women are given equal opportunities, they will actualize their potential and should be rewarded by the dictates of the market demands for their achievements. Liberals believe that the elimination of discrimination based on gender can be accomplished by reform within the structure of American society; they believe that reform can be achieved by the extension of political, legal, and educational opportunities to women. They assume that once these rights and chances are mandated that all women—regardless of race, ethnicity, age, sexual preference, social class, or marital status—will have equal access to all opportunities and be rewarded equally for their talents.

Marxist Feminism

Marxist feminism rejects the possibility that any real equality of opportunity can exist in a society where wealth and power rest in the hands of an elite ruling class. The assumption is that the daughters (and sons) of rich and privileged families will always have the advantage of their inherited positions and that this class will never create or enforce laws, policies, and arrangements that fundamentally threaten its vested interests. Liberal reform is a cruel, deceptive, and ineffective strategy for eradicating the root cause of women's oppression—the existence of a social class system. Thus, Marxist feminists believe that oppression by gender is a derivation of the more primary oppression by social class. Once social classes are destroyed, private ownership and profit abolished, and the means of economic production redistributed to the society as a whole, the oppression of women will disappear.

Radical Feminism

Radical feminism is the least developed and least systematic of the frameworks. Radicals differ considerably among themselves, but they agree that the oppression of women is the historically earliest, the most universal, and the most difficult form of oppression to eradicate. They do not believe, as do the Marxists, that the elimination of social classes will insure women's equality, nor do they accept the liberal position that equalization of legal and educational opportunities will ensure all women an equal chance at self-actualization. What then will? The answers to this question are as varied as the range of radical feminist thought.

Some see the root of women's oppression in biology itself, where enforced child-bearing functions limit women's autonomy by keeping them physically dependent on men. This perspective implies that women's freedom rests on their control over reproduction—birth control, abortion, voluntary sterilization, artificial gestation, and other innovations that would give women real choices concerning childbearing.

Others locate the source of women's oppression in compulsory heterosexuality and call for a woman-identified existence in which a woman "commits herself to other women for political, emotional, physical, and economic support" (Bunch, 1978, p. 136). This extended vision of the woman-identified lesbian concentrates on women granting to other women the range of commitments that society demands be given only to men. Still other radical feminists, like Mary Daly in

Gyn/Ecology (1978), call for a total and continuing exploration of new forms of being-in-the-world. They ask for no less than a complete reevaluation of such taken-for-granted ideas as culture, society, and human nature. In Daly's words, "the radical being of women is very much an Otherworld Journey. It is both discovery and creation of a world other than patriarchy" (p. 1).

Socialist Feminism

Socialist feminists attempt to bridge the gap between Marxist and radical approaches. They argue that economic inequities *and* sexism should be seen as fundamental and equally important forms of oppression, neither having clear predominance over the other. Unlike liberals, they stress the greater struggle of women of color, ethnic groups, and economic classes in gaining equal opportunity; unlike Marxists, they do not assume that a classless society will also eliminate male privilege; unlike radicals, they refuse to consider economic oppression as secondary in importance to women's oppression. They see the oppression of women as a dual problem that must be fought as such: Privilege based on class or sex must be eradicated. The socialist approach recognizes that class inequities must be abolished if all women, not just the more advantaged, are to gain from any enhancement of women's rights. They also recognize the need to abolish patriarchal forms of cultural and social life, such as the nuclear family, enforced heterosexuality, polarized sex roles, and other forces that maintain male privilege even in economically more egalitarian societies. By acknowledging the interaction between sexism and other social forces—classism, racism, ageism, hetero-sexism—this view affords greater flexibility in formulating the problems and potential solutions to overcoming the oppression of *all* women.

Very few participants in this second wave of the women's movement, regardless of the nature or degree of their involvement or their adherence to one or another model of feminism, could have predicted the vigorous emergence of neoconservatism, both in the U.S. and in many other parts of the world, that would come to characterize the '80s. Feminists did not anticipate the failure of the Equal Rights Amendment, the "privatization" (Savas, 1982) of governmental services, the election of conservative politicians, the cutback of federal programs for the less privileged, and the ideological backlash against the movement of women, minorities, and other marginal groups into the national mainstream.

The premature declaration of victory by feminists, especially liberal feminists, proved to be particularly risky in a nation that prides itself on the trappings of pluralism and liberalism. Feminist aspirations for the inclusion of girls and women into the institution of sport were naively neglectful of the power of these new political forces to resist and rescind the progress that had been achieved during the "era of the women's movement." The 1980s witnessed what Uhler (1987) called the "post-Women's Era" during which many of women's gains in the late '60s and '70s have been challenged. One of the best ways to convey this development and the impact of the neoconservative orientation is through a recounting of the history of Title IX.

TITLE IX: LIBERAL LIMITATIONS TO PUBLIC POLICY

The passage of the Education Amendments Act of 1972 and its Title IX provision, which prohibited sex discrimination in educational institutions that receive federal funds, marked the first time that the issue of women's and girls' access to sports achieved the status of a public agenda item. Though the topic of sex discrimination addressed by the entire act was a "highly emotional one (and) the issues involved go to the root of societal sex roles, on which most of the male members of Congress remain extremely traditional in outlook," it was the sport and athletic implications of this act that brought to the surface "expressions of the personal value systems of the members of Congress" (Fishel & Pottker, 1977, p. 132) and produced the greatest controversy. The provisions of Title IX, which sought equalization of sport opportunity and rewards, engendered extreme, organized, and concerted lobbying; generated impassioned pleas; and garnered extraordinary claims about the benefits or disasters that would befall society if the legislative mandates were implemented.

Congress was just the first of many arenas in which liberals seeking the enforcement in sports of the "intent" of Title IX had to fight their battles. Although Title IX was adopted in 1972, colleges were allowed a 3-year grace period to comply with the sports and athletics provisions of the act. The Department of Health, Education, and Welfare's mandate to promulgate regulations and interpretations of how Title IX's sports provisions were to be implemented was delayed. Only on June 18, 1974, 2 years after passage of the act, did HEW release its proposed regulations. At the press conference, then-Secretary Weinberger said the department would allow public response and comment for 4 months rather than the usual 30 days and sarcastically quipped that concern for college sports must be "the most important subject in the United States today" (Fishel & Pottker, 1977, p. 113). On February 28, 1975, after 4 months and over 10,000 written comments to HEW, Weinberger sent the final draft of the regulations to President Ford. This secret document, which was leaked to women's groups, brought another barrage of negative responses to what were perceived as weakened regulations. The regulations were finally published in the *Federal Register* on June 4, 1975 and were scheduled to go into effect on July 21, 1975, some 3 years after the act's passage. However, additional clarifications and modifications were still to follow. On December 6, 1978, HEW issued final guidelines to take effect only in September 1979. It was 6 years after the passage of the act that the enforcement "teeth" appeared. Not until 1979 was loss of federal funds the threatened penalty for noncompliance (Lapin, 1979).

The placement of the oversight function for Title IX was another sign that the forces that had propelled the passage of the act were not strong enough to get it energetically enforced: The Office of Civil Rights was ill equipped to handle this extra task. By February 1982, at least 150 complaints relative to sex discrimination in athletics were pending with the OCR, several of which dated back to 1973 ("Universities Charged," 1982). However, the real battle was yet to be fought, for in 1980 a self-proclaimed conservative, Ronald Reagan, was elected to the White House. Reagan came to office with a conservative ideological agenda that included the task of rolling back the initial successes and sweeping interpretations of Title IX.

It was during the first term of the Reagan presidency that a major legal attack was mounted against Title IX. Opponents argued against the application of Title IX in college athletics claiming that only *programs* receiving federal funds were covered by this law. Because no athletic programs receive direct federal funds (Eitzen & Sage, 1986), opponents argued that the implementation of Title IX should be program-specific and enforced only in those college programs that were federally funded. Proponents and officials in the Office of Civil Rights disagreed and felt that if any federal funds were received by a school, then all its programs must meet Title IX guidelines.

The Reagan administration clearly favored the more limited, program-specific interpretation and took the opportunity to support this policy view when *Grove City College v. Bell* (1984) was heard by the Supreme Court. In this case, the Supreme Court's majority accepted the more narrow, conservative interpretation favored by President Reagan. For all intents and purposes, Title IX was dead. The momentum that Title IX had provided to women's sports had been swept aside. All cases pending with the OCR were discontinued.

The *Grove City* decision meant much more than a conservative victory for athletic programs in America's colleges. It signaled a radical change in the more recent historical role of the Supreme Court itself, which for some 30 years (since the 1954 *Brown* decision) had been the major political institution in the U.S. safeguarding and extending legal, political, and social rights to women and minorities. The Supreme Court had been ideologically reshaped by conservative Reagan appointments. The liberal, judicially activist majority had been replaced by a conservative, judicially passive majority. The extension of constitutional rights (Rosenbloom, 1983, p. 125), which had been the mark of the Supreme Court of the early '70s, was replaced by a strict constructionist majority less willing to intervene in "political issues."

Liberals, feminist and otherwise, now began to learn the real lessons of political power and its effects on public policy. They came to realize that legislation, court decisions, administrative rulings, and patterns of enforcement are not permanently guaranteed, even when codified in official forms; rather, it is the play of political forces and the ideological framework of political officials that actually determines the "rights" and "protections" that citizens have at any given point in time. As blacks, the poor, college students, workers, lesbians and gays, the disabled, and women have learned during the '80s, political will, political organization, and political attention cannot subside when "rights" are enacted. Pluralistic politics entails constant vigilance. The power of interest groups rises and falls. Politics entails the constant application of will, energy, skill, and pressure.

It was only at the end of the Reagan administration that liberal feminists engendered sufficient political support to again reopen the battle of Title IX. With a weakened president in the last year of his final term, the liberal forces in Congress and the bureaucracy prepared for another battle over the issue of Title IX. Resisting to the very end, Reagan vetoed the Civil Rights Restoration Act of 1988, which restored the institution-wide coverage of Title IX, but his veto was overridden by Congress. Once again the OCR would investigate complaints of sex discrimination in sports and threaten the withdrawal of funds should the complaint be found valid. It had taken 3 years after the *Grove City* decision for Congress to clarify the language of Title IX and pass it with sufficient votes to override the Reagan veto. Finally, 16 years after the passage of the Education Amendments Act of 1972, the law had a set of regulations and guidelines, tested in the courts, that would put into effect in 1988 something liberal feminists had expected in 1972.

THE EFFECTS OF TITLE IX:
SOME GOOD AND SOME BAD NEWS

There is little doubt that the passage and the threat of enforcement of Title IX resulted in a vast improvement in the sporting opportunities and resources available to girls and women in high schools and institutions of higher education in the U.S. The expansion of sports and facilities, the increases in levels of participation, the greater allocation of financial and other resources to female school athletic programs have been well documented (Acosta & Carpenter, 1988; Boutilier & SanGiovanni, 1983). To cite a few examples: College women now receive about 25% of all intercollegiate athletics expenditures, up from 2% in 1972 (Garratt, 1989); between 1972 and 1982 the number of female high school athletes in the U.S. rose from 294,000 to almost 2 million (Eitzen & Sage, 1986); from 1972 to 1983, the number of women engaged in college sports jumped from 32,000 to 150,000 (Neff, 1988). A closer look at these gains, however, reveals that not all girls and women benefited equally from Title IX and that many of these gains were drastically eroded during the '80s. More importantly, the larger feminist goal of improving upon the male sports model in school systems went badly awry. Now, some of the bad news about Title IX.

Contrary to many hopes (and fears), Title IX was never intended to transform the structures and processes of sport itself. It was merely going to "force" educational institutions to make room for girls and women and to minimally reallocate scarce athletic resources and rewards. In return for these minor alterations, females were expected to accommodate to the sporting institution as it was structured and to conform to its policies and practices. This accommodation by the female "outsider" has many important consequences for women and sport which Marxist, socialist, and radical feminists highlight.

First, the act clearly legitimates the continued institutional ties between sports and schools. It leaves unquestioned the educational value of athletics and the proper role of sports in schools; the priorities behind the allocation of educational budgets—which programs and groups should be funded and which can be "cut"—are never examined. The issue that arises whenever the controversy over intercollegiate athletics is broached, that is, how do these athletic programs enhance the education and the life-preparedness of the participants, is left unexamined, relegated to the "sports bashers" or academic naysayers who are easily ignored by the major advocates of college athletics.

Second, the emphasis in school sports is on revenue production of spectator sports rather than on the lifelong benefits of sport participation. The vast majority of the budgetary disputes concern the allocation of resources to varsity, interscholastic, or intercollegiate competition rather than to greater participation in less elite, intramural sporting activities. Benefits accrue to elite male and female athletes, and not to the greater number of students, whose role remains a passive one. Sports generate prestige for the educational institution, financial success and a privileged status for the few. Title IX never purported to change this.

Third, another disturbing and unexamined consequence of Title IX has been its failure to enhance the athletic opportunities of minority women, especially in colleges. Legislation expected to enhance equality of opportunity by sex ideally should benefit all women. However, given the dynamics of racism in schools, Title IX is primarily of benefit to white females. In this regard it is useful to distinguish the racial effects of Title IX in secondary schools from those it has in colleges. In the high schools, the resistance to Title IX subsided fairly quickly. Mandatory age requirements for high school attendance and local tax revenues made the task of compliance with the law by high schools a relatively easy one. These changes resulting from Title IX necessarily increased the sporting opportunities for black, Hispanic, and other minorities as well as for poor youngsters. Recent research on the ability of high school sports to enhance the academic as well as the athletic experience of some minority students has been documented (Sabo, Melnick, & Vanfossen, 1989).

A comparison of the participatory trends in high school with those in intercollegiate competition discloses a more marked racial and social class bias at the collegiate level. It is a well-known fact that a substantially lower percentage of minorities, both female and male, continue their education after high school. Thus, the benefits of Title IX for minority females is far less extensive than for white females. High school educations, unlike college opportunities, are far more egalitarian. Despite their high dropout rates, especially in poor urban schools, minorities and the poor in this country still have a far greater chance of completing high school than they do of entering and completing college.

Fourth, the effect of Title IX at the collegiate level has been to reproduce in female sports the same structural inequities found in male sports. The domination of major sports and of certain educational institutions in male sports is well known. UCLA, Ohio State, Michigan, Texas, and so on—in short the ''jock'' colleges and universities—are used as reference points by educational institutions wishing to make a name for themselves in women's sports. It comes as no surprise that the pre-Title IX ''powerhouse'' names in women's basketball (e.g., Immaculata, Queens College, Delta State, Montclair State) have been replaced by the same ''big-name'' schools that dominate men's sports, (UCLA, Ohio, Tennessee, etc.). In the competition for commercial success, the small college cannot contend with the large university, the private college with the public, those that have no male sporting tradition with those that have an established reputation. Colleges with an energetic sports information department win the battle for the scarce resource of athletic talent over those schools with less experience in ''selling the school'' to the potential recruit. The ''rich get richer'' fulfills the ''operative principle . . . that a school must spend to win and must win to spend'' (Weistart, 1987, p. 15).

Not surprisingly, women's intercollegiate programs now experience similar pressures to replicate the male standards of success for athletic programs. Female programs are measured and evaluated by such factors as the number of scholarships offered, the size of gate receipts, the interest shown by the media, the number of victories, and other external criteria of achievement. The abuses such standards have generated in male sports are well documented, and evidence of similar abuses in some women's programs has surfaced. Women's programs have been cited for recruiting violations, providing illegal benefits to players, and other abuses (''Women's Basketball Team,'' 1986). As the coach of the women's basketball team at the University of Texas at Austin recently said, ''. . . women's programs began to model [themselves] after the men's programs. We tried to play like men. We tried to be revenue-producing like men, to draw the big crowds like men, and to offer scholarships like the men. We even fell into a pattern of saying, 'If the men have it, we want it, too' '' (Conradt, 1989, p. 10). Violations of NCAA rules, institutional guidelines, and moral codes apparently are more gender-free than liberal feminists cared to believe 20 years ago.

Fifth, another ominous and unanticipated consequence resulted from the uncritical application of Title IX to women's athletic programs. Consider the matter of coaches for women's teams. In 1972, at the time of passage of the Title IX, over 90% of coaching jobs for women's teams were held by women. By 1977, this figure had *dropped* to 58.2%, and in 1988, the figure stood at 48.3% (Acosta & Carpenter, 1988). Thus, by 1988, over half of these coaching jobs were held by *men*. Several scholars have begun to investigate this phenomenon and search for its causes. In an excellent review of competing explanations of the decline in the number of women coaches, Knoppers, Meyer, and Ewing (1989) argue that ''sex segregation in an occupation such as coaching is not as much a function of women's lack of interest and qualifications (human capital) as it is of economic, cultural, and structural factors'' (p. 25). Our interest here is not to close off debate on this question but rather to call attention to the unexpected results of seemingly benign liberal policies that uncritically accept the status quo of institutional forms.

Similar losses for women can be found in the athletic administrative ranks. In 1972 more than 90% of programs for women's athletics were administered by women. In 1988 only "16% of women's intercollegiate programs are under the supervision of a female head athletic director" (Acosta & Carpenter, 1988, p. 2). In just 16 years women athletic administrators have become an endangered species! If we look at Alpha Anderson's 1977 study of racial status, similar trends emerge. She found that only 5.4% of the coaches were black and only 5.7% of administrative jobs were held by blacks (Anderson, 1977). By 1988, Acosta and Carpenter report that "there is a minority group member in only 1 out of 5 of the athletic administrative structures found in NCAA member colleges and universities" (Acosta & Carpenter, 1988, p. 10). In summary, the work of Anderson, Acosta and Carpenter, and Sabo et al. (1989) illustrate what socialist, Marxist, and radical feminists expected and predicted: The explosion of female collegiate sports has meant more careers and job opportunities for *white males*.

Lastly, perhaps the most profoundly disturbing impact of Title IX in intercollegiate sports is contained in the history of how women athletic administrators lost control over their programs to the powerful NCAA, the national governing body in collegiate athletics. There are several excellent historical accounts of this organizational and policy battle (Grant, 1984; Hogan, 1987; Uhler, 1987), and we wish here to merely highlight its main contours.

Founded in 1971 by female physical educators to act as the governing agency for women's intercollegiate athletics, the Association of Intercollegiate Athletics for Women (AIAW) made great strides in the '70s to strengthen its programs. The number of sports offered to female students increased, the size of women's program budgets were enlarged, more national championships were sponsored, more female athletic scholarships were awarded, and more women athletes competed than in previous years. The progress under the aegis of the AIAW was substantial, and yet the AIAW continued to maintain an educational philosophy that tried to strike a better balance between the roles of student and athlete than was evident in men's collegiate programs. "Participants were to be students first and athletes second" (Grant, 1979, p. 414). This meant that the AIAW produced rules and guidelines that protected the student athlete and placed her academic and general welfare above that of the institution or external interests, such as alumni, media, fans, and commercial concerns. In a play to gain control over the increasingly successful women's programs, the NCAA voted in 1980 to sponsor women's intercollegiate sports championships. The end of the AIAW was in sight. Loss of membership, income, championship sponsorship, and media rights all combined to force the collapse of the AIAW only 2 years later, in 1982. Since then, the major governing body in control of both male and female intercollegiate sports has been the NCAA.

What the history of the AIAW-NCAA bureaucratic struggle proves is the "attractiveness" of the male-model of sports for those who seek merely to "get into the game," not to change it. What college would be willing to forfeit, even in women's sports, the increased revenues, exposure, titles, and prestige associated with high-level competition? What women's athletic program would turn down the money, scholarships, gate receipts, the travel and meal allocations, and the growing budgets and salaries just to fend off the incursion of commercialism into the women's athletic arenas? Unfortunately the answer to these questions seems to be, hardly any. Consciously or not, happily chosen or forcefully fed, the desire for money and power moved women "toward full replication of practices of male athletics" (Nyquist, 1979, p. 388). The demise of the AIAW meant there was no longer an organization that would recall a different history, that would speak in a "different voice" (Gilligan, 1982) for different values, either for women or for sport.

We believe that one of the major reasons why the AIAW was unable to withstand the political pressures of the NCAA was that although the AIAW espoused an educational philosophy, it had only a meagerly developed feminist consciousness. At best, the members were liberal feminists preoccupied with "equal opportunity," and their uncritical grasp of Title IX dominated the AIAW. However, Title IX hardly speaks to the "publics" who have been traditionally ignored. "Public" policy in this case is for that public primarily composed of white, single, 18- to 22-year-old, middle- to upper-class women whose sexual orientation is expected to be heterosexual and whose contact with sports is expected to be channeled into a relatively elite educational setting. The benefits for marginal groups who do not normally attend college—what might be termed "forgotten publics"—were minimal.

At the broadest level, the debate over Title IX and public policy has completely avoided questioning the sex-role polarization that sports creates and the long-held belief that sports is a masculine domain. Though social scientists and public policy makers are content to leave to philosophers and radical theorists any questions regarding the ultimate nature of the human experience, they do so at the cost of leaving a vacuum to be filled by the dominant cultural and institutional definitions that have been shaped by *men's* values, *men's* understandings of the world, and *men's* experiences. Women's alienation from sport, their indifference to it, and their reluctance to enter it stem in large measure from the fact that, as it has existed historically, what sport celebrated, what sport offered, what sport demanded, what sport rewarded do not reflect much of women's experience of the world.

It is apparent from the history of the battle over Title IX that women are being asked to embrace the masculine model of sport. Yet liberal feminists believed that Title IX was a significant victory in the battle *against* sexism. It would not be entirely accurate to suggest that Title IX has meant no gains for women who wish to pursue athletics and sports; however, the retrenchment of neoconservatism during the Reagan years, the post-woman's era, and the emergence of attacks on opportunities that may be even more vital to women's interests—such as reproduction rights—should demonstrate even to those who hold the most radical vision of the impact of liberal feminism (Eisenstein, 1981) that progress and advancement is not inevitable; that "rights" once given can be taken away; that the challenge of liberal politics is to be active, involved, and ever vigilant. Title IX and liberal feminism challenge us to recognize both the benefits and the limits of such legislation and to use caution and intelligence to demand that present policy serve the widest possible public in the most humanistic manner.

REFERENCES

Acosta, R.V., & Carpenter, L.J. (1988). Women in intercollegiate sports. (Available from Brooklyn College, Department of Physical Education, Brooklyn, NY.)

Anderson, A. (1977). *Status of minority women in the Association of Intercollegiate Athletics for Women.* Unpublished master's thesis, Temple University.

Boutilier, M., & SanGiovanni, L. (1983). *The sporting woman.* Champaign, IL: Human Kinetics.

Bunch, C. (1978). Lesbians in revolt. In A.M. Jaggar & R.P. Struhl (Eds.), *Feminist frameworks* (pp. 135-139). New York: McGraw-Hill.

Conradt, J. (1989, November 12). Why must women pay for men's mistakes? *New York Times.*

Daly, M. (1978). *Gyn/Ecology: The metaethics of radical feminism.* Boston: Beacon Press.

Eisenstein, Z. (1981). *The radical future of liberal feminism.* New York: Longman.

Eitzen, S., & Sage, G. (1986). *Sociology of North American sport.* Dubuque, IA: Wm. C. Brown.

Fishel, A., & Pottker, J. (1977). *National politics and sex discrimination in education.* Lexington, MA: D.C. Heath.

Garratt, L. (1989, September). Women in Sports, *CitySports*, **3**(7), 10-12.

Gilligan, C. (1982). *In a different voice.* Cambridge: Harvard University Press.

Grant, C. (1979). Institutional autonomy and intercollegiate athletics. *Educational Record*, **60**, 409-419.

Grant, C. (1984, July). The gender gap in sport: From Olympic to intercollegiate level. *Arena Review,* **8**, 31-47.

Grove City College v. Bell, 104 S. Ct. 1211 (1984).

Hogan, C. (1987, June). What's in the future for women's sports? *Women's Sports and Fitness,* **9**, 43-48.

Jaggar, A.M., & Struhl, R.P. (Eds.) (1978). *Feminist frameworks.* New York: McGraw-Hill.

Knoppers, A., Meyer, B., & Ewing, M. (1989, September). *The structure of athletic obstacles to women's involvement in coaching.* Paper presented at the annual forum of the Council of Collegiate Women Athletic Administration, Washington, DC.

Lapin, J. (1979). Law without order. *Women's Sports,* **1**, 43-45.

Neff, C. (1988, March). Equality at last, Part II. *Sports Illustrated,* **68**, 70-71.

Nyquist, E. (1979). Win, women and money: Collegiate athletics today and tomorrow. *Educational Record,* **60**, 374-394.

Rosenbloom, D. (1983). *Public administration and law.* New York: Marcel Dekker.

Sabo, D., Melnick, M., & Vanfossen, B. (1989). *The Women's Sports Foundation report: Minorities in sports.* New York: Women's Sports Foundation.

Savas, E. (1982). *Privatizing the public sector.* Chatham, NJ: Chatham House.

Uhler, G.A. (1987, July-August). Athletics and the university: The post-woman's era. *Academe,* **73**, 25-29.

Universities charged with sex discrimination in athletics under Title IX. (1982, Feb. 3), *In the Running,* **5**, p. 4.

Weistart, J. (1987, July-August). College sports reform: Where are the faculty? *Academe,* **73**, 12-17.

Women's basketball team in Louisiana penalized for recruitment violations. (1986, January 22). *Chronicle of Higher Education,* **31**, 29.

Chapter 7

The Status of Women
in Intercollegiate Athletics

R. Vivian Acosta
Brooklyn College

Linda Jean Carpenter
Brooklyn College

Sports for girls and women were not born in 1972 with the passage of Title IX,[1] and intense athletic competition for females was not introduced for the first time with the formation of the Association for Intercollegiate Athletics for Women (AIAW).[2] Rather, sports for girls and women have been progressing, albeit slowly at times and often in the face of great hardships, for many decades.

The significance of 1972 is not as "the beginning" but rather as a year that accelerated change. The formation of the AIAW and the passage of Title IX in 1972 were indicative of changing societal views toward gender equity in society at large and sports in particular. How would these changes manifest themselves in the following decades? What would be the effect on leadership roles and participation rates for females in sport?

Although Title IX was passed by Congress in 1972, post secondary educational institutions under its jurisdiction were not required to comply with its ban against discrimination on the basis of sex until 1978. In effect, the institutions were given 6 years in which to develop game plans, gather funds, interpret implications, and otherwise gradually arrive at a state of full compliance with the requirements of Title IX. Even though compliance was not required until 1978, many changes were effected before 1978.

In 1977, a year before the compliance date, we began a longitudinal study of the status of women in intercollegiate sport. This study has involved sending questionnaires to all AIAW member institutions and, with the demise of the AIAW, to all NCAA colleges and universities in the country that offer intercollegiate programs for women. Over the years the number of such schools has varied but it has always been around 800 or more. The rate of questionnaire return has been consistently high, ranging from 70% to 76%. The discussion that follows uses data gathered from our longitudinal study with baseline reference to the early data of Carolyn Lehr and others.

THE STATUS OF WOMEN
AS INTERCOLLEGIATE ATHLETES

Girls and women had been participating in sport in increasing numbers before 1972. Title IX helped open the doors even further, and although the status of women as leaders in sport is grim, the status of women as participants is brighter. It is estimated that in 1972, colleges and universities offered their female students an average of 2.5 varsity teams a campus. Eighteen years later, in 1990, the number had grown to 7.24.

The sporting experiences available to the female college student have increased since 1972. However they comprise a different variety of sports than in 1972. Basketball is the most widely offered sport for females on college campuses, followed by volleyball and tennis (see Table 7.1). Cross-country, soccer, and softball have experienced the fastest growth in the past two decades.

Budget constraints have forced the general abandonment of junior varsity teams thus limiting access to intercollegiate athletics to only highly skilled athletes. The loss of junior varsity teams also eliminates entry-level coaching positions. In the place of the junior varsity teams are found a larger variety of "major" sports and a smaller variety of "minor" sports.

Twenty-five years ago, only about 16,000 women participated in intercollegiate athletics. No doubt, for the individual participant, the competition among that 16,000 felt as strong, the importance of win-loss records was as great, and the sense of personal achievement was as important as it is today. Today, 10 times as many women are experiencing the positive benefits of intercollegiate athletics. Although their choice of sports is different and the postgame get-togethers with opponents over orange slices and cookies are missing, 1972 has had a great impact on the 160,000 intercollegiate female athletes of today.

THE STATUS OF WOMEN IN ATHLETIC ADMINISTRATION

Early research (Homen & Parkhouse, 1981; Lehr, 1981; & Mathison, 1980) supported the fact that in 1972, 90% to 100% of women's intercollegiate athletic programs were administered by women, and women filled 90% to 100% of the coaching positions on women's teams. These data serve as a baseline for the changes that were accelerated by the events of 1972. There has been a marked

Table 7.1   Percentage of Schools Offering Sports for Female Intercollegiate Athletes

Sport	School year														
	77/78	78/79	79/80	80/81	81/82	82/83	83/84	84/85	85/86	86/87	87/88	88/89	89/90	90/91	91/92
Archery	3.0	3.3	2.8	2.2	1.8	1.6	1.2	0.8	0.8	1.2	1.1	0.8	0.8	0.3	.5
Badminton	5.9	6.1	5.4	4.4	3.6	2.2	1.9	2.0	2.0	1.2	1.1	1.5	1.0	0.9	0.9
Basketball	90.3	96.4	97.5	95.9	97.3	93.8	95.7	96.8	97.1	97.2	97.0	96.2	96.2	97.1	97.2
Bowling	3.4	3.6	3.6	3.3	2.9	1.9	1.9	2.0	2.0	1.9	1.6	0.8	0.8	0.3	0.5
Crew	6.9	6.9	7.2	7.7	7.4	7.0	6.9	8.1	8.4	10.9	11.1	10.4	10.5	8.6	5.6
Cross-country	29.4	39.6	46.6	54.0	59.5	59.9	64.0	75.2	78.5	80.1	82.4	82.2	82.1	79.0	80.1
Fencing	9.8	9.5	9.6	9.8	10.4	8.0	8.0	9.1	8.8	9.5	9.2	7.4	7.4	7.2	7.0
Field hockey	36.3	38.2	37.1	36.1	34.6	30.3	30.2	35.5	34.8	33.5	32.6	29.9	29.4	28.9	28.1
Golf	19.9	20.8	24.1	18.5	19.7	19.8	20.5	23.0	24.5	22.5	24.3	25.0	25.8	22.9	24.0
Gymnastics	25.9	28.2	25.6	23.0	22.1	20.0	18.6	20.4	20.6	17.5	16.8	16.0	15.5	11.3	11.5
Ice hockey	1.3	1.5	1.8	2.9	2.9	2.4	2.8	2.7	2.5	3.2	3.0	2.6	2.6	2.7	2.4
Lacrosse	13.0	13.8	13.9	13.7	13.5	13.3	13.5	17.1	16.9	18.2	18.3	16.9	16.9	16.1	16.0
Riding	2.0	2.5	3.1	2.2	2.4	2.4	2.6	2.4	2.7	2.6	2.6	3.5	3.5	2.2	2.4
Riflery	3.8	3.3	3.4	1.9	1.8	2.7	2.8	4.2	4.2	3.2	2.6	3.2	2.6	2.4	2.2
Sailing	2.3	2.5	1.9	2.4	2.7	2.8	2.7	2.7	2.9	3.2	3.4	3.8	4.0	3.6	3.8
Skiing	3.6	4.6	5.2	5.4	5.7	5.0	4.9	6.6	6.7	5.8	5.8	5.3	5.3	5.6	5.7
Soccer	2.8	4.6	8.2	12.5	16.4	16.4	18.7	26.8	29.7	35.1	38.3	38.5	41.3	44.4	45.8
Softball	48.4	58.9	62.3	65.6	67.1	65.6	65.6	68.4	69.6	72.7	72.5	69.2	70.9	70.6	72.4
Squash	2.3	2.5	2.8	2.7	2.9	2.0	2.0	3.3	3.4	3.0	3.2	3.6	3.6	3.6	3.9
Swimming-diving	41.0	44.8	46.9	48.6	49.1	42.5	44.8	53.5	54.2	54.9	55.0	53.3	53.6	51.1	51.1
Synch. swim	3.3	3.4	3.2	3.3	2.7	1.3	1.5	1.3	1.5	0.7	0.7	0.5	0.5	1.4	1.2
Tennis	80.0	86.5	88.6	85.4	85.5	82.6	82.6	87.0	88.5	90.3	89.9	88.8	88.8	85.0	85.8
Track	46.1	54.3	58.6	59.3	62.0	57.2	58.7	63.8	67.2	64.6	66.8	68.1	68.6	64.3	66.4
Volleyball	80.1	85.9	87.8	84.9	85.7	83.6	84.0	86.3	87.7	91.0	91.2	90.8	90.6	89.1	91.1

increase in the number of jobs within the administrative structures of women's intercollegiate programs in the last few years; however, the actual number of such jobs estimated to have been held by females in the early 1970s is far greater than the 704 such positions actually held by women in 1992. That is to say, in 1992, of the 2,286 administrative positions in intercollegiate athletics for women, only 704 are held by women.

By 1992 the number of women's intercollegiate programs that were administered by women had declined from 90% to 17%. The years from 1972 to 1992 are marked by the entrance of males into the head administrative ranks in women's intercollegiate programs (see Table 7.2), though there has been no similar entrance of females into the administrative ranks of men's programs. In fact, in 1972, less than 1% of head administrative positions in men's intercollegiate programs were held by women.

As might be expected, the percentage of men who head women's athletic programs is highest in Division I. The woman who entertains the hope of advancing to the position of head administrator over the women's program and assumes she can work her way up by obtaining an entry-level position in a Division II or III school may be disappointed. Our data show that such a classic American achievement scenario is more myth than reality (see Table 7.3). Division II and

Table 7.2   Percentage of Women's Intercollegiate Athletic Programs With Male Head Athletic Directors

Division	1972	1980	1984	1986	1988	1990	1992
Division I	—	—	90.00	90.65	91.63	92.99	91.4
Division II	—	—	84.10	84.78	85.36	84.80	85.0
Division III	—	—	78.80	79.58	77.08	75.20	75.2
All divisions	10*	80	83.00	84.79	83.95	84.10	83.2

*No specific data are available for 1972. However, this figure is generally agreed upon.

Table 7.3   Percentage of Schools With No Female Athletic Administrator at Any Level

Division	1984	1986	1988	1990	1992
Division I	21.40	23.36	25.61	21.83	14.6
Division II	36.90	34.05	33.33	39.86	38.8
Division III	36.90	38.33	37.91	32.78	31.9
All divisions	31.60	31.92	32.45	30.26	27.8

III athletic programs offer fewer administrative opportunities: 39% of Division II schools and 32% of Division III schools have no woman involved in the administrative structure of women's sport, compared to 15% at Division I schools. About 28% of all programs for women have *no* woman at all involved in the administrative structure.

There are no specific personnel data that track the career opportunities for female administrators, but it appears that for women, entry-level positions are more likely to be found in Division I and head administrator positions are more likely to be found in Division III programs.

Although 1992 has seen 412 more administrative jobs in women's inter-collegiate athletic programs than were available in 1986, only 704 women hold one of those 2,286 jobs. Thus, the impulses unleashed in 1972 have served to *decrease* the representation of women as administrators in women's inter-collegiate athletics.

STATUS OF WOMEN IN INTERCOLLEGIATE COACHING

The percentage of women who coach women's teams has also decreased markedly since 1972. In 1978, 58% of all coaches of women's sports were women; by 1992, the majority of women's sports (52%) were coached by men. Some sports have had a more dramatic change in their coaching staffs than others (see Table 7.4).

Swimming, tennis, and cross-country have seen drastic changes; when team or coaching responsibilities of these sports are combined, the male coaches are chosen to head the program. Only in field hockey, which in the United States is traditionally a female sport, has the percentage of female coaches remained quite high.

The number of coaching positions in women's athletics has increased from 4,208 in 1978 to 5,952 in 1992. However, the vast majority of new opportunities went to men. Of 1,744 new positions created from 1978 to 1992, 24% (425) went to women and 76% (1,319) to men.

PERCEIVED CAUSES
OF THE DECLINE IN REPRESENTATION
OF FEMALE COACHES AND ADMINISTRATORS

What has caused the decline in the representation of women in coaching and administrative positions in women's intercollegiate athletic programs? We might never know the true nature of any actual causes, but we can investigate the factors perceived to be the cause. To define the perceived causes, and thus provide updated information from which intervention strategies might be developed, we

Table 7.4 Percentage of Women's Intercollegiate Sports Coached by Women

Sport	77/78	78/79	79/80	80/81	81/82	82/83	83/84	84/85	85/86	86/87	87/88	88/89	89/90	90/91	91/92
Archery	83.4	75.0	76.5	60.0	58.3	83.3	77.7	80.0	60.0	71.4	66.7	80.0	80.0	50.0	33.3
Badminton	75.0	73.0	72.7	72.4	70.8	62.5	57.1	75.0	66.6	71.4	66.7	33.3	50.0	80.0	80.0
Basketball	79.4	77.7	76.5	73.7	71.2	66.6	64.9	62.7	61.0	59.9	58.5	56.0	59.0	60.7	63.5
Bowling	42.9	36.4	40.9	45.5	47.4	35.7	28.6	16.7	16.7	9.1	11.1	0.0	0.0	0.0	0.0
Crew	11.9	19.1	18.2	29.4	26.6	26.9	23.5	29.1	22.0	21.0	27.0	34.9	39.1	46.0	44.0
Cross-country	35.2	29.9	25.0	22.0	21.6	22.4	19.7	21.1	21.8	18.7	19.5	20.0	20.6	20.3	20.1
Fencing	51.7	46.6	37.3	35.4	34.7	40.7	37.2	35.2	32.7	33.3	30.8	28.9	28.9	35.7	31.7
Field hockey	99.1	97.4	98.3	98.3	99.6	96.9	98.2	93.8	97.1	96.8	96.2	97.3	97.8	97.0	97.0
Golf	54.6	55.1	46.3	49.6	48.9	40.4	39.7	37.5	44.1	37.5	41.3	45.4	41.4	47.8	45.7
Gymnastics	69.7	68.0	66.6	68.7	67.3	60.1	59.1	55.4	55.7	55.6	53.7	59.8	57.5	53.0	52.2
Ice hockey	37.5	11.1	18.2	26.4	21.1	11.1	9.5	37.5	46.7	0.0	0.0	0.0	12.5	18.8	21.4
Lacrosse	98.7	100.0	100.0	96.7	96.9	93.9	95.0	90.1	89.0	95.1	95.2	94.2	95.1	91.5	95.7
Riding	75.0	73.4	73.7	93.4	93.8	94.4	89.5	78.6	81.2	100.0	100.0	85.7	85.7	100.0	100.0
Riflery	17.4	10.0	19.0	7.7	0.0	0.0	4.8	12.0	16.0	5.6	13.3	8.3	12.5	7.1	7.7
Sailing	7.1	13.3	8.3	31.3	22.2	19.0	15.0	6.2	5.9	5.6	5.3	4.3	12.5	4.8	8.3
Skiing	22.7	25.0	25.0	16.7	15.8	13.5	13.8	7.7	48.6	15.2	18.2	18.8	21.9	18.2	21.2
Soccer	29.4	35.7	28.0	27.7	33.0	30.6	26.8	23.9	30.7	24.1	23.0	23.9	23.1	23.5	25.8
Softball	83.5	83.1	82.9	75.8	74.6	70.9	68.6	64.9	68.0	67.5	67.2	64.6	63.8	61.5	63.7
Squash	71.4	73.3	53.0	61.2	63.2	53.3	40.0	50.0	60.0	70.6	66.7	72.7	68.2	57.1	52.2
Swimming-diving	53.6	50.9	44.8	41.4	36.5	35.0	33.2	31.2	30.0	25.7	25.3	24.4	26.4	26.8	28.2
Synch. swim	85.0	90.5	95.0	95.3	100.0	90.0	72.7	100.0	100.0	100.0	100.0	100.0	100.0	75.0	71.4
Tennis	72.9	71.6	68.9	69.1	65.3	61.5	59.7	56.9	54.8	54.9	52.2	50.7	49.8	47.1	48.0
Track	52.3	46.5	43.1	34.8	33.7	30.6	26.8	24.1	23.1	20.8	21.6	18.4	19.6	21.3	20.4
Volleyball	86.6	83.8	83.7	78.0	74.8	76.7	75.5	72.0	71.3	70.2	71.0	70.5	68.4	69.1	68.7

School year

mailed 400 questionnaires in Spring 1988 to men and women involved in athletic administration in colleges and universities across the nation. Over 60% were completed and returned.

Gender differences in perceived causes are striking. The five most important factors perceived by women are:

1. the success of the "old-boys-club" network
2. the failure of the "old-girls-club" network
3. the lack of support systems for females
4. (tie) unconscious discrimination in selection and hiring process
4. females burn out and retire from coaching and administration earlier than males

Men, on the other hand, listed these top five factors:

1. the lack of qualified female coaches
2. the failure of females to apply for job openings
3. the lack of qualified female administrators
4. (tie) time constraints placed on females due to family duties
4. females earlier burn-out and retirement from coaching and administration

It is interesting to note that the three most important reasons cited by women have to do with communication and interpersonal interactions, whereas the three most important factors cited by men have to do with job market dynamics.

It has been hypothesized that the decreasing representation of females as coaches and administrators in sport, and thus as role models of decision makers, and leaders, is in some part responsible for the declining numbers of females submitting applications for administrative and coaching positions. Although this may be possible, it is important to realize that the pool of qualified female coaches and administrators is sufficient for the need, yet the cycle of diminished representation deepens.

One effect of Title IX was an increase in the salaries and other forms of compensation for coaches of women's teams. Although in most instances, the compensation remains grossly unequal today, it is, at least, more nearly equal. Of course, when the compensation for coaching women's teams began increasing, such jobs became more attractive, and men who previously had not considered coaching a women's team began applying for the jobs. Title IX banned discrimination both in participation and in personnel decisions so that the pre-Title-IX practice of hiring a woman to coach a women's team could no longer be maintained. In addition, more and more of the administrators who were doing the hiring were men, and either through their networks or through unconscious discrimination in reviewing resumes, these men hired men. Thus, a dangerous cycle of male control of women's sport has been established.

With the increase in women's participation in intercollegiate athletics has come a decrease in women's leadership opportunities at the administrative and coaching levels. If the women who currently enjoy collegiate athletics are to have the opportunity to remain in college athletics and exert leadership over the activities they enjoy, we must recognize the patterns of exclusion that presently exist in women's athletics and work to reverse this undesirable trend.

REFERENCES

Homen, M., & Parkhouse, B. (1981). Trends in the selection of coaches for female athletes: A demographic inquiry. *Research Quarterly for Exercise and Sport*, **52**, 9-18.

Lehr, C. (1981, April). *Sex of coaches in women's intercollegiate athletics from 1973 to 1986*. Paper presented at the 1981 American Alliance for Health, Physical Education, Recreation and Dance National Convention, Houston, TX.

Mathison, C.M. (1980). *A selective study of women's athletic administrative settings involving AIAW Division I institutions*. Unpublished manuscript, University of Pittsburgh.

NOTES

1. Title IX of the Education Amendments of 1972 barred sex bias in "any education program or activity receiving federal financial assistance" [Title IX of the Education Amendments of 1972, 20 U.S.C., Section 1681 *et seq.* (1972)].

2. The AIAW was an outgrowth of the Division of Girls' and Women's Sports, now called the National Association for Girls and Women in Sport.

Chapter 8

Gender and the Coaching Profession

Annelies Knoppers
Michigan State University

The influx of females into the male collegiate sport domain has been a recent phenomenon, as numbers concerning their participation have indicated (Acosta & Carpenter, 1985a; Boutilier & SanGiovanni, 1983; Coakley, 1986). In 1970 approximately 16,000 women participated in intercollegiate athletics and about 90% of the women's teams were coached by women. By 1984 the impact of feminism and the passage of Title IX had increased the number of female collegiate athletes to about 150,000. However, there was no concomitant increase in the proportion of women coaches (Acosta & Carpenter, 1985a; Holmen & Parkhouse, 1981). Acosta and Carpenter (1985a) have documented a gradual decrease so that by 1984, only 49.9, 52.2, and 58.8% of the women's teams at Division I, II, and III schools, respectively, were coached by women, and the percent of women coaching men's teams was less than 1%. If one counts all full-time head and assistant coach positions in women's and men's programs and assumes those positions are more likely to exist primarily in Division I, then by extrapolation the percent of full-time women coaches would be close to 25%. In other words, coaching is a male-dominated profession and the skewness of the gender ratio is increasing.[1]

This demise in the number of women coaches is problematic especially since the number of women in other male-dominated professions such as law and medicine has been steadily increasing since the 1970s (Harkess, 1985; Patterson & Engelberg, 1978). The National Collegiate Athletic Association's (NCAA) Long

---

Range Planning Committee has publicly expressed its concern about the "diminishing opportunities for women in intercollegiate athletics and coaching" (*NCAA News*, 1986, p. 1). According to Mathes (1983), the decline in the number of women coaches means there are fewer visible role models for women in sport and this could have a detrimental effect on female athletes. Mathes argued that teachers and coaches serve a function for female athletes that goes beyond the technical aspects of coaching.

Although young girls see female role models in a variety of male-dominated occupations, a lack of female coaches could be especially problematic. The high value placed on sport in the United States gives coaches an aura of power, prestige, and status as well as visibility as decision makers (*Miller Lite Report*, 1983; Sage, 1975). The absence of women from such positions may reinforce the gender stereotyping traditionally associated with the sports world and women in general. This absence may mean not only that fewer women than men will consider coaching as a career, but also that fewer women will be able to continue their sport involvement once their own college athletic participation is over. In addition, since coaching is the entry-level job for careers in athletics, fewer women will have careers in sport and possibly will miss opportunities for mobility through such involvement. Thus it is important to explore dimensions that may diminish the number of female coaches.

In this paper I will explore factors related to the coaching profession that perhaps perpetuate this skewed gender ratio. The discussion will be characterized by the functional perspective centering on the coaching profession as it exists in the collegiate sports world.[2] I will not discuss the desirability of women, or of anyone, becoming a coach in a male-dominated sport world nor include a critique of coaching practices or of institutionalized sexism in sport.[3] The latter may also serve to keep women out of the coaching profession however, and their effects should not be ignored. The discussion will focus on those collegiate coaches whose job assignment is primarily coaching. This narrow focus should eliminate possible confounding that emanates from dual career responsibilities in teaching and coaching (Massengale, 1984) and therefore enable the discussion to center on coaching as a full-time occupation.

THEORETICAL PERSPECTIVES ON OCCUPATIONS

Theoretical perspectives best suited for exploring the dynamics of the coaching profession are those that have been used to study aspects of the business world and occupations in general. The many similarities between the sport and business worlds enhance the applicability of such a perspective. Qualities such as hard work and self-discipline, which are purportedly developed through sports participation, have often been described as the same qualities needed for success in the business world (Berlage, 1982; Borman & Frankel, 1984; Nixon, 1984). Two facets of a coach's job, that is, the objective measure of success as well as total accountability for outcome (Coakley, 1986; Sage, 1975, 1980), seem to parallel criteria used for evaluation in the business world. In addition, the commercialization of college athletics has given many athletic programs a business-like character. Frey (cited in Nixon, 1984) claimed that coaches are becoming more and more like corporate managers. Therefore, the use of theories from the business world to study a part of the sport world seems justified as long as this is done with an awareness that no business-oriented model will capture entirely the dynamics of the coaching profession, especially those aspects related to the role of the coach as educator and to the place of sport in an academic institution.

Most studies of occupations have been grounded in either the individual or the organizational model, with the former being used most frequently, especially when women have been studied in the workplace (Harkess, 1985; Kanter, 1977; Wortman, 1982). The individual model is based on the assumption that the worker shapes the workplace (Kanter, 1977); thus research based on this model entails a study of the characteristics of the individual worker. Consequently when researchers have explored occupation-related gender differences, their intent was usually to identify specific characteristics that held women back. These identified characteristics were usually attributed to gender differences in schooling, in socialization patterns, and in some cases to biological determinism (Kanter, 1977). The assumption that the worker shapes the workplace suggests that the factors which lead to occupational differences and inequities are inherent, especially for minorities and women. For example, Parkhouse and Lapin (1980) in their book, *The Woman in Athletic Administration*, discussed in depth 21 "failings common to many women in management" (p. 5) followed by three short paragraphs of "traits women possess which can benefit them, traits which men do not have" (p. 8). This approach encourages the belief that women bring more deficiencies than assets to the athletic workplace.

In order for these deficiencies and differences to be eradicated, people must be "repaired." Women who work in a male-dominated profession are taught to dress for success, to be assertive, to be objective, and to develop management skills, whereas managerial men are taught to be sensitive to the needs of women and to eliminate overt differential treatment based on gender. If women coaches were to be repaired, they would have to be taught how to behave during a game, to be authoritarian with their players, to recruit, to develop winning programs, to court alumni and wealthy boosters, to handle the press, and so on. In other words, they would be taught all the aspects of coaching which, up until the NCAA dominance of women's sport programs, had been part of the written and unwritten job descriptions of coaches of men's teams. Male athletic administrators, on the other hand, would be taught how to write nonsexist memos, how to use inclusive language, and to attend a few women's athletic events. Consequently, gender inequities and differences would be assumed to have been eradicated through the "restructuring" of employees (coaches) and of employers (athletic administrators).

When such repair programs have been used in organizations, they have increased skills and self-esteem but have had little impact on occupational gender differences because the individual model has been inadequate in this respect (Kanter, 1977). For example, Greenfeld, Greiner, and Wood (1980) tried to predict the gender ratio, that is, sex dominance, of jobs on the basis of the characteristics of the women in them. They found that educational attainment explained 10.2% of the variance. Degree of perceived sex discrimination on the job, age of participant, and success values together explained 13.5% of the variance. All other individual characteristic variables did not explain a significant amount of variance. Overall individual characteristics that could be altered or repaired explained only 26.7% of the variance in predicting the gender ratio of a job or occupation. In other words, 73.3% of the variance may have been due to factors that are not affected by repair programs. Similarly, the use of only the individual model to explain the low number of female coaches may fail to capture gender dynamics in the coaching profession. Ultimately, repair programs may do little to change gender ratio and instead may only make women coaches more like men coaches.

A major weakness of the use of this model in the athletic context is that it overlooks the structural causes of inequity and the institutionalization of sexism in sport and in the athletic workplace. If for example one of the requirements for an assistant coach's position is that the applicant must have played that sport in college, then no amount of repair (except for a sex change) will qualify most women for a football coaching position. In the same vein, it would be interesting to discover how many men coaching women's teams had collegiate experience in that sport. Acosta and Carpenter (1985b) found that female athletic administrators attributed the loss of female coaches partially to discrimination in the hiring process. A repair of women coaches would therefore have little impact on gender-differentiated standards for hiring coaches of women's and men's teams.

One other critique of most studies that have looked at characteristics of workers is that the data gathered by the male employees are often considered to be the norm (Harkess, 1985). Comparing women to this norm will inevitably lead to the conclusion that they, rather than the men, need to be repaired. Thus gender-related dynamics tend to be overlooked or not captured. A study of gender-related factors in the coaching profession requires, therefore, a model that explains the occupation for both genders and that captures institutionalized sexism.

The weaknesses of the individual model have caused theorists to focus on the workplace instead of the worker, assuming it is primarily the workplace that shapes an individual's behavior (Kanter, 1977). "What people do, how they come to feel and behave, reflects what they can make of their situation" (p. 251). "To a very large degree, organizations make their workers into who they are" (p. 263). Whereas the individual model assumes a static organization or workplace, the organizational model assumes that the structure of the workplace shapes the behavior of the workers. Seemingly contradictory results in studies of characteristics of professional women may therefore be due largely to the variations in their experiences in different organizations (Cabral, Ferber, & Green, 1981). Miller and Garrison (1982), after reviewing the research on gender-differentiated outcomes in professions, concluded that "Research to date suggests that the major emphasis should be directed toward institutionalized factors channeling men and women into sex segregated work roles'' (p. 249).

It may seem that if both women and men work in the same workplace, then that workplace should be a constant for both. Acker (1978) has argued however that women and men can experience the same workplace differently. Similarly, Kanter (1977) has developed a theory, based on the organizational model, which posits that three interacting structural determinants of the workplace are experienced differently by women and men and may explain gender differences in behavior.[4] She named these structural determinants: opportunity, power, and proportion. Each will be discussed in detail and applied to the coaching profession to explain the scarcity of women coaches.

STRUCTURAL DETERMINANTS OF WORK BEHAVIOR

Opportunity

Opportunity is described by the shape of one's career ladder, perceived obstacles and satisfaction, access to training, and availability and type of feedback. Opportunity in the coaching profession is often gender-related. The shapes of women's and men's career ladders are quite different. As the data indicated earlier, women are rarely hired to work in men's programs, yet positions in women's programs are occupied by men as well as women. In addition, opportunities for receiving money from television shows, shoe contracts, and speaking engagements more often accompany coaching positions in men's than in women's programs. Similarly, male coaches who wish to step up to administrative positions seem to have a greater chance to do so than do females, since ''over 80 percent of all intercollegiate programs have two or more administrators, yet many have absolutely no female input on the administrative level'' (Acosta & Carpenter, 1985a, p. 32). Coaching therefore may be a dead-end career for women, while for men it provides a career ladder with many possibilities.

The type of obstacles encountered in the coaching occupation that affect the degree of opportunity also vary by gender. One obstacle common to women in all-male-dominated professions is sex discrimination (Harlan & Weiss, 1980). Such discrimination may begin with how one discovers the position is available and who does the hiring. Female athletic administrators have attributed the demise in the number of female coaches to the success of the ''old boy'' network, failure of the ''old girl'' network, and discrimination on the part of the male administraors doing the hiring (Acosta & Carpenter, 1985b). Indirect evidence of gender-differentiated hiring standards was revealed in the data collected by Anderson and Gill (1983). They found that compared to men who coached males and women who coached females, men who coached females had fewer years of collegiate athletic experience, were less likely to have majored in physical education, and had received fewer collegiate athletic awards. Thus the first obstacle in the career ladder in coaching for women may come at the entry point into the profession.

Direct evidence of sex discrimination in the hiring process would be difficult to obtain since such discrimination might be grounded in the perception that since sport is a masculine domain, males are inherently more competent to coach than females are (Boutilier & SanGiovanni, 1983). The extent to which the sports world is sexist and dominated by males has been discussed elsewhere and will not be repeated here (e.g., see Boutilier & SanGiovanni, 1983). Greenfeld et al. (1980) in their study of gender ratio in jobs found that the greater the male dominance in an occupation, the more likely women in those occupations experienced discrimination based on sex. Thus gender ratio or proportion, another structural determinant of work behavior, is intertwined with opportunity and the two are not isolated factors (Kanter, 1977).

Once a female is hired in a male-dominated profession, her next obstacle may be sexual harassment (Harlan & Weiss, 1980). The extent to which this occurs in the coaching world has not been determined quantitatively. Such harassment would include questioning the sexual orientation of single female coaches (Nelson, 1984). Since such questioning already occurs with respect to female athletes (Boutilier & SanGiovanni, 1983), it would probably be reflected in attitudes towards women coaches as well. Hall (1984) has argued that female physical educators may refrain from espousing feminism to avoid being labeled lesbians. Thus women coaches may encounter not only forms of sexual harassment experienced by women in other male-dominated professions but also may have to face an unrelenting homophobic environment.

Another obstacle that often has an impact on careers of both women and men coaches is the conflict between time required for coaching and time for family responsibilities (Coakley, 1986; Sabock & Jones, 1978). Traditionally, coaching has been a two-person single career for men in which wives were primarily responsible for raising the children, entertaining recruits and coaches, doing the housekeeping, and attending the games and other athletic events. As Sabock and Jones (1978) discovered in a study of spouses of coaches, the number of husbands who are willing to do the same for a coaching spouse is limited.

The expectation that married male coaches have a two-person single career while married female coaches have a one-person dual career was clearly conveyed by Sabock (1979) in his book, *The Coach*. Sabock spelled out in great detail the duties of female spouses and seemed to assume that either these wives do not have paid careers or that they will subordinate their careers to those of their coaching husbands. In contrast, Sabock's discussion of male spouses of coaches was confined primarily to a presentation of the results of a questionnaire that focused on the attitudes of such husbands. The responses of coaches' husbands indicated that they felt their main responsibilities were to show tolerance for the disruption of household schedules and to share in doing household chores. Sabock and Jones (1978) in another study of such husbands found an unwillingness to do so. In both studies as well as in *The Coach*, no mention was made about the husband's role in recruiting, in creating staff rapport by hosting social functions for spouses, in washing uniforms, hosting team picnics, and so forth. Clearly, coaches' husbands are not expected to be involved in their wives' careers to the same extent as are the wives of male coaches.

Whether one is a male or female coach may also determine the extent of one's own family responsibilities. Research has shown that married women who work outside the home still are responsible for most of the household chores (Miller & Garrison, 1982). Although data concerning those in the coaching profession are not available, it would seem likely that often male coaches are absolved from many family-related responsibilities while female coaches are not but instead carry those responsibilities in addition to those related to coaching. The difficulty of this task is reflected in the data that showed female coaches are more likely to be single than male coaches are (Caccese & Mayerberg, 1984; Hart, Hasbrook, & Mathes, 1986; Mathes, 1982).

Two important points should be made concerning these data. First, the skewed gender ratio in the coaching profession will show little change if for females a coaching career is seen as being incompatible with marriage. Coaching may not be seen as a viable career option by married women and/or by women who wish to have children. A labor pool that consists primarily of single childless women is more constricted than one in which marital and parental status is not a factor.

Second, although many single female coaches may not have a responsibility for children, they must still do the same amount of work as a male coach and spouse combined. The single female coach not only goes on the road to recruit, as does her male counterpart, but she must also clean the house before entertaining recruits, do the wash, and make a dish to bring to the athletic department's potluck supper, duties usually not performed by her male counterpart.

In sum, female coaches, regardless of marital status, may have a one-person dual career while male coaches tend to have a two-person single career. Female coaches therefore may perceive lack of time as an obstacle to opportunity more so than do males.

One other area that enhances or inhibits opportunity is that of feedback and appraisal. Harlan and Weiss (1980) found that male workers were more likely than females to receive informal constructive criticism and praise on a frequent basis. Constant feedback is important to a coach since the lack of formal academic training in coaching per se requires that most occupational socialization and training occur on the job (Chu, 1980; Sage, 1975). Thus, informal feedback would be essential to this process. Women who fail to receive such feedback would be severely handicapped in their attempt to learn the job.

Harlan and Weiss (1980) found no significant gender differences in formal evaluations but did not determine the salience of gender in those evaluations. Similar gender-related data on formal evaluations of coaches are lacking; however, Parkhouse and Williams (1986) found that athletes of both sexes preferred male coaches and perceived them to be more competent than their female counterparts. Although evaluations by athletes may not always be part of the formal feedback, if any, received by coaches, such negative attitudes toward female coaches may create another gender-related obstacle in their career ladders.

The foregoing detailed a few examples of the salience of gender with respect to opportunity in the coaching profession. These gender-related differences in opportunity may partially explain the scarcity of women coaches and may discourage women from entering the profession. Specifically, Bridges and Bower (1985) found that female college students were most likely to select occupations with good job opportunities for women. Similarly female athletes may avoid the coaching profession because they may have noticed the gender-related differences in opportunity.

Lack of opportunity may not only inhibit the number of women entering coaching, it may also directly affect the work behavior of those who do become coaches. Kanter (1977) found that white-collar workers who perceived little opportunity for advancement tend to be lower in self-esteem, tend to limit their career aspirations, and are mainly concerned with survival. Those with high opportunity prospects tend to be higher in self-esteem, are competitive, and tend to identify with the organization and with high-power people. Thus, gender differences in work behavior may result from differences in opportunity rather than from inherent sex characteristics.

Early exits from a career are also often due to lack of opportunity (Kanter, 1977). This may partially account for demographic data which have shown that the average woman coach has fewer years of experience than does her male counterpart (Caccese & Mayerberg, 1984). In addition, Mathes (1982) found that for high school women coaches, lack of opportunity was the best predictor of dropping out. Lack of opportunity therefore may affect not only work behavior but also entry and exit rates.

An increase in opportunity for women in coaching would require a substantial change in the status quo. For example, women coaches could be encouraged to apply for positions with men's teams and in administration. Head coaches could be rewarded for developing assistant female coaches and then "losing" them to head coaching positions. An on-site day care center as well as a staffed hospitality room for entertaining recruits could help to alleviate family time constraints. Another alternative would be to pay for the duties that many spouses of male coaches have traditionally undertaken. Such changes, as well as others, may not only increase perceived opportunities for women but may also ensure that married status does not influence dropping out of the profession or require women, but not men, to have dual careers.

Power

The second structural determinant of work behavior is power. This does not refer to the extent to which one dominates others but rather to one's capacity to mobilize resources (Kanter, 1977). Power consists of job and social-related components in that it is shaped both by formal job description and by informal alliances. A person with power can make decisions in unexpected problems and events without obtaining approval from a superior (Agassi, 1979), has easy and frequent access to mentors and those of higher rank (Rosen, 1982), is able to obtain above average salaries and rewards for subordinates, and is able to influence organizational policy (Harlan & Weiss, 1980). Persons with power have autonomy and freedom of action, having access to whatever is needed to reach their goals.

An application of this concept of power to the coaching profession would mean that coaches with power are those who are able to obtain a full-time secretary, who are consulted about departmental policy, whose budgets and assistants are approved with little question, and who interact both at work and on social occasions with athletic administrators. Coaches with little power are those (a) who have a say, but not a final say, in the hiring of assistants, (b) who continually must plead for budget items, (c) who, when an unexpected problem arises, must receive approval before implementing a decision, (d) who learn about athletic department news and policy by reading the newspaper, and (e) whose only contact with the athletic director is at contract time. Coaches who coach men's football and basketball would tend to have power since they usually insist and receive full control over their program (Coakley, 1986). Since women are rarely found in such positions, the number of women coaches with power in any athletic department is virtually nil. Mathes (1982) reported that the second best predictor of female coaches leaving the profession was lack of control over one's program, in other words, lack of power.

The extent of power one has tends to be related to work behavior. South, Bonjean, Corder, and Markham (1982) in a direct test of this hypothesis found a positive and significant relationship between power and job satisfaction of federal workers. Kaplan and Sedney (1980) have argued that possession of power is accompanied by feelings of respect, credibility, and security which are acquired from the support of mentors, high expectations of supervisors, and reactions of subordinates. Kanter (1977) found that lack of power resulted in cautious and inflexible behavior.

Change in the dynamics of power in the coaching profession may be more difficult to implement than changes in the structure of opportunity.

> To empower those women and others who currently operate at a disadvantage requires attention to both sides of power. It is always hard to get at real power issues or make impactful changes in a power structure, since almost by definition, those with power have a stake in keeping it for themselves . . .
> Just as opportunity-enhancement begins with change in the formal organization (career paths and job ladders), empowerment must also start with, and rest fundamentally on, modification of official structural arrangements. (Kanter, 1977, p. 276).

Kanter suggested that the hierarchy for decision-making be flattened by making all workers as autonomous as possible. For example, all coaches could hire their own assistants without detailed scrutiny by the assistant athletic director as well as the athletic director. Similarly, the administrative staff could be instructed and trained to move from control to facilitation and planning, which would include refraining from paternalistic actions and from circumventing decisions made by women coaches.

Since knowledge is power, a concerted effort should be made to share information. For example, the knowledge of all salaries and budgets could be made available to each coach. Coaches should have the opportunity to give input into departmental policy and to be informed of resultant changes before those policies are published in the newspapers. New coaches should receive an extensive orientation concerning departmental philosophy and policy. Such procedures would give all coaches knowledge of the system and consequently decrease the importance of informal alliances.

Since informal alliances can be a source of power, they could be partially institutionalized through policies that reward or emphasize mentoring. For example, each new coach could be assigned a mentor who has power. Mentors could be rewarded for their mentoring and for the success of their protégées. "Organizations should also routinely schedule meetings and events which give women an opportunity to come into contact with power-holders" (Kanter, 1977, p. 279). Consequently, by investing all coaches with as much power as possible and by giving all coaches formal and informal access to administrators, the gender-related power differences could be minimized.

Proportion

The third structural determinant of a worker's behavior is number or proportion. In the study of gender and occupations, proportion is defined by the ratio of women to men. Kanter (1977) called a ratio of .15 or less as skewed and one of .16 to .35 as tilted. If all coaches and athletic administrators are included in the total count, then in most athletic departments the gender ratio is probably tilted or close to being skewed. The smaller this ratio, the greater the possibility that women are treated as tokens.

According to Kanter such treatment can take three forms. First, it may occur in the form of status leveling. For example, if female coaches are rare then they may be mistaken for secretaries. Second, tokenism occurs in the form of slotting. This means that since every committee needs a female member the few females end up being overburdened with committee work. The third form of tokenism consists of occupational stereotyping, that is, males are considered the norm in the profession and therefore are preferred by subordinates. Evidence of this with respect to athletes preferring male coaches was presented earlier in this paper.

Both skewed or tilted ratios are disadvantageous for women. A tilted ratio might seem more beneficial to women than a skewed ratio. However, South, Bonjean, Markham, and Corder (1982) found that when women comprised a large minority in an organization, they had more same-sex support but also less access to male networks than did women in organizations with skewed ratios. The investigators concluded that a greater number of women in an organization may have little effect on organizational behavior if the structure of power and opportunity has not changed.

The inner psychic costs of being a woman in a profession with a skewed ratio are immeasurable (Kaplan & Sedney, 1980). For example, women coaches may simultaneously represent all women and yet be exceptions. When they lose or have problems with an athlete, they typify all women; when they do well, they are considered exceptions. Women coaches may be aware they are treated differently from men coaches but must pretend those differences do not exist, especially when it comes to budget, salary, publicity, responsibility, and so on. They may suffer from aloneness, yet departmental dynamics may create pressure for them to disassociate from other women such as secretaries. Coaching behaviors may provide dilemmas. Should a female coach behave in an authoritarian manner as do many male coaches? (Coakley, 1986). If she does not do so, her losses may be attributed to her nonauthoritarian manner. Does she have to behave like a man to gain credibility? If she perceives inequities and strives to correct them, she may be categorized as a ''women's libber.'' Male coaches have often been categorized as conservative (Sage, 1975, 1980); athletes who rebel, protest, or question have usually been selected out. Feminist coaches could meet the same fate.

Obviously then, being a woman in an occupation such as athletics in which the gender ratio is skewed takes extra energy and courage. No investigators have examined this extra cost with respect to coaching, perhaps because women have always coached. However, coaching by women until recently was done in an entirely different climate and rarely full time. Full-time coaching has always been part of the male profession and thus women are the ones who are expected to adjust.

Kanter (1977) has given several applicable suggestions with respect to changing a skewed gender ratio and tokenism. One obvious solution is for athletic departments to increase the number of female coaches hired. However, as long as women are considered only for positions associated with women's teams, women will always be in the minority since female athletes comprise only one third of all collegiate athletes. Obviously this structural determinant interacts with opportunity.

Kanter (1977) makes other suggestions applicable to coaching which seem to echo those grounded in the individual model. However, the purpose of the suggestions would be to change the work climate rather than the worker. For example, she suggests that administrators be educated about the dynamics of tokenism and that women's networks and support programs should be encouraged. Thus women coaches could collaborate with each other and with women in central administration to share knowledges concerning the power structure, the use of power in dividing and controlling, and the dynamics of the social organization of gender (Lopiano, 1984). The use of such knowledges often requires a feminist consciousness, and thus women coaches could benefit from forming alliances with feminists on campus. Such alliances may have ramifications, as Hall (1984) has pointed out, since they may result in an increase in the negative stereotyping of women coaches. Yet to the extent to which such alliances give women coaches badly needed support as well as dignity, they may often be worth the cost.

CONCLUSION

Opportunity, power, and proportion have been identified as structural determinants of gender-differentiated work behavior of women and men. These determinants are not static independent entities but dynamic interacting forces. For example, an increase in one's access to power may in turn enhance one's opportunity. Similarly, an increase in the proportion of women may create more positions for women.

Researchers who wish to investigate the skewed gender ratio in the coaching profession should therefore not ignore the structural determinants of work behavior. The delineation of gender-related dimensions of opportunity, power, and proportion and how they shape work behavior of women and men coaches can be accomplished through two types of research. Quantitative methodology could be used to quantify the determinants and to compare them across gender of coach, gender of team, and type of sport. Qualitative methodology such as ethnography could be used to describe the work climate in the athletic department and to determine ways in which the structural determinants enhance or inhibit work behavior. Naturally such studies need to be followed by action and change in organizational aspects. The implementation of such changes may make coaching a viable career option for women.

Although this paper began with a critique of the individual model, an analysis of the work behavior of coaches should not totally ignore that model since it may partially explain such behavior (Greenfeld et al., 1980). Astin (1984) has hypothesized that work behavior may best be explained by an interaction paradigm that incorporates both the individual and structural model. Such a paradigm may explain more dimensions of gender-differentiated work behavior of coaches than either model could do alone. The foregoing discussion merely suggests that the facets of the organizational climate might have a greater impact on a coach's behavior than would the characteristics the coach brings to the job.

REFERENCES

Acker, J. (1978). Issues in the sociological study of women's work. In A. Stromberg & S. Harkess (Eds.), *Women working: Theories and facts in perspective.* Palo Alto, CA: Mayfield.

Acosta, R.V., & Carpenter, L.J. (1985a). Women in athletics: A status report. *Journal of Physical Education, Recreation and Dance*, **56**(6), 30-34.

Acosta, R.V., & Carpenter, L.J. (1985b). Status of women in athletics: Changes and causes. *Journal of Physical Education, Recreation and Dance*, **56**(6), 35-37.

Agassi, J.B. (1979). *Women on the job*. Lexington, MA: D.C. Heath.

Anderson, D.F., & Gill, K.S. (1983). Occupational socialization patterns of men's and women's interscholastic basketball coaches. *Journal of Sport Behavior*, **6**, 105-116.

Astin, H.S. (1984). The meaning of work in women's lives: A sociopsychological model of career choice and work behavior. *The Counseling Psychologist*, **12**(4), 117-126.

Berlage, G. (1982). Are children's competitive team sports socializing agents for corporate America? In A. Dunleavy, A. Miracle, & O.R. Rees (Eds.), *Studies in the sociology of sport*. Fort Worth: Texas Christian University Press.

Borman, K.M., & Frankel, J. (1984). Gender inequities in childhood social life and adult work life. In K.M. Borman, D. Quarm, & S. Gideonse (Eds.), *Women in the workplace: Effects on families*. Norwood, NJ: Ablex.

Boutilier, M., & SanGiovanni, L. (1983). *The sporting woman*. Champaign, IL: Human Kinetics.

Bridges, J.S., & Bower, M.S. (1985). The effects of perceived job availability for women on college women's attitudes toward prestigious male-dominated occupations. *Psychology of Women Quarterly*, **9**, 265-277.

Cabral, R., Ferber, M., & Green, C. (1981). Men and women in fiduciary institutions: A study of sex differences in career development. *Review of Economics and Statistics*, **63**, 573-580.

Caccese, T., & Mayerberg, C.K. (1984). Gender differences in perceived burnout of college coaches. *Journal of Sport Psychology*, **6**, 279-288.

Chu, D. (1980). Functional myths of educational organizations: College as career training and the relationship of formal title to actual duties upon secondary school employment. In V. Crafts (Ed.), *NAPEHE Proceedings, Volume II* (pp. 36-46). Champaign, IL: Human Kinetics.

Coakley, J. (1986). *Sport in society: Issues and controversies* (3rd ed.). St. Louis, MO: Times Mirror/Mosby.

Greenfeld, S., Greiner, L., & Wood, M.M. (1980). The 'feminine mystique' in male-dominated jobs: A comparison of attitudes and background factors of women in male-dominated versus female-dominated jobs. *Journal of Vocational Behavior*, **17**, 291-309.

Hall, M.A. (1984). Towards a feminist analysis of gender inequality in sport. In N. Theberge & P. Donnelly (Eds.), *Sport and the sociological imagination*. Fort Worth: Texas Christian University Press.

Harkess, S. (1985). Women's occupational experience in the 1970's: Sociology and economics. *Signs: Journal of Women in Culture and Society*, **10**, 495-510.

Harlan, A., & Weiss, C. (1980). *Sex differences in factors affecting managerial career advancement* (Working Paper No. 56). Wellesley, MA: Wellesley College, Center for Research on Women.

Hart, B., Hasbrook, C., & Mathes, S. (1986). An examination of the reduction in the number of female interscholastic coaches. *Research Quarterly for Exercise and Sport*, **57**, 68-77.

Holmen, M.G., & Parkhouse B.L. (1981). Trends in the selection of coaches for female athletes: A demographic inquiry. *Research Quarterly for Exercise and Sport*, **52**, 9-18.

Kanter, R.M. (1977). *Men and women of the corporation.* New York: Basic Books.

Kaplan, A., & Sedney, M.A. (1980). *Psychology and sex roles.* Boston: Little, Brown.

Lopiano, D. (1984). A political analysis of the possibility of impact alternatives for the accomplishment of feminist objectives within American intercollegiate sport. *Arena Review*, **8**, 49-61.

Massengale, J. (1984). Role conflict and the teacher/coach. In S. Greendorfer & A. Yiannakis (Eds.), *Sociology of sport: Diverse perspectives.* West Point, NY: Leisure Press.

Mathes, S.A. (1982, April). *Women coaches: Endangered species?* Paper presented at AAHPERD Convention, Houston.

Mathes, S.A. (1983, November). *Socialization of women in sport: The case of the vanishing female sport role model.* Paper presented at the New Agenda National Conference, Washington, DC.

Miller, J., & Garrison, H. (1982). Sex roles: The division of labor at home and workplace. *Annual Review of Sociology*, **8**, 237-262.

Miller Lite report on American attitudes toward sports (1983). Milwaukee: Miller Brewing Co.

NCAA News (1986, February 26). Committee recommends special attention to women's interests. **23**, p. 1.

Nelson, M.B. (1984). Are women coaches headed for extinction? *Women's Sports*, July Coaches' Clinic insert.

Nixon, H. (1984). *Sport and the American dream.* New York: Leisure Press.

Parkhouse, B.L., & Lapin, J. (1980). *The woman in athletic administration.* Santa Monica, CA: Goodyear.

Parkhouse, B.L., & Williams, J.M. (1986). Differential effects of sex and status on evaluation of coaching ability. *Research Quarterly for Exercise and Sport*, **57**, 53-59.

Patterson, M., & Engelberg, L. (1978). Women in male-dominated professions. In A. Stromberg & S. Harkess (Eds.), *Women working: Theories and facts in perspective.* Palo Alto, CA: Mayfield.

Rosen, B. (1982). Career progress of women: Getting in and staying in. In H.J. Bernardin (Ed.), *Women in the work force.* New York: Praeger.

Sabock, R.J. (1979). *The coach* (2nd ed.). Philadelphia: W.B. Saunders.

Sabock, R., & Jones, D. (1978). The coaching profession: Its effect on the coach's family. *Coaching Review*, **1**(6), 4-13.

Sage, G. (1975). An occupational analysis of the college coach. In D.W. Ball & J. Loy (Eds.), *Sport and social order*. Reading, MA: Addison-Wesley.

Sage, G. (1980). Sociology of physical educator/coaches: Personal attributes controversy. *Research Quarterly for Exercise and Sport*, **51**, 110-121.

South, S.J., Bonjean, C., Corder, J., & Markham, W. (1982). Sex and power in the federal bureaucracy. *Work and Occupations*, **9**, 233-254.

South, S.J., Bonjean, C., Markham, W., & Corder, J. (1982). Social structure and intergroup interaction: Men and women of the federal bureaucracy. *American Sociological Review*, **47**, 587-599.

Wortman, M.S. (1982). An overview of the research on women in management: A typology and a prospectus. In H.J. Bernardin (Ed.), *Women in the work force*. New York: Praeger.

NOTES

1. The word ''profession'' will be used synonymously with ''occupation.'' The question of whether coaching meets the criteria for being called a full fledged profession is beyond the scope of this paper.

2. The functional perspective views society as consisting of interrelated parts (institutions), each of which functions so as to enhance the stability of the social system. One such institution is sport. The coaching role therefore is viewed as being embedded in an institution that is assumed to contribute to maintenance of the social system.

3. Institutionalized sexism refers to the depth of sexism in the daily practice of sport to the extent that it is no longer recognized as such but is instead justified on the basis of factors such as economic and spectator interests. For example, the amount of energy, publicity, and money spent on men's football programs is justified because these programs bring in revenue that purportedly support all the other sport programs. The fact that these football programs involve only men is overlooked or ignored.

4. Although Kanter's research led her to conclude that all other individual and organizational characteristics seem linked to these three determinants, she did not explore why these and not others were central to gender-differentiated work behavior. This question certainly deserves further exploration.

Chapter 9

Unequal Exchange and Exploitation in College Sport:
The Case of the Female Athlete[1]

Elaine Blinde
Southern Illinois University

Critiques of intercollegiate sport frequently point with alarm to the growing incidence of athlete exploitation. It is often suggested that a fair exchange does not take place between the athlete and the institutional sport structure as athletes are denied the benefits of and impeded from the desired and expected outcomes of the college experience (Adler & Adler, 1987; Figler, 1981). Such critiques suggest that many intercollegiate sport programs strip athletes of the normal benefits of a college education and thus are inattentive to the needs and interests of the student-athlete (Figler, 1981; Nixon, 1984; Sack, 1977). Moreover, the intercollegiate sport context is portrayed as one in which social arrangements are characterized by a system of inequality that is inherently exploitive as coaches, teams, athletic departments, universities, and governing bodies use college athletes for self-serving purposes (Sage, 1988).

Most of the critiques of college sport have been particularly concerned with the so-called "big-time" college sport programs—equated in many circles with men's basketball and football at Division I universities (Sage, 1988). These programs are highly professionalized and commercialized with "win-at-all-costs" philosophies (Nixon, 1984; Sack, 1987-1988). On the other hand, it is frequently assumed that "minor sport" athletes, non-Division I athletes, and female athletes do not experience serious problems in terms of athlete exploitation

From "Unequal Exchange and Exploitation in College Sport: The Case of the Female Athlete" by E. Blinde, 1989, *Arena Review*, **13**(2), pp. 110-123. Copyright 1989 by the Center for the Study of Sport in Society, Northeastern University. Reprinted by permission.

(Sack, 1987-1988; Wheeler, 1987-1988). With regard of women, several individuals have suggested that exploitation is not a serious problem for female athletes given the findings that female athletes are better prepared for college (Wheeler, 1987-1988; Eitzen, 1987-1988; Purdy, Eitzen, & Hufnagel, 1985), perform better academically (Eitzen, 1987-1988), and have higher graduation rates (Jacobs, 1983; Sack, 1987-1988) than their male counterparts. Moreover, it is assumed that women are somewhat immune to the problems associated with big-time college sport since, compared to men's programs, their sources of revenue are different (Wheeler, 1987-1988) and degree of commercialization is less (Sack, 1987-1988).

Since it is assumed that exploitation is not as severe a problem for women athletes, the experiences of women have not been studied to the extent of male athletes. Moreover, when the issue of exploitation has been examined in women's sport, it has usually been through a comparison of male and female athletes on those items that are assumed to characterize the exploitive demands traditionally associated with men's intercollegiate sport (Leonard, 1986; Sack & Thiel, 1985). Such an approach eclipses forms of exploitation that may be unique to the female athlete.

Therefore, the purpose of this study was to examine both the manifestation and prevalence of exploitation in women's college sport. Not only did this study examine traditional forms of exploitation similar to those experienced by male athletes, but an attempt was also made to identify forms of exploitation not covered in the literature or forms which might be unique to the experiences of women.

PROCEDURES

In order to explore this phenomenon, data were synthesized from several research studies which have previously analyzed various facets of the college sport experience of female athletes (Blinde, 1986, 1987, 1989; Blinde & Greendorfer, 1987; Greendorfer & Blinde, in press). These studies utilized both quantitative and qualitative data collection techniques. For example, survey data were used from samples of 697 and 433 former athletes from a large Midwestern athletic conference, 482 former athletes from 10 Division I universities across the United States, and 301 athletes who participated in ''big-time'' Division I intercollegiate sport programs during the 1986-87 school year. These athletes had participated in the total spectrum of both team and individual sport activities available in women's programs. Moreover, 25 in-depth interviews with both current and former athletes in several Division I sport programs were examined. These interviews were designed to shed additional light on the patterns that had emerged in the various survey studies.

The original research studies utilizing this survey data compared various aspects of the sport experience of female athletes who had participated in sport programs characterized by differing structures and philosophies. For example, comparisons were made between the sport experiences of (a) pre-Title IX vs. post-Title IX athletes (Blinde, 1986), (b) athletes of the 1970s vs. the 1980s (Blinde & Greendorfer, 1987), (c) athletes participating in sport programs emulating the male sport model to varying degrees (Blinde, 1987, 1989), and (d) Division I vs. Division III athletes (Greendorfer & Blinde, in press). For this paper, however, data from these survey studies were re-examined with the intent of identifying responses that reflected traditional forms of athlete exploitation—those forms commonly used in the study of male athletes. Relative to the interview data, a content analysis was undertaken on the interview responses to again identify potential instances of exploitation. Rather than creating a profile that characterized the majority of interview subjects, the content analysis was more concerned with identifying various types of exploitation, particularly those forms which are not typically identified in the research on male athletes.

In order to develop a classification system for identifying instances of exploitation and unequal exchange, the stated purposes of college sport were examined. The National Collegiate Athletic Association (NCAA), the primary governing body for women's sport programs, purports that college sport is a vital part of the total educational system and that student-athletes are to remain an integral part of the student body (National Collegiate Athletic Association, 1987). The NCAA further states that intercollegiate sport programs are to provide educational, physical, mental, and social benefits for the student-athlete.

Given these purposes of college sport, it would be reasonable to assume that a fair exchange should take place between the athlete and the university. Although student-athletes may be forced to sacrifice time and energy in their pursuits as college sport participants, these individuals are nevertheless entitled to the pursuit of their academic, physical, social, and psychological well-being. Whenever college sport participation jeopardizes any of these aspects of the athlete's life or college experience, the potential for exploitation exists. Therefore, situations that appeared to run counter to the well-being of the student-athlete were grouped into one of the following four categories: (1) academic exploitation, (2) physical exploitation, (3) social exploitation, and (4) emotional or psychological exploitation.

RESULTS

Academic Exploitation

Given the stated objectives of intercollegiate sport, as well as the concept of fair exchange, it can be assumed that athletes will be given the opportunity to receive a viable college education while participating in intercollegiate sport. In situations where the athlete is deprived of or impeded from pursuing the desired or expected benefits of a college education (i.e., meaningful college degree), it can be argued that academic exploitation occurs (Figler, 1981).

The intense professionalization and commercialization of college sport may lead to conditions that frequently challenge the educational focus and mission of universities (e.g., recruitment of academically deficient athletes, excessive pressure to win). Conflicting orientations and messages arising from such conditions can subsequently create difficulties for individuals who must occupy the athlete and student roles simultaneously. Based on findings from the various survey studies, it was obvious that conflicts between the athletic and student roles existed and that such conflicts were more characteristic of athletes participating in sport programs in post-Title IX periods and the 1980s (Blinde, 1986; Blinde & Greendorfer, 1987). In particular, as women's programs increasingly emulated those found in men's sport, female athletes were more likely to indicate that they had to sacrifice schoolwork and classes and that college sport placed major demands on their time and energy (Blinde, 1987). An example of the prevalence of such feelings was reflected in the findings from the study which compared the sport experience of Division I and Division III athletes (Greendorfer & Blinde, in press)—over 50% of Division I athletes indicated that the demands of college sport conflicted to a "large" or "great extent" with the demands of school work and studying (compared to only 12% of Division III athletes). The academic well-being of the student-athlete is certainly suspect in such instances.

The interview responses also contained evidence of academic exploitation. Many athletes indicated that during the sport season their grades suffered and that they were forced to take fewer classes. The number of semesters to graduate thus increased, although financial support in the form of an athletic scholarship was usually limited to four years. Athletes also indicated that they were not able to enroll in certain classes because of conflicts with practice sessions and that they frequently missed classes and exams due to travel and game conflicts. In some instances, coaches and academic counselors advised athletes to switch to less strenuous academic majors so as to minimize conflict with their sport participation and to remain academically eligible. One athlete described a conversation with her coach upon entry into college:

> I told my coach I was good at math when I was in high school and I said to her I might want to go into math. And she said it might be too difficult for me to start with math and so she enrolled me in physical education.

Athletes also admitted that the physical demands of college sport sometimes made it difficult to concentrate on their academic work, frequently mentioning that they were physically drained after practice and thus unable to put their best effort into their school work.

Interview responses also revealed that athletes did not feel their coaches were sympathetic to their conflicts as student-athletes and they often perceived inconsistencies in the messages relayed by coaches. As one athlete stated:

He put such a great emphasis on swimming. He didn't really care much about anything else. He'd say school was important. He'd say we don't want to interfere with your school work, but you just better be here on time and that was it. He didn't give much.

Although these instances of academic exploitation parallel those commonly cited in men's intercollegiate sport, it can be argued that many sacrifices may have more serious consequences for women athletes. The college sport structure encourages women to make great sacrifices and commitment to the athletic role, yet in the process exploits females since they have few professional or post-college sport opportunities in which to utilize the sport skills that they have developed. Without this career option, the importance of a college education and a college degree becomes even more important in terms of career advancement. Thus an overemphasis on the development of athletic skills and a neglect of academic skills may seriously handicap women once they leave the college environment. Given the documented obstacles and discriminatory practices that women frequently face in the job market, a viable and meaningful college degree may be even more critical for women than for men as a necessary avenue of upward social mobility.

Social Exploitation

Not only is the college experience viewed as an avenue for the acquisition of an academic degree, but it is viewed as a means to broaden social contacts and experiences. These experiences and contacts may serve as a springboard for success in other life pursuits during and after college (Nixon, 1984). In the event that the athletic role forces an individual to reduce involvement in the social role to the point that the social role cannot be adequately fulfilled or must simply be excluded, social exploitation occurs.

Results of the various survey studies suggested that female athletes of the 1980s, post-Title IX athletes, and athletes in programs resembling those of men's sport were more likely to sacrifice their social life and friendships as a result of college sport (Blinde, 1986, 1987; Blinde & Greendorfer, 1987). These athletes were also more likely to view sport participation as inhibiting their social development. To demonstrate the prevalence of these social conflicts, the study comparing Division I and Division III athletes (Greendorfer & Blinde, in press) found that over 60% of Division I athletes indicated that college sport participation forced them to sacrifice friendships and social life beyond an "average extent" (compared to 22% of Division III athletes).

Relative to responses obtained from the interviews, it was not uncommon for athletes to indicate that their social life was extremely limited by the time commitments of intercollegiate sport and that the majority of their social contacts were with other athletes. As one athlete stated:

> It's hard enough for me to spend time with my roommates, let alone any outside activities, like getting to know other people, keep new friends, meet new friends, have a relationship . . . it was a big sacrifice.

Another athlete commented on the major sacrifices of college sport:

> I sacrifice trying to have a social life. You've got school, classes and homework and studying and basketball and road trips and you can't see your friends very often. I'd say my social life was the number one sacrifice.

Along with sacrificing friendships, several athletes talked about sacrificing other college activities in which the typical college student participates (e.g., dorm functions, sorority activities, student government). Some athletes were not even aware of the type of activities that were sponsored by the university or dormitory associations due to the demands of college sport. Such instances suggest that athletes may not have the opportunity to pursue activities that lead to the development of diverse interests and well-rounded individuals. Moreover, athletes are frequently prevented from experiencing social life and interpersonal relationships in a broad-based social context.

Such responses would seem to somewhat parallel those of male athletes in big-time college programs. As discussed by Adler and Adler (1987), athletes are often socially isolated from the rest of the student body, thus leading to the development of a peer subculture that is often anti-intellectual and anti-academic in character. It is certainly possible that both the demands of sport and the limited contact athletes have with peers alienate them from the rest of the student body—an outcome that indeed runs counter to the stated purposes of inter-collegiate sport.

Physical Exploitation

College sport is obviously designed to enhance the physical well-being of the athlete. However, in situations where the athlete is placed in a position of sacrificing long-term health in favor of short-term competitive goals, it can be argued that physical exploitation occurs.

Since the surveys were not designed to tap potential instances of physical exploitation, it was only through an examination of the interview responses that this form of exploitation became evident. Two potential forms of physical exploitation were identified in the responses of athletes. One dealt with concerns related to training techniques and the handling of injuries. The second, which appears to be a growing phenomenon in college sport, related to the imposition of weight limitations/standards and the subsequent development of eating disorders in athletes.

Relative to the first form of physical exploitation, some athletes expressed concern about the training philosophy espoused by their coaches and trainers. Athletes sometimes felt that their coaches were more interested in getting them "back to action" than in their long-term health and mentioned receiving conflicting messages from coaches and trainers. Some athletes acknowledged the short-term benefits of training techniques but questioned their long-term effect. Comments also addressed the issue that athletes in non-revenue sports and female athletes in general were sometimes slighted in the care and attention they received in the training room (compared to that received by revenue sport athletes or male athletes). The following response points to such concerns (as well as the athlete's possible reservation to indict her coach or program):

> The coach was eager to have everyone running. I think if I had listened to him and not the trainer I would have gotten worse instead of better as far as my injury went. Sometimes it seemed like the coach didn't [pause], well, let me leave it at that . . .

The second potential form of physical exploitation which emerged in the interviews related to the emergence of eating disorders in athletes. Although athletes were not specifically asked about this problem during the interviews, several volunteered this personal information. Athletes in the sports of diving, gymnastics, and cross-country appeared to be most affected by this phenomenon. Several athletes, while discussing their own eating disorder or that of a teammate, mentioned the coaches' preoccupation with body composition measures (e.g., percent body fat ratio), body type and image, and weight limitations. According to some athletes, this preoccupation led to the development of stress and tension for the athlete, which in turn led to a preoccupation with eating habits/behavior. The following comment captures the essence of this conflict within these female athletes:

> I was uncomfortable with the stress on body type. College women have enough trouble with eating. It was to the point that about six members of the team were bulimics. We were weighed every week my freshman and sophomore year. It made me crazy. We had to worry about our weight till the point where we didn't care.

Another diver added the following regarding her conversation with a teammate and her realization of how widespread the problem may have been:

> A teammate of mine said that she was nervous about her weight the whole time she was diving and she was crazy about the tension that the coach had created within her. It did not make her feel good about herself and actually led to a bulimic disorder for over a year. I thought I was the only one in the john at two in the morning since I was so paranoid about gaining weight. The emotional hell the coach put me through at age eighteen.

According to the responses of some athletes, coaches used the weight issue as a means to control athletes. Athletes who did not give up to the coaches notion of the ''ideal'' body type were sometimes subjected to manipulation and exclusion. Athletes cited instances where the coach would ignore those who did not meet a certain weight limit or would not allow athletes to either practice or compete until they met a prescribed weight. Some coaches were very inflexible regarding their imposed weight limitations—in one instance denying an athlete the right to participate because she was a half pound over the limit. On more than one occasion, athletes cited the insensitivity of male coaches to problems related to this issue and commented that male coaches did not understand the problems with which a female athlete had to deal. Such a position was described by one diver:

> The coach has a lack of sensitivity to female issues and weight in our culture. He [the coach] has been so idiotic as to actually tell a diver at some point in time she wasn't going to get dates unless she had a 15% body fat ratio. I mean which is insane logic. I don't know, but with women coaches, I found much more sensitivity involved and not this brutal authoritarian, you know, lose weight or you're off of the team. I don't know why men do that and I don't know why they think it is so easy to lose weight. They just obviously haven't been there—they haven't been an adolescent female.

Along with the emotional turmoil caused by this obsession with weight limits, some athletes cited their vulnerability to injury when they were preoccupied with weight and eating behavior. One track and cross-country athlete indicated that her injury may have been the result of her extremely low weight and the lack of nutrients in her diet. She went on to mention that six athletes had broken bones on her team and felt that poor eating habits may have attributed to this given the rigorous training that was required of them.

Although questionable training techniques and conflicts between coaches and trainers are undoubtedly concerns of male athletes, it can be argued that the issue of weight restrictions and body image are more serious concerns for female athletes. Even though weight limitations or standards may be found in a limited number of male programs (e.g., wrestling), the additional factor of body image most likely has its strongest influence on women. In an attempt to achieve the perfect socially prescribed body of a female athlete, particularly that of a diver or gymnast, women may be sacrificing both short- and long-term physical well-being.

Emotional or Psychological Exploitation

A final form of exploitation was emotional or psychological in nature. Rather than facilitate personal development, sport participation was sometimes seen as a force that stifled the emotional and psychological development of athletes. This form of exploitation was manifested in many different ways and was most obvious in the interview responses of subjects. Several examples from the interviews are presented.

A common response throughout the interviews was that athletes were not treated as adults; they found themselves in an overprotective environment with limited input. Athletes resented being told what to do in a variety of situations (e.g., what to eat, what to wear, when to go to class, when to go to bed, what sports not to participate in) and frequently indicated that they felt their coaches kept track of their personal activities outside of the sport context. Several athletes reacted negatively to such treatment. As one athlete stated:

> Sometimes our coach doesn't treat us like adults. I don't like that. Just the assumption that athletes are so immature and not able to handle their own life. We need to be treated more like adults instead of like kids. . . . Sometimes the coach doesn't really think we're responsible enough to go to class.

As suggested earlier in the discussion of weight limitations, coaches sometimes used manipulation and exclusion as techniques to control athletes. Other athletes stated that coaches sometimes ignored them if their performances did not live up to their expectations and, in some instances, coaches used athletic scholarships as a means to manipulate and control athletes.

It was interesting to note that in some cases athletes believed that male coaches took advantage of female athletes. Male coaches were at times accused of being condescending, intimidating, and coddling relative to their interactions with women athletes. A few athletes also indicated that they felt male coaches sometimes manipulated the female athlete's value system. As described by one athlete:

> The scary thing about it is that if men control programs like our male coach and our female diving team is you get a lot of manipulation of female values of competitiveness, which may be different than male values of competitiveness. If our coach says win, win, win for his own purposes, his male ego, or whatever; that may be different than a woman's need to compete.

Another athlete described the manipulative behavior of her male coach as follows:

> Our coach likes to play with words and he is very emotionally manipulative, specifically with women. He talks down to them, he puts his hand on your shoulder and you know, ''Oh, Mary, how are you feeling, today?'' And you just want to belt him across the face. I had the gall to tell him that this is incredibly demeaning and that I don't mind him asking how I am, but that I am an adult and that I don't need to be coddled. His bottom line is that he is going to revert to behaviors that he is safest with and that's coddling and intimidating women. . . . another instance of being used by yet another male hierarchy.

Others indicated that as athletes they found the atmosphere surrounding their sport participation stifling. Program structure and rules, along with coaches' behaviors, were frequently identified as the source of such feelings. As one diver described her experience:

> I'm crawling into the pool like I cannot believe I'm part of this. I don't know why the coach is crushing my motivation that he damn well knows exists. I don't know how program rules could become that stifling.

In some cases the emotional strain of college sport participation clearly impacted on the psychological well-being of the athlete outside the sport context. One athlete discussed the emotional strain of college sport participation:

> There is only so much physical energy and emotional energy and I started feeling so empty that all I was doing was diving and sleeping and I couldn't even hold a conversation. I just wanted to sit in front of the television—I wasn't even watching it—just to not have to think or do anything. It was a very stressful time.

Some athletes indicated that they felt their coaches were using them to advance their careers as coaches. Such responses were most typical of athletes in individual sports such as diving and gymnastics. Athletes indicated that their coaches would sometimes concentrate their coaching efforts on those athletes most likely to enhance their reputations. One athlete described her reaction to such a situation:

> The coach's inability to help more than one person go forward at a time was obvious. It's like ''All I want Mary to do is make me an important coach.'' That's really the way diving coaches do it. God, they're political. The coach hangs his whole reputation on the name of one of his athletes. That really sucks. It just comes out really obvious—I'm forwarding my career, I'm using you. That's another set of emotional tensions that you deal with.

Several other interview responses would appear to be indications of other forms of personal or psychological exploitation. These included invasion of personal life by mandatory drug testing, dishonest and unfulfilled recruitment promises, and harassment of female athletes by male athletes in weight rooms and training areas.

Again, several of the cited examples of psychological exploitation may be similar to those experienced by male athletes. However, it appears that female athletes may be subject to some unique forms of psychological exploitation given the fact that they are frequently (and increasingly) placed under the direction of male coaches. Patterns of interaction between male coaches and female athletes may sometimes parallel the dominant-subordinate roles usually accorded males and females respectively in a patriarchal society.

DISCUSSION

Given the findings that emerged, it can be suggested that female athletes are subject to many diverse forms of exploitation. In some instances these forms of exploitation parallel those that have been documented in research on male athletes. On the other hand, however, female athletes appear to be subject to several unique forms of exploitation as well.

In attempting to account for the incidence of exploitation in women's intercollegiate sport and to understand why women athletes frequently find themselves in exploitable positions, it can be argued that athletes possess little power in the intercollegiate sport structure and are far removed from any potential power sources. Without power or recourse, these athletes find themselves in potentially exploitable roles. This "institutionalized powerlessness" may be attributed to two sources: (1) their status as athletes, and (2) their status as women.

Relative to their status as athletes, it can be suggested that both male and female athletes are situated outside the power structure of college sport. Input is rarely sought from athletes as decisions are made by various power brokers (e.g., coaches, athletic directors, governing body officials, boosters) who may not necessarily put the interests of student-athletes first and foremost. Thus, those holding power assume a position of domination and control as they gain an unequal share of the benefits of college sport.

It is interesting to note that such a characterization, while typifying the relationship of male athletes to the college sport structure for decades, has only recently been applied to women athletes. This is undoubtedly due in part to the fact that many structural and philosophical features of men's intercollegiate sport have been incorporated into women's programs during the past 15 years (Boutilier & SanGiovanni, 1983; Lopiano, 1984). Data from the various survey studies suggest that increasing incidence of exploitation is most typical of athletes in sport programs that emulate men's intercollegiate sport to a large extent. With an increasing emphasis on winning and financial gains, means and techniques that bring about such outcomes are pursued—sometimes without regard for the academic, physical, social, and psychological well-being of athletes. Athletes thus represent commodities that serve the interests of those with power in the system.

Relative to their status as women, female athletes are exploited at the hands of patriarchal values and structures and are disadvantaged in a sport system that is overwhelmingly organized, administered, and dominated by men. Women are assigned secondary roles and positions while decisions related to the design and conduct of women's sport programs are usually made by male administrators and coaches. This context stresses definitions, values, and standards that are largely male-defined and which may not correspond to those of women (Boutilier & SanGiovanni, 1983). Women's unique value system and woman-centered sport are sacrificed in order to conform to this male sport model. Moreover, the sport practice merely reinforces the patterns of patriarchal domination which reside in the larger society, including the objectification and domination of women's physicality and sexuality (Theberge, 1985b).

Several of the unique forms of exploitation experienced by female athletes may stem in part from the fact that female athletes are increasingly being placed under the direction of male coaches. As suggested earlier, interactions between male coaches and female athletes may parallel the dominant-subordinate positions that males and females respectively hold in the larger society. Male coaches may adopt techniques in their interactions with female athletes that are used in the larger society to control women and keep them ''in their place'' (e.g., intimidation, coddling). Female athletes may also be victims of exploitation as male coaches attempt to both construct and control women's physicality, forcing female athletes to conform to male prescriptions of the ''ideal'' female body type and image (Theberge, 1985a). Manipulation of the female athlete's value system and an imposition of the male coach's value system represents yet another way in which women athletes are exploited. Since research suggests that men and women do not experience sport in a similar fashion (Birrell & Richter, 1987; Grant, 1984), women may be denied many positive experiences in sport if they are placed in sport structures that devalue and de-emphasize these unique aspects of women's experiences.

Given this preliminary interpretation, it is possible then that female athletes are victims of more diverse forms of exploitation than male athletes. Not only must female athletes contend with their position of powerlessness as athletes, but they must also exist in a sport structure that devalues and uses them as women. Although the forms of exploitation in the latter instance may be more subtle and difficult to document, further research needs to focus on these unique forms of exploitation. This knowledge should be useful for those concerned with the sport experience of athletes—particularly those concerned about the design and conduct of women's intercollegiate sport and the quality of the sport experience provided female athletes.

REFERENCES

Adler, P., & Adler, P.A. (1987). Role conflict and identity salience: College athletics and the academic role. *The Social Science Journal*, **24**(4), 443-455.

Birrell, S., & Richter, D.M. (1987). Is a diamond forever? Feminist transformations of sport. *Women's Studies International Forum*, **10**(4), 395-409.

Blinde, E.M. (1986). Contrasting orientations toward sport: Pre- and post-Title IX athletes. *Journal of Sport and Social Issues*, **10**(1), 6-14.

Blinde, E.M. (1987). *Contrasting models of sport and the intercollegiate sport experience of female athletes*. Unpublished dissertation, University of Illinois, Urbana-Champaign.

Blinde, E.M. (1989). Participation in a male sport model and the value alienation of female intercollegiate athletes. *Sociology of Sport Journal*, **6**(1), 36-49.

Blinde, E.M., & Greendorfer, S.L. (1987). Structural and philosophical differences in women's intercollegiate sport programs and the sport experience of athletes. *Journal of Sport Behavior*, **10**(2), 59-72.

Boutilier, M.A., & SanGiovanni, L. (1983). *The sporting woman*. Champaign, IL: Human Kinetics.

Eitzen, D.S. (1987-1988). The educational experiences of intercollegiate student-athletes. *Journal of Sport and Social Issues*, **11**(1-2), 15-30.

Figler, S.K. (1981). *Sport and play in American life*. Philadelphia: Saunders.

Grant, C.H.B. (1984). The gender gap in sport: From Olympic to intercollegiate level. *Arena Review*, **8**(2), 31-47.

Greendorfer, S.L., & Blinde, E.M. (in press). Structural differences and contrasting organizational models: The female intercollegiate sport experience. In J. Humphries & L. Vander Velden (Eds.), *Psychology and sociology of sport: Current selected research* (Vol. 2). New York: AMS Press.

Jacobs, K.J. (1983). *A comparison of the graduate rates of student-athletes with the overall student body who enrolled at the University of North Carolina at Chapel Hill from 1966 to 1976*. Unpublished Masters Thesis, University of North Carolina at Chapel Hill.

Leonard, W.M., II. (1986). Exploitation in collegiate sport: The views of basketball players in NCAA Division I, II, and III. *Journal of Sport Behavior*, **9**(1), 11-30.

Lopiano, D.A. (1984). A political analysis of the possibility of impact alternatives for the accomplishment of feminist objectives within American intercollegiate sport. *Arena Review*, **8**(2), 49-61.

National Collegiate Athletic Association. (1987). *NCAA manual*. Mission, KS: The National Collegiate Athletic Association.

Nixon, H.L., II. (1984). *Sport and the American dream*. New York: Leisure Press.

Purdy, D.A., Eitzen, D.S., & Hufnagel, R. (1985). Educational achievements of college athletes by gender. *Western Georgia College Studies in the Social Sciences*, **24**, 19-32.

Sack, A.L. (1977). Big time college football: Whose free ride? *Quest*, **27**, 87-96.

Sack, A.L. (1987-1988). College sport and the student-athlete. *Journal of Sport and Social Issues*, **11**(1-2), 31-48.

Sack, A.L., & Thiel, R. (1985). College basketball and role conflict: A national survey. *Sociology of Sport Journal*, **2**(3), 195-209.

Sage, G.H. (1988, May). *Power and ideology in intercollegiate sport*. Paper presented at the R. Tait McKenzie Symposium on Sport, University of Tennessee, Knoxville, TN.

Theberge, N. (1985a). Sport and feminism in North America. In A.L. Reeder & J.R. Fuller (Eds.), *Women in sport: Sociological and historical perspectives* (pp. 41-53). Atlanta, GA: Darby.

Theberge, N. (1985b). Toward a feminist alternative to sport as a male preserve. *Quest*, **37**, 193-202.

Wheeler, S. (1987-1988). Knowns and unknowns in intercollegiate athletics: A report to the President's commission. *Journal of Sport and Social Issues*, **11**(1-2), 1-14.

NOTES

1. Revised version of a paper delivered at the annual meeting of the North American Society for the Sociology of Sport, Cincinnati, Ohio, 1988.

Chapter 10

A Postmodern Paradox?
Cheerleaders
at Women's Sporting Events[1]

Laurel Davis
Springfield College

For most of us, the very word "cheerleader" conjures up notions of a petite blonde female jumping up and down on the sideline of men's sporting events. Cheerleaders are perceived as being there "to support the boys" and to provide flashy and/or sexy entertainment for the crowd. The public seems to have an extremely gendered view of cheerleading and has come to expect the presence of cheerleaders as part of men's sporting events.

But what happens when cheerleaders are present at women's sporting events? The female athlete, as a feminist symbol of the female who is active and independent, provides a stark contrast to the traditional image of the female cheerleader as the male athlete's feminine supporter and the male spectator's sex symbol. The female cheerleader as feminine support for female athletes, or female athletes as receptors of feminine support, goes against all traditional notions of gender appropriate meaning. Our everyday notion of cheerleading and athletics would seem to get turned upside-down.

It is truly remarkable that the presence of cheerleaders at women's sporting events appears to go unquestioned. This is especially curious because our common sense view of cheerleading is rigidly gendered. Why is it that this change has not led to controversy? This paper focuses on the presence of cheerleaders at

From "A Postmodern Paradox?: Cheerleaders at Women's Sporting Events" by Laurel Davis, 1989, *Arena Review*, **13**(2), pp. 124-133. Copyright 1989 by The Center for the Study of Sport in Society, Northeastern University. Reprinted by permission.

women's sporting events and attempts to examine this phenomenon as it relates to the struggle over meanings of gender.

The general lack of controversy over cheerleading at women's sporting events can be read as a decidedly postmodern way of dealing with paradoxical meaning. Two aspects of the situation seem especially incongruous. First, the situation itself presents a paradox, with its conflicting messages regarding proper gender behavior and women's proper place in sport. The second paradox occurs when those involved in the situation are self-contradictory, articulating a liberal degendered narrative to justify the spectacle while at the same time articulating views that conflict with that liberal narrative. These individuals neither recognize nor reflect on this self-contradiction. Because some postmodern theorists such as Lyotard (1985) claim that comfort with paradox is a specifically postmodern phenomenon, the practice of cheerleading at women's sporting events will be examined with postmodern theory in mind.

The following analysis of the paradox of cheerleading at women's sporting events is based on data from field observations of cheerleaders, analyses of manuals, guidebooks and popular literature on cheerleading, and 22 indepth semi-structured interviews. The subjects interviewed include 10 collegiate cheerleaders, 6 collegiate basketball players and 6 spectators.[2] All three of these subject groups consisted of equal numbers of females and males.

Cheerleaders at women's sporting events present a paradox because the roles of athlete and cheerleader have always been gendered within our society. In the 1980's these roles are understood as symbolic of oppositional messages regarding proper female gender behavior and the female place in sport. Moreover, historical forces have worked to naturalize these roles as oppositional. When cheerleading emerged in the late 1800's, it was considered an activity exclusively for males. Those females who entered the cheerleading world during World War I were seen as treading in the male territory of sport and as being in danger of becoming "masculinized" (e.g., Gonzales, 1956; Hatton & Hatton, 1978; Morton, 1952). A quote by Gach from 1938 illustrates these concerns:

> [The female cheerleaders] frequently became too masculine for their own good . . . we find the development of loud, raucous voices . . . and the consequent development of slang and profanity by their necessary association with the squad members . . . (p. 301)

Protest against female entrance into cheerleading continued until the 1950's (Hatton & Hatton, 1978). Nevertheless, in the 1940's and 1950's cheerleading came to be dominated by females, and males dropped out of the activity in large numbers (Manfredi, 1983). By 1970 cheerleading was considered a "natural" female activity.

The historical roots of cheerleading have been so obscured that today most people seem to think that cheerleading is and always has been a naturally "feminine" and female activity. As one female cheerleader observed, "It's just the girl thing to do." Modern cheerleading manuals and articles about cheerleading in the popular media make it clear that female cheerleaders are popularly worshiped as "ideal females." One male cheerleader stated that female audience members love cheerleading and look at it as a "feminine sport," and that males, ". . . can whistle at the females [who are cheerleading] out there . . . the females are pretty to them . . ." Because cheerleading is perceived as an ideal activity for females, it reproduces notions that cheerleading should be an exclusively female activity and the proper role for females in sport. The place for women in sport is seen as on the sidelines engaged in supportive activities which should not be taken too seriously by the sport community.

In contrast to the dominant image of the female cheerleader and the meanings associated with this image are the dominant image and meanings of female athleticism. Like the first female cheerleaders of the early 1900's, female athletes in the 1960's and early 1970's were seen as treading in male territory and thus in danger of becoming "masculinized." Ironically, these female athletes were often told that their proper role in sport was that of cheerleader. Although athletic activity for females today is acceptable within certain bounds, much of the ideological baggage of the past remains. A symbolic and real struggle over the proper place for women in sport is waged between those who assert that a women's proper place is on the fields and courts as an athlete and those who feel that women's place in sport should be that of supporters. A paradox exists when females performing these two activities, and therefore symbolizing these two positions, are present in the same context.

Another way in which this situation is paradoxical is when the display of modern cheerleading, which is partially designed to further heterosexual male voyeurism, is performed in front of an audience which consists of a substantial number of females. As noted in another paper (Davis, 1990), the assumption that males not only make up the majority of the men's sport audience but are also the important viewers of female cheerleaders has helped to structure the presentation of modern cheerleading. Just as the gaze of the cameraman and his assumptions of male viewership can work to construct and frame female subjects as sexual objects (e.g., Berger, Blomberg, Fox, Dibb & Hollis, 1985; Kaplan, 1983; Mulvey, 1985), the assumption of a sport audience which is primarily made up of voyeuristic heterosexual males seems to influence the construction of the cheerleading performance. The paradox exists because a cheerleading performance designed for the heterosexual male voyeur does not seem to be modified for an audience that is assumed to contain a large number of females.

The second major paradox occurs when those involved in the situation are self-contradictory. Many of the cheerleaders, spectators and athletes involved in women's athletic events seem to feel comfortable when cheerleaders are present and do not recognize or pose as problematic the contested meanings that are discussed above. In fact, many people associated with this spectacle seem to hold self-contradictory views about the phenomenon, yet do not reflect on these contradictions. The collegiate female athletes tended to vacillate between a liberal narrative (which ignores gendered meanings and demands the same treatment for all) and a reading which recognizes gendered meanings and critiques traditional gender ideals, while cheerleaders and spectators articulated both a conservative narrative about gender (which recognizes gendered meanings and approves of traditional gender ideals) and a liberal narrative. The one narrative that was commonly used by all three groups is liberalism.

Liberal feminists argue that women and men are naturally equal and alike, and that apparent differences between them are the result of social conditioning (e.g., Donovan, 1985; Jaggar, 1983). Within the context of sport, liberal feminists argue that male and female athletes deserve equitable treatment, from the lavishness of locker rooms to the presence of cheerleaders, and that women's sport programs should receive "their 'piece of the pie' " (Boutilier and SanGiovanni, 1983, p. 244). Thus cheerleading at women's sporting events can be understood within a liberal perspective as "only fair" because it signals equality for the male and female athletes. As one male spectator put it, "If they have it for the boys they should have it for the girls or not have it at all." Such attitudes are the logical outcome of the effects of liberal feminism on women's sport.

The liberal feminist reading of the presence of cheerleaders at women's sporting events rests on the premise that all roles should be perceived as "genderless" and free of traditional gender meanings. According to this way of thinking, women athletes should be perceived primarily as athletes, not as women, and cheerleaders should be seen as cheerleaders, not as males and females. By the same logic, the sport spectator should be perceived of simply as an ungendered spectator, and the sex of the spectator should be considered irrelevant to how she/he might observe any sport spectacle.

The interviewed collegiate female athletes vacillated between a liberal reading and a reading which is critical of traditional gender ideals. When articulating the latter position, the women athletes asserted that cheerleading is frivolous, ridiculous and gendered. They derogatorily labeled the cheerleaders as, "cutesy, pritzy, little girls" or "dizzy blonde preppy types." One athlete commented that cheerleaders are the ones who "fall all over the guys." Another athlete sarcastically commented that many people think that female cheerleaders are "just gorgeous." These young athletes assumed that people who value traditional notions of femininity view cheerleading very differently than they do. The female athletes were also somewhat aware of the gendering of athletics itself. As one female athlete commented, ". . . it's always been a man's role of sport. So, the women are the ones that are supposedly supporting the men who are out there working."

Despite these comments that reveal that the female athletes were associating gender with the roles of cheerleader and athlete, the collegiate female athletes also articulated a liberal perspective when they categorized cheerleaders as genderless and viewed cheerleading as instrumental. Comments by two of the athletes revealed that they adopted a liberal perspective only after experiencing the presence of cheerleaders at their games. One athlete said that she "seriously hated" the cheerleaders in high school, but as a collegiate athlete who performed in the presence of cheerleaders she now respected them and saw them as stimulating "school spirit." Another female athlete said that when she first started playing in the presence of cheerleaders she thought they were a distraction, but that now she has learned to "use them to my advantage." In summary, the three female athletes interviewed assumed a gender-sensitive perspective criticizing cheerleading at the same time that they assumed a liberal degendered perspective to justify the presence of, or usefulness of, cheerleaders at their games.

In general, the cheerleaders in this study negotiated between conservative views on gender relations and a liberal justification for the presence of cheerleaders at women's sporting events. They believe that female athletes deserve cheerleaders at their games, yet most of them felt that male athletes are more deserving of cheerleaders than female athletes, and that it is understandable and acceptable that many cheerleaders prefer to cheer for males or refuse to consider cheering for females.

Cheerleading for the women's teams was viewed by the cheerleaders as "practice," or as at best a second choice and at worst as something that they would not consider doing at all. For many cheerleaders, it "just doesn't feel right" to cheer for women. The possibility of feeling degraded when cheering for women was something that the interviewed cheerleaders regularly brought up, especially the male cheerleaders. As one male cheerleader explained:

> I was always kind of embarrassed a little bit [cheering for women] . . . just 'cause . . . My parents weren't really into me being a cheerleader, and when they found out I was cheering for women, they were just like, "What are you doing?" You know, 'cause usually it's the other way around, girls cheer for guys. And I kind of had the same way of thinking. And, I don't know, it was fun, but it just, it was kind of embarrassing, you know.

The lack of status attained by cheerleading for females is illustrated in the following quote by a female cheerleader:

> The [men's basketball] squad would always call the women's [basketball] squad "the J.V. squad," and that's just not true, because it has never been the "J.V. squad," but just the other squad. And they called it "the J.V.," and they're "the Varsity" . . . It bothered me so bad.

Part of the lack of status in cheering for a women's team is attributed to a lack of respect for women's athletics, as this woman's comments illustrate:

> I'd go to the gas station, [and] I'd be wearing my university cheering jacket, like, when I was on the women's squad last year, and someone would say, "Oh, you're a football cheerleader," and I'd say, "No, a women's basketball cheerleader. It's great, you should come to some of the games." And they're like, "Ugh, that sucks! No way," or something like that.

In summary, most of the cheerleaders used liberal rhetoric to advocate their presence at women's sporting events while they simultaneously upheld a conservative view of gender that privileges the role of cheerleading for male athletes.

The interviewed spectators seemed to have most fully adopted a liberal reading of the spectacle. The spectators all felt unequivocally that cheerleaders should be present at both women's and men's sporting events. The spectators apparently attempt to read the spectacle in a gender-free manner, categorizing people by roles and not by sex. The women athletes are categorized primarily as athletes rather than female athletes, and male and female cheerleaders are discussed as cheerleaders not as male cheerleaders and female cheerleaders. This practice of degendering the cheerleaders clearly ignores the prevalence of the distinctly drawn male and female cheerleading roles which reflect traditional notions of gender. Among other things, stylized motions and dancing are viewed as central to the female cheerleading role, while tumbling and performing strength moves in stunts are viewed as central to the male cheerleading role. Thus, in modern mixed-sex cheerleading, male and female cheerleaders construct a sexual division of labor which works to naturalize masculine and feminine ideals, maintaining images of the cheerleader as naturally female and the sexual division of labor as naturally the only way to perform (Davis, 1990). The spectators' use of the liberal perspective to ignore gender broke down when they considered the relationship of the female cheerleader to the male spectator. In regard to this relationship, the spectators tended to assume a conservative stance where the female cheerleaders and male spectators are viewed in terms of traditional gender meanings, and male spectators are assumed to be voyeuristically interested in female cheerleaders.

Overall, it is clear that those involved in women's athletic events accepted a liberal narrative to justify the spectacle of cheerleading at these events. While this narrative contradicts other perspectives that they hold, they remain oblivious to, or unbothered by, the contradictions.

Perhaps public comfort with the paradox of cheerleaders at female sporting events can be seen as an indication of the postmodern condition. According to Lyotard (1985), one characteristic of the postmodern world is the presentation of paradox:

> The postmodern would be that which, in the modern, puts forward the unpresentable in presentation itself; that which denies itself the solace of good forms, the consensus of a taste which would make it possible to share collectively the nostalgia for the unattainable; that which searches for new presentations, not in order to enjoy them but in order to impart a stronger sense of the unpresentable. (p. 81)

Perhaps the symbolic presentation of paradoxical gender ideals when cheerleaders are present at women's sporting events is part of a postmodern trend that reflects a desire for or tolerance of the unpresentable and of contradiction of taste.

The simultaneous adoption of self-contradictory narratives by the subjects of this study is consistent with Lyotard's (1985) observation that individuals in the postmodern world seem unconcerned with consensus of meaning and are comfortable with contradiction. He comments that, "Consensus has become an outmoded and suspect value" (p. 66), and he argues that people are no longer concerned with the pursuit of a totalizing grand narrative that can be used to legitimate all. In the postmodern world, each narrative is viewed as just one discourse among many. Legitimation has become plural, local and immanent.

Whether these changes are viewed as a positive or negative development is an important theoretical issue. Lyotard (1985) sees the move toward multiple perspectives as a positive move that discredits grand narrative. He emphatically concludes that we should "be witness to the unpresentable" and "wage war on totality" (p. 82).

Lyotard's positive position on this issue has been critiqued as politically naive because in calling for the delegitimation of all grand narratives he excludes many positions of social criticism. As Fraser and Nicholson (1988) argue:

> . . . Lyotard insists that the field of the social is heterogeneous and nontotalizable. As a result, he rules out the sort of social theory which employs general categories like gender, race and class. From his perspective, such categories are too reductive of the complexity of social identities to be useful. And there is apparently nothing to be gained, in his view, by situating an account of the fluidity and diversity of discursive practices in the context of a critical analysis of large-scale institutions and social structures. (pp. 378-379)

Fraser and Nicholson (1988) assert that social theory must be able to employ general categories and move beyond small localized boundaries. According to these views, comfort with the paradox of cheerleaders at women's sporting events would not be automatically perceived as a positive political step. By accepting multiple and contradictory perspectives as equally valid, one takes an apolitical position on the perspectives themselves and powerfully entrenched traditional notions of gender are left uncritiqued. Perhaps it is easy for some to argue for the freedom of pluralistic contradictory perspectives and practices when their own perspectives are dominant.

Moreover, Kellner (1988) questions the implication by Lyotard that no narratives are superior to others. Kellner (1988) asserts that we need to be able to distinguish between better or worse narratives in order to provide a position from which to critique. Fraser and Nicholson (1988), agreeing with Kellner (1988), argue that feminists can learn from postmodernist theory to be anti-foundationalist and anti-essentialist, and yet must retain their traditional position of social criticism. In the case of the phenomena discussed in this paper, a critical feminist theorist can then privilege a more radical feminist narrative over the narrative of liberalism or conservatism.

Many critical and feminist theorists point out that history can be distorted and contradictions can be covered-up by processes that encourage us to view the world from a perspective that best serves those who dominate. Arguing from a neo-Marxist position, critical theorist Guy Debord (1970) has offered some insights in regard to spectacle. He states that, "The spectacle is not a collection of images but a social relation among people mediated by images" (No. 4), and that spectacle can function "to make history forgotten within culture . . ." (No. 192). Jameson (1983), a postmodern theorist who leans toward a critical perspective, feels that we live in a world where we are experiencing, "The disappearance of a sense of history . . ." (p. 125). We live in a world of perpetual present in perpetual change, where tradition is obliterated and we lose the capacity to retain the past. One can easily see that within this framework, divergent images of gender-appropriate behavior or of women's place in sport could be perceived simply as images representing different but equally acceptable narratives. And perhaps the history of these images, such as women's oppression in sport, is simply ignored or forgotten. Yet, it is not just history which is ignored, but the present realities of gender oppression in sport and other areas as well.

The liberal perspective encourages an abstract degendered view of cheerleading and athletics that assumes an ideal world where a person is free to choose from many nongendered sport roles. Acceptance of the narrative of liberalism works against the interests of many women by obscuring gender in a world where gender is highly relevant to oppression. The liberal justification of cheerleaders at women's sporting events works as a myth, in the Barthesian (1986) sense, because it works to organize the world without contradictions, reducing otherness to sameness, reducing the complexity of human action, and eliminating a concern for history. According to Barthes (1986), myth "transforms history into nature . . ." (p. 129). Such is the case here where the myth of an abstract liberal reality creates a situation where historical and current gender meanings are ignored, forgotten and distorted. Moreover, history and conflict are not innocently forgotten, rather they are removed by the politics of an overarching liberal narrative that covers up and encourages one to forget.

Why a liberal reading has been accepted as justification for this spectacle is interesting. One thesis is that the spectacle of sport itself has been constructed with liberal goals in mind and therefore encourages a liberal reading. At a deeper level, another possible thesis is that the challenge of female athleticism to sport as a male preserve, which is even more glaringly evident when in a context with cheerleaders, is glossed over by the acceptance of a liberal narrative. The adoption of this narrative encourages us to remove gender from our vision at the spectacle, and therefore the criticism of contemporary gender relations is temporarily silenced. The contradictory relationship between liberal philosophy and feminist concerns are explicitly discussed by Jaggar (1983) who argues that liberal philosophy does not serve feminist needs because it sets out to ignore gender. Moreover, she argues that liberal feminists themselves have historically had to challenge abstract liberal assumptions by recognizing gender in their politics in order to facilitate social change. Perhaps it is fairly easy for those opposed to feminist critiques to accept the liberal ideal as justification for cheerleaders at female sporting events, because by accepting liberalism, more profound feminist criticisms are rejected.

In conclusion, the presence of cheerleaders at women's sporting events is a paradox because of the existence of conflicting messages about appropriate gender behavior and about the female place in sport. This type of paradoxical spectacle seems to be an example of what Lyotard (1985) might consider to be characteristically postmodern. Critical feminists may be uncomfortable with this spectacle when they read the spectacle with an overarching feminist narrative that wants to see traditional notions of gender challenged and feminist ideals privileged. Yet, the conflicting messages that may be glaringly evident to a critical feminist seem to be left unquestioned by most of the people involved in the spectacle itself. This comfort with the paradox of conflicting messages is consistent with Lyotard's (1985) observation that people are no longer concerned with consensus in meaning. In addition, it is also paradoxical that those involved in the spectacle seem to feel comfortable being self-contradictory, articulating a liberal narrative to legitimate the phenomenon while at the same time articulating views that contradict the liberal narrative.

Lyotard (1985) views the postmodern acceptance of multiple narratives as inherently oppositional, in that he sees this acceptance as a move that undermines the logic of grand narrative. In this particular case, the apparent comfort with multiple or contradictory narratives does not appear to undermine grand narratives of conservative gender meanings. In addition, the acceptance of the liberal narrative seems to work against significant feminist change because it encourages one to view the spectacle in a degendered and ahistorical manner, and therefore discourages oppositional feminist critique of the spectacle. As recent critiques of postmodern theory point out, we must attend to changes in the social processes of the contemporary world, yet remain critical and politically committed.

REFERENCES

Barthes, R. (1986). *Mythologies*. New York, NY: Hill & Wang.

Berger, J., Blomberg, S., Fox, C., Dibb, M., & Hollis, R. (1985). *Ways of seeing*. London, England: British Broadcasting & Penguin Books.

Boutilier, M.A., & SanGiovanni, L. (1983). *The sporting woman*. Champaign, IL: Human Kinetics.

Davis, L. (1990). Male cheerleaders and the naturalization of gender. In M. Messner & D. Sabo (Eds.), *Critical perspectives on sport, men and the gender order*. Champaign, IL: Human Kinetics Press.

Debord, G. (1970). Society of the spectacle. *Radical America*, **4**(5), Detroit, MI: Black & Red.

Donovan, J. (1985). *Feminist theory: The intellectual traditions of American feminism*. New York, NY: Ungar.

Fraser, N., & Nicholson, L. (1988). Social criticism without philosophy: An encounter between feminism and postmodernism. *Theory, Culture & Society*, **5**(2-3), 373-394.

Gach, J.J. (1938). The case for and against girl cheerleaders. *School Activities*, **9**(7), 301-302.

Gonzales, A.F. (1956, November). The first college cheer. *The American Mercury*, **83**, 101-104.

Hatton, C.T., & Hatton, R.W. (1978). The sideline show. *Journal of the National Association for Women Deans, Administrators, & Counselors*, **42**(1), 23-28.

Jaggar, A.M. (1983). *Feminist politics and human nature*. Totowa, NJ: Rowman & Allanheld.

Jameson, F. (1983). Postmodernism and consumer society. In H. Foster (Ed.), *The anti-aesthetic: Essays on postmodern culture* (pp. 111-125). Port Townsend, WA: Bay Press.

Kaplan, E.A. (1983). Is the gaze male? In A. Snitow, C. Stansell & S. Thompson (Eds.), *Powers of desire: The politics of sexuality* (pp. 309-327). New York, NY: Monthly Review.

Kellner, D. (1988). Postmodernism as social theory: Some challenges and problems. *Theory, Culture & Society*, **5**(2-3), 239-270.

Lyotard, J. (1985). *The postmodern condition: A report on knowledge*. Minneapolis, MN: Univ. of Minnesota Press.

Manfredi, J. (1983). Peptalk: The history of cheerleading. *Seventeen*, **42**, p. 94.

Morton, C.W. (1952). Accent on living. *Atlantic Monthly*, **189**, 92-93.

Mulvey, L. (1985). Visual pleasure and narrative cinema. In G. Mast & M. Cohen (Eds.), *Film theory and criticism: Introductory readings* (3rd ed.) (pp. 803-816). New York, NY: Oxford Univ. Press.

NOTES

1. Revised version of a paper delivered at the annual meeting of the North American Society for the Sociology of Sport, Cincinnati, Ohio, 1988.

2. All but the spectators were of traditional college age. Six of the cheerleaders have cheered for both women's and men's sport, 2 for just women's sport, and 2 for just men's sport at the collegiate level. Two of the spectators attend both women's and men's events, 2 solely men's events, and 2 solely women's events. All sub-groups consist of equal numbers of females and males.

PART III

WOMEN IN THE MALE PRESERVE OF SPORT

In recent years, scholars interested in sport have come to appreciate and respond to the thesis advanced by Kenneth Sheard and Eric Dunning that sport serves as a male preserve—a site for the production and reproduction of gendered relations of power. Some sports and the practices that surround them are particularly complicitous with the exclusion and degradation of women, ensuring that those women who persevere in their sporting interests do so in an environment of hostility. Thus, women's marginalization and experiences are structured through ideological and exclusionary practices. These processes have managed to naturalize sport across generations as a masculine activity. They also contain fissures when feminist resistance is possible.

In his reconsideration of his and Sheard's thesis, Eric Dunning argues that the need to preserve male spaces manifests itself during times of encroachment by women into traditionally masculine arenas and privileges. Thus, changing relations between the sexes lead men to stake out and fiercely protect clearly demarcated masculine space.

In an analysis that builds on Dunning's and Willis's arguments that sport reproduces gender inequality by subtle extension of its model of male physical superiority into a model of male social superiority, Nancy Theberge examines the implications for women of sport as a male preserve. She argues that "sport . . . has contributed to the oppression of women through the objectification and domination of their physicality and sexuality." Yet, she argues, the implication of physicality in sport also makes sport a potential site for subverting male dominance through women's growing ability "to experience their bodies as strong and powerful."

The remaining three articles demonstrate concrete instances of the process of cultural resistance. First, Elizabeth Wheatley examines women's rugby as a subculture, emphasizing and comparing the songs produced and associated with men's and women's rugby subcultures. She describes how the men's subculture has served as a male preserve in which the players actively construct a "macho" identity through which they define themselves and reproduce meanings that serve masculine interests. In part, these meanings are produced and articulated through song lyrics constructed within the men's rugby subculture that degrade and objectify women and fetishize female body parts. Wheatley suggests that the women's rugby subculture is marked by the active appropriation of those songs.

Wheatley demonstrates how women's rugby intersects with men's rugby and lesbian subcultures to expropriate the male singing ritual and even some of the same songs. By reorganizing the meanings produced within men's rugby subculture, the women denaturalize and disrupt heterosexist and misogynist discourses. Some of the songs actively challenge heterosexist ideology by articulating and celebrating an overtly lesbian sexuality. Wheatley acknowledges the contradictions in the lyrics, the complexities of "resistance," and the possibilities of different interpretations among feminists regarding women's rugby practices.

In "Challenging the Hegemony," Shona Thompson considers the historically dominant position of rugby in New Zealand and its links to the reproduction of patriarchy, capitalism, and white supremacy. Thompson points out that although rugby in New Zealand excluded women, exploited women's domestic labor, and perpetuated misogyny, rugby was historically accepted and glorified, and women actively participated in its reproduction by permitting men the leisure time to play rugby.

Thompson draws attention to the women-organized demonstrations against New Zealand's approval of apartheid as implied by its participation in competitions against teams representing South Africa. During the 1981 South African Spingbok tour of New Zealand, Women Against Rugby (WAR) withdrew their domestic labor (e.g., refusing to wash their men's dirty soccer clothes), and protested in large numbers outside stadiums. Thompson suggests that although the protests were primarily organized against apartheid and drew attention to racism in New Zealand, they were also motivated by and against exploitative gender relations embedded in and symbolized through the sport. Thompson suggests that the protests contributed to an emerging politics in New Zealand through which patriarchal power relations and the position of rugby have been modified.

The section concludes with Susan Birrell and Diana Richter's analysis of the active development of an oppositional sport model produced by self-identified feminists. These women's critique of dominant, institutionalized sport focuses on the win-at-all-cost sport mentality, which depends on the hierarchy of authority embedded in the coach-player relationship, elitism and exclusivity, the construction of the opponent as Other, and physical risks that jeopardize safety. The softball established through feminist sensibilities challenges hierarchy, emphasizes inclusion and cooperation, is based on an ethic of care and support, and is process oriented.

Like Wheatley, who documents an instance of resistance in women's rugby subculture but who ultimately questions the relationship between that resistance and the reproduction of broader gender relations, Birrell and Richter problematize the concept of resistance, suggesting that what counts as resistance must be reconsidered. The question of resistance, especially that of local resistance, opens a space for the ongoing process of theorizing.

Chapter 11

Sport as a Male Preserve:
Notes on the Social Sources of Masculine Identity and its Transformations

Eric Dunning
University of Leicester, England

INTRODUCTION

Few sociologists would disagree that the changing relations between the sexes are one of the most important social issues of our times, though the majority would probably see them as less important than, say, poverty, starvation, unemployment and racial conflict. However, with the sole exception of the threat of nuclear war, which has universal implications and which would, in all probability, be universal in its consequences if the threat became reality, there is a sense in which relations between the sexes are *more* fundamental than these other issues. That is the case, even though it is mainly middle class women in the more industrialized countries who have begun to become conscious of male dominance, or patriarchy, as socially problematic and have started to fight against it. There is a sex/gender dimension to all other fundamental social issues such

An earlier version of this paper was given at the Fourth Annual Conference of the North American Society for the Sociology of Sport held in St. Louis, Missouri, in October 1983. My thanks are due to my colleagues Clive Ashworth, Pat Murphy, Tim Newburn, Ivan Waddington and John Williams from whose critical comments I have benefited greatly.

as class and race. However, despite the universality and social significance of gender differentiation and the increasingly problematic character of relations between the sexes in more industrialized societies—something that is especially evident in the break-up and/or transformation of traditional forms of marriage and the family that appears to be currently occurring—such issues cannot be said to have been adequately theorised sociologically as yet.[1] Nor, as part of the overall nexus that is relevant in this connection, has much attention been paid to sport, traditionally one of the major male preserves and hence of potential significance for the functioning of patriarchal structures. Possible reasons for this twofold failure of the sociological imagination are not difficult to find.

In recent years, mainly as a result of the feminist challenge, it has become increasingly clear that sociology arose as a subject shot through with patriarchal assumptions. Comte (1853, p. 134ff), for example, saw women as 'intellectually inferior' to men and believed that the family has to be based on the dominance of the husband.[2] Not dissimilar assumptions can be found in Durkheim's (1952, p. 384-86) work and they continue to pervade more modern contributions to the subject. The sociology of sport is one of the least developed areas of sociology (Dunning 1983) but, given the patriarchalism implicit in the discipline in general, it is hardly surprising that assumptions indicative of an unquestioned male dominance have been widely incorporated into such contributions as have been made to this field so far. One of the consequences of this has been that the patriarchal character of modern sport and the part that it may play in maintaining male hegemony have been questioned only by a handful of feminist writers. However, they have tended, for the most part, to focus on such issues as discrimination against women in sport (exceptions are Boutilier & SanGiovanni 1983, Hargreaves 1984) and, although their work has helped to bring about a situation where it is possible, none of them has yet attempted a systematic theorisation of the forms of male dominance that exist in and through sport or of the transformations that have occurred in that regard. I want to make a *start* in that direction in this paper. More particularly, using British data, I want to look at sport as a male preserve and at the part it plays, relative to other sources, in the production and reproduction of masculine identity. Before I become more concrete, however, I shall set forth some of the principal sociological assumptions on which my substantive arguments are based.

The first point to make is that, like all other social interdependencies, the interdependency of men and women is best conceptualized, at least in the first instance, in terms of the balance of power, or 'power-ratio', between the parties involved. This constitutes a 'deep structure' within which the ideologies and values that govern relations between the sexes are generated and sustained. Although such ideologies and values constitute an active ingredient in the balance of power between the sexes, in the sense, eg, that they can play a part in mobilizing men and women to fight for what they perceive their interests to be, it is the case that transformations in sexual relations and in the ideologies and values that govern them are often dependent on prior changes in the underlying balance of power that are unintended and not embedded in specifically articulated ideologies and values.

The second point is that the balance of power between the sexes will tend to veer in favour of men to the extent that violence and fighting are endemic features of social life. That is the case, for example, in warrior societies but it also tends to hold true in industrial societies where the power of military relative to civilian élites is high. It also tends to be the case in those areas of social structure where social conditions lead to the production and reproduction of fighting gangs. The balance of power between the sexes will also veer in favour of men to the degree that their chances for engaging in unified action are greater than those of women, and to the extent that men monopolize access to and control of the principal institutional determinants of life chances, especially in the economy and the state. Furthermore, the more extreme the forms of male dominance in society are, the greater will be the tendency for strict segregation between the sexes to prevail. A corollary of these assumptions is that the power chances of men will tend to be reduced and those of women correspondingly increased whenever relations in a society or part of a society become more pacified, when the chances for women to engage in unified action come to approximate or to exceed those of men, and to the degree that the segregation of the sexes begins to break down. A further corollary is that *macho* values will tend to play a more important part in masculine identity under social conditions where fighting is frequent and the balance of power is skewed more heavily in favour of men. Correspondingly, the *macho* tendencies of men will undergo what might be called a shift in a 'civilizing' direction to the extent that social relations are pacified, the power chances of women are greater, and sexual segregation is broken down.

Underlying these assumptions are two ostensible facts: firstly that, although there is a degree of overlap between the sexes in this regard, men tend in general to be bigger and stronger than women and, therefore, better as fighters; and secondly, that pregnancy and the nursing of children tend to incapacitate women, among other ways, as far as fighting is concerned. Of course, modern weapons technology has the potential for offsetting and perhaps for removing altogether the in-built fighting advantages of men. Similarly, modern birth-control techniques have reduced the time spent by women in pregnancy and nursing children. In other words, the power chances derived by men from their strength and capacity as fighters tend to vary inversely with technological development, ie to be greater when technological development is low and *vice versa*. However, it is reasonable to suppose that the level of state-formation, more especially the degree to which the state is capable of maintaining an effective monopoly on the use of physical force, is probably the most significant influence of all.

This way of approaching the problems of male power and masculine identity derives from the work of Norbert Elias (1978a, 1978b, 1982, 1983). It is rather different from that of those Marxists who attribute the *macho* complex largely to the demands and constraints of performing manual work (eg Willis 1977). More particularly, whilst such constraints may play a part in sustaining the more extreme forms of *macho* identity, eg by placing a premium on physical strength, it is difficult to see how they could have generated *on their own* an ethos in which toughness and ability to fight are central and which celebrates fighting as a principal source of meaning and gratification in life. Indeed, it is arguable that such an approach is itself an exemplification of the kinds of patriarchal assumptions that have been implicit in a lot of sociological theorising so far. That is the case to the extent that the production and reproduction of material life are conceived as located primarily in the economy, and that the significance of the family and relations between the sexes are relegated, at least implicitly, to a subordinate position in this regard.

A point has now been reached at which some of the relationships between sport and patriarchy can be considered. In order to illustrate these relationships, three case studies will, fairly briefly, be discussed. These case studies are: (i) the development of modern 'combat sports'; (ii) the emergence and subsequent (relative) decline of the *macho* subculture that traditionally come to be associated mainly with Rugby Union football; and (iii) the phenomenon of 'football hooliganism' as it exists in contemporary Britain.

ASPECTS OF THE DEVELOPMENT OF MODERN COMBAT SPORTS

All sports are inherently competitive and hence conducive to the arousal of aggression. Under specific conditions, such aggression can spill over into forms of open violence that are contrary to the rules. In some sports, however,—rugby, soccer, hockey and boxing are examples—violence in the form of 'play fight' or 'mock battle' between two individuals or groups is a central and legitimate ingredient. In present-day society, sports of this kind are enclaves for the socially acceptable, ritualized and more or less controlled expression of physical violence. It is solely with such 'combat sports', more particularly those involving a play fight between two teams, that I shall be concerned with in this essay.

The roots of modern combat sports such as soccer, rugby and hockey can be traced directly to a set of locally variable medieval and early modern folk games that went by a variety of names such as football, hurling, knappan and camp ball (Dunning & Sheard 1979). They were played according to oral rules through the streets of towns and across country. There were no agents of 'external' control such as referees and linesmen, and sometimes as many as a thousand people took part on either side. Despite the differences between them, one of the central characteristics of such games, relative to modern sports, was the high level of open violence they involved. The players engaged in the relatively free expression of emotion and exercised only a relatively loose form of self-control. In fact, such games were a kind of ritualized fighting in which groups were able to pit their strength against local rivals whilst, at the same time, generating, in a relatively pleasurable form, excitement akin to that aroused in battle. Games of this type evidently corresponded to the structure of a society where the levels of state-formation and of social development more generally were relatively low, where violence was a more regular and open feature of everyday life than it is today, and where the balance of power between the sexes was skewed more heavily in favour of men. In short, these folk games were expressive of a fairly extreme form of patriarchy. As such, they embodied the expression of *macho* values in a relatively unbridled form.

The first significant developments in the direction of the 'modernization' of such games took place in the nineteenth century public schools (Dunning & Sheard 1979). It was in that context that players began to be subjected to the restraint of written rules, many of them expressly concerned with the elimination or control of the more extreme forms of violence. In other words, the incipient modernization of football and related games involved a complex of changes that made them more 'civilized' than their antecedents had been. The comparative is significant. That is, they did not become 'civilized' in an absolute sense but only more so. They continued to reflect the patriarchal assumptions characteristic of a society still at a relatively early stage in its emergence as an urban-industrial nation-state. This can be seen from the fact that such games were justified ideologically, partly as training grounds for war, partly in terms of their use in the education of military and administrative leaders for Britain's expanding empire, and partly as vehicles for the inculcation and expression of 'manliness'.

A good idea of the norms of manliness involved in the public school games of that stage is given in an account by an Old Rugbeian which appeared in the school magazine in 1860. In it, he contrasted the then current game with the rugby football of his schooldays, some two or three years earlier. The Old Rugbeian (Anon, 1939, p. 52) wrote:

> You should just have seen the scrummages in the Sixth Match two years ago . . . Fellows did not care a fig for the ball then except as it gave them a decent pretext for hacking. I remember a scrummage! . . . we'd been hacking for five minutes already, and hadn't had half enough, in fact, the swells had only just begun to warm to their work, when a bystander . . . informed us that the ball was waiting at our convenience on top of the island . . . And then there was Hookey Walker, the swell hack on the Sixth side; my eye! didn't he walk into the School! only shut up ten fellows for the season and sent half a dozen home for the rest of the half . . . (M)erely to see him come through scrummage was a signal for all the ladies to shriek and faint. Bless you, my dear fellow, they enjoy looking on at a scrummage of all things now—more shame to us. And there was none of the underhand shuffling play with the ball then that there is now; no passing it along from one to the other; all was manly and straightforward. Why, to let the ball go after you had once got into scrummage was considered to be as flagrant a transgression of the rules of football as to take it up when you were off your side. Nor did you see any of that shirking outside scrummages that's always going on nowadays. No one thought you worth your salt if you weren't

the colour of your mother earth from head to toe ten minutes after the match had begun. But, dash my buttons! you haven't a chance of getting a decent fall in the present day; and no wonder either when you see young dandies 'got up regardless of expense', mincing across Big Side, and looking just as if their delicate frames wouldn't survive any violent contact with the ball. Hang the young puppies! We shall have fellows playing in dress boots and lavender-coloured kid gloves before long . . . My maxim is hack the ball on when you see it near you, and when you don't, why then hack the fellow next to you.

This account gives a good idea of the norm of 'manliness' which governed Rugby football at that stage. It also provides evidence for the contention that the game was being transformed in a 'civilizing' direction. Thus the Old Rugbeian recommended a return to the glories of his schooldays when, he claimed, 'hacking'—kicking opponents on the shins—had occupied a more central place. At the same time, he deplored the advent of 'passing' since, in his opinion, it was leading to the 'emasculation' of the game. The earlier standard he described is reminiscent of Ancient Greek boxing and wrestling which, as Elias (1971) has shown, were based on a warrior ethos which decreed it to be cowardly to dodge or retreat from an opponent's blows. Since the Old Rugbeian considered it to be 'underhand' and 'unmanly' to feint or pass to a team-mate in order to avoid being hacked, it seems that rugby football was at first based on a similar ethos. The ball was relatively unimportant to the game at that stage. Scrummages were indiscriminate kicking matches in which the 'manly' thing to do was to stand up to an opponent and engage in toe-to-toe hacking. It followed that strength and courage as a 'hack' were the main criteria for establishing a reputation of 'manliness' in the game.

The Old Rugbeian's account also gives an idea of the upper middle and middle class male ideal of feminine identity at that stage. Thus, whilst the ideal male is portrayed as swaggering and physically tough, the ideal female—in male eyes—is portrayed as timorous, weak and dependent. This corresponded to the image of masculine and feminine roles embodied in the form of the patriarchal nuclear family which was then becoming norm among the expanding middle classes. It is possible to speculate that, contrary to what is currently a widespread if not the dominant feminist view, this form of family may, in one respect at least, have represented a shift towards the equalisation of power chances between the sexes. That is because it tied more males more firmly into the family than had tended to be the case before, thus subjecting them to the possibility of a greater and more regular degree of female influence and control. Also possibly working towards an equalisation of power chances between the sexes was the overall 'civilizing' transformation that has been depicted here through the medium of sport. It would have had such an effect by placing a complex of internal and external restraints[3] on the expression of aggressiveness by men, eg via the code of 'gentlemanly' behaviour, thus restricting their opportunities for using one of their principal power advantages relative to women—their physical strength and superiority as fighters. This, in turn, would have increased the chances for women to engage in unified action *on their own*, eg by organizing marches and demonstrations. It would have had that effect by reducing the likelihood that such demonstrations of nascent female unity and power would be responded to violently by men, eg in a domestic context by their husbands and fathers, and, in the context of demonstrations by the police and general public. More particularly, to the extent that a non-violent response from men to such political acts of women could be expected, the fears of women would have been reduced and their confidence correspondingly enhanced to go ahead with the struggle for what they believed to be their rights. In short, it seems reasonable to hypothesize that the power shift between men and women that first received public expression in the movement of the suffragettes may have been at least partly inherent in the 'civilizing' development that accompanied Britain's emergence as an urban-industrial nation-state.

An implication of the discussion so far is that, despite the fact that it continues to be suffused by patriarchal values and buttressed by predominantly patriarchal structures, modern sport emerged as part of a 'civilizing' transformation one aspect of which was an equalising shift, however slight, in the balance of power between the sexes. However, this had the consequence of contributing to the development in certain spheres of symbolic expression of *machismo*. An example is the pattern of socially tolerated taboo-breaking which, in Britain at least, came to be principally, though not solely, associated with the game of Rugby Union football (Sheard & Dunning 1973). It is to some salient aspects of this development that I shall now turn.

THE RISE AND DECLINE
OF A *MACHO* SUBCULTURE IN RUGBY FOOTBALL

The traditions involved in the *macho* subculture of Rugby Union are enacted after the match either in the clubhouse bar or, if the team has been playing away, on the bus that is carrying the players home. Its central constituents include the male 'striptease', a ritual mocking of the female stripper. The traditional signal for this ritual to begin is a song called, 'the Zulu warrior'. Initiation ceremonies are also a customary part of the rugby subculture. In the course of the ceremonies, the initiate is stripped—often forcibly—and his body, especially his genitals, is defiled, for example, with shoe polish or vaseline. Drinking beer to excess, often accompanied by rituals and races which tend to increase consumption and the speed with which inebriation is reached, also came to be firmly embedded in the rugby club tradition. When drunk, the players sing obscene songs and, if the wives or girlfriends of any of them are present, a song, 'Goodnight Ladies', is sung as a signal for them to leave. Events, henceforward, are to be exclusively for males, and any women who choose to stay are regarded as degraded.

These obscene songs have at least two recurrent themes: the mocking, on the one hand, of women, and on the other, of homosexuals. At first sight, these two themes may appear to be unrelated but it is reasonable to hypothesize that both reflect the growing power of women and their increasing threat to the traditional self-image of men. Rugby began to become a game for adults in the 1850's. It was, at first, exclusive to the upper middle and middle classes, a fact which is perhaps significant because the majority of suffragettes came from the same social strata. In other words, it is reasonable to suppose that women at these levels in the social hierarchy were, in that period, increasingly becoming a threat to men and that some of the latter responded by developing rugby football—it was not, of course, the only enclave where this went on—as a male preserve where they could bolster their threatened masculinity and, at the same time, mock, vilify and objectify women, the principal source of the threat. A brief content analysis of a couple of 'rugby songs' will illustrate how that may have been the case.

A principle recurrent aspect of rugby songs consists in the fact that they embody a hostile, brutal but, at the same time, fearful attitude towards women and the sexual act. In the ballad, 'Eskimo Nell', for example, even the champion womanizer, 'Dead Eye Dick', is unable to provide Nell with sexual satisfaction. This is left to his henchman, 'Mexican Pete', who performs the task with his 'six-shooter'. In 'the Engineer's Song', the central character, an engineer whose wife 'was never satisfied', had to build a machine in order to fulfil the erotic component of his marital role. The machine succeeded where he had failed but, in the process, his wife was brutally killed. Seldom, if ever, are 'normal' men or women featured in these songs. Superhuman or extra-human powers are required before the 'hero' can satisfy the 'heroine's' voracious sexual appetite. Nothing could be more revealing of the function of these songs in symbolically expressing but also, perhaps, to some extent in symbolically reducing the fear of women who were experienced as powerful and demanding. Such fears are likely to have grown commensurately with the factual increase in women's power.

The second recurrent theme of these obscene songs is the mocking of effeminate and homosexual males. One of the songs traditional in rugby circles has as its chorus:

> For we're all queers together—
> Excuse us while we go upstairs.
> Yes, we're all queers together;
> That's why we go 'round in pairs.

The function of this chorus appears to be to counter the charge before it is made, to stress and reinforce masculinity by mocking, not only women but also homosexuals. In recent years, as women have grown more powerful and become able to challenge their factual subordination, if not their symbolic objectification, with a slight but nevertheless growing measure of success, less segregated patterns of relations between the sexes have increasingly become the norm. In that situation, men who clung to the old style and continued to enjoy participation in all-male groups must have had doubts cast upon their masculinity. Some may even have begun to doubt it themselves. Doubts of this kind must have been doubly threatening in a social situation such as that of the rugby club where the principal function was the expression of masculinity and the perpetuation of traditional norms in this regard.

British rugby clubs are now no longer such clear-cut male preserves as they used, formerly, to be. The loosening of the structures and ideologies that once held rugby players together in close-knit, all male groups has been a complex process but just as, if the hypothesis advanced here has any validity, the emancipation of women played an important part in their development, so, too, has the continuation of this process made a significant contribution to the weakening that has subsequently occurred. A stage has now been reached where women are frequent and, what is more important, *welcome* visitors to rugby clubs. In part, it was financial contingencies, more particularly the use of dances in order to raise funds, that began to bring about this change. But this economic fact reflects wider changes in social structure, particularly in the position of women within that structure.

Dances brought women into the rugby male preserve with official approval. This does not mean that their presence had been entirely disallowed before. On the contrary, they have always been welcome—to make tea, prepare and serve meals, and to admire and cheer on their menfolk. But traditionally, their presence was only tolerated if they were content to remain in a subordinate position. The more emancipated women who have now begun to enter clubhouses, however, whether in order to attend dances or simply in order to drink with their men, are increasingly unwilling to accept this. They tend to value independence, to be desirous of equality, and to realize the power which their desirability as mates gives them in relation to men. They are unwilling to accept behaviour which they regard as aggressively intentioned or, alternatively, they use obscenities themselves as a sign of emancipation.

Since one is dealing here with an activity where women accompany men into a social enclave where the principal activity is male, male dominance remains very definitely involved. Nevertheless, the changes just discussed give an indication of the degree to which male dominance in British society has begun to be challenged and, to a limited degree, eroded. Of course it shows at the same time how far women still have to go in order to achieve anything approximating to a measure of full equality with men. For one of the reasons why, in this case, they have to follow the men, is the fact that few comparable leisure activities are available for women. They remain, to a much greater extent than men, locked into domestic and family roles. The lack of leisure facilities for women reflects this fact. So, too, does the fact that it is still difficult for women to enter pubs alone without loss of status or without attracting the unwanted attention of men. This, in its turn, is largely the result of centuries of male dominance and an overall social structure that continues, by and large, to reflect and reinforce that dominance. It also reflects the existence of patterns of socialization which fit women principally for domesticity and the performance of subordinate occupational roles, and which limit their horizons, not only in the occupational sphere, but in the leisure sphere as well.

The changes described here as having occurred in British rugby clubs are, it seems reasonable to hypothesize, symptomatic of the social changes more generally associated with the development of modern sport. There is not sufficient space in this essay for a full discussion of the social roots of these changes. It must be enough simply to say that they occurred as part of the emergence of Britain as an urban-industrial nation-state and that this process involved, among its central, interacting components, the emergence of a social structure characterized by more 'civilized' standards of behaviour and a greater measure of equality between the sexes. There is, however, at least one apparent exception to this generalisation: the phenomenon of 'football hooliganism'. That is because it appears to run counter to the hypothesis that 'civilizing' changes have formed part and parcel of the continuing development of Britain as an urban-industrial nation-state. I shall now offer a brief analysis of football hooliganism before developing some concluding remarks.

THE SOCIOGENESIS
OF FOOTBALL HOOLIGAN VIOLENCE

The most immediately evident characteristics of football hooliganism (see Dunning et al 1981, 1982, 1984) are fighting and the display of aggression between opposing fan groups. Football hooligan fighting takes a number of different forms and can occur in a variety of different contexts besides the football ground itself. It can, for example, take the form of hand-to-hand fighting between two rival supporters or between two small groups of them. Whatever the scale of the fighting, weapons such as knives are sometimes used in these confrontations, but not invariably. Football hooligan fighting can also take the form of aerial bombardments using as ammunition missiles that range from seemingly innocuous items such as peanuts and paper cups to potentially more dangerous ones such as darts, coins, bricks, slabs of concrete, fireworks, smoke bombs and, as has happened on one or two occasions, petrol bombs.

Missile throwing usually takes place in the context of the football ground itself, though it is not unknown outside it, especially when a heavy police presence prevents the rival fan groups from establishing direct contact. As a consequence of the official policy of segregating rival fans—a policy introduced in the late 1960's as a means of combatting football hooliganism but one of the principal effects of which has been to displace the phenomenon and increase the frequency of its occurrence outside grounds—hand-to-hand fighting is relatively rare on the terraces, though small groups of fans still occasionally succeed, eg by not wearing identifying favours, in infiltrating the territory of their rivals in order to start a fight. Participating in a successful 'invasion' is a source of great kudos in football hooligan circles. More usually, nowadays, however, fighting takes place either before the match, eg in and around city centre pubs, or afterwards when the police are trying to shepherd the away fans to the railway or bus station. It is then that the largest scale confrontations tend to take place. These often start with a 'run' ie with some four or five hundred adolescent and young adult males charging down the street searching for a breach in the police defences that will enable them to make contact with the 'enemy'. When they successfully invade police control—what you might call 'hard core' football hooligans use elaborate strategies in order to achieve this end—what typically takes place is a series of skirmishes, scattered over a fairly large territorial area, each one involving up to, say, twenty or thirty youths. Confrontations also take place when rival fans meet accidentally, eg on underground trains and at motorway cafés. In addition, fights sometimes occur *within* particular fan groups, rival participants being drawn, for example, from different local housing estates or different areas of a town. Combined 'fighting crews' are also not unknown. For example, the fans of several different London clubs sometimes congregate at Euston or at one of the other main railway terminals in the capital in order to engage in a united attack on visiting supporters from the north.

During the match, the rival fan groups direct their attention as much or more to one another as they do to the match itself, singing, chanting and gesticulating as expressions of their opposition. Their songs and chants have, as a recurrent theme, challenges to fight and threats of violence. Particular fan groups tend to have their own repertoire of songs and chants but many of these are local variations on a stock of common themes. Central in this connection, as Jacobson (1975) has shown, is the fact that their lyrics are punctuated with words like hate, die, fight, kick and surrender, all of which convey images of battle and conquest. Here are a couple cited by Jacobson, from the repertoire of Chelsea fans:

(Sung to: 'Those were the days my friend').
We are the Shed,[4] my friends,
We took the Stretford End.[5]
We'll sing and dance and do it all again.
We live the life we choose.
We fight and never lose.
For we're the Shed,
Oh Yes! We are the Shed.

(Sung to: 'I was born under a wandering star').
I was born under the Chelsea Shed.
Boots are made for kicking,
Guns are made to shoot.
Come up to the Chelsea Shed
And we'll all lay in the boot.

Apart from violence, symbolic demasculinization of the rival fans is another recurrent theme of hooligan songs and chants, eg the reference to them and/or the team they support as 'poofs' or 'wankers', the latter accompanied by a mass gestural representation of the male masturbatory act. Yet another is degrading the community of the opposing fans, as, for example, with the following song:

(Sung to: 'In my Liverpool home').
In their Highbury slums,
They look in the dustbin for something to eat,
They find a dead cat and they think its a treat
In their Highbury slums

As one can see from this description, at least a significant proportion of the football fans who attract the 'hooligan' label appear to be as, or more, interested in fighting as they are in watching football. For them, the match is principally about expressing their *machismo*, either factually by inflicting defeat on the rival fans and making them run away, or symbolically, *via* the medium of songs and chants. Take the case of 'Frank', a twenty six year old lorry driver and self-confessed 'football hooligan' who was interviewed by Paul Harrison after the Cardiff City-Manchester United game in 1974. Frank is reported by Harrison as having said:

I go to a match for one reason only: the aggro. It's an obsession, I can't give it up. I get so much pleasure when I'm having aggro that I nearly wet my pants . . . I go all over the country looking for it . . . (E)very night during the week we go around town looking for trouble. Before a match we go round looking respectable . . . ; then if we see someone who looks like the enemy, we ask him the time, if he answers in a foreign accent, we do him over, and if he's got any money on him we'll roll him as well.

From this and the earlier discussion, it is clear that a central component of football hooliganism is the expression of a particular masculine identity, what one might call a 'violent masculine style'. The currently available evidence suggests that the majority of hard core football hooligans come from sections of the socio-economically most deprived levels of the working class, and it seems reasonable to hypothesize that this violent masculine style is generated by specific structural features of lower working class communities. Gerald Suttles (1968) has coined the term, 'ordered segmentation', to describe such communities and, he argues, one of their dominant features is the 'single-sex peer group' or 'street-corner gang'. Such groups, he suggests, seem 'to develop quite logically out of a heavy emphasis on age-grading, avoidance between the sexes, territorial unity and ethnic solidarity'. However, he documents the occurrence of intra-ethnic conflict between such groups and recognizes elsewhere that ethnic differentiation and solidarity are contingent rather than necessary factors in their formation.

That is, age-grading, sexual segregation and territorial identification appear to be the crucial internal structural determinants. In a community where these are central elements of social structure, adolescent males are left largely to their own devices and tend to band into groups determined, on the one hand, by ties of kinship and residential closeness, and on the other, by the threat posed by the development of parallel 'gangs' in adjacent neighbourhoods. Such communities also tend to be internally fragmented. A partial exception, Suttles argues, is provided by an actual or rumoured 'gang' fight, for these can mobilize the allegiance of males throughout a community.

In a later development of this analysis, Suttles (1972) introduced the concept of 'the defended neighbourhood', suggesting that the adolescent street groups that grow up in slum communities can be seen as 'vigilante gangs' which develop out of 'the inadequacy of the formal institutions that have authorized responsibility for the protection of property and lives'. This is an interesting idea, in some ways consistent with Elias's theory of 'the civilizing process' with its stress on the part played by developing state control in the emergence of 'more civilized' social standards. That is, if Elias is correct, one would expect to find, even in an urban-industrial nation-state, relatively high levels of overt violence in communities where the state and its agencies have been unable or unwilling to exert effective control. Let me now explore the way in which the structure of such communities leads to the production and reproduction of 'violent masculinity' as one of their dominant characteristics.

To the extent that their internal structures approximate to 'ordered segmentation' and to the extent that they are not subject to effective state control, lower working class communities tend to generate norms that, relative to those of other social groups, tolerate a high level of violence in social relations. Correlatively, such communities exert comparatively little pressure on their members to exercise self-control over their violent tendencies. Several aspects of their structure tend to work in this direction. Thus, the comparative freedom from adult control experienced by lower working class children and adolescents means that the latter tend to interact relatively violently and to develop dominance hierarchies of which age and physical strength are central determinants. This pattern is reinforced by the standards characteristic of the dominant adults in communities of this sort. Sexual segregation, the dominance of men over women and the consequent lack of 'softening' female pressure all work in the same direction. Indeed, to the extent that the women in such communities grow up to be relatively violent themselves and to expect violent behaviour from their men, the violent propensities of the latter are compounded. Further reinforcement comes from the frequency of feuds between families, neighbours and, above all, 'streetcorner gangs'. In short, lower working class communities of this type appear to be characterized by a kind of 'positive feedback cycle' which tends to maximise the resort to violence in virtually all areas of social relations, especially on the part of males.

One of the effects of this cycle is the conferral of prestige on males who can fight. Correlatively, there is a tendency for these males to develop a love of fighting, to see it as a central source of meaning and gratification in life. The central difference in this regard between lower working class communities and those of their more 'respectable' counterparts in the upper, middle and working classes appears to be that, in the latter, violence in face-to-face relations tends to be normatively condemned whilst, in the former, it tends to be normatively condoned and rewarded. A further difference is the fact that there is a tendency in the 'respectable' classes for violence to be 'pushed behind the scenes' and, when it does occur, for it to take, on balance, a more 'instrumental' form and to lead to the arousal of feelings of guilt. By contrast, in the communities of the 'rough' working class, violence tends to be expressed to a greater extent in public and to take, on balance, an 'expressive' or 'affective' form. As such it tends to be associated to a greater extent with the arousal of pleasurable feelings.

It is reasonable to hypothesize that it is the 'violent masculine style' which is generated in this manner in the 'rough' working class that is principally expressed in football hooligan fighting. That is today, the currently available evidence suggests that it is youths and young men from this section of the working class who form the hard core of those who most persistently engage in the more violent acts that take place in a football context. Of course, football is not the only venue where this style is expressed. It is, however, in many ways a highly appropriate setting. That is because the football match itself is a play fight that is centrally about the expression of masculinity, though in a form that is socially approved and controlled. The football team also provides a focus for the identifications of young and young adult males from the working class, and the latter came to see the ground, more particularly the goal-end terraces, as their own 'turf'. At the same time, football regularly brings into their territory an easily identifiable 'enemy', the supporters of the opposing team, and the latter are seen as 'invaders'. Finally, the large crowd at a football match provides a setting where what are officially perceived to be 'anti-social' acts can be engaged in with relative anonymity and impunity, and the large police presence provides the added excitement of regular brushes with the law. I have now reached a point where I can offer some concluding remarks.

CONCLUSION

In this essay, I have suggested that the origins of a number of modern 'combat sports' can be traced to a set of folk games the violence of which is indicative of their rootedness in a society that was more violent and hence more heavily patriarchal than our own. I then traced the incipient modernization of these sports in the public schools, suggesting that the 'civilizing' changes that occurred in that connection were symptomatic of a wider complex of changes, one effect of which was to increase the power of women relative to men. Some men responded to this power shift by establishing rugby clubs—they were not, of course, the only enclaves developed for this purpose—as male preserves where they could symbolically mock, objectify and vilify women who now, more than ever before, represented a threat to their status and self-image. The continuing emancipation of women has now substantially eroded this aspect of the rugby 'subculture'. Finally, I examined the apparent contradiction posed for my thesis by 'football hooliganism' and suggested that one of its central features is a 'violent masculine style' that is structurally produced and reproduced among specific sections of the lower working class. As such, it does not constitute a contradiction of my thesis but is indicative of the unevenness with which the 'civilizing' and state-formation processes have occurred and of the fact that there still exist in present-day Britain areas of social structure that continue to generate *macho* aggressiveness in a more or less extreme form.

A central difference between the *macho* complex expressed in football hooliganism and, more generally, in the violent masculine style of the 'rough' working class, and that expressed in rugby football, consists in the fact that the physical violence and toughness of rugby players tends to be channelled into the socially approved medium of the game, whilst that of the 'rough' working class tends to be a more central life commitment. It is noticeable, furthermore, that whilst rugby players, when the subculture of their male preserve was at its height, tended to mock, objectify and vilify women *symbolically* through the medium of rituals and songs, women do not figure in the songs and chants of football hooligans at all. This is, perhaps, indicative of the lower power of women in the communities of the lower working class and, consequently, of the fact that they pose a lesser threat to men. Under such conditions, they are *factually* objectified and exploited to a greater degree, and subject much more to the open violence of men.

Probably the main implication of the present analysis is the fact that sport appears to be of only secondary importance with respect to the production and reproduction of masculine identity. Of far greater significance in this regard, it seems, are those features of the wider social structure that affect the relative power chances of the sexes and the degree of sexual segregation that exists within the necessary interdependency of men and women. All that sport appears to do in this connection is to play a secondary and reinforcing role. As such, however, it is nevertheless crucial in sustaining more modified and controlled forms of *macho* aggressiveness in a society where only a few occupational roles, such as those in the military and the police, offer regular opportunities for fighting, and where the whole direction of technological development has been for a long time reducing the need for physical strength. Of course, to the extent that the socialization of women continues to lead them to be attracted to *macho* men, sports, especially combat sports, will play a part of some significance in perpetuating both the *macho* complex and the dependency of women that flows from that source. It is probably idle to speculate about whether combat sports would continue to exist in a more fully 'civilized' society than our own. One thing, however, is relatively certain in that regard: namely that, even though equalization tends to increase the occurrence of conflict in the short and medium term, such a society would in the longer term have to embody a far higher measure of equality between the sexes, the classes and the 'races' than has so far been achieved.

NOTES

1. Feminist writers, of course, have made a number of important advances in this regard but, on account of the strength of their ideological commitments, much of what they have written *appears* at least, even to many who sympathize with their cause, to be lacking in object-adequacy.
2. To be fair to Comte, whilst claiming that women are 'constitutionally in a state of perpetual infancy' and 'unfit . . . for the requisite continuousness and intensity of mental labour, either from the intrinsic weakness of (their) reason or from (their) more lively moral and physical sensibility', he also saw them as 'spiritually' superior to men and hence as socially more important.
3. From Elias's standpoint it is strictly speaking wrong to dichotomize 'internal' and 'external' restraints. The terms he uses are 'Selbstzwange' (self-constraints) and 'Fremdzwange' ('other', literally 'stranger' constraints), and he focuses in his analyses on the changing balance over time between them.
4. 'The Shed' is a stretch of covered terracing at Stamford Bridge, the ground of Chelsea FC.
5. 'The Stretford End' is one of the goal-end terraces at Old Trafford, the ground of Manchester United. The 'Stretford Enders' were notorious for their hooligan exploits in the early and mid-1970s.

BIBLIOGRAPHY

Anon (1939), The New Rugbeian, Vol. 3, 1860, quoted in C.R. Evers, *Rugby* London: Blackie.

Boutilier & SanGiovanni (1983), *The Sporting Woman*, Champaign, IL: Human Kinetics.

Comte, A. (1853), *The Positive Philosophy of Auguste Comte*, trans and condensed by H. Martineau, London: Chapman.

Dunning, Eric (1983), Notes on Some Recent Contributions to The Sociology of Sport, *Theory, Culture & Society*, 2, 1, pp135-142.

Dunning, Eric & Sheard, Kenneth (1979), *Barbarians, Gentlemen and Players. A Sociological Study of the Development of Rugby Football*, Oxford: Martin Robertson.

Dunning, Eric, Murphy, Patrick & Williams, John (1981), If You Think You're Hard Enough, *New Society*, 27th August.

Dunning, Eric, Murphy, Patrick & Williams, John (1982), The Social Roots of Football Hooligan Violence, *Leisure Studies*, 1, 2.

Dunning, Eric, Murphy, Patrick & Williams, John (1984), *Hooligans Abroad: The Behaviour and Control of English Fans at Football Matches in Continental Europe*, London: RKP.

Durkheim, E. (1952), *Suicide*, London: RKP.

Elias, Norbert (1971), The Genesis of Sport as a Sociological Problem, in E. Dunning (ed) *The Sociology of Sport: A Selection of Readings*, London: Cass.

Elias, Norbert (1978a). *What Is Sociology?* London: Cass.

Elias, Norbert (1978b), *The Civilizing Process*, Oxford: Blackwell.

Elias, Norbert (1982), *State Formation and Civilization*, Oxford: Blackwell.

Elias, Norbert (1983), *The Court Society*, Oxford: Blackwell.

Hargreaves, Jennifer (1984), Action Replay: Looking at Women in Sport, in J. Holland (ed) *Feminist Action*, London: Battle Axe.

Harrison, Paul (1974), Soccer's Tribal Wars, *New Society*, 5th September.

Jacobson, S. (1975), Chelsea Rule—OK, *New Society*, 31.

Sheard, Kenneth & Dunning, Eric (1973). The Rugby Football Club a Type of Male Preserve: Some Sociological Notes, *International Review of Sport Sociology*, 5, 3, pp5-24.

Suttles, Gerald D. (1968). *The Social Order of the Slum: Ethnicity and Territory in the Inner City*, Chicago and London: Chicago UP.

Suttles, Gerald D. (1972), *The Social Construction of Communities*, Chicago: Chicago UP.

Willis, Paul (1977). *Learning to Labour*, London: Saxon House.

Chapter 12

Toward a Feminist Alternative to Sport as a Male Preserve

Nancy Theberge
University of Waterloo

This paper examines two related issues that follow from the fact that sport is a male preserve. First, it explores the effects of male and masculine dominance of sport upon gender relations and women's experience in sport and in other institutional settings. Stated too simply, the paper addresses the question "So what?" or "Why does male dominance of sport matter?" The answer developed here argues that sport as a gendered cultural form bears significant relation to gender segregation and inequality in other realms of social life. While this assertion is probably widely accepted, it is argued further that most accounts of the impact of sport as a male preserve upon other manifestations of gender inequality misrepresent the nature of this relationship and underestimate its impact.

The concluding section of the paper discusses the potential of sport to transform gender relations and contribute to the liberation of women. This section develops some ideas from recent feminist social theory on the centrality of sexuality and physicality to male power and dominance. The purpose is to show how these writings provide the theoretical underpinnings for an analysis both of the capacity of sport as an agent of women's oppression and, by extension, its potential as an agent for the transformation of gender relations.

From "Toward a Feminist Alternative to Sport as a Male Preserve" by Nancy Theberge, 1985, *Quest*, 37:2, pp. 193-202. Copyright 1985 by The National Association of Physical Education and Higher Education. Reprinted by permission.

SPORT AND GENDER INEQUALITY

While this paper begins from the premise that sport is a male preserve, it will help to indicate here how this is so. Perhaps the first and simplest way in which to indicate male dominance of sport is to examine gender differences in rates of participation. Although there is evidence that the gap is narrowing in rates of participation between men and women, in general sport is still largely organized for men. For example, recent Canadian national survey data show that while almost as many females as males participate in unorganized physical activity, males have considerably higher rates of participation in organized competitive sport (Fitness Canada, 1982). A similar pattern exists in the United States (Sporting Goods Dealer, 1980). Additional data (Vickers et al., 1982) show that 70% of students participating in programs affiliated with the Canadian Interuniversity Athletic Union are male. In international sport, of the events included in the 1984 Winter and Summer Olympics, 66% were contested by men only, 28% by women only, and 6% by men and women competing together.[1] And, professional sports still remain largely a male preserve. Thus, despite recent gains in participation by women, sport still is an activity mostly organized for males.

A second instance of sport as a male preserve is male dominance in the administration and organization of sport. Historically, leadership positions in sport have been held almost exclusively by men. In contrast to the limited recent gains achieved by women in sport participation, in the past few years women have experienced losses in their proportion of leadership positions in sport. Specific examples of this include recent declines in the number of women in coaching and administrative positions in athletic departments in American (Holmen & Parkhouse, 1981) and Canadian universities (Vickers et al., 1982). At the same time, positions on the International Olympic Committee, national Olympic committees, and in the control and administration of professional sport in North America remain the near exclusive domain of men.

A full analysis of the forms and implications of sport as a male preserve must show the connections between these differences and patterns of power and domination. This matter will be addressed shortly. There is, however, an important point to be noted in a discussion of rates of involvement. These differences indicate women's relative exclusion from an activity that is culturally valued and to a considerable extent publically supported. Public support of sport takes place in a variety of ways including the location of programs in educational institutions, direct government support of sport organizations, and indirect support through tax incentives for corporate donations and sponsorship of events and programs. Thus, women's underrepresentation in sport is an instance of their unequal access to the valued goods and resources of our society.

Still another aspect of sport as a male preserve is seen in the cultural images of women's sporting activity. For example, in both its quantity and quality, media coverage of women's sport in North America often serves to denigrate and trivialize women's sporting experience. While the limited amounts of coverage of women's sport in both the printed and electronic media provide a straightforward indication of the valuation—or devaluation—of women's sport, the images portrayed in this coverage offer complementary ideological messages. Television ads celebrating the glory of male athleticism and activity while women appear as background props, and references by commentators to sex-role stereotypic characteristics of women athletes (their marital and family status and physical appearance) suggest that women's athletic experience is unimportant and inappropriate.

The trivialization of women's sporting experience has perhaps reached its nadir in the current feminization of the fitness craze embodied in some instances of the activities labeled Dancercise and Jazzercise and in the televised "Twenty-Minute Workout." I would argue that in many instances these activities are concerned with developing women's potential not in sport and athletics but in the sexual marketplace. The suggestive poses assumed by activity leaders, and breathy voices exhorting participants, convey images of dominance and submission. The ideal or goal is not the development of physical strength or even fitness but the development of women's sexual attractiveness and appeal. Thus, these programs are a further embodiment of sport as a male preserve.

Of course, much more could be said to demonstrate male and masculine prerogatives in sport. However, this is a point likely to be accepted by most observers and critics and one that is well documented. I turn now to the implications of sport as a male preserve—or the question "So what?" Restrictions upon women's sporting activity and denigration of this activity are important not only as distributive questions of equality of opportunity but also as relational questions concerning the associations among groups. The point here is that sport does not simply represent gender inequality but contributes to its maintenance in social settings that transcend sport.

THE IMPLICATIONS OF SPORT AS A MALE PRESERVE

Several writers have recently offered interpretations of the manner in which sport operates as a male preserve. In their recent book, *The Sporting Woman*, Boutilier and SanGiovanni (1983, pp. 100-101) argue that sport and masculinity are "social realities" that "support, inform and reinforce" each other and together contribute to the traditional polarization of sex roles. They cite three reasons why men resist women's entry into sport: because of a desire to maintain sport as a socializing agency that prepares men for adult roles in the public sector, particularly the workplace and political life; to maintain the hierarchical ranking of sex roles, specifically in the valuation of masculine over feminine roles; and to preserve an exclusively male realm that allows for expressiveness and intimacy—qualities that are typically absent from what is generally viewed as appropriate behavior for men.

Boutilier and SanGiovanni's (1983) analysis is predicated on their argument that there is an isomorphism between sporting roles and male-dominated instrumental roles in the public sector, and on the assumed (by educators and other policymakers) socialization effects of sport. This argument is supported by their discussions of the connections between sport and the educational system, the media and public policy, and in a chapter by Susan Greendorfer on family socialization. The particular form of the association between sport and other institutions that they discuss differs for the various institutions. For example, the chapter on education emphasizes the presumed socialization effects of sport while the chapter on public policy examines policy determinants of women's sporting experience. The overall effect of their analysis is to present a strong case for the connection between gender differentiation and inequality in sport and other institutions.

Although this connection is well brought out by Boutilier and SanGiovanni's (1983) analysis, some elaboration may be in order. In an attempt to specify further the process by which sport interacts with other institutions in the reproduction of gender relations, I cite three recent discussions of sport as a cultural form, two of which are concerned with gender and sport. The works are Richard Gruneau's *Class, Sports and Social Development*, an essay by Paul Willis entitled ''Women in Sport in Ideology,'' and a detailed and systematic investigation by Helen Lenskyj of the role of physical education in the socialization of girls in Ontario between 1890 and 1930.

Class, Sports and Social Development is a study of the development of Canadian sport that is grounded in a theoretical perspective that sees play, games, and sports as social practices ''indissolubly connected to the making and remaking of ourselves as agents'' (Gruneau, 1983, p. 50). After a lengthy review and critique of writings on play, games, and sports that view these as ''some sort of transhistorical essence, need or transcendent metaphysical form,'' or ''as activities simply reducible to a 'separate' material reality'' (1983, p. 50), Gruneau develops his own position that sports (or, in his broader formulation, play, games, and sports) are concrete, material social practices that are outcomes of human agency. Fundamental to this position is an emphasis upon play, games, and sports as practices that players and organizers *produce*, albeit within the context of historically specific social limitations. This theoretical formulation provides the basis for the author's analysis of class relations, reproduction, and transformation in Canadian sport.

Gruneau's (1983) book provides one of the most theoretically sophisticated accounts we have of the relationship between sport and social relations. His view of sport as social practice has considerable relevance to the study of gender relations, although Gruneau himself does not develop this topic. The works by Willis (1982) and Lenskyj (1983) offer useful complements to *Class, Sports and Social Development* because they are grounded in similar perspectives that see sport and physical activity as forms of cultural production. Lenskyj and Willis, however, are concerned with the connections between physical activity and gender relations.

Willis' (1982) article is an analysis of women's sporting practice as an ideological process that lends legitimation to certain dominant versions of social relations. In Willis' formulation, the ideological process that legitimizes women's sporting experience begins with the general belief that the sexes are innately different and that males are superior. Concerning women in sport, the innate or biological difference between the sexes is recognized as discrepancy, but is not necessarily translated into a notion of *social* inferiority. The social reality of women in sport may be unconnected with biological differences and may be based, say, on an appreciation of the *process* of athletic activity. The transformation of the biological differences between the sexes into the reality of the social inferiority of women takes place when these differences come to define and limit the practice of sport. To illustrate how this takes place, Willis cites the sexualization of women's sport, including media images of sporting women that concentrate on their sexuality, and the assumption of male models of sport as "natural" forms of athletic experience.

What is important for the present discussion is Willis' (1982) account of how a general ideological belief comes to operate in a particular social subregion, where it in turn comes to assume a life of its own, thus reinforcing the general form of the belief. Willis argues that sport provides an extremely useful subregion for the recreation of the ideology of male superiority because of its apparent autonomy and separation from other areas of life and the relatively "voluntary" nature of sporting activity. Sport also offers a "bonus" to the ideological process: the importance of physical capacities in sporting performance. Biological differences between men and women are a matter of fact, but what is important ideologically is the reinterpretation of these differences into social distinctions and male superiority. This is accomplished through the trivialization and degradation of women's sporting experience.

The research by Helen Lenskyj (1983) cited above is a recently completed doctoral dissertation at the Ontario Institute for Studies in Education. The dissertation is an extensively documented sociohistorical account of the major influences upon the definition and implementation of girls' physical education in Ontario from 1890 to 1930. Lenskyj's work adds to the analysis of how sport as a male preserve is a social practice and the outcome of human agency. In the period she discusses, the major agents acting upon the physical education of girls were "experts" from the medical, physical education, and education fields who exerted a powerful influence upon the social construction of girls' physical activity.

This social construction was informed and limited by concerns for femininity, defined both physically and psychologically. Lenskyj shows how the aims of physical education programs, as formulated by these experts, served the interests of patriarchal ideology by confirming and perpetuating sex differentiation in sport. This differentiation in turn gave meaning to assumptions that legitimated women's personal and economic subordination by "demonstrating" innate differences or the "facts" of women's physical and psychological frailty. In short, Lenskyj underscores the process whereby girls' physical education emerged as a social practice defined by and defining women's subordinate status. Her analysis also provides empirical support for the interpretation of women in sport in ideology that Willis offers.

The works by Gruneau (1983), Willis (1982), and Lenskyj (1983) reviewed here help to specify the connections between sport as a male preserve and other forms of patriarchal control by elaborating the process by which sport comes to embody and recreate male power and domination. In emphasizing the relationship between sport and gender relations, however, it is important not to read women out of the analysis. That is, it must be emphasized that there are limitations to an analysis of sport that focuses exclusively upon the role of men and masculinity. An important area of research is the identification of women's participation in the construction of their sporting experience. This part usually, if not always, has been restricted by their lack of power, as in the events discussed by Lenskyj which are reviewed here.

Powerlessness, however, need not signal acquiescence or capitulation. Examples of counter-hegemonic sport practices are provided by Lenskyj in an analysis of data from interviews conducted with women who pursued sporting careers in the period she studied. Some of these women clearly rejected patriarchal notions of female frailty and inferiority. An additional example is provided by Nancy Theriot (1978), who argues that in the United States in the 1920s, the Women's Division of the National Amateur Athletic Federation mounted a successful challenge to male and masculine dominance of school sport programs. The Division, according to Theriot, was "a group of women dedicated to a uniquely feminine direction for women's sport" (1978, p. 1). That direction was player- rather than spectator-oriented and emphasized the joy of participation over an excessive emphasis upon competition. Theriot contends that accusations that the Division's philosophy was based on conservative ideas about women's capacities and proper feminine roles are mistaken. Rather, she argues, the Division represented a rejection of models of sport based on men's experiences.

Sport as a male preserve, then, is an important cultural practice that contributes to the definition and recreation of gender inequality. As noted earlier, this point may not be contentious. What has been emphasized here is that sport's capacity to recreate—or transform—gender relations arises from its capacity to give meaning and realization to patriarchal forms of power and domination. The analysis of how sport contributes to gender inequality must therefore attend to the connections between sport as social practice and broader patterns of gender relations, and must indicate how women's sporting activity is part of a broader ensemble of patriarchal relations.

RESEARCH ON WOMEN AND SPORT

While there is now a substantial and growing body of research on the "problem" of women and sport, I would argue that much of this literature has been seriously deficient. It has been based on a misunderstanding of sport as social practice and, thus, the conclusions drawn from this research have underestimated the impact of sport upon gender relations and inequality. In support of this claim, a sample of the literature on two topics is reviewed below.

Role Conflict Among Women Athletes

Much of the research on this topic is based on the assumption that sport is a stereotypically masculine activity and that women who participate in sport experience conflict between their feminine and athletic roles. The research on role conflict among women athletes has been evaluated by Hall (1981) and Boutilier and SanGiovanni (1983). As these authors show, this research is flawed both methodologically and conceptually. Relevant problems include issues of scaling and measurement, inconsistent and imprecise conceptualization of variables, sampling biases and restrictions, and failure to identify the contextual and other mediating influences (e.g., the level and type of sport involvement) upon the hypothesized relationship between sport participation and role conflict. Boutilier and SanGiovanni make the additional point that research on role conflict is marred by philosophical problems in its uncritical acceptance of both the traditional role of women and conventional arrangements in sport. They argue that research that examines whether women in sport experience conflict due to cultural proscriptions against their participation in a masculine activity accepts both the notion of sex-appropriate behavior and the power of proponents of these ideas to limit women's behavior.

These criticisms of role conflict research, in my view, are accurate. With respect to the issue raised in this paper, however, the manner in which sport recreates gender inequality, the most important problem with research on role conflict is that it depoliticizes women's sporting experience by emphasizing individual attributes, perceptions, and "felt states." The problem of women in sport, as suggested by this formulation, lies with the individual and the psychological characteristics she brings to sport. There is little recognition in this work of the broader ideological and structural forces that inform and limit women's sporting experience.

To be sure, both Hall (1981) and Boutilier and SanGiovanni (1983) recognize the political limitations of the literature on role conflict. But elaboration seems to be in order. Psychological interpretations of limits on women's involvement in sport serve to define the problem as one that lies within women. This approach begs the question of how women's sporting experience came to be degraded and judged to be inappropriate for their sex. It does not view sport as a dynamic and politicized activity, shaped and contoured by human agents who bring different resources and capacities to the experience. Rather, it views sport as a static and often apolitical "fact" which can be "captured" in statistical analysis. Viewed from this perspective, studies of role conflict among women athletes, like research based in role theory generally, are lacking an adequate sociological perspective.

Sport and Socialization

This literature often is presented as two separate subtopics, socialization into sport and socialization through sport. While the distinction may be useful in helping to order material, it is limited by implying a false separation between sporting and other social practices. Notwithstanding this limitation, the analysis of both kinds of socialization warrants comment.

At first glance it may appear that the literature on socialization into sport avoids the error of separating sport from other practices. Much of this research attempts to examine the influence of significant others upon the learning of sport behavior in different institutional settings. Thus, for example, research is directed at identifying the impact of individuals in the family, school system, and community. This formulation apparently recognizes the connections between sport and other social experiences, and in this respect it is well conceived. Unfortunately, however, the manner in which this connection is explored often obscures the association.

This holds especially for research that employs statistical analysis. This research fails to capture the dynamic aspect of sporting practice, the manner in which socialization into sport is less a process of taking on roles than of actively creating them, albeit within the limits and constraints of social practice. Moreover, much of this research fails to consider these limits and constraints: Significant others are conceived as units of analysis that are roughly equivalent rather than as cultural agents characterized by different degrees of power and ability to mobilize resources. The implication of this for research on women's socialization into sport is that this research often fails to uncover the political and social factors that define and constrain women's sporting practice.

The conclusions drawn from the literature on socialization through sport are equally misleading in their implications for an analysis of women and sport. This research attempts to identify the socialization effects of sport experience. It asks how sport participation influences the development of particular characteristics and the learning of nonsport roles. The historical development of this research presents an interesting case study in the sociology of sport. Probably much of the interest in the "effects" of sport participation was motivated by skepticism concerning some common beliefs about the purported benefits of sport participation (the idea that sport builds character) and was an attempt to debunk these beliefs. As the sociology of sport developed as a scholarly undertaking devoted to the rigorous analysis of social behavior and relationships, long cherished beliefs about sport's "effects" were put to test. The results of this analysis were succinctly stated by Stevenson, who in a frequently cited review of the literature reported that "there is no valid evidence that participation in sport causes any verifiable socialization effects" (1975, p. 287).

In view of this conclusion, what then are we to make of the "obvious" isomorphism between sport and other institutions? This isomorphism, it is argued, facilitates men's socialization into instrumental roles in the workplace and political arena and, because sport is largely a male domain, denies these experiences to women. It appears that in their zeal to put to test conventional views about the presumed benefits of sport participation, researchers have again missed the mark. While the concern to move beyond an uncritical faith in the benefits of sport to rigorous investigation and analysis of these alleged effects was a much needed advancement, the results of these efforts have been misleading.

Again, the problems are errors of conceptualization and methodology. Quantitative analyses that attempt to isolate experiences and to establish cause and effect relationships between them will inevitably fall short, for the experiences of sport and other social practices are not, in the end, separate and amenable to causal analysis. As the literature suggests, sport participation *per se* or "by itself" (if it could be so conceived) does not result in the development of particular characteristics or the learning of particular roles. But if we broaden our analysis to a consideration of sport as social practice imbedded in a social and cultural context characterized by forms of power and domination and legitimized by ideology, the importance of sport may be recaptured.

Sport is *not* critical to socialization in the sense that participation in sport is necessary or sufficient for the learning of gendered social roles by individual men and women. It is important, however, as one among many mutually reinforcing forms of cultural production that give meaning to and reinforce gender inequality and male domination. The previous section of this paper, which reviews works by Gruneau (1983), Willis (1982), and Lenskyj (1983) suggests how this is the case. There is a need for more research from the perspectives that these authors employ to identify how sporting practices contribute to—and challenge—gendered social arrangements.

A FEMINIST ALTERNATIVE
TO SPORT AS A MALE PRESERVE

A vision of the potential of women's sporting experience to transform gender relations could be based on the conception of sport as social practice, as is emphasized above. Additionally, this vision of the potential of sport as *feminist* social practice stresses the importance of sport as *physical* activity which expresses, embodies, and gives meaning to women's experience.

Jennifer Hargreaves (1982, p. 16) has recently argued that "historically, the political relevance of the body has been given scant attention in our society which is dominated by verbal language." She states that this position is a cultural expression of a mind-body dualism which conceives of sport as a physical activity rather than a mental one. An alternative conception is the view of sport as a united physical and mental process, in which the physical is an integral and organic expression of individual and social experience. This conception sees sport as comprising "the mental and emotional response, whether of an individual or of a social group, to many inter-related events and the many repetitions of the same event" (Hargreaves, 1982, pp. 16-17).

Hargreaves correctly identifies the historical inattention to the political relevance of the body, although this is *relative* inattention. Important writings on the topic include those of Freud, Wilhelm Reich, and Marcuse, as well as those of de Beauvoir and other feminist writers, as noted below. Hargreaves may also be correct in attributing this inattention to a false mind-body dualism. But, I would add that this relegation has served patriarchal interests by obscuring the relationship between sport and male oppression. Like Hargreaves, it is contended here that sport should be conceived as an integration of the physical and social. A word of caution, however: In redirecting attention to the political dimensions of sport, we should be careful not to deemphasize the physical aspect of sport, for it is this aspect that leads, ultimately, to an explanation of the relationship between sport and women's oppression.

Recent writings in feminist social theory have provided further correctives to the historical inattention to the political relevance of the body. Among these are Shulamith Firestone's *Dialectic of Sex* and Barbara Ehrenreich and Deirdre English's *For Her Own Good*. A recent essay that is particularly relevant to the thesis of this paper is Catherine MacKinnon's "Feminism, Marxism, Method and the State: An Agenda for Theory" (1982). In this essay, MacKinnon argues that sexuality is the primary social sphere of male power and that feminist political theory centers upon sexuality—"its social determination, daily construction, birth to death expression, and ultimately male control" (1982, p. 529). In MacKinnon's formulation,

> each element of the female gender stereotype is revealed as, in fact, *sexual*. Vulnerability means the appearance/reality of easy sexual access; passivity means receptivity and disabled resistance, enforced by trained physical weakness; softness means pregnability by something hard. Incompetence seeks help as vulnerability seeks shelter, inviting the embrace that becomes the invasion, trading exclusive access for protection . . . from the same access. (1982, p. 530)

And,

> One "becomes a woman"—acquires and identifies with the status of the female—not so much through physical maturation or inculcation into appropriate role behaviour as through the experience of sexuality: a complex unit of physicality, emotionality, identity and status affirmation. Sex as gender and sex as sexuality are thus defined in terms of each other, but it is sexuality that determines gender, not the other way around. (1982, p. 531)

MacKinnon's (1982) argument has considerable relevance to an analysis of the experience of women in sport. This relevance lies in the capacity of women's sporting practice to reflect and realize or challenge gendered social arrangements and their basis in sexuality. Moreover, it is argued that the potential of sport in this regard is quite powerful because of the particular place of the body and physicality to women's sporting experience.

Earlier reference was made to the degradation of women's sporting experience contained in Dancercise, Jazzercise, and "Twenty-Minute Workout" programs. Additional examples are publications that sexualize women's physical activity and fitness. These are not isolated or trivial instances of the mislabeling of practices as athletic or physical activity. They are meaningful realizations of the oppression of women through the objectification and commodification of their sexuality. They leave little doubt that these instances of women's experience with their bodies are defined by and directed toward the attainment of sexual attractiveness.

Sexualized fitness programs and publications are perhaps the most blatant recent forms of the oppression of women through the degradation of their physical activity. An important area of research is the investigation of how other forms of physical activity and sporting practice reinforce and realize patriarchal domination through the objectification and domination of women's physicality and sexuality. Lenskyj's (1983) analysis of the power exercised by "experts" during the early 20th century to define and limit girls' physical education in the interests of sexual and economic servitude to men is evidence of another such occurrence. More research is needed on this issue.

Although there is little theoretical or empirical work in the sociology of sport to guide and inform such study, relevant work from elsewhere is available. Recent writings on women and health (e.g., *For Her Own Good*; Gordon, 1977; Rich, 1977; Roberts, 1981) are concerned with issues that also affect women in sport: the objectification and commodification of women's bodies; male domination of institutions (the medical and health professions, sport governing bodies and associations, athletic departments in educational institutions); and an ideology that transforms biological differences between the sexes into the social inferiority of women. Consideration of applications and extensions of the literature on women and health to the analysis of women and sport provides an appropriate starting point for needed work in this area.

In conclusion, it is argued that the potential for sport to act as an agent of women's liberation, rather than their oppression, stems mainly from the opportunity that women's sporting activity affords them to experience their bodies as strong and powerful and free from male domination. If, as MacKinnon (1982, p. 537) argues, sexuality is the linchpin of gender inequality, then women's sporting practice can challenge gender inequality by challenging sexual stereotypes and patriarchal control of women's bodies.

NOTE

1. These percentages were calculated from information on Olympic events provided in Wallechinsky (1984).

REFERENCES

Boutilier, M.A. & SanGiovanni, L.C. (1983). *The sporting woman*. Champaign, IL: Human Kinetics.

Ehrenreich, B. & English, D. (1979). *For her own good*. Garden City, NY: Anchor Books.

Firestone, S. (1971). *The dialectic of sex*. New York: Bantam Books.

Fitness Canada. (1982). Canada's Fitness: Preliminary Findings of the 1981 Survey. Ottawa: Government of Canada.

Gordon, L. (1977). *Women's body, women's right*. New York: Penguin.

Gruneau, R. (1983). *Class, sports and social development*. Amherst, MA: University of Massachusetts Press.

Hall, M.A. (1981). Sport, Sex Roles and Sex Identity. The CRIAW Papers/Les Documents de l'CRIAF No. 81-01. Ottawa: The Canadian Research Institute for the Advancement of Women.

Hargreaves, J. (1982). Theorising sport: An introduction. In J. Hargreaves (Ed.), *Sport, culture and ideology*. London: Routledge & Kegan Paul.

Holmen, M.G., & Parkhouse, B.L. (1981). Trends in the selection of coaches for female athletes: A demographic inquiry. *Research Quarterly for Exercise and Sport*, **52**(1), 9-18.

Lenskyj, H. (1983). *The role of physical education in the socialization of girls in Ontario, 1890-1930*. Doctoral dissertation, Ontario Institute for Studies in Education, University of Toronto.

MacKinnon, C. (1982). Feminism, Marxism, method and the state: An agenda for theory. *Signs: Journal of Women in Culture and Society*, **7**(3), 515-544.

Rich, A. (1977). *Of woman born*. New York: Bantam.

Roberts, H. (1981). *Women, health and reproduction*. London: Routledge & Kegan Paul.

Sporting Goods Dealer. (1980). *The sporting goods directory*. Sporting News Publ. Co.

Stevenson, C. (1975). Socialization effects of participation in sport. *Research Quarterly*, **46**, 287-301.

Theriot, N. (1978). Toward a new sporting ideal: The women's division of the National Amateur Athletic Federation. *Frontiers*, **3**(1), 1-7.

Vickers, J., Inglis, S., Appleton, M., Bean, G., Bedingfield, W., Fromson, J., Knox, S., & Savoy, C. (1982). A Comparative Study of Relative Opportunities for Women in the C.I.A.U. (update 1981-82). Report Presented to the Canadian Interuniversity Athletic Union, Ottawa.

Wallechinsky, D. (1984). *The complete book of the Olympics*. Harmondsworth: Penguin.

Willis, P. (1982). Women in sport in ideology. In J. Hargreaves (Ed.), *Sport, culture and ideology*. London: Routledge & Kegan Paul.

Chapter 13

Subcultural Subversions:
Comparing Discourses on Sexuality in Men's and Women's Rugby Songs

Elizabeth E. Wheatley
University of California–Santa Cruz

The decades of the 1960s and 1970s gave rise to a growing sociological literature on sport and sport subcultures. A number of studies within this tradition examine occupational, avocational, and deviant sport subcultures (Donnelly, 1985; Loy, McPherson, & Kenyon, 1978) and insightfully identify various sport forms and practices as well as the particular cultures they generated. Despite these contributions to our understanding of the intersection of sport and culture, few accounts contextulize sport subcultures within the broader social relations surrounding them (Donnelly, 1984).

Especially lacking are accounts that address the important intersection of gender or gender relations with sport and its subcultures. There is a relative absence of analyses that considers how sport functions in the production, reproduction, and possible transformation of gender relations. Much past sociological work has accepted without question that sport and sport subcultures are male privileges and masculine activities and portrays predominantly male and masculinist cultural groups. The continued neglect and marginalization of women in subcultural accounts has led to theoretically inadequate conceptualizations of subcultures that both obscure and distort not only how women's social position

Note. We recognize that this chapter contains language that may be offensive to some readers. The chapter is included to permit scholarly analysis of the subject.

From " 'Stylistic Ensembles' on a Different Pitch: A Comparative Analysis of Men's and Women's Rugby Songs" by E. Wheatley, 1990, *Women and Language*, **13**(1), pp. 21-26. Copyright 1990 by University of Illinois at Urbana-Champaign. Adapted by permission.

and experience function in subcultures, but also how prevailing patterns of gender relations severely structure and limit women's social position and experience.

Further, few studies of sport subcultures have used the concept of "style" (Clarke, 1976; Hall & Jefferson, 1976) as a basis for understanding the emergence of subcultures and subcultural identities. Few have examined how particular sport subcultural styles intersect with, overlap, and are influenced by other subcultures and their corresponding styles.

This paper is a small part of a project (Wheatley, 1988) that traces various points of convergence and departure between men's and women's rugby subcultures. I also examine points of coincidence and difference between the women's rugby subculture and features of lesbian culture as articulated through, and marked by, their distinctive subcultural styles.[1] I offer a reading of selected rugby songs that demonstrates how such songs represent one feature of the men's rugby subcultural style that has been appropriated by and incorporated into the women's "stylistic ensemble" and is simultaneously transformed, translated, and reorganized to express different meanings. Effectively, the songs are reworked and reworded by the women in a way that enables a "homologous" fit between the songs and other features of the women's subcultural style, values, and everyday practices. In this capacity, the women's rugby subculture simultaneously reproduces and transforms various features of the men's rugby style, while establishing a cultural space in which lesbian identity, culture, and style are constructed, lived out, struggled over, and sometimes resisted in complex and contradictory ways.

STYLE

Generally, subcultures are created out of and are marked by "styles." A subcultural style consists of combinations of objects, fashion, and ritual used by a cultural group to communicate a distinct image and identity. Through the construction and expression of style, a subculture articulates difference from and resistance to the "mainstream" or dominant order. Clarke (1976) utilizes Lévi-Strauss's concept, bricolage, to explain the process by which styles are created through the appropriation of objects from other cultural realms and fitted into a form of collage that generates new meaning for the objects.

> Together object and meaning constitute a sign, and, within any one culture, such signs are assembled, repeatedly, into characteristic forms of discourse. However, when the bricoleur re-locates the significant object in a different position within that discourse, using the same overall repertoire of signs, or when that object is placed within a different total ensemble, a new discourse is constituted, a different message conveyed. . . . The generation of subcultural styles, then, involves differential selection from within the matrix of the existent. What happens is not

the creation of objects and meanings from nothing, but rather the *trans-formation* and *rearrangement* of what is given (and borrowed) into a pattern which carries a new meaning, its *translation* to a new context, and its adaptation. (pp. 177-178)

Thus, subcultural bricoleurs appropriate, adapt, and subvert a given discourse from one cultural context to another and thereby produce new meanings for it. In this capacity, the women's rugby group's song repertoire can qualify as a product of subcultural bricolage.

RUGBY AS A MALE PRESERVE

As a new discourse, the women's song ensemble borrows from yet transforms and rearranges features of the men's discourse, which constitutes rugby as a male preserve. Repeated accounts of the men's rugby subculture depict a male preserve in which members establish a male enclave and construct a particularly macho identity (Dunning, 1986; Hilliard, 1987) through engagement in a physically demanding sport involving daredevil pursuits, mischievous party practices, and overtly misogynist rituals.

Hilliard (1987) describes the macho presentational style as the central feature of men's rubgy identity. Men embracing this identity continuously degrade women, treating them as sexual objects. Hilliard suggests that the most popular pastimes of the members of the rugby tour group he studied included the sexual pursuit of women and the subsequent boasting of such sexual exploits. The men's rugby subcultural repertoire has been described by others who detail adventures involving vandalism, petty theft, and public nudity (Donnelly & Young, 1985; Sheard & Dunning, 1973).

Beyond this, Thomson (1977) describes men's behavior toward women in the subculture as "consistently offensive" (p. 147). Often referred to derogatorily as "rugger huggers," women who attend rugby parties are frequently victims of "butt biting" or "the sandwich," a ritual in which two men squeeze a woman between them while simulating sexual intercourse. Generally, women tend to be marginalized as spectators or objectified victims of such ritual.

Dunning (1986) suggests that women have always been welcome in the male preserve of rugby, inasmuch as they served their men food and drink and enthusi-astically applauded the men's sporting endeavors. As cooks, dance partners, or cheerleaders, however, women remain in subordinate positions relative to men in the subculture. The prevailing gender arrangements and social practices inher-ent to this form of rugby serve to reinforce and perpetuate male dominance and the masculine hegemony of the rugby subculture.

More recently, however, women have begun to challenge and undermine the taken-for-granted notion of rugby as a male preserve by taking up the sport themselves. Though in its earliest forms, women's rugby developed on the coat-tails of the men, it has shifted toward an increasingly separate and distinctively women's cultural form. Whereas the earliest players were frequently girlfriends or wives of the men and often relied upon the men to teach and encourage them, today's groups have become more exclusively enclaves of women, often independent of and requiring little or no tutelage from their male counterparts.

Rather than objectified and marginalized observers who must tolerate the humiliation and ridicule that indicate their position and status, women who play rugby have become increasingly independent of men and are primary participants whose identities are neither determined nor defined by men. Although the women's subculture has retained residual features of the men's rugby style, it has also imbued various practices and traditions with distinct meanings. My discussion focuses on the significance of rugby songs as discourses that occupy a pivotal space and perform an important function in this process.[2]

MEN'S MELODIES: SEXUAL INVENTIONS, VIOLATIONS, AND OBJECTIFICATIONS

Many of the men's rugby songs demonstrate a penchant for producing violent imagery of women as objectified through and victimized by their sexual anatomy and through heterosexual intercourse. Two songs of the men's subcultural repertoire that provide stark imagery of women as sexual objects of men's violation are "The Engineer's Song" and "The Ten Wise Men of Montana":

"The Engineer's Song"

An engineer told me before he died,
And I don't know if the bugger lied,
That he had a wife with a cunt so wide
That she could never be satisfied.

And so he built a prick of steel
Driven by a bloody great wheel,
Two brass balls all filled with cream,
And the whole bloody issue was driven by steam.

Round and round went the bloody great wheel
And in and out went the prick of steel
Until at last the maiden cried,
"Enough, enough, I'm satisfied!"

But this was a tale of the bitter bit:
There was no way of stopping it.
She was rent from cunt to tit
And the whole bloody issue was covered in shit.

(Thomson, 1977, p. 131-132)

"The Ten Wise Men of Montana"

There were ten wise men with knowledge quite fine—
To build a great cunt was their design.
From all of Montana they searched and they sought
To find the materials to build a great twat.

The first was an axe-man, whose swing was quite swift;
With double bit-axe, he made a great slit.
The second was a miner—with drill and with bore,
He bore and he bore and he made a great pore.

The third was a trapper quite short and quite stout;
With marten and beaver he lined it without.
The fourth was a tailor, quite tall and quite thin;
With finest red velvet he lined it within.

The fifth was a plumber who whistled with bliss;
With faucet and washer he made it to piss.
The sixth was a gourmet who worked with great haste;
He threw in a chicken to give it a taste.

The seventh was a fisherman who knew his job well;
With herring and kipper he made it to smell.
The eighth was a drummer with one extra skin;
He stretched it and tacked it and made a hymen.

The ninth was a doctor whose hands were quite small;
With ten pounds of vaseline he greased up the wall.
The tenth was a rabbi—that damned little runt—
He blessed it, he fucked it, he called it a CUNT!

(Thomson, p. 130-131)

"The Engineer's Song" includes several themes common to men's rugby ballads. First, the song demonstrates a fetish for features of the female anatomy—in this case, "cunts." Second, the song addresses men's insecurity about their incapacity to provide sexual satisfaction for women. In addition, the song shows an aggressive, physically abusive, graphically violent image of the sex act itself, often described in gory detail in men's rugby verse. For the engineer, providing pleasure for his wife in a mutual act of sexual sharing is less important than satisfying his own self-serving obsession with demonstrating sexual performance. He resorts to fabricating a machine to perform a sexual function that he is incapable of performing—providing his wife with a satisfying sexual experience. The vile disfigurement and demise of the woman is her punishment for failing to experience sexual pleasure with her husband.

"The Ten Wise Men of Montana" also reveals an obsession with what is termed "the cunt." In this case, the cunt begins as a "twat," which is an object of the imaginations and machinations of men from diverse walks of life who offer their knowledge and special skills in its production. The small-handed doctor carefully places the finishing touches on the virginal twat so that it can become a fully fledged and finally "fucked" cunt, an outcome of the rabbi's action upon and designation of it.

The song celebrates aggressive and exploitative versions of masculinity through highlighting the physically impressive feats of men of archetypically rugged outdoor occupations: axe-men, miners, trappers, and fishermen. Simultaneously, the song mocks the less overtly physical, nonmanual professional contributions of the thin tailor, the hurried and hasty gourmet, the small-handed doctor, and the little, runtlike rabbi. The song subtly derides these professional men of refinement, who are depicted as weaker and less impressive than their more virile counterparts. The nonmanual labor of these "refined" men serves as a cause for suspicion of their true masculinity. Nonetheless, all the men manage to cooperate in the production, use, and abuse of women's sexual anatomy, the cunt.

The song separates women's sexual anatomy from their humanity because the cunt is construed as an object of men's creation intended for men's pleasure. Effectively, the woman is no more than "A Vagina Surrounded by a Woman" (Vance, 1987). As a fully dehumanized object, manufactured, used, and abused by men, the cunt is featured in scores of men's rugby songs.

SEXUAL INVERSIONS:
RECLAIMING SEXUALITY THROUGH RUGBY VERSE

Whereas songs such as "The Engineer's Song" and "The Ten Wise Men of Montana" invoke images that are consistent with the masculinist status of rugby as a male perserve, depicting women as objects to be manufactured, manipulated, and acted upon by men, one of the women's songs that originated in "Coastal Town" paints a very different portrait:

"My Favorite Things"

I

Loose rucks and good fucks
And aunts that are crazy;
Girls that are horny
And guys that are lazy;

Good moves make good screws
For those one night flings—
These are a few of my favorite things.

Scrummies that tackle and backs that have hands
All come together to astonish the fans.
When the game's over the party begins—
That's when those studs think that we'll let them in.

When the prick grows, when the juice flows,
When he's feeling grand—
Just fart in his face, and tell him his place,
And that he can use his HAND!

II

Deep cigarette burns
And slight razor slashes;
Cum drops that dry on
My nose and my lashes;

Leather-clad partners
All tied up in strings—
These are a few of my favorite things.

Spike studded collars and partners with zippers,
Partners in bondage and women with clippers,
Silken restraining straps, joy anguished screams—
These are a few of my favorite things.

When the spurs dig,
When the whip cracks,
When I've got the crabs—
I simply remember my favorite things
And then I don't feel so bad.

Taken together, the two verses of the song illuminate the complex and contradictory character of the women's discourse. Each verse presents contrasting
images for and conveys different experiences of sexual practice and women's
sexuality. Sung to the tune of the popular song from "The Sound of Music,"
the first verse creates a social discourse that repositions and empowers women
in sexual relations and thereby reclaims and redefines women's sexuality. The
verse asserts that women's sexuality is primary and privileged over pervasive
versions of sexuality or sexual practice as desired by men. By indicating that
"girls that are horny" are among her favorite things, the subject/singer not
only implies that a sexually aroused woman in pursuit of sexual gratification is
appealing to her, but assigns women to an active sexual role. This is implied
further by the next line, which contends that "guys that are lazy" are among
her favorite things, too; this suggests that she prefers men who are sexually

passive over those who act in a sexually aggressive or conquering manner. The description in the following line, of "good moves" as another favorite thing suggests that the subject/singer is able to assume a sexually active role, which leads to "good screws" (i.e., a pleasureable sexual experience). Later, her stated appeal to "those one night flings" suggests that she *can* be promiscuous and is able to enjoy somewhat anonymous sexual encounters, or multiple sexual partners, while pursuing sex for pleasure without personal commitment.

After the party begins, the subject/singer asserts "that's when those studs think that we'll let them in." This not only implies refusing "those studs" admittance to the party, but suggests a sexual reading—that vaginal penetration by the "studs," though anticipated by them, will not be welcomed. The final stanza describes men's physiological response to sexual arousal and advises the listener to deny their requests outright by rejecting men's advances in a gaseous fashion while telling them what they can do. By showing the "stud" "his place" and telling him that "he can use his hand," the singer asserts that she is not interested in the man's sexual advance and that he can relieve his sexual arousal through masturbation.

The verse allows the repositioning of men and women in sexual relations and in sexual practice. By asserting that sexual gratification achieved by manual stimulation is preferred to that obtained by vaginal penetration by a "prick," the subject/singer places women's sexuality in the forefront, and women's desires over those of men. Such discourse challenges heterosexual ideology through demystifying and denaturalizing how women achieve sexual gratification. Additionally, it repositions women in heterosexual relations, thereby empowering them to dictate sexual procedure and to define and judge what qualifies as "good" in sexual practice.

The second verse, contrary to the first, conveys sado-masochistic imagery in which the woman assumes the submissive position while engaging in violent eroticism. Enslaved by and within this form of sexual domination, the defaced and diseased woman screams out in joyful anguish, certain that such an experience is among her favorite things.

Though both verses place primary importance on deriving pleasure and excitement from sexual practice, each endorses different strategies for achieving it. Overall, the song represents a calculated and deliberate effort to disrupt and antagonize the audience with stark sexual imagery and language. Once used by heterosexually identified women to shock heterosexual men's audiences with its obscene and brutal verses, the song is now employed by lesbian and heterosexual women in rugby. In either case, the song serves as a form of retaliation and rebuttal to the men's songs and stands as proof that women, like their male counterparts, not only know how to play rugby, but are equally adept at producing bawdy verses. Though the song may be differently interpreted and intended by heterosexual and lesbian women, it nevertheless produces vivid imagery that matches the most disturbing of men's songs while confronting and alarming male and female audiences alike.

One song in the women's repertoire, "Please Eat Me", manages to combine both functions of the previous song. Its purpose is both to shock and to reposition women in sexual relations so as to empower them to dictate sexual practice:

"Please Eat Me"

You start from the very beginning—
It's a very fine place to start.
When you sing you begin with Do Re Me
And when you fuck, you begin with PLEASE EAT ME!
Please Eat Me, Please Eat Me . . . (Echo)

P   A Penis, a too limp penis,
L   The Lick that gets it up,
E   Erect—it's my turn now;
A   All done? It's just not fair!
S . . o it's time to lick my clit
E . . ven if it takes all night;

EAT ME now or else get out—
And that will bring us back to PLEASE EAT ME!

After providing her male partner with sexually arousing oral stimulation, the subject/singer waits her turn for sexual pleasure, anticipating his reciprocal duties. When she is not satisfied through his conventional means, she orders him to proceed with alternative techniques "even if it takes all night."

Another song empowers women relative to men by depicting both prostitution and "gang bangs" (gang rapes) to be liberating to women. "I Don't Want To Be a Housewife" is highly popular among those in "Coastal Town" and has inspired T-shirts and sweat shirts that assert the same claim.

"I Don't Want to Be a Housewife"

I don't want to be a housewife;
I just want to be a whore.
I'd rather turn tricks involving footlong pricks—
Housework is such a bore, oh blimey.

I don't want to mop his fucking floors up,
I don't want to cook his fucking food;
And if I'm getting laid, I should be getting paid,
But as it is I'm only getting screwed.

Monday I walk the streets of Stratford,
Tuesday I beat some meat in Wales,
Wednesday on the Thames I lay them ten by ten,
And Thursday's saved for all that's female;
Friday's for buggars, whips, and hand jobs,
Saturdays are gang bangs occupied,
And Sunday at the palace, I'll mount my royal phallus
And take his heinous for a regal ride, oh blimey.

I don't want to be a housewife;
I just want to be a whore.
I'd rather turn some tricks involving footlong pricks—
Housework is such a bore, oh blimey.

I don't want to have a batch of babies.
I'll leave this fucking flat this very day
And walk the streets of Coastal Town—
Merry, merry Coastal Town—
And fornicate my fucking life away.

In the song, the subject/singer insists that she would prefer to service men with sex than to be subjected to the tedious duties of housewife who is exploited by her male partner. Effectively, prostitution and gang bangs are considered liberatory and enabling to women who find housework, domestic labor, childbearing, and childrearing highly oppressive and constraining.

SIMILAR SONGS, DIFFERENT MESSAGES

Though the preceding songs are unique to either the men's or women's respective repertoires, other songs are common to both groups. Certain songs have been reorganized by the women to suggest a new, preferred reading, whereas others have been left unchanged. A song sung similarly by both men and women is "If I Were the Marrying Kind":

"If I Were the Marrying Kind"

If I were the marrying kind—
But thank the lord, I'm not, sir—
The kind of woman I would marry
    (Some women substitute *man* for *woman*)
Would be a rugby _____.

In the women's version, sexual preference is signalled through pronoun choice in the third line. Also significant in the song is how the women view marriage.

The women seem to recognize that marriage is not necessarily a heterosexual and heterosexist institution, although it has been historically constructed as such within a capitalist patriarchal order. Wittingly or unwittingly, the women suggest that marriage can be appropriated and remade into something that can have meaning for homosexual couples as well. Both men and women fill in the blank in the fourth line by naming an object or player's position pertinent to rugby. Depending on the word selected, the verse that follows is suggestive of the sexual practices that the couple would perform if married. For example, if the object "goal line" was named, the verse might read:

> Cause she'd get laid, I'd get laid
> We'd both get laid together
> We'd be alright in the middle of the night
> Getting laid together.

Since the lines on the field, and in this case the goal line, get "laid" down prior to a game, the players can use it as a symbolic resource for its sexually suggestive connotations.

Another song that is shared and sung similarly by both groups is "Gang Bang":

"Gang Bang"

> I like to gang bang, I always will
> Because the gang bang gives me such a thrill.
> When I was younger and in my prime
> I used to gang bang all the time.
> But now I'm older and getting gray,
> I only gang bang once a day.

(Thomson, p. 131)

The chorus is followed by ever-evolving verses that are invented in the process of singing the song. Here, the effusive enthusiasm expressed by both men and women is problematic. At first glance, it seems understandable that men would enthusiastically vocalize their verse, as men are more typically participants in such acts and seem more likely to experience pleasure through their involvement in gang bangs. As women who define themselves independently of men, the women rugby players' enthusiastic singing of the song seems ironic. Such enthusiasm seems to express their approval of and consent toward women's objectification and use by pleasure-seeking men. Yet, their eager enthusiasm for the song might also be interpreted as an articulation of women's superior sexual powers in their capacity to experience multiple or frequent orgasms. Rather than objects or victims sexually abused in gang bangs, such women might perceive themselves as using gang bangs for their own continuous sexual pleasure. An experience of exceedingly violent sexual abuse and objectification is pleasurably redefined through expression of women's sexual superiority and advantage.

SONGS OF RIDICULE, SONGS OF CELEBRATION: SPEAKING OF HOMOSEXUALITY

Beyond song variations based on separate gendered experiences, a noteworthy distinction between the two song repertoires exists in the treatments of and references to homosexuality. Typically, in men's rugby verse, homosexuality is mocked and ridiculed. One song that conveys this is "For We're All Queers Together":

"For We're All Queers Together"

For we're all queers together—
Excuse us while we go upstairs.
Yes, we're all queers together;
That's why we go 'round in pairs.

(Thomson, p. 132)

Perhaps by confronting the subject of homosexuality in the open, the men hope to quell any suspicions about their sexual preference (Thomson, 1977). By playing the aggressive, intimately physical game, particularly when grasping hold of one another in the scrum (suggesting "male bonding"), the men may perceive that they are "suspect." Perhaps they ease their concern about the potential of being labelled *homosexual* by mocking homosexuals through seeming to openly admit that they are "queers" (Sheard & Dunning, 1973). Conversely, the women's frequent proclamation through lyric messages of their homosexual preference directly confronts and oversteps gendered sexual boundaries.

The women's preference for lesbianism also "comes out" in selected verses of the song, "The Twelve Days of Rugby," which draws on themes from the men's version, "The Twelve Days of Training," sung to the tune of "The Twelve Days of Christmas":

"The Twelve Days of Rugby"

On the first day of rugby
My true love gave to me . . .
  1. A hand job in a soft bush
  2. Two bathroom doors
  4. Four French whores
  5. Five pubic hairs
 11. Eleven lesbians loving

"The Twelve Days of Training"

On the first day of training
My C.O. gave to me
1. A pamphlet on V.D.
2. Two shithouse doors
4. Four fucking fools
5. Five fairies
7. Seven severed scrotums

(Thomson, p. 132)

Though the women celebrate lesbian practice and preference, the men mock homosexuality. In "The Twelve Days of Training," men sing "five fairies" while producing exaggerated hand gestures to invoke the stereotypic image of effeminacy frequently used to ridicule homosexual men (Thomson, 1977).

Another song that the women sing, which celebrates rather than condemns or ridicules expressions of sexuality that deviate from the heterosexual norm, is "Bestiality's Best." The song suggests imaginative possibilities for experiencing sexuality other than standard sexual intercourse between men and women and also produces a shock effect for unsuspecting listeners. "Bestiality's Best" advocates this conventionally considered, outrageous sexual practice as superior to all others:

"Bestiality's Best"

chorus
Bestiality's best, girls, bestiality's best.
Don't waste your time with the rest
'Cause bestiality's best!

verse
Intercourse with a horse, girls,
Intercourse with a horse;
Intercourse with a horse
'Cause bestiality's best!

Other verses include:
Sixty-nine with a porcupine,
This-and-that with a cat,
In the dark with a lark, etc.

Already considered deviant by traditionalists, a consequence of their frequently pronounced lesbian identities, singers proclaim bestiality as an invigorating experience that should be fully explored and thoroughly enjoyed. Overstepping social constraints and ignoring any physical ones, singers advocate the pursuit of sexual pleasure through "intercourse with a horse," "sixty-nine with a porcupine," "this-and-that with a cat," or any other nonprocreative sexual activity with a multiplicity of species. Imaginative and enthusiastic participants add to and invent verses as they sing along, so quite literally "anything goes" in this song of bestial sexuality. Though it is doubtful that they engage in such unconventional practices, their eager proclamations of the superiority of bestiality to all other sexual practices signals their inventive, open-minded, and nonjudgmental approach to sexuality, sexual relations, and sexual practice.

THE MULTIPLICITY OF MEANINGS

The various readings I provide are not intended to represent the authoritative readings for the women's rugby songs. I offer what I consider to be the preferred readings or dominant meanings of the songs among those who regularly sing them. Different singers and audiences will produce different meanings for them depending upon their distinctive experiences within the women's rugby subculture. Hence, there is no single reading or essential meaning to be derived directly from the text. The songs might even have different meanings for the same person at different times or in front of different audiences. When singing in front of male comrades, heterosexual teams, or lesbian-identified teams, the singers may have different motives for, and different thoughts about, the verses they vocalize. In front of men, the purpose may be simply to shock, whereas in front of teams with heterosexually identified members, the motivation may be a desire to initiate unsuspecting newcomers through this exuberant exposure to rugby culture.

Additionally, songs may produce different meanings for those players differently positioned with respect to sexual identity or their degree of experience in the subculture. "If I Were the Marrying Kind" is an example of a song in which lesbian and heterosexually identified women insert different words at critical points to convey their respective sexual preferences. Yet, some heterosexually identified women sing the song in the same way that lesbian-identified women do in order to avoid asserting heterosexual privilege.

Effectively the context in which the songs are sung is crucial to how particular meanings are both collectively and individually negotiated and experienced. What is more, the singers and audience often interact in ways that determine not only what songs get sung, but also how meanings are produced and transformed within the songs by singers and audience alike.

WOMEN'S RUGBY AS CULTURAL RESISTANCE

Analysis of these and other songs suggests that rugby as a sport form and as a cultural event represents an experience with highly different meanings for men and women. For men, rugby offers a social space to act and be supermasculine. Courage and strength are constantly called for on the pitch, whereas boisterous beer drinking is required at the party. Songs for sexists and songs of sexism are shared by all while women watch passively from their appropriate place.

The social arrangements and corresponding repertoire of songs that pertain to men's rugby reinforce the naturalized view of sport as masculine territory. Simultaneously, these social arrangements and the practices that coincide with them reflect and reproduce the ideology of men as athletes and sexual conquerers and of women as cheerleaders and passive sexual objects to be exploited and enjoyed by men. Women's rugby departs from men's rugby by creating a version of sport in general (and of rugby, specifically) that provides an alternative to male-centered, -defined, -controlled, and -practiced sport.

Eric Dunning (1986) demonstrates the recurrent theme of men's rugby songs as discourses that convey a hostile yet fearful attitude toward women and the sex act. He suggests that such songs as ''The Engineer's Song'' symbolically express, and thus reduce, men's fear of women and women's increasing social power.

Curiously, the fear and perceived threat expressed through this discourse is *exploited* by women. Through open announcement and celebration of lesbianism, many women's songs symbolically express the social and sexual irrelevancy of men.

Other songs reciprocate in a manner that mimics the men's shocking and lewd verse while reproducing the sexist and misogynist features of the men's lyrics. Yet, in this new context, these lyrics are transformed into discourses that express a woman-defined, -determined, and -dominated sexuality, which often involves lesbian identification. Such lyrics celebrate and promote women's active desire for and aggressive pursuit of sexual pleasure while explicitly describing a wide range of sexual possibilities.

The women's version of rugby disrupts the male, heterosexual hegemony of the rugby subculture by exposing female physical capability in a typically male enclave, while openly expressing a distinct identity and lifestyle through its social proclivities. The women's rugby style challenges patriarchal ideology in sport and leisure and in social and sexual relations. Through this means, the women are responding to and resisting features of the gender and sexual oppression that they experience in their daily lives. The subculture enables its participants to cultivate alternative sporting, social, and sexual identities through violating and disrupting socially dictated gender prescriptions.

PROTEST OR PLEASURE?: CONTRADICTORY TENSIONS

Though women construct a multiplicity of resistant cultural practices through their appropriation and rearticulation of men's rugby discourse, several compelling issues remain. First, a definitive and final statement as to the significance of such resistant practices is neither desirable nor likely to do justice to the complexities and contradictions that characterize women's rugby as a subcultural form and social practice. The rugby style, including the song repertoire, is not unanimously endorsed, agreed upon, or settled. Instead, the songs (and other features of the women's rugby style) are lived out and experienced in contradictory ways. The songs and the singing rituals are sometimes as unsettling to the rugby group as they are unsettled by the group.[3]

Second, the resistance is largely temporal. Restraints imposed by time and space clearly limit the visibility of their resistant style. Off the field and after the party, many of the women return to the "real world" and live out identities that often differ dramatically from the style they construct and live out in rugby. Because they are both primary producers and primary consumers of this discourse—performers of and audience for the songs—it is difficult to claim that such women disrupt or dismantle mainstream sporting or social relations beyond a "localized" or even "hyper-localized" level (Grossberg, 1986).

Finally, our interpretations of and responses to the women's rugby songs and style depend on our particular vision for social change as well as our theoretical understanding about how women generally, and lesbians particularly, are socially positioned and variously oppressed. Though some may condemn the group for mimicking and reproducing the atrocities of "male" sport and sexuality, others may offer an appraisal of the song repertoire as an instance of counterhegemonic resistance to heterosexist, male-dominated sport and sexuality.

Those who endorse what is often termed a cultural feminist position (Alcoff, 1988; Echols, 1983; Segal, 1987) may find the femininities and sexualities performed or advocated by the women in rugby deplorable.[4] The social practices and tendencies of rugby players are incompatible with the cultural feminist vision for social change and severely contradict and challenge basic cultural feminist tenets about gender difference, sexuality, and lesbianism. From the cultural feminist perspective, women rugby players may appear "unliberated" and "male-identified" (Echols, 1983) as a consequence of their reenacting a violent, aggressive, competitive sport form while promoting the promiscuous and aggressive pursuit of sexual pleasure in a way that mimics "male" tendencies. The women's rugby group's aggressive and outspoken articulation of sexual desire, promotion of promiscuity, and celebration of a multiplicity of ways for experiencing and experimenting with sex stand in direct contradiction not only to the cultural feminist assumption that women's sexuality is inherently more spiritual than sexual, but also to cultural feminists' desexualized views of lesbian relationships as egalitarian affectional bonds bewteen women (Echols, 1983). In the view of cultural feminists, women rugby players construct a distorted version of male-identified and -defined sport and sexuality and thereby reveal their lack of any form of feminist consciousness.

Other feminists may view the group differently. For example, those I would label "antiessentialists," or social constructionists, are committed to and preoccupied with illuminating and challenging cultural practices that subordinate women through constructing and reproducing ideologies of gender and sexual difference.[5] From this perspective, the resistance cultivated by and lived out through women's rugby may be interpreted as a challenge to commonsense beliefs about women's essential "difference" from men. Effectively, women's interest and involvement in rugby serve as proof that women can be physically aggressive and highly competitive and are capable of both withstanding pain and inflicting pain upon others. The rugby players' social activities can be seen as violations of common conventions for "appropriately feminine" behavior; engagement in the heavy, competitive drinking that accompanies the profoundly profane songs shows that women can be as boisterous and obnoxious as their male counterparts. Finally, women rugby players demonstrate that some women, like men, may seek and derive pleasure through active, aggressive expressions of sexual fantasy and pursuits of sexual experience.

Social constructionists may applaud the fact that the women's rugby group rearranges features of the men's rugby style and appropriates them to their own ends. In this fashion, the women transform not only features of men's rugby but also the gender and sexual relations constituted through rugby. Thus, women not only transform the form of rugby, they also change its fundamental meaning and content. This can be viewed positively as marking a moment of struggle, and an effort, whether conscious or unconscious, to resist and transform oppressive gender and sexual relations and prescriptions. In this capacity, women can be seen as challenging male and heterosexual dominance in sporting, social, and sexual relations.

As feminists, variously and multiply identified and positioned, our task is not to judge women's rugby practices as inherently good or bad. Neither should we dismiss their resistance as "male-identified" or "politically incorrect" behavior nor naively offer a romanticist appraisal, celebrating such resistance as an idealized reponse to patriarchal oppression. The important question is not whether their resistance is self-consciously inspired or carefully calculated counterhegemonic, "revolutionary" practice, but to what extent such resistant practices contribute to or cultivate a critical, feminist sensibility among these women. Regardless of their degree of feminist consciousness, these women have constructed an alternative to male, heterosexually dominated sport and sexuality. We must understand how their practices can be liberating and empowering while being fun and pleasurable. At the same time, we must recognize the limits of such cultural resistance for dismantling social structures that systematically position and oppress all women in diverse ways.

By examining cultural struggles, such as those articulated through women's rugby, we enhance our understanding of power and gender relations and the limits of women's resistance to our patriarchally dominated social order. Simultaneously, we can begin to assess what potential sport holds for transforming the social order.

REFERENCES

Alcoff, L. (1988). Cultural feminism versus post-structuralism: The identity crisis in feminist theory. *Signs: Journal of Women in Culture and Society,* **13**(3), 405-436.

Clarke, J. (1976). Style. In S. Hall & T. Jefferson (Eds.), *Resistance through rituals: Youth subcultures in post-war Britain* (pp. 175-191). London: Hutchinson.

Donnelly, P. (1984, July). Sport subcultures: A new agenda for research. Paper presented at the 1984 Scientific Congress, Eugene, Oregon.

Donnelly, P. (1985). Sport subcultures. *Exercise and Sport Science Reviews*, **13**, 539-578.

Donnelly, P., & Young, K. (1985). Reproduction and transformation of cultural forms in sport: A contextual analysis of rugby. *International Review for the Sociology of Sport,* **20**(1-2), 19-37.

Dunning, E. (1986). Sport as a male preserve: Notes on the social sources of masculine identity and its transformations. *Theory Culture and Society,* **3**(1), 79-90.

Echols, A. (1983). The new feminism of yin and yang. In A. Snitow, C. Stansell, & S. Thompson (Eds.), *Powers of desire: The politics of sexuality* (pp. 439-459). New York: Monthly Review Press.

Grossberg, L. (1986). Is there rock after punk? *Critical Studies in Mass Communication,* **3**(1), 50-74.

Hall, S., & Jefferson, T. (1976). *Resistance through rituals: Youth subcultures in post-war Britain.* London: Hutchinson.

Hilliard, D. (1987). The rugby tour: Construction and enactment of social roles in a play setting. In G. Fine (Ed.), *Meaningful play, playful meaning* (pp. 173-192). Champaign, IL: Human Kinetics.

Loy, J., McPherson, B., & Kenyon, G. (1978). *Sport and social systems.* Reading, MA: Addison-Wesley.

Segal, L. (1987). *Is the future female? Troubled thoughts on contemporary feminism.* New York: Peter Bedrick Books.

Sheard, K., & Dunning, E. (1973). The rugby football club as a type of "male preserve": Some sociological notes. *International Review of Sport Sociology,* **8**(3-4), 5-24.

Sherry, J. (1980). Verbal aggression in rugby ritual. In H. Schwartzmann, (Ed.), *Play and culture* (pp. 139-150). Champaign, IL: Leisure Press.

Thomson, R. (1977). *Sport and deviance: A subcultural analysis.* Unpublished doctoral dissertation, University of Alberta, Edmonton, Canada.

Vance, C. (1987, May). The Meese Commission on pornography, 1985-1986: A vagina surrounded by a woman. Public lecture, University of Illinois, Urbana–Champaign, IL.

Wheatley, E. (1988). A women's rugby subculture: Contesting on the "wild" side of the pitch. Unpublished master's thesis, University of Illinois, Urbana–Champaign, IL.

NOTES

1. My analysis is based on evidence gathered as a team member and participant observer with three university-based women's rugby teams over a period

extending from February 1986 to January 1989. The teams, which I refer to as "Twin City," "Midwest City," and "Coastal Town" respectively, are located in the midwestern and west coastal United States.

2. Elsewhere (Wheatley, 1988) I provide a more elaborate ethnographic description and analysis that highlights the intersection of the women's rugby subculture with both the men's rugby subculture and gay and lesbian subcultures. Apart from the rugby songs, features of overlap and difference between the women's rugby subculture and both the men's rugby subculture and gay and lesbian subcultures are articulated through fashion, humor, language, ritual, and numerous traditions.

3. For example, not all women in the subculture view the songs positively. Some dissociate from and object to the singing and drinking traditions characteristic of rugby parties. Some view the rugby parties as detrimental to and incompatible with their desire to become serious athletes. Others are less willing to sing the songs in front of heterosexually identified teams or men in attendance at rugby functions. Finally, some contend that the song singing tradition is less popular than it once was and has declined in recent years with the increasingly competitive and serious attitudes of some athletes.

4. Though there is no fully systematic rendition of this theoretical and political position, cultural feminists generally seek to promote and celebrate women's special virtues and qualities, which they view as distinct from and preferable to men's values and practices. (i.e., Men and women are inherently different from one another.) Cultural feminists seek to cultivate and preserve rather than eradicate what they view as essential gender difference (Alcoff, 1988; Echols, 1983). Effectively, this line of theory celebrates what it considers the superior virtue, sensitivity, humanism, pacifism, and nurturance of women, while denouncing the aggressive, competitive, violent tendencies it considers inherent to maleness (Segal, 1987). This position envisions and aspires to a "world of women," which seeks to cultivate and promote "women's special nature" (Echols, 1983).

5. From this perspective, the differences between men and women are seen as culturally constructed and historically shifting rather than "natural," monolithic, fixed, or biologically determined. A major feature of this feminist project is to resist, challenge, and subvert culturally produced notions of femininity, masculinity, and the "natural" difference between women and men, which maintain and reproduce women's subordination.

ACKNOWLEDGMENTS

I especially want to thank Paula Treichler, John Loy, Jeremy Howell, Cheryl Cole, Susan Birrell, Mike Messner, Simon Jones, and Toni Bruce for their thoughtful and constructive commentaries on this paper. I'd also like to thank the rugby players from coast to coast who helped out with the songs—most notably Betsy Hill and Val Scott.

Chapter 14

Challenging the Hegemony:
New Zealand Women's Opposition to Rugby and the Reproduction of a Capitalist Patriarchy

Shona M. Thompson
Murdoch University, Western Australia

RUGBY IN NEW ZEALAND AND THE TOUR OF 1981

The sport of rugby football in New Zealand has been interpreted and documented as being the country's major passion and religion (Laidlaw, 1973; Thompson, 1975; Pearson, 1979; Phillips, 1980). It is played only by men. Because New Zealand rugby teams had regularly competed against South Africa, New Zealand's sporting policies and practices had become an international concern. It is not the intention of this paper to detail the controversies surrounding previous sporting links (see Hain, 1971; Thompson, 1964; Thompson, 1975; Pearson, 1979). It is reasonable to state however, that over the years many New Zealanders had become embarrassed by the reputation gained of covertly supporting apartheid, and increasingly angry at the Rugby Union's insistence on continued competition with South Africa.

In 1981 a rugby team selected to represent South Africa (the 'Springboks'), was invited by the Rugby Union and came to New Zealand for a 57 day tour. The question of rugby's importance then became of prime concern and caused conflict to an extent never before seen in New Zealand. The protest against this

From "Challenging the Hegemony: New Zealand Women's Opposition to Rugby and the Reproduction of a Capitalist Patriarchy" by S.M. Thompson, 1988, *International Review for the Sociology of Sport*, **23**(3), pp. 205-212. Copyright 1988 by Oldenbourgverlag. Reprinted by permission.

visit was huge and as the tour continued protesters became more committed and determined. Eventually confrontations with the pro-tour rugby supporters and the police resulted in disorder and violence which shocked all sectors of New Zealand society.

One aspect which differentiated opposition to this tour from those previous was the extremely high profile played by women in the protest action. The protests were overtly against racial discrimination in South Africa. But women, it is argued were mobilised in their opposition by a compelling frustration with and resentment of the sport of rugby. Yet to them it was more than simple opposition to a sport played and administered exclusively by men. It was a challenge to many of the symbols and values that have been institutionalised in rugby, to the gender relations it perpetuates, and to the power invested in the sport which was clearly demonstrated by the events of the 1981 tour. Such power, with a material and ideological base in patriarchy, capitalism and white supremacy, is a source of exclusion, subordination and oppression of New Zealand women.

RUGBY AND PATRIARCHY

Hartmann's definition of patriarchy describes well the conditions in which rugby has thrived. She sees it as ". . . a set of social relations between men, which have a material base, and which . . . establish or create interdependence and solidarity among men that enables them to dominate women" (1981:14). Millet (1970:5) sees the evidence of our patriarchal society in the fact that every avenue of power, ". . . military, industry, technology, universities, science, political offices, finance and even the coercive force of the police" is in male hands. The major components of patriarchy as women experience them are outlined as male control of institutions, decision making, female labour and sexuality, as well as homophobia, male expressed or threatened violence and an ideology of male superiority (Hartman, 1981). There are many examples of how rugby has contributed through these components to patriarchal power and control of New Zealand women.

Thomson, studying the rugby sub-culture in the U.S.A. concluded that rugby players' ". . . behaviour towards women, both within and outside the subculture, can only be regarded as consistently offensive" (1977:147). Women involved in rugby circles as wives, girlfriends and supporters are systematically submitted to ritualised harassment, mostly with highly sexual overtones and are coerced into being passive, adjusting, accepting and being 'good sports' in the end. It is legitimate to consider rugby in North America as subcultural. However in New Zealand, where it is decidedly dominant culture the 'woman as object' attitude has been similarly documented as prevalent (Laidlaw, 1973; Phillips, 1987). There are slight cultural differences but the central theme of mocking, objectifying and defiling women and homosexuals has, as described by Sheard and Dunning

(1973), spread throughout the world in very similar forms wherever rugby is played as part of what is considered 'the rugby tradition.'

In spite of this, the domestic labour of New Zealand women has always serviced rugby. One is able to cite an almost endless list of chores traditionally done by women for the benefit of the men and boys who play rugby. It would include providing meals, catering for visiting teams, shopping for, laundering, mending and ironing team uniforms, transporting sons to practises and games, waiting on the sideline, attending to injured bodies and egos. Baker (1981) and Deem (1982) have both written of the ways in which women's domestic labour services men's leisure, usually at the expense of their own. The socialisation of New Zealand women into their roles of mothers, sisters, wives, and daughters has been very powerfully influenced by an ideology which accepts and glorifies rugby. The 1981 Springbok tour however, forced this acceptance into question. For many women, the first political step taken in opposition to the power of rugby was in their own domestic realm, opposing the men in their own families. One organised protest group (called WAR, ''Women Against Rugby'') deliberately used the withdrawal of domestic labour servicing rugby as a political tool. The huge and vehement divisions that went through New Zealand during the tour can be partly explained by the factions that appeared in many individual households which were frequently split down gender lines. Chapple (1984) recounts many incidents during the tour where the men were inside the stadium watching the rugby game whilst their female relatives and friends were outside marching with the protesters, and sometimes being severely batoned by the Police Riot Squads.

Women's reproductive labour has also been of concern to rugby men. For one, the production of strong healthy sons to play rugby was an important commodity. The patriarchal power of Government, debating the abortion issue in 1937 justified their argument against abortion in terms of protecting potential male babies who were likely to become rugby players, especially ''All Blacks,'' the National representative team. Brookes (1981:130) recounts the debate during which the Parliamentary speaker emphasised this point by stating,

> Tomorrow the Springboks play the All Blacks in Auckland. I wonder
> how many of the 55,000 people who will be present watching the match
> will realise that during the actual period of play . . . one child, perhaps
> a potential All Black, will have been willfully destroyed in the womb
> of its mother.

Decisions concerning women's fertility and reproductive labour were thus made and rationalised by men in relation to their importance to the future of an exclusively male sport.

RUGBY AND CAPITALISM

Hartmann (1981) suggests that society can best be understood when we recognize it is organised in capitalistic and patriarchial ways, as in a necessary partnership.

They must co-exist to reproduce the means of production (a continued work force and the social conditions of work) as well as to produce goods and accumulate wealth. Men therefore have a material interest in women's continued oppression.

New Zealand's economy has traditionally been based on agriculture. Capital interests and rural interests were one and the same, and the connection with rugby was implicit. Rugby's deemed importance to international trade was highlighted in 1971 when the National Government withdrew what was then Rhodesia from the itinerary of a pending rugby tour. The Prime Minister at the time reasoned Rhodesia's inclusion would be "practically worthless, since sanctions against the Smith regime rule out the possibilities of trading benefits" (Hain, 1971:94).

The relationship of sport to capitalism has been explored by John Hargreaves (1982) who gives for example, the training of a docile labour force and the development of a marketable commodity for profit as two of the 'uses' of sport in a capitalist society. The State, Hargreaves argues, as a representative of capital interests, is actively complicit in these uses.

Throughout New Zealand's history a huge proportion of women, in their unpaid positions as farmer's wives have been working both on the farms and in maintaining the rural family unit, reproducing the conditions of the country's agricultural production. At the same time the control of government and decision making remained with the men. Here too, the country's dominant sport has contributed to that control. It would not be over simplifying the relationship to suggest that rugby has traditionally made a major contribution to the social relations between males that have created and supported the fabric of New Zealand's economic and political structure. A huge network of sporting competition and social cameraderie spreads throughout the country linking schools, communities, rural districts, businesses, and provinces. This proliferation of hundreds of clubs functions as a hierarchial administrative structure which is prestigious, lucrative and highly interrelated with other institutions (Waring, 1985). The 'gentlemen' roots of rugby still feature, and it has been traditionally strong in all male private schools attended by the sons of major land owners. The power structures of New Zealand—the Government, the directors of the economy, the Police and the Army have for the most part played and supported rugby together, which has provided a central and binding focus. Women do not belong to the rugby network, nor are they often found in positions of power. When present, frequently they are silenced. In 1981, when a female member of Parliament spoke out against the rugby tour and the country's relations with South Africa, she was prohibited from speaking further in the Parliamentary debates (Waring, 1985).

WHITE SUPREMACY

Most documentaries of the tour noted the contrast between the predominantly male rugby crowds and the large number of women among the protesters

(Barrowman, 1981; Shears and Gidley, 1981; Chapple, 1984). However, it was obvious at the time that women were prominent not just in numbers. They played a major role in leadership of the organised opposition. Coney commented (1981:8),

> New Zealanders watching the latest episode of the Tour Troubles un-folding on their tellies can't have missed the fact that marshalling the marches, facing the batons, and directing the invasions of jet planes, motorways and rugby pitches are women. For women, and especially Maori women, form the backbone of the anti-tour movement.

Many accounts by the protesters were characterised by a very high conscious-ness of the issues involved. One woman is quoted in Hall as saying (1981:10), ''How could I not march? I'm female, black, lesbian and a feminist. What other reason do I need?'' White supremacy was a major issue. On the face of it, opposition on the tour was concerned about sporting contact with white supremist South Africa. It had the effect however, of focusing attention on white supremacy at home. Maori New Zealanders make up approximately 20% of the population but are over represented in lower socioeconomic groups, unemployment and poor health statistics and prisons. For them, the issue of opposition to apartheid highlighted their own inequality. But the tour also split the Maori community along gender lines. Evans (in Coney, 1981) explains that Maori men had more to lose over stopping the tour; for them rugby had always been a bargaining ground. In an earlier analysis of sporting contacts with South Africa, Thompson explained (1964:40), ''It is doubtful whether there is any aspect of life in which the reputation of the Maori stands higher in European estimation than on the rugby field.'' Throughout the tour many Maori men found themselves in extremely contradictory positions, particularly those who were members of the teams playing against the visiting South Africans, or those in the police Riot Squads.

SPORT, ORDER AND CHANGE

Whereas the tour had a divisory effect on Maoris, and men of all classes, it brought women together. However the presence in such large numbers of females among the protesters seemed to have particularly incensed both the pro-tour rugby fans and the police. Chapple's (1984) account of the aftermath of a game cancelled at the last minute due to the success of protest action, describes how women were singled out for attack by raging rugby fans. The police too, appeared frequently to deliberately choose female victims in their baton charges (Aitken and Noonan, 1981). The impression given was that the challenge by women to rugby and to 'law and order' was more unforgivable than a similar challenge by men, and more deserving of violent control mechanisms.

We have been reminded by John Hargreaves that ''. . . one cannot begin to understand the structure and meaning of sport without also appreciating that it is intimately tied up with conceptions and evaluations of social order'' (1982:33). Sport symbolises an idealised version of that social order. As such, an attack on sport can be viewed as threatening to society itself. From this perspective, Hargreaves argues for the complex and previously under-rated influence of dominant class power in the institution of sport. He cites historical developments of sport in Britain showing a pattern of policies and actions more accurately evaluated as impositions from above, from the organised interests of those powerful. Further,

> Though these policies and actions were and are, no doubt sincerely felt to be in keeping with the needs of society as a whole, they involve the bringing to bear of pressure on subordinate groups: pressure ranging from outright coercion and the use of material incentives to moral exhortation. (John Hargreaves, 1982:38)

Such pressure has traditionally surrounded the perpetuation of rugby in New Zealand and was particularly obvious during the 1981 Springbok tour. During the tour however, the organised interests of dominant power, concentrated in the inter-related patriarchal structures of the rugby administration, National Party government, agriculturally based capitalism and the state power enforcement agencies of the police and the army, came into conflict with emerging conceptions of a different social order.

Social order theory has been criticised for its failure to address oppositional sporting ideologies (Jennifer Hargreaves, 1982) and for its elimination of consciousness (John Hargreaves, 1982). Both criticisms are valid, should such theory be applied to analyses of the 1981 Springbok tour of New Zealand. Developing from these criticisms, sport has been discussed in relation to the concept of hegemony, which relates the social structure to specific distributions of power and influence, so that it becomes a lived process of dominance and subordination (Williams, 1978). Essential to the understanding of the hegemonic process is the acceptance of conflict and the possibility of change. In this respect the dynamics of New Zealand culture exemplified in the conditions surrounding rugby and the 1981 Springbok tour could well be considered as a highly visible form of hegemonic process in action. Whitson (1984) has argued that the scope for change of the dominant culture is limited by our ability only to reject rather than to initiate alternatives, because the all encompassing power of the hegemony disallows 'space' for alternative experiences. It would appear that the rugby tour in New Zealand provided the 'space' to reject aspects of lived subordination. Additionally, the continuation of the tour and the escalated conflict extended that space to allow the beginnings of an authentic break from dominant hegemony which has lead to some obvious changes in the relations of domination and subordination in New Zealand.

CONCLUSION

In the years since 1981, New Zealanders have witnessed the gradual incorporation of an emerging ideology, much of which contributed originally to the mass mobilisation against the rugby tour. Rugby no longer holds the same position of unquestionable importance (Dann, 1982; Campbell, 1985). The power of government and capital interest has shifted considerably, with a change of political party governing and a restructured economy reducing the reliance upon traditional agriculturally based trade. The country's international policy reflects changed values, and internally there is evidence to suggest that both women's interests and Maori interests have been very much more readily accommodated. Both groups, separately and in combination are demonstrating lived identities and relationships of enhanced power.

It is argued that much of the women's protest against the tour, particularly as it continued, was motivated by emerging conscious opposition to the forces of patriarchal power over women in New Zealand society, intricately linked with the power of capitalism and white supremacy, in which the sport of rugby has played an exceedingly strong symbolic and reproductive role. New Zealand women were seen to present a strong challenge to that previously held dominance, and from a position of subordinance made a substantial contribution to the emerging hegemony.

REFERENCES

Aitken, Judith and Ros Noonan, 1981: "Rugby, Racism and Riot Gear." In: *Broadsheet*, No. 94, 16-19.

Baker, Andrea, 1981: "Team Mates or Tea Makers." In: *Papers and Reports from the 1981 Conference on Women and Recreation*. Wellington: New Zealand Council for Recreation and Sport.

Barrowman, Rachel, 1981: "A Report on the Molesworth Street Incident". In: *The Police and the 1981 Tour*. History Department Occasional Paper, Wellington: Victoria University.

Brookes, Barbara, 1981: "Housewives' Depression". In: *New Zealand Journal of History*, 15(1), 115-134.

Campbell, Gordon, 1985: "Is Rugby Dying?". In: *New Zealand Listener*, June 29, 22-23.

Chapple, Geoff, 1984: *1981: The Tour*. Wellington: A.H. and A.W. Reed.

Coney, Sandra, 1981: "Women Against The Tour". In: *Broadsheet*, No. 92, 8-14.

Dann, Christine, 1982: "The Game Is Over". In: *Broadsheet*, No. 97, 26-28.

Deem, Rosemary, 1982: "Women, Leisure and Inequality". In: *Leisure Studies*, 1, 29-46.

Hain, Peter, 1971: *Don't Play With Apartheid*. London: Billing & Sons, Ltd.

Hall, Sandi, 1981: "Dykes Against The Tour". In: *Broadsheet*, No. 92, 10.

Hargreaves, Jennifer, 1982: "Theorising Sport: An Introduction". In: Jennifer Hargreaves (ed.): *Sport, Culture and Ideology*. London: Routledge & Kegan Paul.

Hargreaves, John, 1982: "Sport, Culture and Ideology". In: Jennifer Hargreaves (ed.): *Sport, Culture and Ideology*. London: Routledge & Kegan Paul.

Hartmann, H., 1981: "The Unhappy Marriage of Marxism and Feminism". In: L. Sargent (ed.): *Women and Revolution*. Montreal: Black Rose Books.

Laidlaw, C., 1973: *Mud In Your Eye*. Wellington: Reed Books.

Millet, Kate, 1970: *Sexual Politics*. New York: Doubleday.

Pearson, M.M., 1979: "Heads in the Sand: The 1956 Springbok Tour Of New Zealand in Perspective". In: R. Cashman & M. McKernan (eds.): *Sport in History*. St. Lucia: Queensland University Press.

Phillips, Jock, 1980: "Mummy's Boys: Pakeha Men and Male Culture in New Zealand". In: Phillida Bunkle and Beryl Hughes (eds.): *Women in New Zealand Society*. Auckland: George Allen & Unwin.

Phillips, Jock, 1987: *A Man's Country?* Auckland: Penquin Books.

Sheard, K.G. and E. Dunning, 1973: "The Rugby Football Club As A Type Of Male Preserve: Some Sociological Notes". In: *International Review of Sport Sociology*, 8, 5-24.

Shears, Richard and Isobelle Gidley, 1981: *Storm Out of Africa. The 1981 Springbok Tour of New Zealand*. Auckland: Macmillan.

Thompson, Richard, 1964: *Race and Sport*. London: Oxford University Press.

Thompson, Richard, 1975: *Retreat from Apartheid*. Wellington: Oxford University Press.

Thomson, Rex, 1977: Sport And Deviance: A Subcultural Analysis. Unpublished Ph.D. Dissertation, University of Alberta.

Waring, Marilyn, 1985: *Women, Politics and Power*. Wellington: Allen and Unwin.

Whitson, David, 1984: "Sport and Hegemony: On the Construction of the Dominant Culture". In: *Sociology of Sport Journal*, 1. 64-78.

Williams, R., 1978: *Marxism and Literature*. Oxford: Oxford University Press.

Chapter 15

Is a Diamond Forever?
Feminist Transformations of Sport

Susan Birrell
University of Iowa

Diana M. Richter
University of Iowa

Any feminist can tell you that if you are a stranger in town on a hot summer evening and you want to find the feminist community, you should head for the nearest softball diamond.[1] There, during the summer months, members of the women's community can be found engaged in what at first glance appears to be the great American pastime but on closer inspection turns out to be a ritual of resistance to dominant male structures and values. How it happened that softball rather than volleyball, field hockey, or some other sport came to be so fully identified with the women's community is a significant topic awaiting the attention of other writers. This paper addresses how that connection is maintained and how women who define themselves as feminists consciously construct and maintain alternatives to what has been called the "male preserve" of sport (Eric Dunning, 1986; Kenneth Sheard and Eric Dunning, 1973; Nancy Theberge, 1986). This paper shows that women can colonize an activity which in its unaltered state serves as a site for the reproduction of patriarchal ideologies inimical to their interests as women (Susan Birrell, 1984; Mary Boutilier and Lucinda SanGiovanni, 1983; Ann Hall, 1983; Nancy Theberge, 1985). Through reflexive social action, women (and by extension other traditionally disenfranchised groups) can overcome the hegemonic grasp of alienating ideologies and institute social

Note. We wish to thank Cheryl Cole for her help with many aspects of this paper.
From "Is a Diamond Forever?: Feminist Transformation of Sport" by S. Birrell and D. Richter, 1987, *Women's Studies International Forum*, **10**(4), pp. 395-409. Copyright 1987 by Pergamon Journals Ltd. Reprinted by permission.

practices which have authentic meaning in their own lives. Thus this paper documents one instance of the process of cultural resistance to rituals of hegemony.

The analysis is based on data drawn from intensive interviews and observations collected over a four year period.[2] The women involved in the study were participants in women's summer recreational slow-pitch softball leagues in two neighboring towns. Both towns offer opportunities for women to play at one of two or three levels generally defined by skill.

The sample was a purposive one: women who define themselves as feminists were purposely sought out and interviewed about their feminist attitudes, their attitudes toward sport and softball, and the relationship they saw between a feminist consciousness and the practice of sport. Many of the women in the sample had been in the communities for several years, playing on a number of different teams, and thus their accounts are historically informed.

ANALYTICAL FRAMEWORKS

The analysis draws most heavily upon feminist theory and methodology, particularly as they are affected by interactionist principles and cultural studies approaches (Cheryl Cole and Susan Birrell, 1986). As a strategy for understanding the way women organize and understand the world, feminist analysis must be based on self-conscious ontological and epistemological choices which inform the strategies for collecting information about women's lives (methodological choices) and the explanations of social phenomena and social forces we are willing to entertain (theoretical conclusions). Thus feminist analysis entertains interpretations of findings that are informed by and consistent with women's experiences of the world.

One sensible way to collect and interpret the stories of women's everyday life experiences is to utilize the methods of symbolic interactionism and to build theories of the world that are grounded in women's unique experiencing of it. The research approach we advocate is qualitative and interactionist, and it listens to what women say in their own voices.

Many feminists interested in sport are ambivalent about the recent changes in girls' and women's sport in the United States. The boom in female participation in high school, college and recreational sport, largely due to Title IX[3] and the Association for Intercollegiate Athletics for Women (AIAW)[4] has managed to enfranchise more females into the existing structures of sport. Massive as these changes appear to be,[5] they actually represent the accommodation of women within a system of male sport which remains virtually unchanged despite the increased presence of women. Moreover, while many applaud the increased opportunities now available to girls and women, gains at the participation level have been accompanied by a virtual takeover by men of coaching and administrative positions (Vivian Acosta and Linda Jean Carpenter, 1985; Milton Holman and Bonnie Parkhouse, 1981). Thus the liberal remedy to women's exclusion from sport has merely resulted in incorporation and has failed to accomplish the far-reaching changes in sport some feminists had advocated.

This paper focuses on the possibility of a radical remedy for women in sport by presenting one community's attempts to shape sport into a practice which has relevance within their lives as those lives are informed by feminism. In a sense, their constructions represent one version of what women defined sport would look like. Thus the study investigates the social construction of sport by focusing upon how feminist consciousness can inform and structure feminists' experiences of sport.

From an analytical standpoint, understanding feminist softball takes place on two levels: the level at which the social actions and meanings are created, negotiated, and communicated to teammates and opponents, and the level at which those meanings can be apprehended by one purporting to do cultural analysis. Thus the procedures feminists use to create a sport form recognizable to themselves as feminist, however they understand that term, are precisely those procedures which must be observed, questioned and understood by the analyst.

Feminist softball is not a *product* turned out by inventive minds but rather an ongoing *process of invention*, and that process can be observed. Teams and individuals reflect on their own experiences, talk about how they feel, make decisions, act and react in observable ways, recount incidents to one another as object lessons and offer accounts for their actions. From these speeches and actions, the conclusions and interpretations of this paper are drawn.

FEMINIST CONSCIOUSNESS AND FEMINIST ACTION

We purposely selected as informants women who called themselves feminists who played softball in one of the leagues mentioned. We were particularly interested in interviewing and observing four teams within the leagues which had reputations as "feminist teams." However the term "feminist team" had two different meanings. At one level it meant simply comprised of women from the feminist community. For three of the teams, it meant more, for they actively sought to transform sport through feminist practice. The fourth team assumed that, by definition, feminist softball was whatever feminists played.

Individuals who subscribed to these different definitions differed in terms of the connection they saw between feminist principles and playing softball. While both groups willingly accepted the label of feminist as an accurate description of themselves and their teammates, some saw little reason to apply feminist principles to sport.

> Feminism is prevalent in most of the teams we play but it's not overt. It's subtle but there. It's a feeling among women. If these attitudes affect

sport, great. But in the process of playing, consciously applying feminism at every turn is not important and it could be a drag.

We are not, well, radically or maybe collectively proclaiming (feminism). Political terms should be left out of sport especially at this level . . . Right now our team is effective and inwardly liberated. Whether or not we are feminist just doesn't come up or isn't important for us as a softball team.

One woman aptly summarized this position when she said: ''How about a feminist unconsciousness?'' Another woman who considered herself a feminist but did not play for a team actively attempting to transform sport through feminism made a comment which reveals her feminist consciousness but shows how a commitment to feminist action is a further step:

I guess feminists would reconstruct sport in terms of women, but I'm not sure how. Maybe to emphasize women's experiences and values and not just men's would be different. It's hard to say, but women do experience sport and softball differently. Feminists would use this to redefine or reconstruct sport so that it fits women's experience also.

By contrast those on feminist teams had made some analysis of the problems of sport and what their team might do to remedy the situation. This quote from a coach summarizes some typical elements of that consciousness:

Our team is built on a certain number of agreements that make me feel it's . . . compatible with a feminist spirit, being that everyone who comes plays, that while we're in the season, I try to equal out amount of playing time. Now there's some factors that go into it that I feel, that's fairness: if someone doesn't come to any of the practices, I do not feel compelled that they play equal amount of time . . . I think on the team there's alot of support for people trying, and people don't really get upset with mistakes and the criticism is relatively supportive. And I think basically the two things people want to do is have a good time and play well. It's nice if we win, but if we don't win, we don't win—as simple as that.

While the interviews focused on the transformative effect feminism had on softball, several players clearly felt that sport had served as an arena for their developing feminist consciousness:

I think that maybe playing softball and socializing with other women . . . has shaped my attitudes. I think that there is alot more that goes on in the field than just the game.

Sport enhances (feminism) by allowing me to be with other liberated women and probably feminist women. Sport can be a meeting ground for not only strong women physically but also mentally and emotionally.

DECONSTRUCTING MALE SPORT

Those feminists who see a clear connection between feminism and sport and who work to strengthen that connection—and that was the majority of our respondents—follow unconsciously the two step process of feminist analysis and action discussed by Sandra Harding and Merrill Hintikka (1983): deconstruction and reconstruction. Their decision to enact feminist softball, as they understand it, entails a critical analysis of dominant American sporting traditions and how sport has failed to satisfy women's leisure needs. While the level of sophistication of the analysis differed by individual and by team, their critiques of sport and their solutions for change are logically related. Moreover the source of their critique and their strategies for change are clearly understood by themselves as grounded in their feminist sensibilities, i.e., their own notions of what it is like to be women in a world constrained by patriarchal pressures.

A major feature of their criticism is aimed at institutionalized forms of sport, specifically those contained within educational structures. The proximity of these leagues to a large university and the relationship many players had to that university account for some of their reservations. As a group, they find institutionalized sport to be rigid, hierarchical, conservative, elitist and alienating, and they are determined to keep the dominant values represented in institutionalized sport from reasserting themselves in other levels of recreational play.

Few of these women had had positive experiences in high school or college, stating that "in high school it was cut-throat competition" and that

> I didn't feel good and I definitely felt, even then in the 70's, that you played for the *school*, you played to keep your coach's job by winning, and *then* maybe you played because you liked sports. The priorities were all wrong.

Other criticisms focused on the elitism and exclusivity of institutionalized sport:

> Some sports are only played at a high competitive level or in such a way so you have to be very rich to be a part. You know, that bothers me.

> I think that sports are extremely important for women, both individually and in a recreational setting, even in an organized sense. but when it starts to be in an institutional setting, alot of times I think we get really far away from how it supports feminism . . . You think of the budget in (intercollegiate) athletics and how it supports the activity of, what,

100 athletes? To me there is something terribly elitist and classist about
that that I don't buy. I don't like it at all.

One woman had a plan for saving intercollegiate sport by restructuring it:

> I would get rid of all the major college sport organizations like the
> NCAA and the AIAW and put all the sports at the school at the club
> level, that are funded like any other group that the student center funds
> . . . and have it be a return to the true "amateur sport" . . . You would
> not play to represent any organization, you'd play because you love
> playing . . . I'd get rid of all this extraneous status that has been laid
> on sport, that has nothing to do with sport. Winning for (the coach, the
> university). Winning to go to States . . . Schedule people from your
> region and enjoy the game.

But most were concerned with presenting oppositional meanings in their own
recreational sphere.

The dominant view of sport which these feminists deplore is labeled by them
"the male model." Males are seen as the keepers of the tradition and as beneficiaries of the dominant arrangement of sport. One woman stated

> Sport is generic, yet so many think sport is male, and in alot of ways
> traditional sport is. When I think of even what we play now, you know,
> women today play men's games by their rules and how they want us
> to play.

Another commented

> There is a tremendous amount of pressure to keep up with the men and
> to mirror their programs, and winning starts to be everything.

Because these women's experiences in male constructed sport have been negative, they were actively seeking an alternative, even if that meant they would
have to invent it themselves. From the standpoint of these women, men make
sport and sport makes men, and women are effectively kept out of the entire
process unless they take dramatic steps to accommodate themselves.

Males involved in the league as coaches or umpires were almost invariably
seen as antithetical to the production of meaningful sport experiences for women.
Often they appear in stories as foils against which the players' feminist philosophies were developed or tested. Male coaches are sometimes seen as exemplars
of the worst that male definitions of sport represent. Concerning the difference
between the way men and women play sport, one softball player used her observations of men's pick-up basketball games as an exemplar:

It's *absolutely* violent. They are totally abusive to each other. There is not an ounce of support. It's completely competitive, you know, everyone is really showy. They don't work together whatsoever. It's amazing. Maybe their worst stage is at 19, I don't know. It's a real heavy dose if you watch men play pick-up basketball.

According to another woman

A lot of the coaches annoy the hell out of me . . . I don't know why they've got to show off that they're strong and stuff. I think it's because it's about the only thing they have going for them . . . that we don't have going for us.

And a third observed

You also have male coaches who, hearing them on the baselines and having talked to the batters and players, they sort of treat the game in a very traditional way, which is you absolutely have to win and try to bad-mouth the other team, and try to interfere with their concentration, and cheer when the other team makes mistakes. You know, it's a whole different mind set.

Some of the women had played for male coaches in the past but would not repeat that experience.

I would never choose to (play for a male coach) again . . . The mind games and abuse is unbelievable as I look back. I received more from my female coaches—things I can never replace or have obtained with men. My skills were enriched and myself built. I will only play for a woman coach now.

Most women on the team wouldn't play for a man because it would just be another domination thing and win-at-all-cost attitude. The women on our team want quality, not quantity.

Another woman offered this astute summary:

Male coaches try to treat you like a male. They want you to act the same way. We might be serious about playing, you know, and we might be cracking jokes, dancing around, you know, doing some things . . . I had a male coach who did not like that kind of behavior. He said, you know, ''You are acting like a bunch of women out there.'' That's what we *are* you know, and we are serious. We don't have to walk around with our jaws jutted out, feeling our biceps and strutting into the park. You don't have to do those things. It's just not a part of us.

As many recognized, having men coach women recreated the whole power structure between men and women in society. One woman noted,

> I don't see what's in it for them except this power of having those girls under them.

An example from another woman verifies this point:

> This one coach . . . he never called any of them by name. He called them all "girl"—"nice going, girl." And I finally said—he was coaching third base and I was on the mound—and I said "Don't you know any of their names?" And he just pretended not to hear me."

The incidents which most clearly focused attention on the distinction between male coaches and feminist teams concerned close calls by the umpires. While most of the women on feminist teams would shrug off unfavorable calls, male coaches habitually disputed close calls. Their behavior was read by the feminists as proof of "the way men deal with sport." This argumentative male behavior, and the win-at-all-cost attitude that apparently fostered it, were not shared by all the women who played for them. Sometimes their reaction to such incidents was resigned embarrassment.

> Sometimes it seems that they are embarrassed at how their coaches are acting. There was one game this year when their coach was being a real jerk. He was being real abusive to the umpires, and he challenged every call and told them they were blind. He was just a real asshole. And the players were real embarrassed. When we did the hand shaking ritual at the end of the game they said, "Oh we're sorry about our coach. Please don't pay attention."

In other similar situations, the feminist teams took the opportunity to engage their opponents with understanding glances that were statements of solidarity with one another as women. But one feminist coach was discouraged that more women did not confront their male coaches about their behavior.

> Alot of times, I know I don't hear the women speaking up and saying, "Shove it. I don't want to hear it. We can think for ourselves." Well, maybe a handful of times over the years I've finally seen some of the women—they've had enough and finally they tell a guy to shut up. I've seen it a few times. Maybe some other stuff goes on behind the scenes. I'm just talking about the ball diamond because that's the only way I know these teams.

Players on feminist teams were much less reticent and far less tolerant of such behavior from male coaches as two incidents from the lore of the league attest.

We were playing (a team) and the umpire made a call that (the male coaches) didn't agree with, and instead of just letting it go, they stormed out onto the field and started arguing. And that's when I said, "This is bullshit. If we want to argue, we will. You fuckers stay off the field and stop turning this game into a power struggle." I just lost it, and we had this huge argument. And it was just like venom, because I had been repressing so much anger.

On another occasion when a male coach was abusing an official by belaboring a close call and the action on the field was being delayed, one feminist had had enough. "This is *women's* softball," she shouted from the dugout. "*Get that boy off the field.*"

The league employed both men and women as umpires, and while rumors in the league occasionally identified a male umpire who "has some trouble" with feminist teams, the quality of the umpiring was rarely affected. However, on one occasion, an incident occurred between a player and an umpire "known" to be antagonistic to feminist teams. The issue had to do with a close call in which a woman was called for interference when she chose not to slide into second base because of the condition of the field, and the second base player had to hold the ball rather than throw to first.

I was arguing with him about the call, and I said things like, "If you're going to make that kind of call, then I want you out there fixing this field so we can play that kind of game," and trying to make some connections with him about his concept of what was being a good sport and how the sport was being played and what they were giving us to play with . . . And then there was a foul ball hit and I went after it, which is sort of unusual. I could tell I was really angry and over-compensating, because I really went after it . . . And as I was coming back, we were facing each other and he said something like, "Boy you've got all kinds of problems. Why don't you complain to me about world problems now?"[6] And it really made me mad, really made me mad, to the point where if I talked about it I would have cried and lost control. And I thought, "This is *not* having fun. I am *not* having a good time." Me and this umpire were just going at it, and it's pointless. So I walked off the field and told (the coach) to send someone else in.

What most upset this woman was the fact that the umpire's behavior was beginning to control her own and to interfere with her enjoyment of the game.

I was going to get my whole self shifted into being very competitive and very edgy and very aggressive because of him, which meant I would have thrown the ball harder and probably over-thrown alot of things, and would have swung harder and struck out and it would have built and built and it wouldn't have been a good time.

In such moments, however unpleasant, discoveries about the dimensions of feminist sport are made and feminist principles are affirmed.

In this light, it is not surprising to find that one feature of softball these women particularly treasured was the opportunity to share their experiences with other women. One woman explained,

> We want to be away from men, playing our sport for ourselves, with ourselves. So what if we lose a few? We have a good time, stay in shape, and share being women—but mostly without men. It's refreshing.

Another said

> I'm playing to be with other women, to get closer to women. Summer softball gives us a chance to have our own little group—exclusive.

For a third, feminist softball meant "enjoying women enjoy sport together."

These examples demonstrate a few feminist complaints about sport as it is practiced by or influenced by men. Many of the women on the teams observed were determined to intervene in this process of cultural reproduction. To the extent that the problems in sport are understood by these women as male constructed and male sustained, the solutions they offer are understood to be female constructed or feminist. As one woman was asked to speculate:

> Q: Do you think a feminist perspective of sport is a viable perspective for the future?
>
> A: I want to hope so. At least in recreational or amateur sport . . . Creating options for women to continue to participate and contribute to sport are important. I guess a feminist perspective would enhance women's chance of continuing to advance in and create the sport world.

To this process of creation and to an analysis of the specific critiques of the male-defined sport world we now turn.

AN ANTI-RATIONALIST VIEW OF SPORT

Although many minor complaints were voiced by the women interviewed and observed, several critiques emerged most frequently and seemed to hold particular importance to the women. In this section, six areas of concern are explored: (1) the overemphasis on winning at the expense of enjoying the process of play; (2) the hierarchical nature of sport, symbolized by the traditional power relationship between player and coach; (3) the elitism based on skill; (4) the exclusivity represented by sexism, racism, classism, ageism, heterosexism, and sizism; (5) the disparagement of opponents which alienates players from one another; and (6) an ethic of endangerment that often places outcome above the safety of the individual, a teammate or an opponent. To a great extent these criticisms might be termed ''anti-rationalist'' for they confront directly the rationalist ideology of dominant American sporting traditions. While none of these feminists contexted their critiques within a theoretical framework, their analyses are consistent with those of Allen Guttmann (1973), Richard Gruneau (1983), Nancy Theberge (1981), Harry Webb (1969) and many others who argue that the heavy emphasis placed on winning in sport almost invariably leads to rational strategies for ensuring that end.

The Primacy of Winning

The most clearly voiced sentiments from these feminists were their refusal to elevate winning to the principle of ultimate worth, their refusal to subvert the process of play to the product of winning, and their insistence on measuring the value of the activity for themselves against the joy of playing. They were strongly opposed to an approach to softball that so highly valued winning that friendship, sensitivity to others and safety were disregarded. They wanted to play a highly skilled game, to challenge the skill of their opponents, to play hard and to have a good time. All of that, they felt, could be accomplished whether they won or lost. Thus outcome could be rendered less relevant than the process of play. One woman stated simply, ''Winning in an all out way is not as important as actually playing and experiencing the sport.'' Others develop this theme:

> I think you can have a game that there is a winner and loser and you do keep score and in the end people feel good about what they do. I mean, *everybody* whether they are on the winning team or the losing team. Perhaps those on the winning team maybe enjoyed it more because they won—I don't know—but I think those two things, when you're careful, can exist side by side.

> I want the satisfaction of playing the game well and the beauty of the well-executed double play, and strike-outs and spectacular catches. I want the pleasure and satisfaction of playing well, and when the importance of winning gets in the way of having a good time playing the game, that's where the line is drawn for me.

> It's more an atmosphere that people are having a good time, that the outcome may or may not be important to anybody. And I know definitely that that's happened when we've been on the losing side. You know alot of people say ''that's true until you lose,'' but I know we have lost a couple of these games, and it's usually later when someone says ''did

you have a good game?'' and I think, ''Yeah. Yeah. We lost, but it was a good game.''

Another saw feminist sport as providing ''opportunities for people to run and to laugh at the same time.''

But these feminist teams do not exist in a vacuum, but play most of their games against more traditional women's teams. Most games are enjoyable affairs in which teams with different philosophies go home satisfied with their experiences. Occasionally, however, the philosophies clash, and the result is not always pleasant.

> It becomes difficult when it matters *alot* to the people you're playing, and that's something I ran into this summer. We were just getting trounced by this team, and generally it doesn't bother me, except it mattered alot to that team that they trounced us—not just that they win, but that they kill us . . . I believe that the coach breeds that in them. They were the type of team that kept statistics on each other, and if you were beating a team, it was an opportunity to run the statistics up. Right? They were in no way interested in a fun, competitive game. There was sort of a selfishness involved in their participation in the game. So I didn't have fun then at all.

> If the other team is being nasty . . . those games aren't fun . . . Even if we win a game like that it's not as much satisfaction as a game that maybe we would lose against a team that was a friendly team, it was a close game, it was a good game and there were good plays—there was a lot of satisfaction.

A coach who had been involved in the softball leagues for many years recounted this historical note:

> I remember a team we used to play in fastpitch a number of years back . . . that . . . a number of the teams including us . . . ended up boycotting. We refused to play them because they were so competitive and they were also extremely homophobic—I mean, it was rather complicated, the situation. But they were in it for totally different things, it felt like, and finally the teams just said it's not what this league is about, and refused to play them.

Concerning a similar situation, another woman provided this insight into the transformative power of feminist resistance:

> We began to realize we didn't like what was going on. This isn't fun.
> We're not having a good time. We feel lousy when we do it—*so what's
> wrong?* And I think as feminists we train ourselves to ask those questions
> and be reflective, and we know we can organize groups in different
> ways, that we can structure activities differently.

These negative experiences can be nicely contrasted to the games during the
season when two feminist teams meet. On one such occasion, both teams decided
to dress up for the game. The members of one team all showed up with neckties,
while the other sported tuxedoes, high school gymsuits and old dresses and hats
obtained from the second-hand stores downtown. Despite the flippancy of the
costumes, the game was played as a serious contest. For the hundred or so fans
from the feminist community who had gathered to watch, the game was a highlight
of the summer. But the fans' behavior mystified some onlookers who couldn't
figure out why they would cheer when a woman got a hit and then cheer when
she was caught out. The fans were truly indiscriminate: they cheered with delight
for every play.

Another story from community lore concerned a game played a few years past
between two feminist teams of widely differing talent. One team was comprised
mostly of beginners, while the other was in contention for the league title. To
make the game more competitive and more fun, the more skilled team decided
not to play their usual positions but to try new ones. When the rookies actually
pulled ahead, the skilled team remained true to their commitment—eventually
losing the game and falling in the standings. But they were convinced they had
created something more important than winning—an enjoyable, competitive
game.

The Hierarchy of Authority

The feminist transformations attempted by these softball teams occurred mostly
within the context of the prevalent rules and structures of the sport. Rule changes
were not sought, and the structure of the game was challenged only in one
area—coaching.

The general feminist distrust for hierarchical chains of authority was evident
in the ways in which different teams dealt with the role of the coach. One player
voiced the concerns of many when she said

> I don't know if coaching is on the edge of an abuse of power. I suspect
> that just the nature of the job makes it a possibility. A coach would
> have to be pretty sensitive to not abuse it, because it is a lot of power.

The best solution, it appeared, was to entrust that sensitive position to a woman.
Generally she was concerned with equalling out the playing time and accommo-
dating the needs of the players, and generally she was successful.

We have a coach and positions and play the game traditionally for most parts. But it's more relaxed and the coach listens to the players and sometimes will ask for advice, so there is a sharing atmosphere, more than in the usual coach/player relationship in which the coach is the boss. All the women contribute and support the team. They also support each other.

Our structure is very traditional, but the input level is different. Everyone contributes and it is more team effort than anything. The coach guides and instructs, but we can change decisions if need be.

Well, she tolerates all of our opinions and tries to accommodate everyone regardless of skill or status. Winning is important, but not as to sacrifice people's feelings and stuff. She realizes we want fun as well as glory, I guess.

Nevertheless minor problems occasionally surfaced:

Gail and I would share in the pitching . . . It was all (the coach's) decision, how it was set up. We'd show up at the game and (the coach) says "You're pitching. You're not pitching," or "You're pitching the first three innings and you're pitching the next four" or something. Maybe a better thing would have been for (the coach) to say "You and Gail set up a plan for who's going to pitch for the next four games. Divide it between you." So we would be forced to deal with one another, instead of we were just these competitors with no power and no say-so.

However the lore of the league also includes stories of good feminist intentions gone awry:

We were winning, and at first the team got real relaxed about it, like, "Wow, we're winning. Isn't that neat?" But it wasn't like "Aw, we're going to go out and win the title." It was like, "Wow, we won." Each game was like living in the present moment. The goal wasn't so much down the road, as it was just at each present moment doing your best and appreciating that in each other—supporting each other in mistakes, offering advice, things like that. But once our coach became so intent on focusing on the fact that we were winning and that meant we had to win even more, it was like we got uptight and anxious and starting puking on each other.

To help guard against such problems, some teams met before the season to discuss their team philosophy. At one such meeting, mindful of a similar problem that had engulfed them the year before, the women reaffirmed their feminist principles and vowed not to reset their priorities if the team turned out to be very successful.

Some teams tried another system—collective management. On one such team, interested players took turns managing a game. This responsibility included discovering who would be available to play, setting the line-up and acting on behalf of the team in conversations with umpires or scorers. The purpose of this system of rotating coach was to share power and responsibility and to avoid creating a structure in which one person made all the decisions. With minor squabbles and accommodations, this system worked well for that team.

The Elitism of Skill

When outcome is privileged over the process of play, those whose skill levels are less developed are often disenfranchised from sport. The feminist solution was to offer opportunities for women with little sport experience to learn the game in a supportive environment.

Most teams were successful in their attempts to provide a supportive environment for their players:

> If someone is having a bad night, it's like people caring, you know, "Don't worry about it. It will be ok the next time." These types of things, whereas with male sport . . . it's been like a real negative thing to make a mistake. It's very natural in sport, and it's always going to happen, and women can handle them a little better.

> I remember there was one game . . . We were losing, and I think we were down to our last out, and Karen was up, and we might have had people on base. And instead of putting pressure on her, or being mad that she made the last out . . . we all started making fun and a lot of noise from the bench. It was making it a fun situation, to make it very easy for that person to make the last out, so she wouldn't have to feel bad that she was the last out of the game.

> Alot of people on the team use humor to let the person know it's not the most earth-shattering thing that just has happened . . . Part of it is just so people don't feel so devastated, you know, like they really have done something bad. So what, they dropped the ball. In the great universe of things what does that mean? . . . But on the other hand, I think we give each other alot of encouragement for things done well, because we do like to play well.

And the players feel the support:

I've never felt bad when I've struck out. I've never felt like I've let anybody down when I haven't hit the ball (well). I think in fact I did something really dumb once, like not running very fast to the base, or giving up on something. And you know if there's a certain amount of self-disappointment, then that's one thing, but I've never felt like that was projected on me by the rest of the team. You're just what you are on the team and that's it.

Another saw support as

The presence of a real comfort with our own abilities. We knew our weaknesses and strengths and we were glad to say to Kate for instance, "You are a good shortstop and we want you there. Let's put Nancy in center field because she has more speed than I do, she had just something I didn't have. Let's move me to left because this, that or the other." A real acceptance, a real cuing in on each other. People could admit their weaknesses and be told these things without a sense of being kicked in the rear, and there wasn't alot of behind the scenes maneuvering so that people were grumbling.

Concern for providing support was not confined to skilled performances. This woman gives her account of the incident between the player and the umpire cited earlier:

There was an umpire that, apparently there was some old bad blood between him and Becky, and she challenged one of his calls—and I think it was a bad call—and he just rode her . . . Things were happening really fast and we were on the field and Becky was on first base and I was pitching. I could hear him riding her . . . I should have stopped pitching. I should have held that ball and said, "When you're done, then I'll play." I knew I shouldn't have started to pitch, but I did. And then I felt like I shouldn't have. I felt real bad, like none of us supported Becky very good in that.

The issue of skill had another aspect to it: how to deal with different levels of skill. The league's solution to different levels of skill was structural: two or three divisions differentiated by skill. Some feminist teams followed this approach and were specifically designed for players just learning the game. Other feminist teams chose a different solution and tried to accommodate heterogeneous levels of skill within one team. These teams tried to provide safe space for a few newcomers by placing them in positions—such as shortfield or second base— where they could be backed up by other players so that errors would not seem so devastating. This system worked part of the time, but despite the best supportive intentions of veteran players, some newcomers still felt the stress that unequal skill imposes.   No issue raised as much discussion or required as much feminist work as the accommodation of players with different levels of skill on the same team. One woman who had been playing softball in the community for many years spoke quite pointedly about her experiences in the earliest days of feminist consciousness and softball.

> I got criticized for being too good, because if I threw a ball too hard to someone it was oppressing them. Just bullshit, absolute bullshit. And I'll never forget this one woman, she came up to me at a party one time and she said, "You know, you really oppress me because you're so good at softball." It's like people were struggling with that whole feeling of how women are discouraged from sport, and how people who weren't good at it are put down in phys. ed. in grade school, and (they were) dumping all that confusion on people who are good athletes . . . It's not that I discredit their feelings about these things, but they were so in the middle of the analysis that they were just throwing shit around at people, and I just caught a lot of it, and I didn't appreciate it.

Her next experience was more positive, and in general shows that while the problem may always exist, creative feminist responses can successfully deal with it.

> I then played for (another team) which was coached sort of collectively. And once again we ran into that feeling of what to do with people who aren't good enough or people who are too good. How do we protect their feelings? And really that was ok. We handled that ok because we all loved each other and cared about each other together as a collective. So we knew how to do it together and it worked.

Another woman with many years in the softball community spoke to the gradual evolution of community consciousness.

> Maybe we have sort of evolved ourselves to what we're willing to put up with in a sport atmosphere and know much clearer what we want to have happen. When I think of those (bad) experiences—they were in the first few years I was in (town), so we're talking 7-10 years ago—those were sometimes nasty exchanges. I mean, you got two women's teams together and it was not a good experience. But I also think we were talking very much at the time about how we wanted to make it different.

Three final statements describe other ways that the issue of different skill is handled individually and collectively:

> Something that's very annoying to me (is) the way people are fooling around so much that the game loses any kind of continuity . . . I get annoyed when that happens and I generally find that if that's happening,

I just need to remove myself from the game, mostly because it's serving other people's needs and not mine . . . Or I need to say "This isn't going to work seriously" and just calm down and have a good time.

Some people have been fairly competitive over the years and in a sense are natural athletes. They just seem skilled out of who knows where? And even with this year's team, there are a couple of people who occasionally have a hard time with it being a not very skilled team and things being real smooth and being real serious. But then they catch themselves and they are fine.

Part of (the solution) has been a weeding out process too. I've (coached) for 5 years and I think within those 5 years some people who've played haven't come back because they haven't agreed with the philosophy, and other people join because they know that's what our team is about. So there has been a self-selecting process along the way, too.

But regardless of how tolerant of mistakes a team was, their support never reached the extreme feminist sentiment we have heard of in another community, where a team wore this motto on their shirts: "Every error helps another woman." Feminists in this study who were told of this slogan were confused by the mixed message they thought the motto implied. While they were committed to making all women comfortable with their skill level, they were uneasy with the total lack of respect for skill they thought the motto endorsed.

Social Exclusion

A second form of elitism offended these feminist players—exclusion from sport because of social identity. As members of a social category which has historically been denied access to sport, these women were sensitive to exclusion of others because of race, class, size, age or sexual preference.

I have a much broader sense of who's defined as an athlete. Around (the university) who an athlete is, is a really select few. I'd like to know, do fat people become athletes? How do physically challenged people have a sense of being athletic? I do not think there is much support in this (university) for those images. There is a very narrow image of what's athletic. Somehow (we need to) make that more broad. It's not just your 5'6'', 120 pounds, blue-eyed, blond-haired anorexic person.

I've always been a fat girl, so I think that's something that has kept me from sports, you know, that has turned me away when I've not wanted to be turned away from them . . . People don't think you should be there. I think the signals are pretty overt . . . I guess I'd like to see it a little more recognized that it's pretty brave, anyone my size or bigger that is out there in public view, running on a field.

We are older than most of the other teams. Like we probably have more players over 30 than them. I've been conscious of that the last year or so because . . . I mean, 9 o'clock on a Friday night or something, we don't have the steam to be running around with these 18 year old girls, running around the bases, huffing and puffing. Half of us are over 30.

It's bad enough (university sport) supports 100 athletes, but then you look at who's been on those teams and it's basically been a white woman's activity. Now maybe some of that is going to start to change, but as far as who that privilege even gets extended to anyway, seems to me has been fairly racist on a certain level, which is also anti-feminist.

Intercollegiate sport was very alienating. I couldn't deal with it. It was not a safe place to be a lesbian.

One final incident provides a macabre note:

(The team) was called White Way, and it was this group of lesbians who weren't really feminists who were sponsored by this old guy who ran the supermarket downtown—White Way. And the guy put on the back of our shirts, ''The Great White Way'' and I thought, ''Oh my God, we cannot wear these.'' I don't think he realized what he was doing.

The Opponent as Other

Dedication to providing support for one's teammates is not unheard of in the sports world, but extending that supportiveness to one's opponents is a more unusual stand. While some opponents were hard to love, as the anecdotes recounted earlier document, most of the feminist players refused to reduce their opponents to enemies. As one player eloquently put it:

Any sport done with another person, whether it's a team member or another being, is a cooperative venture. You are all cooperating and participating in creating a sporting atmosphere . . . And so no team is ever seen as an enemy. An enemy is something you don't want around.

Others felt the same:

That's something I've noticed makes a difference when you have women who coach women . . . There is a comradery between both teams, there is a lot of congratulations from the bench when good catches are made, when good hits are made.

Sometimes I think that our sportship cuts through some of the shit. Because I think we are awful good sports, and I like that about us. I'm proud of that in us . . . Being gracious to each other or cheering (the other team) if they make a spectacular play or something like that. It's things like that—it's how we are.

But no story is as touching or as illustrative of the transformation feminist softball can accomplish than this one:

She hit the ball, oh so far away out into center field, and she was fast so by the time people were thinking of catching it, or the ball was even coming down, she was by second base. And the woman caught it. And rather than trudge off the field and feel disappointed, this woman ran out into center field—she rounded first base and headed for center field—and hugged the woman that caught it. And it wasn't this touchy, feely thing—it was just "you caught that ball and I hit is *so* hard and you caught it and that's really good."

Endangerment

A final theme expressed by these women was a rejection of the need or desire to put oneself, a teammate or an opponent into a situation of physical danger. This rejection of endangerment as "part of the game" fits within the anti-rationalist stance, for once the outcome is devalued, risking injury in order to win is no longer necessary. Despite best intentions, collisions did occur on the basepaths and injuries sometimes resulted, but players actively discouraged one another from taking risks. One woman who played with a leg brace was moved from second base to a safer position after a teammate realized that playing second made her more vulnerable to injury.

Commitment to safety is illustrated by the following incident in which a woman running to second base was ruled to have interfered with the second baser's throw to first for a double play:

(The argument over the call) had something to do with blocking a throw to first base. They were trying to make a double play and everyone was called out. And I got upset about it, and we asked (the umpire) "What was she supposed to do?" because she was just trying to slow down . . . We don't play that kind of softball where you take somebody out at second. It literally wasn't that kind of situation. And somebody said "Well, what was she supposed to do?" and he said, "*Slide.*" And that's when I made a connection between the umpire wanting us to play that big league stuff. And I looked down at the ground where we were playing and it was *rocks*. The ground was so dry, sliding would have been dangerous, I think, and I would never have asked anybody I knew to slide.

Women on other teams voiced the same concerns, stating that "feminists . . . want an emphasis on more cooperation and skill as opposed to brute strength and aggression," and "more attention (is) paid to cooperation and utilizing aggression for a productive goal rather than to destroy or injure an opponent." Another noted,

> Everyone cares about each other as a person and as an athlete second. And I think that even if we had to play short, I don't think they would let someone play that was injured, you know, to a point that would hurt them worse.

Once again they clearly saw this behavior as oppositional to "the male model":

> They're just cut-throat about winning. Even when they're ahead 15 to nothing, they're just out for blood on every play. They'll purposely slide into you or something like that. It's unnecessary.

> I was very traditional when I was in grade school and high school . . . and it was ingrained in us to go out there and kill 'em and win . . . I always heard the men say this, so I always thought if they do it it was alright for us to maul people and kill, and get a license for anything . . . I don't feel that way anymore.

The accounts of these feminists indicate traditional forms of sport contain elements offensive to their feminist sensibilities. Specifically, their complaints focus upon the over-emphasis on winning, the hierarchy of authority, the elitism of skill, social exclusion, the disparagement of opponents and an ethic of endangerment. These criticisms serve as a blueprint for the changes they were putting into practice: a form of softball that is process oriented, collective, supportive, inclusive, and infused with an ethic of care. In the process of creating these oppositional meanings for sport, feminists claim as their own, territory long inhabited only by men.

THE TRANSFORMATIVE POWER OF FEMINISM

Sport is a significant and pervasive cultural form whose meaning is often taken for granted because the public and scholars alike tend to recognize sport only in its highly institutionalized form. Alternatives to dominant notions of sport, such as the American Negro baseball leagues and the New Games Movement, are marginalized, trivialized or obscured, and they are not accorded the status of "real" sport. As long as feminist scholars focus on the relationship of women to dominant structures of sport, our scholarship will continue to reproduce those dominant notions of sport.

This paper documents one instance of feminist resistance to masculinist hegemony and dominant, male-sustained definitions of sport. The women whose efforts to transform softball are documented here not only challenge dominant images of sport, they show, through that challenge itself, that hegemony is never complete. These women successfully and creatively demonstrate that people can take a text meant to mean one thing and subvert that meaning for their own needs. Under their direction, sport is transformed from a mechanism for the preservation and reproduction of male values to a celebration of feminist alternatives.

We argue that this is a *feminist* alternative less because these solutions are unique to women than because women have labored to produce them. In this argument we rely upon the insight of Laura Nader, who, when challenged with the question, "What could a woman tell us about the war in Vietnam that a man couldn't?" replied, "It's not what a woman *could* say, it's what a woman *would* say." Feminist action may often take this form: it is not so much what women *could* say or do, it is that they choose to take some action. We see little evidence of other groups offering oppositional meanings for sport. Moreover we argue that the specific critiques these feminists offer and their solutions to them emerge from an analysis of the world grounded in women's particular experiencing of it. Neither sport nor society, as presently constituted, serves women's needs particularly well. As one of the softball players observed:

> If you think about it, there is a contradiction between feminism and sport. But when you think about it, there's a contradiction between feminism and life in America, but you keep doing it.

And another noted, "After experiencing the world, being a feminist was the only natural way to combat all the crap."

The transformative efforts of this particular feminist community may appear isolated from the mainstream of sport and culture, and one must examine the extent to which their efforts will effect change on dominant social practices. The power of such grassroots activism lies in a commitment to the radical feminist doctrine that the personal is political. In this community, moreover, feminist softball is not the only product of feminist praxis. Women's health cooperatives, women-owned and women-sustained businesses, and social service agencies created by women to ease the particular social problems of women, such as rape and domestic violence, provide evidence of the strength of women's culture. To the extent that such practices become commonplace elsewhere, feminism can serve as a powerful force for social change.

REFERENCES

Acosta, Vivian and Carpenter, Linda Jean. 1985. Women in athletics—a status report. *JOPERD* **56**(6): 30-34.

Birrell, Susan. 1984. Separatism as an issue in women's sport. *Arena Review* **8**(2): 22-29.

Boutilier, Mary and San Giovanni, Lucinda. 1983. *The Sporting Woman.* Human Kinetics Press, Champaign, IL.

Cole, Cheryl L. and Birrell, Susan. 1986, October. *Resisting the canon: Feminist cultural studies.* Paper to be presented at the annual NASSS meetings, Las Vegas.

Dunning, Eric. 1986. Sport as a male preserve: Notes on the social sources of masculine identity and its transformations. *Theory, Culture, and Society* **3**(1): 79-90.

Gabriner, Vicki. 1976. Come out slugging. *Quest* **2**(3): 52-57.

Grant, Christine. 1984. The gender gap in sport: From Olympic to intercollegiate level. *Arena Review* **8**(2): 31-47.

Gruneau, Richard. 1983. *Class, Sport, and Social Development.* University of Massachusetts, Amherst.

Guttmann, Allen. 1973. *From Ritual to Record.* Columbia University Press, New York.

Hall, M. Ann. 1983. Towards a feminist analysis of gender inequality in sport. In Theberge, Nancy and Donnelly, Peter. eds, *Sport and the Sociological Imagination* pp. 82-103. Texas Christian University Press, Fort Worth, TX.

Hall, Stuart and Jefferson, Tony, eds. *Resistance Through Rituals.* Hutchinson & Co. Ltd., London.

Harding, Sandra and Hintikka, Merrill B. 1983. *Discovering Reality: Feminist Perspectives on Epistemology, Metaphysics, Methodology, and Philosophy of Science.* D. Reidel, Dordrecht, Holland.

Holman, Milton and Parkhouse, Bonnie. 1981. Trends in the selection of coaches of female athletes: A demographic inquiry. *Research Quarterly* **52**(1): 9-18.

National Federation of State High School Associations. 1983-84. *Sport participation survey.* NFSHSA, Kansas City.

NCAA files statement regarding civil rights legislation. 1984, June. *NCAA News.* pp. 21, 23.

Sheard, Kenneth and Dunning, Eric. 1973. The rugby football club as a type of male preserve: Some sociological notes. *International Review of Sport Sociology* **5**(3): 5-24.

Slatton, Bonnie. 1982. AIAW: The greening of American athletics. In Frey, James, ed, *The Governance of Intercollegiate Athletics* pp. 144-154. Leisure Press, New York.

Theberge, Nancy. 1981. A critique of critiques: Radical and feminist writings on sport. *Social Forces* **60**, 2, 341-353.

Theberge, Nancy. 1985. Toward a feminist alternative to sport as a male preserve. *Quest* **37**, 193-202.

Webb, Harry. 1969. Professionalization of attitudes towards sport among adolescents. In Kenyon, Gerald, ed, *Aspects of Contemporary Sport Sociology.* pp. 161-178. The Athletic Institute, Chicago, IL.

NOTES

1. One woman told us that she was playing softball within three hours of moving to a new town. Another recounted the time she was alone in a new town and, hoping to find the women's community, she called the women's information hotline. The woman who answered told her there were no women's restaurants or bars in town, but she brightened considerably when she remembered that there was a woman's softball game in town that night. Other feminists have also explored the role of softball in the feminist community, see Gabriner (1976) and Boutilier and San Giovanni (1983).

2. Interviews with women drawn from all levels were done in the fall of 1983 in private settings not connected with softball. Interviews lasted from twenty minutes to an hour and were taped and transcribed. Observations were collected during the summers of 1983-1986, at games, practices and team meetings.

3. Title IX of the Education Act of 1972 requires that all educational institutions which receive any federal funds must offer programs open to members of both sexes or risk loss of those federal funds. While it covers all extra-curricular activities, its effect has been felt most strongly in athletics.

4. The AIAW was organized in 1971 to provide American college women with the opportunity to compete at an elite level in sport. It was organized by women, for women, and was the largest athletic organization in the United States. In the late 1970s, threatened by the success of women's athletics and mindful of the new economic implications of the growth of women's sport in colleges, the NCAA, a powerful all male organization, launched a campaign to take over women's sport. In 1980 they were successful, and the AIAW folded in 1982. For ten years, the AIAW existed as an all-woman organization which offered an alternative model of sport to women. With its demise, no alternative exists, and the hegemony of male values in collegiate sport, promulgated by the NCAA, is complete. For further reading see Christine Grant (1984) and Bonnie Slatton (1982).

5. At the high school level, participation for girls increased 616% between 1971 and 1982 (National Federation of State High School Associations, 1983-84). At the college level, the increase was 150% between 1971 and 1983 (NCAA News, 1984).

6. His remark is probably a reference to the player's reputation as an outspoken advocate of feminist and lesbian causes.

PART IV

MEDIA, SPORT, AND GENDER

iven the force of media-produced and -circulated images, including those images related to sport, it makes sense that feminism
and cultural studies have taken the media as a central object of
study. Both are concerned with the role of the media in circulating
and legitimating dominant narratives that construct who we are
and how we understand the world around us.

More people are involved in sport through the media than any other means,
including direct, active participation. Though familiar media representations of
sport appear innocent—that is, although "sport" may seem to be transparently
and objectively reported—the media actually re-present and re-construct sport
within certain frames and through routinized codes and conventions to produce
images that benefit particular privileged groups. Understood through a theory of
society informed by feminism, media sport constitutes a site for the display of
gendered, raced, and classed representations and the reproduction of social relations. Thus the media organize the ways we come to think about sport, social
relations, and even ourselves.

While the essays in this section vary in their approach to the media, they share
an emphasis on the power of the media. Grounding their arguments in data
collected from 6 weeks of televised sport in the Los Angeles area in 1989,
Duncan, Messner, Williams, and Jensen's study, "Gender Stereotyping in Televised Sports," documents several patterns of media representations: women's
sports are vastly underrepresented in televised coverage; the quality of technical
production is considerably higher for men's sports; women's sports are trivialized,
whereas men's sports are framed as important dramatic spectacles; and sports
broadcasters routinely infantilize and demean women athletes by referring to
them as "girls" and "young ladies" and calling them by their first names. In
contrast, male athletes are represented as strong and powerful "men" and "young
men" who are engaged in contests of "historical import."

In "Active Women, Media Representations, and Ideology," Margaret
MacNeill widens the scope of the discussion on media and power by examining
the relationship between televisual codes and the active construction of representations consistent with dominant gender ideology. Focusing on aerobics and bodybuilding, MacNeill argues that television offers a preferred reading of active
women consistent with conventional notions of beauty, sexuality, and gender
roles. She shows how visual and auditory signs are used to recuperate potentially
liberatory images of strong, active women into frames that work to contain the
status quo. She argues that the popular Canadian exercise show, "The 20-Minute
Workout," used cinematic techniques to sexualize and objectify female images;
in the same way, the "1985 Bodybuilding Championships" were narrated through
auditory signs which inscribe excessive sexuality on women's bodies. MacNeill
suggests that although these activities can be seen as counterhegemonic in that
they alter the historical relations between women and physical activity, any
subversive impulses are systematically neutralized and incorporated.

Nancy Theberge and Alan Cronk challenge the notion that the media's limited
coverage of women's sports is due to individual journalistic biases against women

and women's sports. Instead, they suggest that the coverage given to sports is continuously shaped by routine practices that construct the news. They suggest that the media construct an imaginary general public or readership that is assumed to be more interested in men's than in women's sports. This assumption is compounded by two related practices that they highlight in their study: the resources available to men's commercial sports and the reporter's beat. The established public relations organizations of men's sports make information more easily accessible to reporters and the "beat" assures ongoing contact with a particular team or event expected to generate news and to be of interest to the readership. Consequently, those events outside the beat, such as women's sports, are covered less frequently and by "stringers" rather than full-time reporters. The standardized format and content of the sports pages and the information from national wire services, whose focus is almost entirely on men's sport events, constitute another element of constraint upon the coverage of women's sport.

Christine Anne Holmlund extends MacNeill's discussion on media, gender, and bodybuilding to cinematic relations, looking, pleasure, and power. Holmlund offers a comparison of two staged documentaries, "Pumping Iron" and "Pumping Iron II: The Women," to demonstrate the relationships between popular film, visible difference, the body, sex, sexuality, race, and power. She locates the body, seen and spoken "commonsensically" through biological discourses, as a cultural element encoded with meanings, embedded in power relations and constrained by the historically specific needs of society. Based on a form of feminist film theory influenced by psychoanalysis, she emphasizes the tension between the fear of difference and the fear of the annullment of difference in terms of sex and race. Despite surface similarities in the structure of the two films, she argues that because of cultural incongruity between muscularity and woman, the narratives of "Pumping Iron II" and "Pumping Iron" are significantly different. In "Pumping Iron II" the competition is displaced and replaced by the standard Hollywood practice of asking "What is woman?" Images of muscular females undermine the common sense of visible difference and thus threaten "normal" sexuality and loss of love in the male spectator. The narrative and images in "Pumping Iron II" work to circumvent these threats by "fetishizing women's bodies and making them the object of heterosexual desire" while maintaining visible difference. The representation of Carla Dunlap, the only black contestant and winner of the Miss Olympia, illuminates the need for visible difference in terms of race as well as sex. Since both films present the body as spectacle, conflate sex/gender/sexuality, and obscure and stereotype race, Holmlund concludes that both films resemble advertising more than sport documentary.

Finally, in her essay on Robert Towne's film, "Personal Best," Linda Williams takes up the relationship between film and sexuality as it is constructed through a sport setting. "Personal Best" is the story of Chris and Tory, two Olympic track athletes who have both a competitive and lesbian relationship. Although the film received positive reviews for "its iconography of physically active, powerful women and its lesbian love theme," Williams contends that contradictions in the narrative work to recuperate potentially resistant or counterhegemonic representations of athletic female bodies and lesbian sexuality. She argues that although the possibility for the film's apparent overwhelming acceptance of homosexual love is established and legitimated through the sport setting and the emphasis on the physical and sensual, the relationsip is never *named* "lesbian." Because the lesbian theme is unarticulated, the implication of the relationship cannot be dealt with, and Chris and Tory must be driven apart (although Williams argues that what drives them apart is a "contrived separation"). The focus of the film shifts to the (re)establishment of Chris's heterosexual identity as well as a maturity marked by a heterosexual relationship.

Chapter 16

Gender Stereotyping in Televised Sports

Margaret Carlisle Duncan
University of Wisconsin–Milwaukee

Michael A. Messner
University of Southern California

Linda Williams

Kerry Jensen

Edited by Wayne Wilson
Amateur Athletic Foundation of Los Angeles

INTRODUCTION

Television both shapes and reflects the attitudes of our society. National networks and local stations broadcast thousands of hours of sports coverage each year to millions of viewers. The way in which television covers, or fails to cover, women engaged in athletics affects the way in which female athletes are perceived and also tells us something about the status of women in our society.

Note. Sponsored by the Amateur Athletic Foundation of Los Angeles, August 1990.
From *Gender Stereotyping in Televised Sports* (p. 1-31) by W. Wilson (Ed.), 1990, Los Angeles: The Amateur Athletic Foundation of Los Angeles. Copyright 1990 by the Amateur Athletic Foundation of Los Angeles. Reprinted by permission.

The Amateur Athletic Foundation of Los Angeles has sponsored research on the topic of television coverage of women's sports with the hope that it will lead to a more informed discussion of the issue.

The study presented here analyzes the quantity and quality of women's sports coverage and compares it to the coverage of men's sports. It examines six weeks of local sports coverage on a Los Angeles television station during summer 1989; the "Final Four" of the 1989 NCAA women's and men's basketball tournaments; and the women's and men's singles, women's and men's doubles, and the mixed doubles of the 1989 U.S. Open tennis tournament.

Our major findings are summarized at the beginning of the report and are followed by several policy recommendations. An explanation of methodology, a more detailed discussion of each finding and an interpretive essay appear later in the report.

While the report does offer some cause for optimism regarding the status of women's sports on television, the weight of the evidence clearly suggests that women's sports is underreported and that what coverage does exist is inferior to that afforded men's sports.

Sport is an important part of the human experience. Television is a powerful medium. Women and girls comprise a majority of our population. Their experience in sport should be reported and reported accurately. Broadcasters who fail to do so fail in their professional responsibility.

This report, "Gender Stereotyping in Televised Sports," identifies problems with the way that the broadcasters we studied treated women's sports and it suggests solutions. Although this study did not examine every national network, all of the networks and their local affiliates can learn from it. We may debate the solutions, but there is no denying the fundamental finding of the study: The television programs that we examined did not cover women's sports as well as they covered men's sports. This inequity is unfair. It is wrong. It can be changed and it must be changed.

Anita L. DeFrantz
President
Amateur Athletic Foundation of Los Angeles

POLICY RECOMMENDATIONS IMPLIED BY FINDINGS

- Televised sports news should provide more coverage of existing women's sports.
- Televised sports news coverage of women's sports should include visual as well as verbal coverage in proportions that are roughly equivalent to the coverage of men's sports. Viewers should be able to hear about and *see* women's sports on the news.

- Sports broadcasters should cease the sexist practice of focusing on female spectators as sexualized comic relief.
- Television networks should commit themselves to more equal amounts of coverage of women's events such as college basketball. Regular season games should be aired regularly.
- Television networks should commit themselves to equal quality of coverage of women's athletic events. The amount of resources and technical and production quality should be equivalent in the coverage of men's and women's sports.
- Women athletes should be called ''women'' or ''young women,'' just as men athletes are called ''men'' and ''young men.'' Announcers should stop referring to adult female athletes as ''girls'' just as they avoid referring to adult male athletes as ''boys.''
- Commentators should consciously adopt a standard usage of first and last names and it should be applied equally to men and women athletes and athletes of all races.
- When gender marking is necessary for clarity, it should be done in ways that are symmetrical and equivalent for women's and men's events. If announcers use phrases such as ''women's game'' and ''women's national championship,'' then they also should refer to gender when discussing men's sport (e.g., men's NCAA final, smartest player in men's tennis, etc.). The same symmetry should apply to the use of graphics.
- Commentators should increase their use of strength descriptors when announcing women's sports. They should reduce the use of descriptors implying weakness in women's sports.

DESCRIPTION OF STUDY: SAMPLE AND METHOD

The study addressed both quantitative and qualitative aspects of televised coverage of women's sports. The major questions, though, concerned the quality of actual coverage of women's versus men's athletic events. Therefore, we chose to examine televised sports programs in which men's and women's coverage could be analyzed comparatively. First, we studied six weeks of televised sports news coverage on KNBC, Los Angeles. Second, we examined the ''Final Four'' of the women's and men's 1989 NCAA basketball tournaments. And third, we analyzed the women's and men's singles, women's and men's doubles, and the mixed doubles matches of the 1989 U.S. Open tennis tournament.

Sample

Televised Sports News

Six weeks of sports news broadcast on the 11:00 p.m. edition, July 2 through August 15, 1989, from a single station, KNBC in Los Angeles, were taped and analyzed. During 1989, KNBC emerged as the top-rated local news broadcast in the Los Angeles market, and its lead sports reporter was awarded the Golden Mike award by the Radio and Television News Association of Southern California for his sports report. Amounts of air-time devoted to men's versus women's sports were measured. In addition to the quantitative measures, researchers analyzed the quality of coverage in terms of visuals and verbal commentary. Finally, visual and verbal presentations of non-athlete women in television news sportscasts were examined.

Basketball

We compared and analyzed televised coverage of the Final Four of the 1989 women's and men's NCAA basketball tournaments that appeared on CBS and ESPN. It should be noted that we chose the Final Four for the comparative analysis, rather than regular-season games, because there were so few women's regular-season games actually broadcast on national television. Final Four coverage amounted to three women's games and three men's games, including introductions/lead-ins and half-time shows. Types and levels of technical production as well as visual and verbal framing of the contests and the athletes were examined.

Tennis

The four final days of televised coverage on CBS and USA Network of the U.S. Open tennis tournament on September 7-10, 1989 were analyzed. Televised coverage on these days consisted of four men's singles matches (two quarterfinals, one semifinal, and the final), three women's singles matches (two semifinals and the final), one men's doubles match (the final), two women's doubles matches (a semifinal and the final), and one mixed doubles match (the final).

Research Method

Stage 1 of the study consisted of an extensive review of the literature on sports media from which the investigators constructed a list of research questions and created the research design. The televised news, basketball games, and tennis matches were then recorded on videotape.

In Stage 2 of the study, the entire research team (the three investigators and the research assistant) conducted a pilot study of the tapes. The pilot study had two outcomes: (1) The research design was fine-tuned—a list of specific questions and verbal descriptors was constructed; (2) the graduate research assistant was trained to analyze visual and verbal commentary. The research design which we constructed aimed to analyze the data both qualitatively and quantitatively.

- Quantitative Analyses: For the televised sports news, we compared the number of minutes devoted to men's sports/male athletes to the number of minutes devoted to women's sports/female athletes for each individual broadcast, and also computed totals by gender for the six-week period. We converted the totals to percentages. For the basketball games and tennis matches, we counted the incidences of verbal and graphic gender markings, strength and weakness descriptors, martial metaphors and power descriptors, types of naming of individual athletes, use of statistics, slow-motion instant replays and on-screen graphics.
- Qualitative Analyses: We employed a descriptive textual method in the analysis of the oral commentary during television broadcasts. We also analyzed the visual aspects of the television broadcasts—production, camera work, editing—by drawing on the research assistant's graduate training in cinematography.

In Stage 3 of the research, the research assistant viewed all of the tapes and compiled a written preliminary analysis.

In Stage 4, one investigator independently viewed and analyzed all of the tapes and then added her written analysis to that of the research assistant.

Finally, in Stage 5 the data were analyzed and compiled for this report by two of the investigators, using both sets of written descriptions of the tapes, and by viewing portions of the tapes once again.

DESCRIPTION AND ANALYSIS OF FINDINGS

A. Six Weeks of Televised Sports News: Women Are Humorous Sex Objects in the Stands, but Missing as Athletes

1. Quantitative Description

During the six-week period, 42 complete evening broadcasts were examined; 21 contained no coverage of women's sports. Male athletes received the lead coverage 40 times, women twice. Women's sports were normally covered, if at all, in the middle or toward the end of the broadcast. Out of approximately 264 minutes of total sports coverage over the six-week period, 244 minutes (92%) covered men's sports, 12 minutes (5%) covered women's sports, and 8 minutes (3%) covered gender-neutral topics.

2. Qualitative Description

The Sunday night sports show (the longest of the week) began with a sophisticated visual sequence accompanied by music with a snappy rhythmic tempo. The visuals were comprised of a rapidly changing montage of 17 sports scenes. Two of these shots were of women—one a tennis player, the other of a bikini-clad body builder strutting across the stage in time to the music. The framing of this show suggested its content: mainly men's sports with one or two token female athletes.

Men's sports tended to receive both visual and verbal coverage; women's sports tended to receive only verbal coverage. The commentators were far more likely to refer to women athletes by their first names and the men athletes by first and last, or simply last names. And actual coverage of women's sports, though occasionally good, was sometimes framed in insulting ways. For instance, on the July 25 broadcast, the only mention of a female athlete was essentially a gag feature. Footage showed golfer Patty Sheehan driving her ball straight into the water, and was accompanied by this commentary: "Whoa! That shot needs just a little work, Patty. She was out of the hunt in the Boston Big Five Classic." The story which followed showed a man making a hole-in-one at a miniature golf tournament.

Though female athletes were rarely covered—and when they were covered, it often was ambivalently—women in non-athletic roles were generously sprinkled throughout these broadcasts. Women appeared most commonly either in the role of comical object of the newscaster's joke, or as a sexual object. In fact, these two roles were often overlapping, and were given significantly more air time than were female athletes. For instance, by far the longest single story (3 minutes, 50 seconds) on a woman in the six-week period focused not on a female athlete, but rather, on "Morgana, the Kissing Bandit," a woman with enormous breasts who has made a name for herself by running out onto baseball fields and kissing players.

The most common depictions of women in these broadcasts were the frequent visuals of scantily clad female spectators, accompanied by verbal sexual innuendo by the commentators. For instance, on July 3, the broadcast showed a clip of a female baseball spectator reaching into her breast pocket and attempting to get something out, accompanied by the commentator's "Be still, my beating heart!" Shots of—and comments about—women's breasts (always large) were frequent. On July 10, viewers saw female spectators in bikinis dancing in the stands, breasts jiggling, with the comment: "Why we love this game—because it's a great sport and it's part of America. Take yesterday in Oakland [shot of one bikinied woman], we're talking great weather, we're talking great atmosphere . . ."

The male commentators appeared to be aware that this sort of locker room humor was not acceptable to all people, but they essentially communicated that they didn't care: It's all in good fun. For instance, on July 14, a broadcast which had no coverage of women's sports, there were several shots of female spectators, including one of a particularly bosomy woman wearing a tank-top at a Minnesota Twins baseball game. The commentator queried, "Isn't baseball a great sport? Just brings out the best in everyone! Okay, I know we'll get complaints, but it's not like we snuck into her back yard and took her picture. We're talking public place here!'' Shortly thereafter, we were shown male tennis star Andre Agassi changing his shirt during a match, and the same commentator declared, ''In tennis the big moment in an AA match is when he changes shirts. Equal time for that incident in the Twins game.''

3. Analysis and Interpretation

The examples above encapsulate the general tone and consistent framing of gender on this televised sports newscast. Women athletes were largely ignored. Instead, women were more often presented ''humorously'' as sex objects. Men, on the other hand, almost never were presented as sex objects (we observed men presented as sex objects only twice in the six-week period). But when men were viewed as sex objects, it was within their roles as athletes—and in the case of Agassi, as an elite athlete. Thus, the framing of women reinforced the image of women as non-athletic sex objects on the sidelines. The rare sexual framing of men reinforced the equation of male sexuality and masculine power. The verbal disclaimer (''it's not like we snuck into her back yard . . .'') echoed the kind of reasoning that frequently is used to rationalize harrassment of and violence against women: ''I couldn't help myself, she was so scantily clad!'' Moreover, the attempt to humorously label this kind of coverage as ''equal time'' can only be seen as extremely cynical commentary which insults women, whether athletes or not.

It is not surprising that men's sports were covered more than women's sports. In fact, during the six-week period studied, there were simply more men's sports to cover. Men's professional baseball, which has no women's counterpart, drew a large proportion of coverage during this period of time. But the 92% coverage of men's sports to 5% women's still amounted to a disproportionately high coverage of existing men's sports. During this six-week period numerous unreported or underreported sports events involving women took place, including five professional women's golf tournaments with $1.6 million in prize money; three Virginia Slims professional tennis tournaments and Wimbledon totaling more than $2 million in prize money; the national gymnastics championships; the U.S. Olympic Festival '89; and major competitions in swimming, diving and cycling. The ignoring or underreporting of women's sports events contributes to what Gerbner (1978) called ''the symbolic annihilation'' of women. Put simply, if it is not reported, in the minds of most people, it simply did not happen.

What was most disturbing about these television news broadcasts was the confluence of, on the one hand, the conspicuous absence of coverage of women athletes with, on the other hand, the ways that women were consistently placed in the role of sexualized comic relief. It should be emphasized that what is presented as ''news''—and how it is presented—is the result of concrete choices made by human beings. In the case of the six-week period of television sports news that was examined, the choices of what to cover and how to cover it reflected a very sexist bias against women.

B. Women's and Men's Basketball: Differences in Quality of Technical Production

We observed demonstrable contrasts between the ways that the women's and men's basketball games were produced and presented. Overall, the production of the men's games was of much higher quality than the women's games.

1. Visual and Aural Framing of Contests

The visuals and the sound in the three men's contests can be summarized as highly professional. The camera angles and the editing of visuals, were technically sophisticated. Graphics were sophisticated, stylish and frequent. The commentators were "high profile," experienced and skillful. The sound was clear. Throughout the games, the shot clock and the game clock appeared on-screen frequently and appropriately. The three women's contests, on the other hand, were characterized by lower sound quality, periodic mistakes in editing, generally less colorful commentary, far fewer appearances of game and shot clocks on-screen, and the use of fewer camera angles. Graphics appeared less frequently, and occasionally incorrectly. For instance, in the Auburn versus Louisiana Tech women's semifinal game, Steve Physioc spoke about Auburn while the graphic pertained to Louisiana Tech. Two examples of these different levels of technical quality, consistent through all the games, were the opening/framing of the contests and the coverage of free throws.

a) Opening/Framing of the Contests.   Verbal and cinematic clarity combined with some form of either emotional, intellectual or narrative development are key elements in the creation of an opening sequence capable of instigating and maintaining audience participation. Camera operators must choose well-composed, focused and ideally evocative shots. The editors must combine the shots in a meaningful, continuously evolving fashion, choosing bits of interview which add excitement, poignancy or information. The opening of the men's games offered a model for this. The opening of the women's games tended to ignore these tenets.

Men's games.   Each of the men's games was introduced with a sophisticated and dramatic montage which drew the viewer into the event. The variety of camera angles, shot distances and shot transitions, artfully edited, created a kinetic, exciting effect and spoke of high production values. For example, the championship game between Michigan and Seton Hall opened first with Quincy Jones playing the piano and singing; followed by a montage of artfully edited sights and sounds of excited fans, team mascots and dome officials discussing preparation for the event; two hands checking the hoop; a bouncing ball accompanied by upbeat music; the coaches yelling instructions to players; scoreboard lights; and the band leader cuing his musicians ("2, 3, 4 . . ."). As the band music began to the beat of a heavy drum, a spinning basketball became the

NCAA logo, a small child wearing an oversized Michigan visor was lifted in time to the music, a baby grinned, a spectator spread a handful of tickets poker-style, the camera zoomed out from the tickets, and then rapidly back in to a Michigan logo on a young woman's cheek, and then to a low-angle shot, with closely miked sound, dramatizing the swoosh of the ball through the hoop. A cheerleader told us she was praying for her team's win. We saw a man dressed as a pirate carrying a large Seton Hall flag. A player emerged from the locker room. And, a Catholic priest blessed the Pirates. Finally, filmed highlights of each team's semifinal wins brought the opening to an emotional climax of ecstatic coaches and players celebrating, jumping on one another. The driving sequence ended on a strong downbeat, and moved us out to the Seattle skyline to orient us geographically, and then we were brought down gently with a lyrical sequence of soft dissolves. The camera slowly swept over the band, continuing the same movement in an extremely wide shot of the dome interior, a shot of the mascot and a tracking shot of the row of cheerleaders. A deep male voice welcomed us to the NCAA championship. Then, commentators Jim Nantz and Brent Musberger began the work of intensifying the dramatic conflict. This is a "remarkable tournament," we heard from Musberger, who then laid out five clearly articulated points, each accompanied by clever graphics concerning game analysis.

As the players were introduced, two cameras kept us close to the players, and low angles emphasized their bulk. The frequent cuts to cheerleaders during introductions were well-composed low-angle shots designed to emphasize the huge dome interior, with star filters over the camera lense enhancing the lights. As we approached tipoff, James Brown of CBS assured us that both teams were "fully armed and ready to do battle," while extremely long shots characteristic of epic drama moved us out of the dome. And, a verbal and visual emphasis on sports luminaries in the audience (Bill Walton, Magic Johnson and a good luck telegram from Senator Bill Bradley) added to the aura of importance surrounding the event.

Women's games.   Generally speaking, even when they were not directly framing the women's contests as "preliminary" to the men's, the opening/framing of the three women's games were far less technically sophisticated and less dramatic than those of the men's. The opening of the women's championship game stood in contrast to the opening of the men's game, described above. Whereas the men's coverage focused on the drama of the event, the opening of the women's game focused, in a sentimental way, on the backgrounds of several of the players. Narration began over images of little girls, many in dresses, playing basketball on a playground, and continued over short photographic histories of several players. Meanwhile, synthesized music played over the sequence of images and softened the images of rough basketball playing. As we viewed the sequence of images of individual players (2-4 photographs, spanning from infancy through high school and college), interspersed with interviews with the players' mothers, a male voice reported the following:

> The familiar sounds of the playground echo with the lifelong dreams
> of youth. For our college stars, there is a kaleidoscope of memories

with the fantasies of yesteryear, and the promise of today. Many of these young ladies have been pushed to peak performance by sibling rivalry. [Brief interview with a mother then voice continues.] To pursue with eagerness the phantoms of hope and expect that age will perform the promise of youth. Talent carries with it authority which makes it preferable to all the pleasures of age. History shows development through the competition of sport. [Another brief interview with a mother.] As their talent blossoms through the years, their expectations become realizations. They have now reached new heights. [The voice over is now accompanied by game footage of jump-shooting players.] It has been said that success is not a destination but a continuous journey and for these women, their journey has taken them down a long and arduous road. And so dreams become reality. The echoes continue to be heard as children emulate luminaries while the heroes of today are the dreamers of yesteryear.

The verbal commentary was flowery and difficult to follow. The music was not as upbeat as that in the men's game. And the visual images were ambivalent: At best, they showed some athletically talented basketball moves that may have built some sense that an important game was about to occur. At worst, they trivialized these athletes as childlike, cavorting on the playground.

As the women's games were being discussed in the openings, at half-time, and throughout the contests, the men's games continually jumped into the frame. For instance, as the audience awaited the Maryland versus Tennessee NCAA semifinal game, ESPN's Bob Ley and Dick Vitale interviewed players and coaches of the *men* who would play the next day. Then, we saw low-angle kinetic shots of women playing ball as the game was introduced. But immediately, we were back to the men: "Certainly, for the men's games some amazing institutions and happenings," and we learned about the annual pilgrimage to Friday's men's open practice. Then we returned to interviews with the women players. This sort of cutting back and forth from coverage of today's women's games and tomorrow's men's games tended to mark the women's game as preliminary, less important. At best, it constructed a frame of emotional ambivalence around the women's game: This game is not an event of great importance in the world of sport.

Player introductions also contrasted sharply with those in the men's games. Usually, a single camera followed a player as she left the bench, traveled down the row of teammates and out onto the floor. The cuts from traveling player to stationary bench sometimes were abrupt and jarring. And, the timing was off somewhat. During the Auburn versus Louisiana Tech introductions, there was a brief period in which nothing was shown before the next player was announced and rose from her seat. Moments later, there was a confusing, noncommittal shot with no clear focus.

b) Coverage of Free Throws.   A comparison of the coverage of free throws in the women's and men's games offered a specific example of the more general issue that fewer cameras, less expert camera work and editing, and lower quality sound equipment characterized the coverage of the women's games.

Men's free throws. A sophisticated narrative structure of free throws repeated itself through the three men's games. For example, in the men's championship game, a close-up of Seton Hall's John Morton concentrating intensely in preparation for his foul shot followed a long shot which established the setting. A wide shot allowed viewers to see the successful drop through the hoop, with a medium shot showing the reaction of Morton's team and a close up of the coach nervously chewing his hand. A camera behind the basket captured Morton's preparation for his second shot with a smooth camera move keeping the ball in frame as it fell through a second time. We then saw the coach's reaction on the bench before returning to watch the game in real time. The narrative structure combined with camera shot variety to dramatically frame the moment.

Women's free throws. The framing of free throws in the women's games was generally far less dramatic than in the men's. In the women's games, only two camera positions alternated. The transition from one position to another was not always smooth. For instance, in the Maryland versus Tennessee semifinal game, viewers saw a wide angle shot of the court as Maryland's Deanna Tate prepared to shoot. This was followed by a confusing shot of another player's back, a close-up of Tate as she shot, a wider shot to view the trajectory of the shot and finally a close-up of the back of a potential rebounder's head. Women's free throws were usually followed immediately by long shots of the court as play resumed. Coaches' and teammates' reactions on the bench and close-ups of the shooter's face were far less frequent than in the men's games. As a result, compared with the men's free throws, the narrative drama of the moment was diluted.

2. Slow-Motion Instant Replays

The number of plays which were shown in slow-motion instant replay was higher in the three men's games (43) than in the three women's games (34). But this gap was actually greater when we take into account the fact that replays in men's games were more likely to be shown from two or more angles (11 times in the men's games; 4 times in the women's games). The average number of instant replays per game was thus considerably higher in the men's games (18.0/game) than in the women's games (12.7/game). The replays in the men's games also were more likely to be accompanied by sophisticated graphics and superlative descriptions.

3. Use of Statistics

The use of statistics—both graphic and verbal—was less frequent and less refined in women's games than in men's games (see Table 16.1). Graphic statistics often

Table 16.1   Use of Statistics (Average per Game, by Sex)

	Verbal	Graphic	Total
Men's games	33.3	24.3	57.6
Women's games	29.0	9.3	38.3

appeared during free throw attempts in men's games, but not nearly as frequently during women's games.

C. Tennis and Basketball: Women Players Are Constantly "Marked" Verbally and Visually, and Are Verbally Infantilized. Male Athletes of Color Share Some of This Infantilization

1. Gender Marking

In women's basketball, gender was constantly marked, both verbally and through the use of graphics. Viewers continually were reminded that they were watching the "Women's Final Four," the "NCAA Women's National Championship Game," that these were "some of the best women's college basketball teams," that coach Pat Summit "is a legend in women's basketball" and that "this NCAA women's semifinal is brought to you by . . ." As Table 16.2 shows, gender also was marked through the use of graphics in the women's games which CBS broadcast, but not in the ESPN game. The CBS logo marked the women's championship game: "NCAA Women's National Championship," as did their graphics above game scores. ESPN's graphic did not mark gender: "NCAA Semifinal." In the three women's basketball games which we examined, team names were gender-marked 53 times graphically, 49 times verbally (a total of 102 times). However, we chose not to count gender-marked team names in our

Table 16.2   Gender Marking in Women's Basketball (Total Number)

	Graphic	Verbal	Total
Mrlnd. vs. Tenn.	2	10	12
La. Tech. vs. Auburn	0	21	21
Tenn. vs. Auburn	26	18	44
Total	28	49	77

tabulations because they were the responsibility of their respective universities, not the networks or commentators.

During the women's games, when commentators were discussing the next day's men's games, the men's games were sometimes gender-marked, (e.g., "The men's championship game will be played tomorrow."). But during the men's basketball games, we observed no instances of gender marking, either verbal or graphic. Men's games were always referred to as universal, both verbally and in on-screen graphic logos (e.g., "The NCAA National Championship Game," "The Final Four").

Women's and men's tennis matches were verbally gender-marked in a roughly equitable manner (e.g., "Men's doubles finals," "Women's singles semifinals"). Verbal descriptions of athletes, though, at times revealed a tendency to gender mark women, not men. For instance, in the mixed doubles match, the commentators informed viewers several times that Rick Leach was "one of the best doubles players in the world," while Robin White was referred to as one of "the most animated girls on the circuit." A notable instance of graphic gender marking in tennis was the tendency by CBS to display a pink on-screen graphic for the women's matches, and a blue on-screen graphic for the men's matches.

2. Hierarchies of Naming by Gender and Race

The data revealed dramatic contrasts between how men athletes and women athletes were referred to by commentators. This was true both in tennis and in basketball. Women were referred to variously as "girls," "young ladies" and "women." On occasion, the naming of women athletes was ambivalent. For instance, Steffi Graf was called "the wonder girl of women's tennis." By contrast announcers never referred to male athletes as "boys." Male athletes usually were referred to as "men," "young men" or "young fellas." Second, when commentators used only a first name to identify an athlete the athlete was more likely to be female than male. This difference was most pronounced in tennis commentary, as revealed in Table 16.3.

In basketball, the degree of difference in the use of first names of players was not as dramatic, but the pattern was similar. In the three women's basketball games, we counted 31 incidents of women athletes being referred to by first

Table 16.3   First and Last Name Use in Tennis Commentary
(Totals and Percentages by Sex)

	First only	Last only	First & last
Men	44 (7.8%)	395 (69.8%)	127 (22.4%)
Women	304 (52.7%)	166 (28.8%)	107 (18.5%)

names only. This occurred 19 times in the men's games. What was most notable, though, was the fact that in each of the cases in which men were referred to by their first names only, the players were men of color (Rumeal [Robinson], Ramon [Ramos], etc.). White male basketball players never were referred to by their first names only.

3. Verbal Descriptors of Women and Men Athletes

There were consistent and clear contrasts between the quality and quantity of certain kinds of verbal descriptors which commentators used in discussing women and men athletes.

a) Attributions of Strength and Weakness. Examples of verbal attributions of strength were: powerful, confident, smart, big and strong, brilliant, gutsy, leader, mature, quick, dominant, takes control and aggressive. Examples of attributions of weakness were: mental mistake, weary, fatigue, frustrated, jittery, not comfortable, panicked, indecision, vulnerable, losing concentration, shaky, worries, lost control, dejected, a little flat and choking.

Commentators' verbal attributions of strength and weakness for men and women athletes contrasted sharply. As the data presented in Table 16.4 demonstrates, commentators in men's tennis used nearly four times the number of verbal attributions of strength as those of weakness. In women's tennis, verbal attributions of strength and weakness were roughly equal in number. Similarly, Table 16.5 shows that in men's basketball, verbal attributions of strength out-

Table 16.4   Verbal Attributions of Strength/Weakness in Tennis (Totals and Ratios, by Sex)

	Strength	Weakness	Ratio (S/W)
Men	146	38	3.84/1
Women	95	103	0.92/1

Table 16.5   Verbal Attributions of Strength/Weakness in Basketball (Totals and Ratios, by Sex)

	Strength	Weakness	Ratio (S/W)
Men	59	10	5.9/1
Women	51	24	2.1/1

numbered attributions of weakness by a nearly six-to-one ratio. In women's basketball, attributions of strength outnumbered attributions of weakness, but by only a two-to-one ratio.

In addition to these differences in quantity, the quality of attributions of strength and weakness for women's and men's events also tended to differ. In basketball, women's attributions of strength often were stated in ambivalent language which undermined or neutralized the power and strength descriptor: "big girl," "she's tiny, she's small, but so effective under the boards," "her little jump hook," etc. A difference in descriptions of coaches also occurred. Joe Ciampi (male) "yells" at his team, while Pat Summit (female) was described twice in the Auburn versus Tennessee game as "screaming" off the bench. Men coaches were not described as "screaming," a term which often implies lack of control, powerlessness, even hysteria.

Even strong descriptors, for women, often were framed ambivalently: "That young lady Graf is relentless." And, whereas for women, spectacular shots sometimes were referred to as "lucky," for the men, there was constant reference to the imposition of their wills on the games and on opponents. In men's doubles, for example, the announcer stated, "You can feel McEnroe imposing his will all over this court. I mean not just with Woodford but Flach and Seguso. He's just giving them messages by the way he's standing at the net, the way he kind of swaggers between points."

There was little ambivalence in the descriptions of men: These were "big" guys with "big" forehands, who played "big games." Clearly, there was the constant suggestion of male power and agency in the commentary. Even descriptions of men's weaknesses often were framed in a language of agency: "He created his own error . . ." Discussion of men's "nervousness" was qualified to make it sound like strength and heroism. For instance, early in the Becker/Krickstein match, the audience heard this exchange by the two commentators: "They're both pretty nervous, and that's pretty normal." "Something would be wrong if they weren't." "It means you care." "Like Marines going into Iwo Jima saying they weren't nervous, something's a little fishy."

b) Verbal Martial Metaphors and Power Descriptors. Examples of verbal martial metaphors and power descriptors used by commentators were: buries, bangs in, yanks, firepower, ambushed, explode, whips, hits, punches, fights, battles, knocks, routed, pounds, misfire, attack, stalk, force, exert pressure, wrestling, squeezing trigger, scorch, fully armed, duel, shootout, bullet pass, penetrate, warrior, big guns, jam, powers ball in, fire away, hit bullets, blasting away, bolo punch, drawing first blood and weapons. Table 16.6 shows that gender differences existed in the use of such descriptors.

In tennis, commentators used twice as many martial metaphors and power descriptors when discussing men's play. In basketball, the quantitative difference was even more dramatic. Martial metaphors and power descriptors were used in men's games nearly three times as often as in women's games. In place of frequent words and phrases that invoke images of power in men's games, fewer

**Table 16.6   Martial Metaphors and Power Descriptors
(Basketball and Tennis Totals, by Sex)**

	Basketball	Tennis
Men	82	34
Women	28	17

and less evocative power descriptors were used for women. For example, instead of one who "attacks" the hoop, a woman might "go to" the hoop. Where a man's play might be referred to as "aggressive" a woman might be called "active." With negative outcomes, there also were differences: Where men "misfire," apparently women simply "miss." Where a man might "crash through" the defense, a woman was described as "moving against" the defense. And the word "nice" was used ad nauseum in describing moves, passes and shots in women's games. Though "nice" also was used at times in men's games, it was not as common.

c) Verbal Attributions of Success and Failure.   Verbal attributions of success used at least once in men's games were: experience, physical condition, strength, hustle, knowledge of game, quickness, skill level, intelligence, good judgment, height of team, good teamwork, good blood lines and genetics, guts, poise, physical ability, speed, gifted physically and mentally, perfect timing, old-fashioned hard work, courage, size, talent, good leadership, good coaching and showing no emotion. Verbal attributions of success used at least once in women's games were: good coaching, getting along with each other, helping each other out, close chemistry, bigger and better, skill and luck, patience in offense and defense, big hearts, good athlete, quick, courage, leadership, hard work, hustle, composure, emotional preparation, execution, skills, teamwork, experience and victory because they are family.

Verbal attributions of failure used at least once in men's games were: bad judgment, too hesitant, lack of concentration, fatigue, wear and tear, impatience and abandoning game plan. Verbal attributions of failure used at least once in women's games were: size disadvantage, nerves, laziness because of dependence on a teammate, inactivity, lack of composure, tight rims and not settled into offense.

As Table 16.7 demonstrates, the ratio of verbal attributions of success to those of failure differed by gender. Attributions of success in men's basketball outnumbered attributions of failure by a better than five-to-one ratio. For women, attributions of success outnumbered attributions of failure by a better than two-to-one ratio.

In both basketball and tennis, there were qualitative differences in the ways that success and failure were discussed for women and men athletes. In fact, two

**Table 16.7   Attributions of Success and Failure in Basketball
(Totals and Ratios, by Sex)**

	Success	Failure	Ratio (S/F)
Men	62	12	5.2/1
Women	21	9	2.3/1

formulae for success appeared to exist, one for men, the other for women. Men succeeded through a combination of talent, instinct, intelligence, size, strength, quickness, hard work and risk-taking. Women also apparently succeeded through talent, enterprise, hard work and intelligence. But frequently cited with these attributes were emotion, luck, togetherness and family. Women also were more likely to be framed as failures due to some combination of nervousness, lack of confidence, lack of "being comfortable," lack of aggression and lack of stamina. Men were far less often framed as failures—men appeared to miss shots and lose matches not so much because of their own individual shortcomings (nervousness, losing control, etc.), but because of the power, strength, and intelligence of their male opponents. This framing of failure suggested that it was the thoughts and actions of the male victor that won games, rather than suggesting that the loser's lack of intelligence or ability was responsible for losing games. Again, we encountered the theme of male agency and control. Men were framed as active subjects, women reactive objects.

D. Less Overt Gender Stereotyping Exists in Basketball and Tennis Commentary, When Compared With Past Studies

Though the televised sports news was clearly biased against women, in the basketball and tennis we found very little of the overtly sexist language, sexualization and/or devaluation of women athletes that was documented in studies over the past two decades. We noted some obviously conscious efforts by commentators to move toward non-sexist reporting of women's sports. For example, in the Maryland versus Tennessee women's basketball game, Steve Physioc at times renamed "man-to-man defense" to "player-to-player" defense.

ANALYSIS AND INTERPRETATION OF FINDINGS

An individual who watches an athletic event constructs and derives various meanings from the activity. These meanings result from a process of interaction between the meanings that are built into the game itself (the formal rules and structure, as well as the history and accumulated mythology of the game) with the values, ideologies and presuppositions that the viewer brings to the activity of watching. But viewing an athletic contest on television is not the same as watching a contest "live." Televised sport is an event which is mediated by the "framing" of the contest by commentators and technical people (Clarke & Clarke 1982; Duncan & Brummett, 1987; Gitlin, 1982; Morse, 1983; Wenner, 1989). Thus, any meanings that a television viewer constructs from the contest are likely to be profoundly affected by the framing of the contest (Altheide & Snow, 1979; Antin, 1982; Conrad, 1982; Duncan & Hasbrook, 1988; Fiske & Hartley, 1978; Innis, 1951; McLuhan, 1964; Morse, 1983).

It is already well-documented that women's sports are undercovered on television (Boutilier & SanGiovanni, 1983; Duncan & Hasbrook, 1988; Dyer, 1987; Felshin, 1974). The vast majority of televised sports are men's sports. Just as with newspaper editors, those who make decisions about what will be covered on television usually argue that they are simply "giving the public what it wants." Programming decisions clearly are circumscribed by market realities, and research does indicate that with few exceptions, men's athletic events draw more spectators than women's. But one question that arises concerns the reciprocal effect of, on the one hand, public attitudes, values and tastes, and on the other hand, the quantity and quality of coverage of certain kinds of athletic events. What comes first: public "disinterest" in televised women's athletics, or lack of quality coverage? Perhaps a more timely question now that women's sports are getting at least incrementally more coverage is: How do the ways that women's and men's sports are covered on television affect the "interest" of the public in these events?

A. Visual and Aural Framing of Contests

It has been well-documented that television is, in its essence, a medium which constructs and manipulates feelings (Corcoran, 1984; Gitlin, 1982; Real, 1989; Wenner, 1989). It follows, then, that television networks' different levels of commitment to producing, editing and presenting men's and women's sports are likely to produce very different feelings in viewers—feelings that operate below the level of conscious thought. The men's games are produced and framed in such a way that viewers are likely to feel that they are privileged to be watching an exciting, dramatic spectacle which is of historic importance. The television crew clearly has done its job in creating an emotionally-charged context. The eyes of the world appear to be focused on this all-important event. The viewer is invited to sit back and enjoy it with everybody else.

By contrast, women's games have a lower budget feel to them. The lower technical quality, less colorful or exciting visuals and less informative verbal commentary, combined with production decisions which frame the women's contests ambivalently combine to add to viewers' perhaps already existing sense that women's basketball is less important, and of lower quality. The overall effect of the presentation of the women's games is that we are viewing not a dramatic, historic spectacle, but rather, a less-than-dramatic game. This ambivalent framing of women's basketball is likely to add to viewers' already-existing doubts about the importance of the women's game. The subtext seems to be that the *real* event is tomorrow "up the road at the Dome."

B. Commentary on Women and Men Athletes

Language is never neutral. An analysis of language reveals imbedded social meanings, including overt and covert social biases, stereotypes, and inequities. There is an extensive body of literature which documents how language both reflects and reinforces gender inequalities (Baron, 1986; Henley, 1977, 1987; Lakoff, 1975; Miller & Swift, 1977, 1980; Schultz, 1975; Spender, 1980; Thorne, Kramarae & Henley, 1985; Van Den Bergh, 1987). In a recent study of the gendered language of sport, sociologists D. Stanley Eitzen and Maxine Baca Zinn (1989: 364) argue that:

> [Gendered] language places women and men within a system of differentiation and stratification. Language suggests how women and men are to be evaluated. Language embodies negative and positive value stances and valuations related to how certain groups within society are appraised. Language in general is filled with biases about women and men. Specific linguistic conventions are sexist when they isolate or stereotype some aspect of an individual's nature or the nature of a group of individuals based on their sex.

The sports media reflect the social conventions of gender-biased language. In so doing, they reinforce the biased meanings built into language, and thus contribute to the re-construction of social inequities. This study identified three general areas of difference in the language used to discuss and describe women and men athletes: (1) differential verbal and graphic gender marking; (2) differential use of first names when discussing players; and (3) differential use of verbal descriptors by commentators. We will discuss briefly the implications of these differences.

1. Gender Marking

Our observations of tennis reveal that women's and men's matches are verbally gender-marked in a roughly equivalent manner, though the pink (for women) and blue (for men) graphic on-screen logos tend to mark gender in a manner which reinforces conventional gender stereotypes. In basketball, the data reveal a dramatic asymmetry: Women's games are constantly gender-marked, while men's games are never gender-marked. Team names (e.g., "Lady Techsters, Lady Tigers, Lady Volunteers") are an example of gender marking that has been criticized by sociologists as "contributing to the maintenance of male dominance within college athletics by defining women athletes and women's athletic programs as second class and trivial" (Eitzen & Baca Zinn, 1989: 362). In the three women's basketball games examined, team names are gender-marked 53 times graphically, 49 times verbally (a total of 102 times). However, we chose not to count gender-marked team names in our tabulations (see Table 16.2) because they are the responsibility of their respective universities, not the networks or commentators.

We can conclude, though, that the combination of on-screen graphics, verbal commentary, and team names and logos amounts to a constant level of gender marking in the women's games. By contrast, the men's games always are referred to simply as "the national championship game," etc. As a result, the men's games and tournament are presented as the norm, the universal, while the women's continually are marked as the other, derivative (and by implication, inferior) to the men's.

2. Hierarchies of Naming by Gender and Race

The language which the commentators use to describe women is often infantilizing, ("girls," "young ladies,") while the language used to describe men ("men," "young men,") linguistically grants them adult status. This occurs despite the fact that the women and men athletes are all roughly the same age, particularly in the case of basketball players who are all college students, and thus are nearly exactly the same age.

As Nancy Henley (1977) has demonstrated in her research, "dominants" (either by social class, age, occupational position, race, or gender) are most commonly referred to by their last names (often prefaced by titles such as "Mr."). Henley points out that "dominants" generally have license to refer to "subordinates" (younger people, employees, lower class people, ethnic minorities, women, etc.) by their first names. The practice of referring more "formally" to dominants, and more "informally" to subordinates linguistically grants the former adult status, while marking the latter in an infantilizing way. This "hierarchy of naming"—by gender as well as by race—is clearly evident in the sports events which we analyzed. Tennis commentators' tendency to utilize the first name only of women athletes (52.7% of the time) far more frequently than men athletes (7.8% of the time) reflects and reinforces the lower status of women athletes.

The data also suggest that it is not simply gender hierarchy which is being linguistically constructed here. There also appears to be a "hierarchy of naming" operating. At the top of the linguistic hierarchy sit white "men," whose last names always are used; followed by black "men," who sometimes are called by only their first names; followed by "girls," and "young ladies," who frequently are called by only their first names. We find no racial differences in terms of how women athletes are named. This suggests, following the theory of gender stratification developed by Connell (1987) and applied to sport by Messner (1989), Messner & Sabo (1990) and Kidd (1987), that sports media reinforce the overall tendency of sport to be an institution which simultaneously (1) constructs and legitimizes men's overall power and privilege over women; and (2) constructs and legitimizes heterosexual, white, middle class men's power and privilege over subordinated and marginalized groups of men.

3. Differences in Use of Descriptors for Women and Men Athletes

The combined effect of focusing more on strength than on weakness, more on success than on failure, and of using many and varied martial metaphors and power descriptors when describing men athletes has the effect of linguistically weaving an aura of power, strength and human agency around male athletes. By contrast, commentators in women's games tend to utilize martial metaphors and power descriptors far less frequently, to employ a much higher proportion of verbal attributions of weakness, and tend to focus on reasons for an individual's failure, rather than reasons why her opponent won. In the USA tennis broadcast, commentator Anne White repeatedly undercut her descriptions of the women's strength, power, and skill with allusions to their emotionality. There was so much discussion of the affective states of the female players that one is left with a sense of apparent emotional fragility of female athletes. As a result of this sort of practice, even attributes of strength for women are often verbally couched in ambivalence (e.g., ''strong girl''). As a result, commentators tend to weave around women athletes a linguistic web of ambivalence.

Can these differences always be interpreted as implying ''sexism'' on the part of the commentators? After all, there are identifiable objective differences in men's and women's style of playing basketball and tennis. For instance, the ''vicious slam dunk'' in men's basketball has very few counterparts in women's basketball. And in mixed doubles tennis, the only example of women and men playing as teammates and as opponents, commentary abounds about the men's power and domination of vulnerable women opponents, and about men needing to ''cover'' for their weaker female teammates. This commentary does reflect a common reality in strategies of mixed doubles play. Men's serves, overheads, and other shots, *do* tend to be more powerful than women's. In terms of ''power descriptors,'' then, the question is not just quantitative, but *how and when* power descriptors are used comparatively. The commentary can either dwell on this in ways that over-emphasize these differences, or commentary can focus on other issues of strategy and on the positive things that the women do. Most of the commentary which we examined does the former. Here, a ''real difference'' constantly is marked and over-emphasized by the commentary, resulting in the reassertion of the association of men and masculinity with power, and the association of women and femininity with weakness (Duncan & Hasbrook, 1988; Messner, 1988, 1990).

4. Less Overt Gender Stereotyping in Commentary Compared With Past Studies

Studies of the 1970's through the mid-1980's, revealed that women athletes, when they were reported about on television at all, were likely to be overtly trivialized, infantilized, and sexualized (Boutilier & SanGiovanni, 1983; Dyer, 1987; Felshin, 1974). Though the televised sports news that we analyzed was obviously overtly biased against women, most of the gender bias in the commentary on women's basketball and tennis was fairly subtle.

Though subtle stereotyping can be as dangerous as overt sexism, we see the decline of overtly sexist language as an indication that some commentators are becoming more committed to presenting women's athletics fairly. For instance, as we noted, Steve Physioc re-named ''man-to-man defense'' as ''player-to-player'' defense. This is an example of a conscious decision to replace androcentric language with language which is not gendered. Though Physioc did not do this consistently, the fact that he did it at all was an indication of his awareness of the gender biases built into the conventional language of sports. Critics might argue that changing language subverts the history or the ''purity'' of the game. The general response to this argument is that terminology used to describe sports constantly is changing. Viewed in this context of change, Physioc's use of ''player-to-player defense'' can be viewed as a linguistic recognition that something significant has happened to basketball: It is no longer simply a men's game. There are women players out there, and the language used to report their games should reflect it.

Language does not simply change as a ''reflection'' of social reality. Language also helps to construct social reality. Thus, it is imperative that those who report and comment on sport become conscious of the values underlying the language that they use on television. They can choose to use the conventional androcentric language—and thus help to shore up an old system of male dominance and superiority. Or they can choose to consciously create and use language which is not gendered. The choice to use non-sexist language is a choice to linguistically affirm the right of women athletes to fair and equal treatment. And it will contribute to the construction of a more egalitarian society (Van Den Bergh, 1987).

We speculate that the differences in our findings, when compared with these recent studies, are an indication that public discussion of these linguistic patterns has raised the consciousness of commentators. What was being done at a less-than-conscious level by well-meaning, but perhaps subtly biased commentators, was revealed by researchers and journalists and discussed in public forums. Commentators then chose to change the ways that they report. If this interpretation is correct, it is indeed a positive phenomenon which speaks optimistically of the possibilities for change.

REFERENCES

Altheide, D.L. & Snow, R.P. (1979) *Media logic*. Beverly Hills, CA: Sage Publications.

Antin, D. (1982) Video: The distinctive features of the medium. In H. Newcomb (Ed.), *Television: The critical view* (3rd ed.) (pp. 455-477). New York: Oxford University Press.

Baron, D. (1986) *Grammar and gender*. New Haven: Yale University Press.

Boutilier, M.A., & SanGiovanni, L. (1983) *The sporting woman*. Champaign, IL: Human Kinetics.

Clarke, A. & Clarke, J. (1982) Highlights and action replays: Ideology, sport, and the media. In J. Hargreaves (Ed.), *Sport, culture, and ideology* (pp. 62-87). London: Routledge & Kegan-Paul.

Connell, R.W. (1987) *Gender and power*. Stanford, CA: Stanford University Press.

Conrad, P. (1982) *Television: The medium and its manners*. Boston: Routledge & Kegan-Paul.

Corcoran, F. (1984) Television as ideological apparatus: The power and the pleasure. *Critical Studies in Mass Communication*, **1**, 131-145.

Duncan, M.C. & Brummett, B. (1987) The mediation of spectator sport. *Research Quarterly for Exercise and Sport*, **58**, 168-177.

Duncan, M.C. & Hasbrook, C.A. (1988) Denial of power in televised women's sports. *Sociology of Sport Journal*, **5**, 1-21.

Dyer, G. (1987) Women and television: An overview. In H. Baeher & G. Dyer (Eds.), *Boxed in: Women and television* (pp. 6-16). New York: Pandora Press.

Eitzen, D.S. & Baca Zinn, M. (1989) The de-athleticization of women: The naming and gender marking of collegiate sport teams. *Sociology of Sport Journal*, **6**, 362-370.

Felshin, J. (1974) The social view. In E.W. Gerber, J. Felshin, P. Berlin, & W. Wyrick (Eds.), *The American woman in sport* (pp. 179-279). Reading, MA: Addison-Wesley.

Fiske, J., & Hartley, J. (1978) *Reading television*. New York: Methuen.

Gitlin, T. (1982) Prime time ideology: The hegemonic process in television entertainment. In H. Newcomb (Ed.), *Television: The critical view* (3rd ed.) (pp. 426-454). New York: Oxford University Press.

Henley, N.M. (1977) *Body politics: Power, sex, and nonverbal communication*. Englewood Cliffs, NJ: Prentice-Hall.

Henley, N.M. (1987) This new species that seeks new language: On sexism in language and language change. In J. Penfield (Ed.), *Women and language in transition* (pp. 3-27). Albany: State University of New York Press.

Innis, H.A. (1951) *The bias of communication*. Toronto: University of Toronto Press.

Kidd, B. (1987) Sports and Masculinity. In M. Kaufman (Ed.), *Beyond patriarchy: Essays by men on pleasure, power, and change*. Toronto and New York: Oxford University.

Lakoff, R. (1975) *Language and woman's place*. New York: Harper & Row.

McLuhan, M. (1964) *Understanding media: The extensions of man*. New York: Signet Books.

Messner, M.A. (1988) Sports and male domination: The female athlete as contested ideological terrain. *Sociology of Sport Journal*, **5**(3) 197-211.

Messner, M.A. (1989) Masculinities and athletic careers. *Gender & Society*, **3**(1) 71-88.

Messner, M.A. (1990, forthcoming) When bodies are weapons: Masculinity and violence in sport. *International Review for the Sociology of Sport*, **90**(3).

Messner, M.A. & Sabo, D.F. (1990, in press) Toward a critical feminist reappraisal of sport, men and the gender order. In M.A. Messner & D.F. Sabo (Eds.), *Sport, men and the gender order: Critical feminist perspectives*. Champaign, IL: Human Kinetics Publishers.

Miller, C. & Swift, K. (1977) *Words and women: New language in new times*. Garden City, NY: Doubleday/Anchor.

Miller, C. & Swift, K. (1980) *The handbook of nonsexist writing*. New York: Lippincott & Crowell.

Morse, M. (1983) Sport on television: Replay and display. In E.A. Kaplan (Ed.), *Regarding television* (pp. 44-66). Los Angeles: American Film Institute/ University Publications of America.

Real, M. (1989) *Super media: A cultural studies approach*. Newbury Park, CA: Sage Publications.

Schultz, M. (1975) The semantic derogation of women. In B. Thorne & N. Henley (Eds.), *Language and sex: Difference and dominance* (pp. 64-75). Rowley, MA: Newbury House.

Spender, D. (1980) *Man made language*. London: Routledge & Kegan-Paul.

Thorne, B., Kramarae, C., & Henley, N. (1985) Language, gender and society: Opening a second decade of research. In B. Thorne & N. Henley (Eds.), *Language, gender and society* (pp. 7-24). Rowley, MA: Newbury House.

Van Den Bergh, N. (1987) Renaming: Vehicle for empowerment. In J. Penfield (Ed.), *Women and language in transition* (pp. 130-136). Albany: State University of New York Press.

Wenner, L.A. (1989) Media, sports and society: The research agenda. In L.A. Wenner (Ed.), *Media, sports and society* (pp. 13-48). Newbury Park, CA: Sage Publications.

Chapter 17

Active Women, Media Representations, and Ideology

Margaret MacNeill
University of Toronto

"Four, three, two, one . . . and take it to the right, left, right, left . . . ooouh you're lookin' good." Across North America, millions stretch and bounce to the tune of the *20 Minute Workout*. Now switch the channel to CBC; *Sportsweekend* is covering the 1985 Women's World Bodybuilding Championships. Someone in the audience yells, "Hey, where's the beef?" Then the hooting and whistling begins. How different are the oiled bikini-clad bodybuilders from the aerobic dancers in high-cut leotards? Are these images progressive or do they stereotype female activity? Initial conceptions of active leisure pursuits often locate aerobics within a "female" realm of activity while placing bodybuilding within a "male" sphere. These arbitrarily defined boundaries between "male" and "female" activities are cultural constructs.

Since the 1970s, growing numbers of women have been attempting to liberate themselves through physical activity. Some would argue that this expansion is primarily individual and has led to changing ideas of femininity. Others would argue that the movement can be attributed to larger social forces. For example, the fashion industry foresaw the potential of increased profits by developing a line of women's sportswear. Entrepreneurs soon realized the business opportunities in women's fitness clubs and other services. The federal government also had an

From "Active Women, Media Representations, and Ideology" by M. MacNeil. In *Not Just a Game: Essays in Canadian Sport Sociology* (pp. 195-211) by J. Harvey and H. Cantelon (Eds.), 1988, Ontario: University of Ottawa Press. Reprinted by permission.

interest in promoting physical activity; its Participation campaign was aimed at reducing health-care costs and improving the productivity levels of the Canadian work force (Labonté, 1982).

The (re)production of these structural considerations through the mass media, specifically televisual representations, is the central focus of this discussion of active women, media representations, and ideology. An episode of the *20 Minute Workout* and *Sportsweekend*'s coverage of the 1985 Women's World Bodybuilding Championships are examined in order to investigate the changing patterns of female physical activity. The discussion locates both aerobics and bodybuilding within the locus of dominant hegemonic relations and ideologies.

IDEOLOGY AND HEGEMONIC RELATIONS

The concept of hegemony allows one to examine agency-structural ties with specific attention to the linking of work and leisure spheres. What women do in their free time, and the media representations of this activity, cannot be examined independently of the external constraints that direct individuals into various patterns of social organization; reciprocally, one must not ignore the capacity of human agency to create change.

Hegemonic relations are so effective because they are legitimated; moreover, they are not based on economic considerations alone—moral, political, and intellectual power are vital determinants as well (Mouffe, 1979:183). Hegemonic power so saturates the common-sense reality of humans that people rarely act or think in ways alternative to those that are legitimated. In other words, in their lives, people operate within a relatively narrow range of practices and beliefs. Alternatives to this range are either never considered or dismissed as inappropriate, that is, they are marginalized. Hegemonic relations are thus "silently" maintained without coercion.

For instance, the everyday practice of sending young girls to figure-skating lessons while their brothers go to arenas to play hockey is an example of hegemonic relations. Without ever being taught or told, children learn that certain activities are more appropriate for girls and others are more suitable for boys.

One should not equate hegemony with the absence of change, however. Hegemonic relations are dynamic in that they must be continually reaffirmed and renegotiated. Without this dynamic component, relationships would remain static. We know that some young girls play hockey and that some boys figure skate. This dynamic nature of hegemony is described by Raymond Williams (1980) as a residual/dominant/emergent set of tensions.

The role of human agency is important in the residual/emergent areas to initiate change. For example, although active leisure for most women was unthinkable in 1886 and was a counterhegemonic (or emergent) practice for those few women who were active, in 1986 such activity was more acceptable. This acceptance of particular forms of female physical activity (such as aerobic classes) is now being challenged by the women's bodybuilding subculture. The emergent notion of the muscular female image is being negotiated in many ways. What is "appropriate" female muscularity? How can bodybuilding competitions, which were an exclusively male domain, be feminized? How can activity be best marketed? All these emergent views are challenging the dominant notions of what is proper female activity.

Sports hegemony in Canada includes specific socialization practices. Although there are obvious differences between individual families in the upbringing of their children, Canadian families have much in common, including notions that result in, reflect, and maintain *gender* stratification. Residual patriarchal ideologies concerning the "inferiority" of feminine practices seem to be at the basis of female socialization.

Research concerning female physical activity often uncovers gender differences in game and sport orientation due to polarized socialization processes for males and females. Further, the history of female opportunities is one of expansion and contraction. For example, in the "Golden Era" of women's sport between the two World Wars, women were indispensable for wartime industry. Attitudes became more liberal and women moved into essential jobs and expanded their leisure opportunities as well. However, attitudes can be just as quickly reversed and the longer history of women's oppression has been accompanied by the channelling of women into expressive, aesthetically pleasing sports such as gymnastics, dance, and figure skating (Cochrane et al., 1977). Duquin (1978) and Hall (1982) note that boys are socialized into *instrumental* activities that teach qualities such as competitiveness, teamwork, and co-operation to aid their later integration into the labour force. Boutilier and SanGiovanni (1983) similarly argue that females are inadequately socialized into sports roles, since the institution of sport in Canadian society embodies the "masculine" values of hard work, competition, and deferred gratification. Sports behaviours are therefore defined as male gender roles.

Socializing women into selective roles in active leisure serves to legitimate the dominant ideology of patriarchy, that is, the system of power relations based on male domination. The problem for women in assuming healthy athletic roles is based on the cultural definitions of the masculine/feminine dichotomy. Aggressive and competitive patterns of behaviour learned through play are considered appropriate for males and inappropriate for females (Hall, 1982). Most sports, therefore, offer few positive status or prestige incentives for females. To socialize girls and women into a wider spectrum of play, games, and sport, a redefinition of the positive aspects of masculine/feminine and athletic traits into *androgynous* traits (that is, neither male nor female) needs to be accepted (Hall, 1981, 1982).

The degree of self-expression located in media representations of active women provides clues to the extent of patriarchal ideology. The next question to be addressed is: how is the dominant ideology reaffirmed through the medium of television?

ACTIVE WOMEN ON TELEVISION

Sportsweekend's televised presentation of the Women's World Bodybuilding Championships and Orion Entertainment's *20 Minute Workout* are, first and foremost, productions constructed by humans. In order to understand how the dominant ideology is reaffirmed through television the theory of semiology must be briefly considered. Specifically, it is necessary to discuss three terms: the signifier, the signified, and the sign. At every level of understanding, semiologists argue, there are signifiers (a physical form) and a signified (the meaning attached to the signifier), which together create a sign. Through the examination of both levels, the physical form and the meaning can be distinguished from each other to display the conventionality of human communication.

For example, the letters w, n, o, a, m are physical forms (the signifiers). Arranged in a particular way they become signified to represent (in the English language) the sign for woman. By combining the physical forms in this particular way, an item of knowledge is denoted. But the sign carries with it a cultural meaning as well as a representational one. The sign "woman" also involves cultural images of what a woman is, what she does, how she looks, etc. Thus a television image of a woman engaged in physical activity may embody the notion of femininity if she is an aerobic dancer, or masculinity if she is a bodybuilder.

The following analysis will deal with two basic categories of communicative modes: visual and auditory signs. For research purposes it is possible to separate the former from the latter but it should be noted that both modes of representation are broadcast simultaneously, and for the most part are received by the audience as a package. However, from this artificial separation, a series of subcategories of popular production techniques emerges. Among the visual signs which could be examined (camera angle, framing, scan and zoom, focus, dissolves and wipes, special effects, lighting, background, body language), only some have been singled out for analysis. A similar selection has been made from the numerous auditory signs (auditory noise, music, commentator's verbal speech, and instructors'/competitors' verbal speech). Those which have been selected provide a good illustration of how the cultural meanings of active women are constructed.

VISUAL SIGNS

The Camera Angle

The camera angle is a common method of lending a particular meaning to the visual. In the *20 Minute Workout*, the models are surveyed from all angles except directly underneath. In the episode examined, 18.28 per cent of the 257 shots were aerial. This highly distortive angle of aerobic movements accentuates "cleavage" shots of the women, in their low-cut leotards, exercising on a rotating stage. The limb movement of criss-crossing arms and the spinning bodies arranged in various line and triangle formations create an interesting human kaleidoscope for the viewer but do not permit the audience to perform aerobics with ease. To maximize participation the camera should be directly aimed at the instructors, thus providing a standard frame of reference for the active viewer. This direct vantage point was displayed in only 36.63 per cent of the shots. The majority of the shots, 47.08 per cent, were from an upwardly tilting angle, usually whenever the women were bent over from the waist. In addition, the cutting rhythm of these shots increased in speed. Thus, the predominance of aerial and upwardly tilting camera angles helps create sexual images rather than images of power activity.

Sportsweekend's production of the Women's World Bodybuilding Championships employs a very different distribution of angles. Of the 69 shots from the routines, 76.6 per cent displayed the bodybuilders through a non-tilted camera. Downwardly tilted shots from behind the stage curtains accounted for 25.37 per cent, and 11.94 per cent of the shots tilted up from the side stage exit. These side stage angles are employed occasionally to capture the entrance and exit expressions of the competitors, and to permit the television audience to closely survey their bodies. Downward tilts from behind the stage are used sparingly. The direct angle is the simplest angle to capture the event without having to contend with other extraneous factors. It allows an audience that is unfamiliar with the sport to view female bodybuilders with little angular distortion; as well, it accentuates the physical rather than the sexual.

The Framing of the Image

The framing of aerobic images differs significantly from that of women's bodybuilding. The camera determines the borders of the image seen by the viewer. For the most part, the bodies of the instructors from the *20 Minute Workout* are fragmented. Rather than capturing complete visual images of the whole body in exercise, 62.75 per cent of all shots, in the episode examined, were close-ups and medium shots (half body). Predominantly, the mid-section (hips, thighs, buttocks) was centered on the screen. The tendency to focus on this part of the anatomy further objectifies an image of the ''sexually active'' female body.

Conversely, the camera coverage of women's bodybuilding frames the entire body of the competitors for most of the show. Since bodybuilders often flex muscle groups in the lower and upper body concurrently, and since sports broadcasting has not yet standardized the presentation of the new sport of women's bodybuilding, the long shot framing is more appropriate. In total, 37.25 per cent of the shots were framed as long shots, 32.39 per cent as medium. Close-ups of facial features during pre-taped personal interviews with the competitors accounted for the remaining 30.36 per cent of the framing. Overall, the sexually oriented (some would say pornographic) nature of the *20 Minute Workout* is absent in the coverage of bodybuilding. The objectification and orientation, in a sexual way, of the female bodybuilder is largely the product of the judging criteria, the women's posing, and the verbal analysis by the commentators.

Camera Techniques

The use of scan and zoom is common to both the bodybuilding competition and the *20 Minute Workout*. However, like the camera angles, their use denotes disparate images of women. In the bodybuilding competition the zoom is used most often to focus on the poses that display back muscularity and during the finale "posedown." In the *20 Minute Workout*, a disorienting zoom and scan occurs continuously. In fact, 32.79 per cent of all aerobic shots zoomed in or out. In addition, the audience is titillated by the constant visual caressing of the female body created by the rotating stage and camera angles.

Like the camera angle and the zoom and scan, the use of the focus transmits a very clearly defined image. In the "cool-down" section of the *20 Minute Workout* the softly focused women wiggle their hips, sway their arms overhead, and look "groggy-eyed" to intensify the significations of sensuality. The body-builders, always in sharp focus while performing on stage, are softly focused during interviews, when the women are carefully "made-up" with cosmetics. The other exception to the bodybuilding sharp focus occurs in brief shots of the women "psyching up" in the "pump-room," which create the illusion that the audience is quietly intruding on this preparation.

Body Language

Body language (locomotion patterns, stances, gestures, and facial expressions) is created by the aerobic instructors and the bodybuilding competitors themselves. The sexually oriented physical gestures in both cases are projected towards the television audience only. The only connections made to other women in either aerobics or bodybuilding are externally constructed by the television viewer or the judges' narrative.

Although it is the women who position and manoeuvre themselves on stage, their choices of body language are not absolutely "free" choices. The locomotion patterns of both activities are founded in dance. The *20 Minute Workout* is choreographed by the lead instructor Bess Motta, with every episode following the same repertoire. Instructors of fitness classes across North America are quickly adopting this procedure, thus presuming that dance is the basis of aerobics. Similarly, although the bodybuilding poses are borrowed from the male counter-part and carry the muscular/masculine connotations with them, female competitors must include a dance transition between poses. These transitions tend to blur muscular definition.

The sexual stances and wiggles help to sell aerobics and bodybuilding to particular audiences. Through the choreography and the directions of the production crew, the aerobic instructors are positioned within an eighteen-inch range (defined as intimate in kinesic theory). In some instances, they are positioned so closely that their legs overlap in the open-legged stance and their buttocks touch in bent-over triangle formation, though there is sufficient room on the stage to space the women further apart. The proximity of the women, the erotic pulsing, and the arched backs unobtrusively sell sex appeal rather than fitness development. The bodybuilding poses separated by dance transitions are also sexualized through bodywaves, arched backs, hand movements, and constant wiggling.

Finally, the facial expressions in these productions are a further visual portrayal of feminine sexuality. While active men in televised sports are usually presented in a serious aggressive manner, women in both aerobics and bodybuilding smile, kiss the camera, and create seductive looks. This sexualization of women's physical activities through the choice of certain signs forces a closure on other possible definitions of female athleticism and activity.

AUDITORY SIGNS

As noted above, the auditory signs (music, verbal commentary), along with the visual, are important carriers of dominant ideologies.

The Use of Music

The "female" activities of aerobics and bodybuilding, with their underlying dance orientation, are always performed to prerecorded popular music. During the *20 Minute Workout* the movements co-ordinate exactly with musical phrases. In the dynamic cardio-vascular section, the music is fast and loud to complement the happy faces and energetic actions of the women. Later, in the cool-down, the music softens in volume and tone to relax participants and enhance the sexual hip sways. The bodybuilders also choreograph their routines to match the style and phrasing of the music. The main difference between the effects of the music in the two shows is that the aerobic instructors talk exactly to the 4/4 beat in a choppy monosyllabic fashion, whereas the verbal commentary of bodybuilding follows the rhythms of normal sentence flow more closely.

The Commentary

The primary role of the commentators is auditory rather than visual. It is their job to introduce the show, describe the activities to educate the audience, provide technical facts concerning fitness or bodybuilding judging criteria, and conclude the show. An important aspect of this narration is the personalization of the show; the commentators talk to ''you'' rather than ''everyone.''

Aerobic participants are told ''you want to look good so com'on let's see you move.'' The female bodybuilding commentator looks directly at the viewer and suggests that ''maybe in five years you'll find yourself on the bodybuilding stage.'' During the *20 Minute Workout* the commentator is never seen. She is an outside authority whose every word is simultaneously reinforced by written graphics across the screen. Her clear enunciation and correct sentence structure starkly contrast with the blurred tones and choppy speech rhythms of the models leading the class.

Because *Sportsweekend* is presented as a live event, the commentators are rarely seen during the performance. They make their appearances before, between, and after major segments to analyse and discuss the proceedings. Carla Dunlap, the ''expert colour commentator'' by virtue of her three-time world bodybuilding championship record, supplements her ''inside scoop'' on what it is like to compete with technical knowledge about women's bodybuilding. This knowledge confirms her presence as the authority and allows Vic Rauter, the co-commentator, to ask Dunlap those questions ''we all have'': ''Is this a show or a sport?''; ''Do these women have to be feminine?'' Vic Rauter plays the role of student; he goes on a learning experience with the audience in viewing women who are muscular. The voice-overs are positive but the audience never sees Rauter's actual facial expressions and reactions to the women as they compete. He appears only in the pre-taped segments in which he asks Dunlap the aforementioned general questions.

Again, it is important to reiterate that members of the audience individually interpret the images of aerobic dancers and bodybuilders. However, it can be argued that the structured verbal mediation also affects the audience's reception of female activity. Whereas the aerobics commentary is presented as factual, the bodybuilding expert is required to defend the activity. In other words, the hegemony of patriarchy intervenes in the auditory encoding of ''muscular'' women. Aerobic dancers reaffirm their femininity, their sexual attractiveness to men; the muscular frame of the bodybuilder is still an area of contestation.

The television viewer is not permitted to individually decide his or her feelings towards this new active image. Decisions are made within the constraints of patriarchy. For example, the eventual winner of the bodybuilding competition, Mary Roberts, is confirmed as a woman as well as a bodybuilding competitor. Rauter mentions that she is a mother, while Dunlap responds, ''See, women can have children and still look this good.'' This exchange guides the audience's interpretation of the image. Rather than concentrating on her muscularity, the commentators present Roberts as still being able to fulfil the traditional female sex and gender roles. Four of the five finalists are congratulated for ''softening'' their posing through dance, that is, enhancing their femininity. At the same time as the narrative provides examples of the residual, there are examples of emergent notions of the female image. Rauter notes that Deanna Panting is very ''thin in the upper body in comparison to the other competitors.'' Paradoxically this new image is also situated in the male/female sexual mediation:

Rauter: ''Look at the lats; even I'm getting into this.''
Dunlap: ''It's very sexy.'' (They both chuckle.)
Rauter: ''It's showbiz . . . and a little wave to the crowd, and there's her boyfriend.''

The viewer ''learns'' that, like Mary Roberts, Deanna Panting, despite her muscularity, can still attract men.

DISCUSSION

However, the question must still be asked: ''to what extent are these activities counterhegemonic or emergent?'' In the historical context, both aerobics and bodybuilding are counterhegemonic to the notion that intense physical activity for women is harmful. But, as noted above, hegemonic relations must be continually reaffirmed. As such, these relations vie for supremacy with emergent ideas. In the case of bodybuilding and aerobics, both contain, within their structure, patterns of the dominant, residual, and emergent. They are emergent in that they symbolize the increased opportunities for physical activity which are opening to women. They are also emergent in that physical activity of different sorts (such as bodybuilding) is increasingly seen as a socially accepted part of female social life. On the other hand, aerobics and bodybuilding are also sites of residual and dominant relations in that they reproduce patterns that subjugate women. Physical activity, yes, but in a form that stresses a preoccupation with beauty, glamour, and sex appeal as status symbols. The fitness boom channels women into traditional but revamped areas of ''female'' public space; simultaneously, the entry of men into aerobics and the possibility of developing men's bodybuilding beyond a few static poses are prevented by these same ideological barriers.

   To leave the analysis at this point overemphasizes agencies/individuals making decisions that are either constraining or enabling. It must also be remembered that structure limits those decisions that can be made. Thus, not only is the range of ''common-sense'' choices a woman considers severely ordered by the ''follow-the-leader'' style of aerobics or the rule-bound nature of bodybuilding, but it is also limited by wider-reaching structural constraints.

   Initially, the contemporary fitness and sport-related activities for women did contain counterhegemonic or emergent impulses. The fitness boom of the 1970s in some ways symbolized the radical notion of freedom from the constraints of waged and domestic work, and liberation from sedentary lifestyles. Being physically active was a visible, concrete display of the discontent with the dominant ideology of femininity. Aerobics and, perhaps to a greater extent, bodybuilding are counterhegemonic activities that eventually may emerge as a reaffirmed dominant hegemony. Yet aerobics is also being reintegrated into the dominant patriarchal and capitalistic modes of life. A greater differentiation from the "norm" is displayed by the female bodybuilders through their musculature and their heavy training program. However, this, too, is not counterhegemonic in the fullest sense because bodybuilders reaffirm their femininity through the dance-like posing and the degree of controlled muscle development. Repeatedly, commentator Dunlap mentions how many of the finalists have "softened" their look or style of posing. The less static posing ensures that the viewer does not see the full extent of muscle definition of which the competitors are capable. In other words, the posing ensures that female bodybuilders do not too closely approximate their male counterparts. Furthermore, the judging criteria for "assessing the female physique" state that:

> . . . first and foremost, the judge must bear in mind that he or she is judging a women's bodybuilding competition and is looking for the ideal *feminine* physique. Therefore, the most important aspect is shape, a feminine shape. The other aspects are similar to those described for assessing men, but in regard to muscular development, it must not be carried to excess where it resembles the massive muscularity of the male physique. (my emphasis) (International Federation of Body Building)

The "ideal" feminine shape is rooted in the patriarchal notion of femininity. It ensures that the distance between male and female muscularity is maintained and the continued common-sense notion that men have a greater biological potential for muscularity is continued. Female physicality has been intentionally obscured. More important, the "choices" for bodybuilders are also tied to the structured judging criteria. With rules and subjectivity of judging that deter full muscle development, bodybuilders must balance their training between an adherence to the sport through muscle development, and the demonstration of "female qualities."

While the rules of competition make it clear how limited the choices are for bodybuilders, even more significant is the way dominant power relations reproduce hegemonic knowledge and practices. Consent and loyalty to the common-sense conceptions constrain the degree to which active women can negotiate new forms. Female involvement is a "partial penetration" because it does not threaten the dominant hegemony. In other words, an active and emergent leisure counter-culture is gradually stripped of its radical impulses. Moreover, the concessions granted to allow for activity also neutralize the more radical counterhegemonic impulses. The dominant hegemony affirms women's rights to adopt an active lifestyle but within a strict social context. Thus, women move back into positions of inferiority by accepting the common-sense notions of a "female" bodybuilding or by participating in aerobics less for reasons of fitness and personal freedom and more for reasons that reaffirm the patriarchal notions of femininity (i.e., to lose weight, to improve sex appeal). The reattachment of patriarchal values defines aerobics as a "female" activity and consequently not as important as "masculine" leisure; and because it is so popular among women, aerobics marginalizes other active leisure possibilities.

But not only is there conformity in the choice of "appropriate" leisure forms, there is also a conformity in the styles and fashions in which the activity takes place. All over North America, active women are wearing mass produced bodysuits to aerobic classes taught by instructors who copy the *20 Minute Workout* style of teaching, movements, and fashions. Similarly, bodybuilding is gradually becoming more acceptable as the dance-oriented style of posing becomes more pronounced and the "ideal feminine" shape is mass-marketed as the form of champions. Generally, the styles of both these leisure forms are packaged within the music, the fashions, the gestures, and facial expression. Through conformity to these patriarchically grounded styles, gender differences are upheld and alternatives are not considered. Even the lead instructor on the *20 Minute Workout* cannot think of any forthcoming changes in aerobics. The only differences between the first and second year of production were stated as "new faces, new music, new colours for the leotards . . . there are not too many ways to make the show different" (Motta, cited in Taylor, 1984). Obviously, ingenuity and imagination have been suppressed during the process of style reification.

The combined influences of media, service, and commodity industries leave little room for personal initiative to mould the styles. These have become quickly institutionalized into hegemonic rituals for women. Ritualization occurs when the articulation of a particular style becomes reified. For example, across North America each episode of the *20 Minute Workout* attracts a million and a half viewers in ritual motion. The show format follows prepackaged standard instructions and motions.

The intent to "feminize" aerobics in the mass media generally is acknowledged by the lead instructor. Bess Motta considers aerobics

> . . . a women's medium because it's soft and very flowing and graceful, and men would look a little klutzy. We could get terrific guys but they'd just look a little funny doing aerobics. (cited in Taylor, 1984)

Because of this ritualization, the presence of aerobics and bodybuilding does not fundamentally reduce the domination of men over women in patriarchal society. Indeed, they complement other roles that are also experienced through femininity. Aerobics and bodybuilding are performed to music in the same way as the "feminine" sports of dance, figure skating, and gymnastics are experienced. Aerobics helps to uphold the feminine values of nonaggressiveness, noncompetitiveness, and gracefulness. Thus, the feminine "self" is learned, developed, and personified in aerobics. Bodybuilding develops the feminine "self" in the graceful sexually oriented dance transitions. It is, however, more competitive by the nature of the sport. Also, given the muscular development of the participants, it contains greater capacity to create new definitions of the feminine self.

As already noted, the production of the World Bodybuilding Championships and the *20 Minute Workout* objectifies female instructors and competitors. One of the reasons for the immense popularity of aerobics is that it caters to the voyeur through the sexualization of the images. The earlier textual analysis of the show demonstrated that the *20 Minute Workout* is produced in such a way that it emphasizes the sexual rather than safe and proper exercise. Similarly, the commentators of *Sportsweekend* noted how "sexy" one competitor's back appeared and yet it was later noted that her upper body musculature was underdeveloped in comparison to that of other competitors. Thus, the television viewer is situated in the role of voyeur capable of exerting domination over the image of active women. Women are voyeurs also, looking through "male eyes" to determine what the "ideal" female body is and to rank themselves according to standards set by the media.

It was also noted that, in the *20 Minute Workout*, the female body is constantly objectified into parts. Entire bodies are rarely framed in the *20 Minute Workout*. This tends to fabricate pornographic and erotic myths about how activity is to be experienced, and what an active woman should look like. The instructors are arranged in carefully planned positions that are intended to arouse. There are no fitness purposes being served through lingering "crotch" shots as arm exercises are being performed. The dehumanizing fragmentation of women into sexual objects is a repressive practice which is tied to the commodities market. "Sex" is marketable and promotes both male and female viewer identification with shows. Commercials describe "how to liven up your afternoon with the 'beautiful' instructors on the *20 Minute Workout*" rather than mentioning "fit" or "professional" instructors. Similarly, the closing comment for the bodybuilding championships noted that "one thing we all have to agree on is that those are very nice swimsuits those girls are *almost* wearing."

Unlike that of the aerobics dancers, the objectification of the female bodybuilders also contains a muscularity component. The objectification creates internal contradictions for the women who must display sensuality to be successful while still developing muscularity. To display maximum muscle definition, the women diet to a dangerously low level of body fat. This process, while enhancing muscle definition, tends to eliminate the ideal curves or "female shape" for which the judges must look "first and foremost." To balance muscle and sex appeal, some contenders are undergoing silicone breast implants to artificially meet the criteria. Dunlap is one of the first bodybuilders to publicly admit this. It goes without saying that, like aerobics, the sport does not have a health-oriented or fitness/bodybuilding-oriented base.

Indeed, these leisure activities have become new forms of the traditional beauty contest. The *20 Minute Workout* instructors are paraded on a revolving merry-go-round before the audience. Over the past two years aerobic competitions, such as the popular Etonic National Championships (U.S.A.), Coppertone Tanercise, or Crystal Light Aerobic Championships, have emerged. These competitions are similar to Broadway auditions based on routines consisting of moves such as leaps and gymnastic poses.

Bodybuilders are also paraded before judges and a very critical audience. Mary Roberts eventually won the 1985 World Championships because of her "perfect combination of round, massive, voluptuous muscles, aesthetic symmetry, balanced proportions and exceptionally sharp muscularity" (Reynolds, 1985:179). These activities have become an extension to the traditional feminine preoccupation with beauty; they are a form of cosmetology or "bodywork."

Throughout this chapter it has been argued that leisure is a site of contestation. Women's participation is presenting new ideas of physicality while reaffirming some of the established ones. Although some redefinition always occurs (such as the place of leisure in the female world), it is evident that residual patriarchal notions are difficult to alter.

In addition to the patriarchal infrastructure that objectifies a particular notion of femininity, capitalism plays an important part in the commodification of the feminine style. The range of commodification includes clubs, fitness classes, testing, and active lifestyle counselling. Clothes for aerobic classes, casual wear with the aerobic "look," published materials on the subject (videos, books, periodicals, and records), exercise equipment, and nonrelated products such as diet aids are all marketed.

Patriarchy is thus reproduced in a newly negotiated form that attracts women to buy the range of narcissistic commodities. This exploits women by creating "needs" that are in reality only wants. Furthermore, the champion bodybuilders and the *20 Minute Workout* instructors are commodities in themselves. They are used to sell boats, condominiums, clothes, and memberships at racquetball clubs. Just as female sexuality and glamour help sell physical activity to women, the sexuality and glamour of these active women help to sell unrelated products.

Advertisers gain the consent of particular groups of people by reproducing and legitimizing various ideologies and types of social organization. In particular, advertising is a major impetus in the acceptance of the aerobic ritual and its style as "feminine." Because it reproduces dominant ideologies, there is no need to coerce women into aerobics. Women learn through the narrative of advertising the "appropriate" social behaviour: "develop your figure as it was meant to be—radiant, fit, alluring" . . . "the joy of cooking" . . . "fitness mate" . . . "fit to be eyed" . . . "exercitement." Physical activity for women is often associated with diet food and beverages, fashions, and beauty aids, just as alcoholic beverages, cigarettes, cars, and computers are the products associated with active male leisure activities. Similarly, men learn the vocabulary of physical fitness: "excel in every direction" . . . "winning is a state of mind—competitive, determined, first" . . . "game-plan for life." Thus, economic forces suggest the direction of leisure and the degree of control that agents have in producing social transformations.

CONCLUSIONS

Media representations of active women, as this case study of aerobics and women's bodybuilding has shown, are aligned with dominant hegemonic relations. While the activities seem divergent because of the nature of aerobics and bodybuilding, they both serve to produce and reproduce images of active women engaged in "feminine" activities. For women to be *active* is an innovative and emergent notion in comparison to earlier periods in Canadian history. However, the alliance of physical activities with motifs of sexualized and feminized participation suggests that the liberating impulses are being reincorporated into residual/dominant hegemonic tendencies. The ideological politics surrounding the presentation of the female body in motion reinforces and perpetuates the patriarchal subordination of women. Thus, patriarchy serves as a major structural determinant of these cultural forms as they develop in North America.

As a critical method for analysing how the mass media orchestrate hegemonic relations, semiology enables us to better understand the various types of signs transmitted to mass audiences by revealing that representations of human social and material life are not neutral or natural. It forces people to question how and what they communicate and suggests the cultural meanings associated with communication. This questioning must necessarily lead to a deeper understanding about how power relations enable us to think, experience, and interact, and how these same relations and practices restrict access to a wider range of possibilities.

SUGGESTED READINGS

Two excellent sources dealing with the interrelationship of gender and sport are Mary Boutilier and Luciana SanGiovanni (1983), *The Sporting Woman*, Illinois, Human Kinetics, and Paul Willis (1982), "Women in Sport in Ideology," in Jennifer Hargreaves (Ed.), *Sport, Culture and Ideology*, London, Routledge & Kegan Paul. For literature dealing with television and cultural representations, see John Fiske and John Hartley (1978), *Reading Television*, London, Methuen, and Umberto Eco (1976), "Articulations of the Cinematic Code," in Bill Nichols (Ed.), *Movie and Methods: An Anthology*, Berkeley, University of California Press.

REFERENCES

Auger, C. (CSN) (1981), "L'activité physique et les travailleurs," Paper presented at the Conference on Physical Activity and Workers, Montréal, U.Q.A.M.

CNTU (Confederation of National Trade Unions) (1984), *Nos loisirs et nos vacances c'est pas du luxe*, Plate-forme de revendications de la CSN, Montréal.

Cochrane, J., A. Hoffman and P. Kincaid (1977), *Women in Canadian Life: Sports*, Toronto, Fitzhenry and Whiteside.

Crawford, R. (1981), ''You are Dangerous to Your Health: the Ideology of Victim-Blaming,'' in *International Journal of Health Services*, VII, 4.

Duquin, M. (1978), ''The Androgynous Advantage,'' in C. Oglesby (Ed.), *Women in Sport: From Myth to Reality*, Philadelphia, Lea & Febiger.

Gramsci, A. (1977), *Gramsci dans le texte*, Paris, Éditions sociales.

Hall, A. (1981), *Sport and Gender*, Vanier, CAHPER Society of Sport Monographs.

Hall, A. (1982), ''Sport and Sex/Gender Role Socialization,'' Paper presented at the Annual Meeting of the Canadian Sociological and Anthropological Association.

Labonté, R. (1982), ''Half Truths About Health,'' in *Policy Options*, III, 1.

Labonté, R. and S. Penford (1981), ''Analyse critique des perspectives canadiennes en promotion de la santé,'' in *Education sanitaire*, April.

Landry, F. (1979), *Kino-Québec et le mouvement international sport pour tous*, Meeting of the Coordinators of Modules, Québec, Kino-Québec.

Merwin, D.J. and B.A. Northrop (1982), ''Health Action in the Work Place: Complex Issues—No Simple Answers,'' in *Health Education Quarterly*, IX.

Mouffe, C. (1979), *Gramsci and Marxist Theory*, London, Routledge & Kegan Paul.

Reynolds, B. (1985), ''Mary Roberts: Toronto Comeback,'' in *Muscle and Fitness Magazine*, September.

Taylor, B.M. (1984), ''Flextime,'' in *Toronto Star Magazine*, August.

Williams, R. (1980). *Problems In Materialism and Culture*, London, Verso Editions.

Chapter 18

Work Routines in Newspaper Sports Departments and the Coverage of Women's Sports

Nancy Theberge
University of Waterloo

Alan Cronk
Winston-Salem Journal, North Carolina

One of the major topics of analysis and criticism about women in sport has been the treatment of women in the media. Despite the recent rise in the number of females participating in sport, and the perhaps less dramatic rise in the social acceptance and appreciation of women's sports, there has been little improvement in the quality and amount of coverage of women in the North American sports media. In a recent review of the evidence, Rintala and Birrell (1984:237) estimate that coverage of women's sports in newspapers hovers around 15% of all articles. The figure for magazines is an even lower 10%. Moreover, as Boutilier and SanGiovanni (1983) argue, the problem is more than one of numerical under-representation. Both in the amount of coverage of women's sports and in the quality of that coverage, the sports media collectively engage in the "symbolic annihilation" (see Gerbner, 1978) of women. By either trivializing women's sports by highlighting such events as the televised "Battle of the Sexes" or focusing the coverage of women athletes on their gender role characteristics, the media continue to present a picture of sport as a man's world in which, should women enter, they do so as strangers.

Because the media form a powerful institution that does not simply reflect but indeed shapes perceptions and behaviors, their treatment of women is important to the larger struggle for women's advancement. As Rintala and Birrell (1984) discuss, one important influence of the media can be to present information about athletic role models to young girls, influencing their ideas about the value of sport and physical activity and the opportunities that may be available to them in the world of sport. More generally, the impact of the media can extend to the broader ensemble of social relations. Despite the advances achieved by women in some sectors of our society in recent years, North American society remains rigidly stratified by sex. Several authors (e.g., Willis, 1982; Lenskyj, 1984; Boutilier & SanGiovanni, 1983) have written recently about sport's ideological contribution to maintaining this inequality. The continued underrepresentation of women in sport and the denigration and trivialization of their sport experience provides strong support for the myth of female passivity and frailty. This myth is manifested in barriers to women's participation in traditionally male activities, perhaps most crucially, in traditionally male occupations. The myth of female frailty, for instance, provides ideological justification for the continuing exclusion of women from physically demanding and hazardous occupations (see Theberge, 1985).

A significant change in media coverage of women's sports could provide a frontal assault on the myth of female frailty. As was evident in some of the coverage of the 1984 Olympic games, for example, media coverage of sport provides dramatic and widely publicized evidence of the varieties of women's physical accomplishments. To be sure, much of this coverage is not progressive: media fixation with women's gymnastics and individual gymnasts, for example, is best seen as a perpetuation of traditional notions of appropriately feminine behavior and demeanor. But coverage of other events indicates the potential impact of the media to record and dramatize an alternative view. Coverage of such events as the women's marathon, cycling, and rowing can transcend sport in its impact and provide a powerful challenge to conventional accounts of women's experiences and capabilities.

Among the explanations for the underrepresentation of women's sports in the media, perhaps the most frequently cited is the dominance of the journalism profession, especially sports journalism, by men. Anderson (1984) found that in a random sample of newspaper sports editors, 2% of the respondents were women. In their discussion of the treatment of women in the mass media, Boutilier and SanGiovanni (1983) emphasize the importance of increasing the number of women sports journalists. They caution, however, that simply bringing more women into the field is not a sufficient challenge to the male domination and masculine orientation of sports journalism. They argue,

> It matters a great deal whether the sportswriter is a feminist. . . . For many feminists, merely increasing the number of women who share the

same sexist orientations and assumptions of their male colleagues is less than a shallow victory. It is a dangerous instance of institutional co-optation whereby women become unwitting accomplices to the dissemination of sexist ideology in sport. (1983:204-205)

A second focus of explanations concerns the market forces that limit the range of coverage in the sports media. The dominant philosophy in journalism remains largely that the media should cover the events and issues that have the widest public interest. In North America this philosophy rarely embraces women's sports. Anderson (1984:20) quotes one of the sports editors in his survey on this topic:

When deciding how much space to devote to a topic and when to staff an event, editors need to look more closely at how many readers really want to know. Unfortunately, this means even less coverage for minor and women's sports.

As Rintala and Birrell (1984:247) observe, this issue comes down to a balance between social responsibility and economic rationality.

Related to marketing pressures are occupational pressures, specifically that the media are limited in the amount of space or time they have for coverage and the staff to handle their workload. Thus, the argument goes, they must devote what limited resources they have to the stories that command the most interest.

The purpose of this paper is to shed light on the exclusion of women from the sports media by exploring the process of newsmaking and news production. The paper is based upon research conducted while the second author, Alan Cronk, was employed at a midsize newspaper in the southwest United States. The analysis begins from the fact that coverage in newspaper sports sections is constrained by limitations of space and staff. A major thrust of recent sociological work on the media has concerned the manner in which the content of the news is socially constructed and constrained by the work routines of journalists. This paper utilizes that approach in order to demonstrate how the production of newspaper sports sections relies on a number of practices that, employed collectively, read women out of the sports news.

RESEARCH METHODOLOGY AND FRAMEWORK

The data for this analysis were collected between April 1983 and June 1984, when the second author was the sports copy editor at a paper he calls the *Pioneer*. Located in a southwestern U.S. city with a population of 250,000, the *Pioneer* has an average daily circulation of 40,000. The community served by the *Pioneer* has professional basketball and football teams and is 500 miles from the nearest major league baseball team. There is also a major university in the community, which fields teams in both men's and women's sports. The sports department at the *Pioneer* includes seven full-time employees (during the time of this study, all were men) and three stringers. Usually students, stringers are hired to cover local events and are paid a fee for each story they cover.

The framework used in this analysis is adapted from earlier research on newspaper production exemplified by the work of Tuchman (1978) and Fishman (1980). Following Fishman (1980:14), "this study takes journalists' routine work methods as the crucial factor which determines how they construe the world of activities they construct." The problem for the newsworker is how to sift and select from among the myriad of happenings in the world of sport those to be reported and analyzed in the sports section, that is, to choose what will become news.

THE *PIONEER* SPORTS SECTION
AND THE COVERAGE OF WOMEN'S SPORT

Tuchman (1978) has likened the process whereby journalists capture news to that of casting a net. Unlike a blanket, a net has holes. As she says,

> Its [the net's] haul is dependent upon the amount invested in intersecting fiber and the tensile strength of that fiber. The narrower the intersections between the mesh—the more blanketlike the net—the more can be captured. Of course, designing a more expensive narrow mesh presupposes a desire to catch small fish, not a wish to throw them back into the flow of amorphous occurrences. (1978:21)

Tuchman continues, "today's news net is intended for big fish" (1978:21). This is so because the practices newspapers follow to get stories consistently lead them to favor established bureaucratic sources as the subjects of their stories (see Tuchman, 1978; Fishman, 1980). In casting the news net, journalists seek connections with subjects that are both deemed newsworthy and able to provide reliable and accessible news material. In the case of sports news, the advantage enjoyed by men's sports lies not simply in the assumption of greater public interest but in the greater organizational and institutional resources of men's sports that guarantee preferred access to the media. The offices of the professional sports leagues and organizations, the NCAA, and individual teams and institutions are well equipped to offer services and materials to facilitate the sports reporter's job. Through the simple device of the press release, whereby they issue statements of current developments, sports organizations in effect offer story material to reporters. Similarly, through their media relations offices, these organizations institutionalize contacts with journalists and again create a bridge between themselves and the news world. The point here is not that journalists' work is done for them or that journalists do not exercise judgment and creativity in their work. Rather, the point is that in order to do their jobs, journalists must have ready and frequent access to reliable news sources. It is the established bureaucratic sources that can best perform this service, and these sources predominantly support male sports.

Of course, the bias toward coverage of established sources results not simply in a bias against coverage of women's sports but against coverage of noncommercial sports. For it is the commercial sports, including professional but also amateur spectator sports such as the Olympics and some university sports, that have the greatest need for media coverage. They also have the resources to invest in obtaining that coverage. The outcome is lack of coverage of ''minor'' sports in general and women's sports in particular. Where commercial sport does include women's sports, the news net is more likely to reach out to women. This is evident in the comparatively better treatment of women in media coverage of the Olympics in recent years.

A particularly powerful form of media dependence on established bureaucratic news sources is the work routine of the reporter's ''beat,'' or assignment to a particular organization in order to provide regular coverage of a subject. Beats are a way of providing predictably available information to reporters and, as such, are an important means of reducing the variability of the news and bringing some order to the news world. They are also another effective means of limiting the coverage of women's sports.

Because regular ongoing contact is required to cover a beat, only formally constituted organizations are the subjects of beats. Moreover, because assigning a reporter to a beat constitutes a significant investment of a newspaper's resources, only organizations deemed likely to produce important news of general interest are assigned beat reporters. Consistent with this philosophy, on the *Pioneer*, beat writers covered the major professional sports of basketball and football and the men's football and baseball teams at the nearby university. Women's sports were covered by stringers or by beat reporters when they were not busy with their regular responsibilities.

The importance of the beat to newspaper work is underlined in Fishman's observation that beat writers are expected to produce stories. He notes that on the newspaper he studied, both beat reporters and their editors agreed that ''nothing happened'' is not sufficient reason for not writing a story (Fishman, 1980:35). Designation of a beat thus ensures continued coverage and attention to an organization and its activities.

From the newsworkers' perspective, beats are essential to providing regular and predictable news material. Quite simply, for newsworkers, beats are necessary to do their jobs. One outcome of the beat system, however, is that the range of content of the daily news is limited, for it is a given that the newspapers will provide regular coverage of the subjects of their beats. Because space and personnel are limited, it is inevitable that activities and organizations not covered by beats will be less frequently captured by the news net. In short, because the beat ''defines the world of possible news'' (Fishman, 1980:16) this institutionalized practice constitutes a barrier to the coverage of women's sports. It is one way in which even enlightened sports editors are constrained from broadening the scope of their news coverage.

A second work practice that limits the range of the news net concerns the structure of the sport section. At the *Pioneer*, the sports copy editor can rely on two structural constants: the first is that page 1 will not have any advertisements and the second is that page 2 will look the same every day. Page 2 includes a feature called the Today Box, which provides a summary of national and local sports developments. In addition, there is a small section that details the local sports events for the day and what events are on local television and radio. Information about national sports events are taken from the wire service files, while accounts of local events are compiled by the *Pioneer* staff. The importance of the Today Box to the copy editor is that it is the same each day—except for the words. As such, it is a structuring device or format for producing the sports section.

On most days, the remainder of page 2 is taken up with agate: the minutiae of statistics, standings, and game results that are vital to newspaper sports sections. Agate is to the sports section what stocks are to the business section. It's not pretty, it's in small type, and it's hard to read. But both have high readership. In a report to the Associated Press, Tim McGuire (1982:14) wrote, "Sports editors have been telling us about the agate addict for a long time. Even managing editors and editors who consider sports disgusting, because as nine-year-old intellectuals they were forced to ride the Little League bench, agree that the sports junkie exists."

The regularity of page 2 is a further aid in structuring the copy editor's work routine. Although the page contains a substantial amount of material, its production is predictably smooth and straightforward. For the copy editor, the production of page 2 is a virtually mindless task and thus the page is another device for reducing the potentially unlimited amount and range of information that might constitute the news each day. An outcome of this routinization, however, is that the practice provides yet another device for excluding women from the contents of the sports section. The principle that page 2 will look the same each day, as well as newsworkers' conviction that readers "demand" the minutiae of statistics and league standings, provide powerful barriers to change in the form of increased coverage of "minor" sports, including of course women's sports.

An additional feature of the newsworker's routine that limits the scope of the news is reliance upon other news organizations, primarily the national wire services. While the largest newspapers employ bureau staff for coverage of national news, medium-sized and smaller newspapers depend on the wire services for coverage of nonlocal news. The *Pioneer* subscribes to the entire UPI service and selected items from the Associated Press and the *Los Angeles Times-Washington Post* services. On a given day, these services will send anywhere from 70 to 200 sports stories to the *Pioneer*. These stories are sent by telephone line and accessed on the video display terminals that are common in newsrooms today. The influence of the wire services on the pages of the *Pioneer* is especially evident on page 2, both in the content of the Today Box and in the agate section.

With the exception of local sports briefs in the Today Box, virtually all of page 2 is taken from the wire services (a main reason why the production of this section is a "mindless" task). In addition, depending on the balance between local and national coverage, much of the rest of the paper is taken from the wire services.

Tuchman (1978:22) has described the wire services as the steel links in the news net—the strongest connectors in the net. With their large staffs and firmly established contacts, the wire services are the main means by which smaller papers such as the *Pioneer* reach out to the sites of major news events. For this reason, material supplied by the services exerts significant influence on the contents of their subscriber papers, including the *Pioneer*. The slant or focus of wire service reporting exemplifies the bureaucratic mentality described earlier. The wire services' extensive resources and connections are directed at subjects that have historically demonstrated their "newsworthiness" in the sense of being easily accessible and in that they are judged to be the subjects of broad public interest. In the case of sport, this of course means that the wire services focus their coverage largely on the major men's professional and amateur spectator sports. The *Pioneer's* reliance upon wire service material results in yet another form of pressure to reproduce this male bias in its own pages.

DISCUSSION AND CONCLUSION

This paper has examined two ways in which the work of the sports staff at the *Pioneer* is routinized and how this leads to the exclusion of women from the newspaper's sports section. One of these is in the structuring of the sports section. Most particularly in the daily repetition of page 2, the copy editor's work is simplified considerably. The beauty of this page to the copy editor is that its construction is taken for granted. In contrast to the minimal work involved in its construction, however, the contents of page 2 exert considerable influence on the presentation of the sports news. Page 2 provides daily confirmation of the fact that in North America, sport is largely men's sport. The attractiveness of the page to newsworkers, its predictability, is also what makes it a powerful barrier to change in the coverage of the sports news.

The second means of simplifying news work is reliance upon other organizations for news material. This reliance is evident in the paper's utilization of wire service reports and in beat assignments. The *Pioneer's* dependence on the wire services for national sports news dictates the selection and slant of this coverage. While the paper would appear to have greater freedom in extending its local news net, it is in fact similarly constrained by its dependence on accessible news subjects. Both the wire services and local beat reporters depend on established bureaucratic sources for news material. Because of their greater resources, the major men's sport organizations fall much more easily under the news net than minor sports, including women's sports.

Our emphasis on the effects of the routinization of newswork practices on the construction of the sports news is not meant to deny the ideological foundations of the news. The primary determinant of the male bias in sports news is not journalists' work practices but the social organization of sport in North America and its domination by commercial spectator sports, which are directed primarily at male audiences (see Rintala & Birrell, 1984; Beamish, 1984). Newsworkers' need for a steady flow of reliable and accessible material is well served by the commercial spectator sports' need for publicity and recognition. As noted earlier, the media and men's commercial sports are engaged in a symbiotic relationship that functions largely to exclude women from the newsmaking process. The fit between the male bias in the sports world and the same bias in the sports pages indicates the systematic nature of this problem and the degree of resistance that will be encountered by those who seek to challenge the bias.

The particular role of the media in recreating this bias is in providing daily "confirmation" of the fact that sport in North America is mainly about men. Molotch and Lester (1975:236) have described the news as "the very processes through which are created—for news professionals and their audiences—the 'things' which are important." Newsworkers, including those in the sports department at the *Pioneer*, routinely define sports news as news about men's sports, in particular about men's professional and amateur spectator sports. The practices they follow in casting the news net and producing the sports section enable the daily realization of that definition, and the elimination of women from the sports news.

Extending this idea, Tuchman describes the manner in which various news practices are a "means not to know":

> The temporal and spatial anchoring of the news net . . . prevents some strips of occurrences from being defined and disseminated as news events. Professional practices, as frames, dismiss some analyses of social conditions as soft news novelties and transform others into ameliorative tinkerings with the status quo. (1978:180)

It may be argued that women's sports are still seen as soft news or tinkerings with the status quo.

This discussion of the ideological foundation of the sports news and its realization through the routine work practices of journalists gives support to Boutilier and SanGiovanni's (1983) argument that merely increasing the number of women in sports journalism will not of itself eliminate sexism in the sports news. Sexism in the sports media is not primarily a function of the prejudices of individual journalists, male or female. Rather, this bias is woven into journalists' beliefs about the makeup of the news and the practices they follow to uncover the news. In turn, these beliefs and practices are outcomes of the dominance of men's commercial sport in North America.

Efforts at change must therefore be mounted on several fronts. No doubt, increasing the number of female, and male, journalists who appreciate the problem of sexism in the media and are committed to improving the situation will help. However, these journalists must become aware of the ways in which their own efforts contribute to the problem. The success of efforts in this regard will certainly vary across newspapers. While Anderson's (1984) survey indicated some sensitivity to problems of sexism in newspaper sports sections among sports editors in the United States, there appeared to be little appreciation of the problem among members of the sports staff at the *Pioneer* during the period of research for this study. We have no figures bearing on the prevalence of enlightened newspaper sports staffs, and can only hope that the situation represented by the *Pioneer* is increasingly the exception.

The most formidable barrier that stands in the way of improved media coverage of women's sports lies not in the newsroom but in the sports world. As this paper has shown, the practices newsworkers follow as a means not to know women's sports are largely determined by the structure of sport. The dominance of men's commercial sport influences newsworkers' beliefs about what is newsworthy and the reach of their news nets. While changes in the composition of newspaper sports staffs and in their work routines may be possible, unless there are corresponding changes in the makeup of the sports world, little will be gained.

REFERENCES

Anderson, D.A. 1984. Changing Thrusts in Daily Newspaper Sports Reporting. Paper presented to Sport Literature Association Conference, San Diego.

Beamish, R. 1984. ''Materialism and the comprehension of gender-related issues in sport.'' Pp. 60-81 in N. Theberge and P. Donnelly (eds.), Sport and the Sociological Imagination. Ft. Worth: Texas Christian University Press.

Boutilier, M., and L. SanGiovanni. 1983. The Sporting Woman. Champaign, IL: Human Kinetics.

Fishman, M. 1980. Manufacturing the News. Austin: University of Texas Press.

Gerbner, G. 1978. ''The dynamics of cultural resistance.'' Pp. 46-50 in G. Tuchman, A.K. Daniels and J. Benet (eds.), Hearth and Home: Images of Women in the Mass Media. New York: Oxford University Press.

Lenskyj, H. 1984. ''A kind of precipitate waddle: early opposition to women running.'' Pp. 153-161 in N. Theberge and P. Donnelly (eds.), Sport and the Sociological Imagination. Fort Worth: TCU Press.

McGuire, T. 1982. ''Rekindled interest in sports agate brought on by information junkies.'' Pp. 14-16 in A Report of the Associated Press Managing Editors Sports Committee.

Molotch, H. and M. Lester. 1975. ''Accidental news: the great oil spill as local occurrence and national event.'' American Journal of Sociology, **81**(2): 235-260.

Rintala, J. and S. Birrell. 1984. "Fair treatment for the active female: a content analysis of *Young Athlete* magazine." Sociology of Sport Journal, **1**(3): 231-250.

Theberge, N. 1985. "Sport and feminism in North America." West Georgia College Studies in the Social Sciences, XXIV:41-53.

Tuchman, G. 1978. Making the News. New York: Free Press.

Willis, P. 1982. "Women in sport in ideology." Pp. 117-135 in J. Hargreaves (ed.), Sport, Culture and Ideology. London: Routledge and Kegan Paul.

Chapter 19

Visible Difference and Flex Appeal:
The Body, Sex, Sexuality, and Race in the *Pumping Iron* Films

Christine Anne Holmlund
University of Tennessee, Knoxville

Pumping Iron (George Butler and Robert Flore: 1977) and *Pumping Iron II: The Women* (George Butler: 1984), two documentaries about bodybuilding contests, provide an ideal opportunity to look at the relationships operating between body, desire, and power in the United States today. Taken as a pair, these films are a veritable melting pot of sex, sexuality, race, and sales. Intentionally and unintentionally, they reveal how the visible differences of sex (to have or have not) and race (to be or not to be) mesh with ideology and economy in contemporary American society, and within film fictions. In both films sexuality is adroitly linked with sex and race at the expense of any reference to history or class. The body is marketed as a commodity in its own right, not just as the silent support for the sale of other commodities.

An analysis of the way popular film reflects and shapes the categories of body, sex, sexuality, and race remains an urgent project for film theory. Despite the incorporation of critiques made by the women's, black, and gay movements of the 1960s, 1970s, and 1980s—indeed, in some ways because of these critiques—we continue to see and speak about the body as the last bastion of nature. While the sexual and civil rights movements make it clear that inequalities predicated

From "Visible Difference and Flex Appeal: The Body, Sex, Sexuality, and Race in the Pumping Iron Films" by C.A. Holmlund, 1989, *Cinema Journal*, **28** (Summer), pp. 38-51. Copyright 1989 Board of Trustees of the University of Illinois. Reprinted by permission.

on sex, race or sexual preference are socially established and maintained, the strategies they employ are nonetheless often based on an idea of the body as unified and unique.[1] Difference is either flaunted (black power and cultural feminism, black and women's separatism) or elided (the "we're just like you" policy of the National Gay Task Force since 1973), but the body remains the support of and rationale for political praxis. Even within theoretical discourses the biological status of the body lingers on, masking and motivating a series of power relations. (One has only to think of the multitude of feminist critiques of Lacan's penis/phallus confusion.)

Everyone has difficulty acknowledging the extent to which the body is a social construction and an ideological support because, to invoke Freud, the body (our own and the Other's) is the object and the origin of our earliest fears and desires. The associations established between the body and power are particularly hard to acknowledge when, as is often the case, several kinds of visible difference or its correlates are intermingled: when sex is added to race, or when gender is conflated with sexuality. The original ambivalent attitudes we hold toward the body are then multiplied many times over.

The rush to ignore and deny sexual, racial, and gender differences so that there will be more money for straight white men—initiated and/or encouraged by the Reagan government and other right wing forces—further obscures the roles assigned to the body today. More than in the sixties and seventies, we forget that the ways we look at and speak about the body are historically variable. Knowledge and power of and over the body function within what Foucault calls an "apparatus." Since we live in and create this apparatus, it is hard for us to realize that it is "a formation which has as its major function at a given historical moment that of responding to an *urgent need*."[2]

The reliance of Western society on images of the body to sell products and promote fictions compounds our confusion. Mass media and advertising see to it that we consume visible difference daily. Foucault notes that starting in the 1960s, "industrial societies could content themselves with a much looser form of power over the body."[3] The joint success of the civil rights and sexual liberation movements, in perverse combination with the post-World War II advertising and mass media boom, has affected "the kind of body the current society needs."[4]

The question for media analysts is to define *what* kind of body, or what kind*s* of bod*ies*, are needed and/or tolerated by current societies, and to describe how the apparatus of body and power functions in popular culture today. The *Pumping Iron* films furnish a wealth of material for such an analysis. Since they deal with bodybuilding, it would seem apparent from the very start that the bodies we see are *not* natural. After all, they are clearly the products of individual obsession, created with great effort in the gym, through dieting and even drugs. Moreover, the contestants clearly try to "sell" their bodies, first to the contest judges, then to a burgeoning group of bodybuilding entrepreneurs who promote a vast array of products. Yet though the contestants' bodies are obviously and necessarily constructions, up for comparison and sale, there is an overwhelming need on the part of the judges, the audiences and even many of the contestants to see bodies as representative of "Body" with a capital B, a natural and God-given essence, segregated and defined, as the films and contests themselves are, according to sex and gender roles.[5]

Body, capital B, participates in myth, not history. References to the mythic status of these extra-muscular bodies appear throughout both films, reinforcing our perception of bodies as "Body." Both men and women are associated with heroes and heroines, gods and goddesses. The contestants compete for the titles of Mr. and Miss Olympia, respectively. The theme song of *Pumping Iron* tells us, "Everybody [every body?] wants to be a hero / Everybody wants to live forever." *Pumping Iron II* opens with shots of mountains and power lines, then shows Bev Francis, the 180-pound Australian power lifter turned bodybuilder, seated next to and looking up at statues of muscular goddesses. Similar shots of other women recur later, though then the emphasis is on femininity via statues of Venus.

A sense of history is not absent from these films, however. On the contrary, because they are documentaries (albeit staged documentaries), the spectator knows that the contests have taken place, and that the characters are real people. Moreover, because these characters are social actors, the spectator also assumes that the issues they discuss in *Pumping Iron II* (and ignore in *Pumping Iron*) are of contemporary concern. Paradoxically, though, the historical references inherent in the form of documentary hide the fact that the *Pumping Iron* films are films, with narrative and visual strategies. Like the bodies they chronicle, they too become part of nature.[6]

In order to distinguish myth from history in these films, and in order to evaluate the representation of men and women bodybuilders in the broader context of the societal organization of body and power today, it is necessary to artificially separate the terms they entangle. Therefore, in what follows, I will look in turn at how sex/gender, sexuality, and race are perceived and constructed as visible, physical differences in the film narratives and images. My conclusion recombines the three categories and discusses how history is obfuscated by representation and sales: within the competitions, within the films, and within society at large.

Because women are the subjects of *Pumping Iron II*, the fact of visible difference based on sex is inescapable. It displaces the competition as the central topic of the film narrative. In order to define which woman has the best and most well-defined body, the judges feel compelled to define "body" in relation to "woman." The contestants, too, wonder about the relationship between gender (femininity or masculinity), sex (female or male bodies), and bodybuilding. The film makes their questions its own, marshalling images and sounds to ask: Is a woman still a woman if she looks like a man? Where is the vanishing point?

In contrast, *Pumping Iron* simply chronicles the 1976 Mr. Olympia contest. The reason why is obvious in retrospect: because men are the norm in patriarchal society, visible difference cannot be an issue. The association of muscularity with men poses no conflict between sex and gender: muscular men are seen as "natural."[7] As Richard Dyer says of male pin-ups: "Muscularity is a key term in appraising men's bodies. . . . Muscularity is the *sign* of power—natural, achieved, phallic.''[8] What then could be more natural, more familiar, more right than men pumping iron?

Images of muscular women, on the other hand, are disconcerting, even threatening. They disrupt the equation of men with strength and women with weakness that underpins gender roles and power relations, and that has by now come to seem familiar and comforting (though perhaps in differing ways) to both women and men. Because of this threat to established values, *Pumping Iron II* has an edge of excitement and danger missing from *Pumping Iron*. Yet *Pumping Iron II* is not wholeheartedly in favor of muscular women; on the contrary, it is both ambiguous and ambivalent. Contradictions abound within the narrative and between the narrative and the images.

On the surface of the narrative, *Pumping Iron II* seems to promote strong women and to treat women in the same way as men. As the sequel to *Pumping Iron*, it has the same narrative structure: both films begin with interviews of the top contenders, intercut with training scenes; both climax with the bodybuilding contest.

On a deeper level, however, *Pumping Iron II* treats women very differently than *Pumping Iron* treats men. *Pumping Iron* does not need to ask "What is man?" while *Pumping Iron II* cannot do anything else. When the question "What is woman?" is asked about women bodybuilders, it seems topical, even liberal. In actuality, however, it is centuries old, and standard Hollywood practice. Steve Neale could be describing the basic plots of the *Pumping Iron* films when he writes: "While mainstream cinema, in its assumption of a male norm, perspective and look, can constantly take women and the female image as the object of investigation, it has rarely investigated men and the male image in the same kind of way: women are a problem, a source of anxiety, of obsessive inquiry; men are not. Where women are investigated, men are tested."[9]

Of course, there are individual moments within the narrative that contradict both the deep and surface levels of the film. At these times the majority of spectators in the contest audiences and the film theater are aligned with the more muscular and articulate women. Although the conventionally prettier and sexier Rachel McLish has her ardent supporters, on the whole, Bev Francis and Carla Dunlap appear more intelligent and more likeable. Throughout the film, Bev and Carla come across as outspoken and independent, good sports and good sportswomen, while time and again, Rachel is characterized as a whining, cheating, Bible-belting brat.

Similarly, the film does not encourage spectators to adopt the positions articulated by the universally white male International Federation of Bodybuilders (IFBB) officials: on the contrary, they look ridiculous. In a key pre-contest sequence, Ben Weider, chairman of the IFBB, intones: "What we're looking for is something that's right down the middle. A woman who has a certain amount of aesthetic femininity, but yet has that muscle tone to show that she is an athlete." The retort of one of the younger male judges seems far more logical and far less patronizing: "That's like being told there is a certain point beyond which women can't go in this sport. What does that mean exactly? It's as though the U.S. Ski Federation told women skiers that they can only ski so fast.'' In the final contest scenes the officials' competence as officials is thrown into question: even with the help of a calculator, they are unable to total the women's scores.

Moments such as these, where the audience is encouraged to identify with strong women and to reject ''dolls'' and patriarchs, are certainly victories for feminism. But they must be evaluated in the context of the entire film and especially in the context of the film images. The images of *Pumping Iron II* are more ambiguous than the narrative because society defines how we look at women's bodies very narrowly indeed.

When bodybuilding is understood just as a sport, the analogy between bodybuilding and skiing made by the young judge and endorsed by a certain part of the film narrative is absolutely valid. The problem is that, unlike skiing, bodybuilding for women entails confronting and judging the near-naked female body. One has only to turn to Freud to appreciate why, for the male spectator especially, the female body is fraught with both danger and delight.

In Freud's analysis, men see women not just as different, but also as castrated, as not men. The male subject simultaneously recognizes and denies difference: the woman is different, *unheimlich* even,[10] yet she is also the same, just missing a part.[11] At one and the same time he desires and dreads the woman's visible difference: it evokes his fears of the loss and/or inadequacy of the penis, while simultaneously establishing male superiority based on possession of the penis. In the essay entitled ''Fetishism,'' Freud maintains that men negotiate castration anxiety caused by ''the terrifying shock of . . . the sight of the female genitals'' in three different ways: ''Some become homosexual in consequence of this experience, others ward it off by creating a fetish, and the great majority overcome it'' and choose women as their love objects.[12]

In *Pumping Iron II* in particular, the problems posed by the images of female bodies provoke responses involving all three of Freud's strategies: homosexuality, fetishism, and heterosexuality. Male ambivalence toward women's bodies is omnipresent. A fear of visible difference and a fear of the abolition of visible difference paradoxically coexist, so tightly are body and power interconnected here.

The images of the more muscular women inflame male anxiety because they threaten the abolition of visible difference. In an article on a made-for-TV movie about women bodybuilders, Laurie Schulze comments: ''The danger to male heterosexuality lurks in the implication that any male sexual interest in the muscular female is not heterosexual at all, but homosexual: not only is *she* 'unnatural,' but the female bodybuilder possesses the power to invert normal *male* sexuality.''[13] Since Bev Francis looks and moves ''like a man,'' homophobic patriarchal ideology whispers that men who find her attractive must be gay, and, further, that women who find her attractive must be lesbians. Bev's muscles, dress, heavy facial features, and ''unfeminine'' body language evoke the stereotype of what a lesbian looks like: the butch, the lesbian who is immediately recognizable as such, visibly different. Women who find Bev attractive would, as a result, be defined as fems, lesbians who, in Joan Nestle's words, are "known by . . . their choices" while butches are "known by their appearances."[14] In each case, the stereotypes of what kind of bodies gay men and lesbians find attractive are constructed around the phallus: gay men are assumed to be wimps who worship "he-men," while lesbians are assumed to be women who *are* "he-men" or women who worship "he/she-men."

The film narrative attempts to circumvent the threats of homosexuality Bev poses by having her repeatedly insist that she is a woman, not a man, and by repeatedly showing her accompanied by her trainer/boyfriend, Steve Weinberger. But these narrative strategies cannot be successful in allaying male castration anxieties and/or homophobia in general, especially since they are reinforced by a fear of loss of love. Where men are concerned, Freud mentions this fear only in passing:[15] for him women, far more than men, are concerned about the loss of love intendant on the abolition of visible difference. Indeed, in Freudian terms, loss of love, not castration, constitutes the most significant *female* anxiety.[16] Adrienne Rich, in contrast, argues that: "it seems more probable that men really fear . . . that women could be indifferent to them altogether" than that "the male need to control women's sexuality results from some primal male 'fear of women.' "[17]

In *Pumping Iron II*, the association of muscularity, masculinity, and lesbianism invokes these fears of a loss of love for spectators of both sexes, though in different ways. If heterosexual men see Bev as a lesbian, she is threatening: lesbians incarnate sexual indifference to men. If heterosexual women see Bev as a lesbian they must reject her: to like her would mean admitting that they themselves might be lesbian, which would in turn entail the abnegation of traditionally feminine powers and privileges.

The overwhelming majority of the female characters in *Pumping Iron II*, from the bodybuilders themselves to the one female judge, fear that a redefinition of femininity will entail the loss of love, power, and privilege.[18] It is fear of loss of love that motivates one of the women to say, rather inanely, but nonetheless quite sincerely and even persuasively, "I hope really that they stick with the feminine look. . . . I mean, really, a woman's a woman. That's my philosophy. I think she should look like a woman. And I think that when you lose that, what's the point of being a woman?"

Most of the images in *Pumping Iron II* espouse the same philosophy. In general, they function to defuse rather than provoke male and female spectators' anxieties about muscular women by fetishizing women's bodies and by making them the objects of heterosexual desire. The differences between the two *Pumping Iron* films illuminate how these strategies work. In four areas in particular—mise-en-scène, costume and props, development of secondary characters, and framing and camera movements—sexuality is surreptitiously linked with sex and gender in such a way as to support heterosexual and patriarchal ideologies.

The settings of both films consist largely of gyms and competition stages. In addition, the "stars" of each film are interviewed at home, in their hotel rooms, and backstage before the final, climactic contest. *Pumping Iron II* adds something more, however. In two sequences involving groups of women bodybuilders, the beauty of the female body is evoked via lyrical images, even as individual women debate the essence of femininity. The first of these is set in Gold's Gym in California. It opens with a series of shots of women lifting weights. The camera then moves with the women through the door marked "Ladies Only" into the shower room. There, through lather and steam, naked female bodies are glimpsed. The scene is a fetishist's delight: the camera pans and cuts from torsos to biceps to necks to breasts to heads. The second sequence again involves a group of women and is shot in a pool outside of Caesar's Palace. The camera movements, editing, even the lighting, echo those of the Gold's Gym sequence, only here doubly frozen bodies—the female statues—add to the camera/spectator's titillation and admiration of muscular but distinctly feminine women's bodies, portrayed as so many water nymphs. In each sequence, the images counteract the threat posed by muscular, active women by placing them in traditionally sexy, feminine environments (showers and pools) and by showing them in stereotypical ways (frozen, fragmented, or both). Needless to say, Bev Francis and Carla Dunlap are not present in either group: they represent alternative possibilities of femininity.

The costumes and props used in both films further align sexuality, nature, and the body. The most striking example of this process occurs in the photo sessions for bodybuilding magazines included in each film. Rachel McLish flexes for the camera, holding dumbbells and wearing feathers, chains, and a tiger suit; Arnold Schwarzenegger wades knee deep in women, then plays in the ocean and poses against the sky; Lou Ferrigno, Schwarzenegger's chief competitor, crouches somewhat awkwardly next to a cheetah. While the shots of Rachel add a spice of sadism missing from the shots of the men, all testify to an imbrication of sexuality, sex, gender, and nature.

Pumping Iron II again differs from *Pumping Iron*, however, in its creation of a category of secondary characters, "boyfriends," with no equivalent in the first film. Again and again not only Bev, but also Rachel and Lori Bowen are shown with their men. Lori's fiancé (a male go-go dancer—the object par excellence of a certain, class-linked, heterosexual female desire) even proposes to her in front of the camera. Throughout, the film imperceptibly but inflexibly imposes what Adrienne Rich would call a "compulsory heterosexual orientation" on the female bodybuilders.[19] Only Carla is seen in an all-female environment, accompanied by her mother and sister and without a boyfriend or male trainer. In an interview, she described how she told George Butler she would be seen with her boyfriend, who was married, only if Butler were willing to pay for the divorce costs.[20] In *Pumping Iron*, on the other hand, only Arnold Schwarzenegger is constantly surrounded by women, glorying in his super-masculinity. But these women are nameless and interchangeable bodies, not secondary characters of note.

Finally, the way in which the two films are shot differs radically. As is obvious from the discussion above of the Gold's Gym and Caesar's Palace pool sequences, *Pumping Iron II* positions women as fetishized objects of the camera's and spectator's gaze far more than *Pumping Iron* does men. Except in the case of scenes involving Bev, the camera movements, editing strategies, framing and lighting, resemble those of soft-core pornographic films. It comes as a surprise to learn that the cameraperson in *Pumping Iron II* is a woman, Dyanna Taylor, best known for a documentary about the first women's team to climb Mount Annapurna. Although in interviews she has said that she wanted to capture the excitement of bodybuilding by using lightweight cameras and multiple setups, this has very little impact on how the spectator, and the film, look at near-naked women. Though muscular, breasts and buttocks still appear as tits and ass. Marcia Pally graphically describes the voyeurism of the opening shots as follows:

> Close to the woman's skin, the camera slides along her nude body. It runs down a leg, around the soft, flat stomach, and over the hip bones like a steeplechaser barely acknowledging a shrub. It sweeps across her back to the nape of her neck, and then to an arm more venous than most. It circles a shapely thigh brushing her body with a motion that is part caress but more a search. It scans her surface and takes note; like the cop in any *policier*, it knows what to remember and what to reveal. The case under investigation is the nature of femininity; the female body lies here in evidence.[21]

The men's bodies in *Pumping Iron* are not filmed in the same way: they are not panned or framed like this, nor is lighting used to the same effect. Because the male body in patriarchal societies is not *acknowledged* to be either mysterious or problematic, it is simply not displayed for the spectator's investigation and consumption to the same extent as the female body. In actuality, however, it is intensely problematic: the threat of castration is everywhere present and everywhere hidden. Repressions of and allusions to the precarious status of the male body permeate the visual strategies of *Pumping Iron*. These male bodybuilders are freaks just as Bev Francis is: they are *all* too muscular. Lou Ferrigno's subsequent casting as the Hulk and Arnold Schwarzenegger's success as Conan the Barbarian and the Terminator are not coincidental. Their excessive muscularity has made them oddities and has only increased male anxiety and awareness that, to quote Richard Dyer again, "the penis is not a patch on the phallus."[22] This is why, unlike the emphasis on tits and ass in *Pumping Iron II*, the camera never focuses on the bulge in Arnold's or Lou's bikinis or pans their naked bodies in the shower: to look might reveal too much or too little, threatening the tenuous equation established between masculinity, muscularity, and men.

The fear of visible difference joined with the fear of an abolition of visible difference thus make it exceedingly difficult to separate sexuality, sex, and gender in the *Pumping Iron* films and in society as a whole.[23] Although *Pumping Iron II* relies for its dramatic tension on the possibility of a separation between sex and sexuality, the contradictions between and within narrative and image throughout reassure us of the continuation of the status quo: sex, gender, and sexuality are one, indivisible.

A similar politics of conflation operates in the films' representation of race. Yet there are significant differences between the way sex and sexuality, and race and sexuality are linked both in these films and in the society they portray and address. Visible difference based on sex must be determined according to secondary characteristics like muscularity due to the fact that the primary characteristic, ownership or lack of a penis, is hidden. But visible difference based on race is right there on the surface, in the color of the skin. Although, or maybe paradoxically *because* it is there in plain sight, racial difference is not incessantly discussed and examined the way sexual difference is. In America today, as opposed to in past or present colonial societies, race is ignored and overlooked, hidden by discourse the way sexual difference is hidden on the body.[24] The majority of Americans avoid acknowledging the continuing existence of racial discrimination at home, preferring instead to export it safely overseas—to South Africa, for example. Where race is discussed, it is usually presented via stereotypes, as it would be in colonial discourse.[25]

The *Pumping Iron* films incorporate both strategies—silencing and stereotyping—in the relationships they establish among race, body, and power. Neither film is about racial difference but, again, especially in *Pumping Iron II*, race plays a significant role. In *Pumping Iron* race is not regarded as an issue, even though the Mr. Olympia competition takes place in South Africa. Here blacks are simply minor characters of no real importance to either the narrative or the images. In *Pumping Iron II*, however, race is constantly visible in the person of Carla Dunlap, one of the four major women characters and the winner of the Miss Olympia title. Yet the film narrative and images and Carla herself downplay her color, concentrating instead on the issues of sex, sexuality, and the body. Carla stands out less because she is black than because she spearheads the revolt against enforced femininity and because, as mentioned earlier, she is the only woman who is not involved with men.[26] Her articulateness, her sensitivity toward and support of the other women athletes, and her interactions with her mother and sister make her extremely appealing to both feminists and nonfeminists. What is interesting is that, despite her autonomy and despite the fact that she is more muscular than many of the other women, she never poses a threat of homosexuality the way Bev does, because, by comparison with Bev, she still looks and moves like a woman. Carla plainly knows how to apply makeup and how to dress seductively. Because images override narrative, the possibility that she might actually be a lesbian or that she might be the object of lesbian desire is passed over, silenced: only the most visible lesbians are recognized as such, in the film and in society as a whole. If anything, *Pumping Iron II* underlines Carla's grace and femininity: a sequence showing her practicing synchronized swimming—that most graceful of sports, one of the few Olympic events so far open only to women—is inserted, not coincidentally, right after she challenges the judges' authority to define women's bodybuilding according to their ideas of what women should be. Accompanied by melodic, andante piano music she swims, slowly and sensuously, in an azure pool. The setting and the sounds could not be more romantic. The dual threat posed by her muscularity and her feminism is contained and displaced by an emphasis on her femininity and sexuality.

The most ambivalent sequence involving race, sex, and sexuality is Carla's free-form posing routine, performed to Grace Jones's song "Feel Up." The song begins with jungle noises, moves on to a sexy, upbeat message of independence and strength, and ends with jungle noises again. Carla's choreography complements the two moods of the song, passing from mystery and bewilderment to flashy self-confidence to mystery again. Although neither the song nor Carla's routine are racist, the jungle sounds and Carla's seductive posing routine might easily be reabsorbed within the framework of racist images and attitudes that permeate mass media representations of blacks. As Gloria Josephs says, "the very presence of black women shrouded in sexual suggestiveness is loaded in particularly racist ways" because racists conceive of black women as "being intrinsically nothing but sexual."[27] The combination of exoticism, blackness, femininity, and sexuality is also, as Sander L. Gilman points out, reminiscent of Freud's equation of female sexuality and the dark continent.[28]

Given the tensions within the film and within society, the judges' choice of Carla as Miss Olympia can be seen, in Foucauldian terms, as a response by the power apparatus to an urgent need in society.[29] Threatened by the specter of the abolition of visible difference (muscular women), the male judges consciously and unconsciously affirm their need for visible difference by choosing a woman who still looks like a woman (different) and who is black (different). The judges' decision can be seen as a simultaneous recognition and disavowal of racial difference. This ambivalence, as Homi Bhabha provocatively argues in "The Other Question," links the racial stereotype with the sexual fetish:

> [F]etishism is always a "play" or vacillation between the archaic affirmation of wholeness/similarity—in Freud's terms: "All men have penises"; in ours "All men have the same skin/race/culture"—and the anxiety associated with lack or difference—again, for Freud, "Some do not have penises"; for us "Some do not have the same skin/race/culture." . . . The fetish or stereotype gives access to an "identity" which is predicated as much on mastery and pleasure as it is on anxiety and defence. . . .[30]

Most important, however, the "identity" of the fetish or the stereotype masks history. It is synchronic, not diachronic. Edward Said offers another, potentially more historical, version of the ambivalence that characterizes how the racial other (in his analysis, the Oriental other) is seen: "The Orient at large vacillates between the West's contempt for what is familiar and its shivers of delight in—or fear of—novelty."[31]

Here, in the appeal to and the denial of history, is the key to how and why *Pumping Iron* and *Pumping Iron II* confront both the threat of sexual and racial difference and the threat of the abolition of sexual and racial difference. The muscular bodies we see, whether black or white, male or female, are all sold to us as new and improved versions of an old product. *Pumping Iron* downplays visible difference in its search for the ultimate meaning of generic ''man.'' The film spectator and the audience at the Mr. Olympia competition take it for granted that Arnold Schwarzenegger should and will win the contest: after all, he is the most muscular, most articulate, most virile, and most Aryan man around. *Pumping Iron II* plays up the visible differences of sex and race in its search for the new woman who can still be admired and loved. The title song, sung by a woman and heard at the beginning and again at the end, betrays the film's preference for a male-oriented, heterosexual eroticism, especially because the start of the film combines the suggestively seductive lyrics with slow pans of a woman's naked body on a tanning bed: ''I am the future / Beyond your dreams / I got the muscles / Future sex / I got the motion / Future sex / I got the body / Future sex / Touch this body / Feel this body.'' From the start, therefore, it is clear that women bodybuilders will be defined by their feminine sex appeal. The men who profit from the sport of bodybuilding, including director George Butler, know that the future of women's bodybuilding depends on ''how well it can be marketed to the general public—on how many women can be made to want to look like . . . Rachel McLish, and, to a lesser degree, on how many men can be made to want to sleep with them.''[32]

The strategy behind *Pumping Iron II* is thus a marketing strategy. As a film, it wants to make, package, and sell history, not just watch it. *Pumping Iron II* aspires to be more than the chronicle of a contest, more than a sequel subtitled ''The Women.'' In his eagerness to promote and sell women's bodybuilding, director George Butler staged not only the events leading up to the contest, but also the contest itself. He spent months booking Caesar's Palace and convincing Bev Francis to participate, confident that Caesar's was the last frontier and that Bev would inevitably cross it. As in television coverage of sports events, ''the worlds of sport and show business meet upon the ground of stardom and competition'' in both *Pumping Iron* films.[33] Unique to these films, however, is the way the spectacle of the competition and the spectacle of the film are merged with the spectacle of the near-naked, and therefore supposedly natural, body.

In the final analysis, because they emphasize and appeal to the body, the *Pumping Iron* films resemble advertising far more than sports documentaries or show business dramas. As Marcia Pally says, watching *Pumping Iron II* is like watching one long Virginia Slims commercial: ''You've come a long way, baby.''[34] The skillful combination of sex, gender, and sexuality, the silencing or stereotyping of race, and the complete bracketing of class, readily recall basic advertising principles. In both films slick images and hip music repetitively say the same thing: there is no history, there is no work, there is only leisure and sex. Both films repress the history of bodybuilding and the largely working-class affiliation of its contestants and audiences, choosing instead to emphasize the body as art, sculpture, and timeless spectacle.[35] Only a few sepia stills of nineteenth-century strong men, glimpsed at the beginning and end of *Pumping Iron*, testify to the popular and fairground origins of the sport. No mention is made in *Pumping Iron II* of early strong women like Mme Minerva, Mme

Montagna, the Great Vulcana, or Katie Sandwina, the Lady Hercules. While it is obvious in *Pumping Iron II* that the Miss Olympia competition in many ways resembles strip tease shows and beauty contests, no mention is made of the very recent (1970s) history of female bodybuilding contests, where models and strippers posed only to titillate the largely male audiences of the men's competitions.

Today female bodybuilding has moved closer to being a sport. Nonetheless the nagging suspicion remains that the "long way" traveled by the women of *Pumping Iron II* dead-ends in the chance to be treated, once again, as advertising objects. Now attractive white female as well as male bodybuilders motivate spectators to buy protein and vitamin supplements, to use certain bodybuilding machines, to join health clubs, and to consume magazines, books and, of course, movies.[36] As always, sales are more important than sports, and much more important than social commentary. Far from abolishing stereotypes based on visible difference, *Pumping Iron II*, and *Pumping Iron* as well, visually position the body as spectacle, then sell it as big business. In both films, the threat of visible difference and the threat of the abolition of visible difference are contained and marketed—as flex appeal.

NOTES

1. In the case of the women's movement, organizing around the issues of abortion, rape, physical abuse of women, and pornography is often based as much on the idea that the body should not be violated as on the idea that women have a right to choose for themselves. Unfortunately, organizing predicated on the inviolability of the body frequently overlaps in highly problematic ways with New Right interests.
2. Michel Foucault, "The Confession of the Flesh," in *Power/Knowledge: Selected Interviews and Other Writings 1972-1977* (New York: Pantheon Books, 1980), 195.
3. Michel Foucault, "Body/Power," in *Power/Knowledge*, 58.
4. Ibid.
5. No doubt because the *Pumping Iron* films seek to legitimate bodybuilding as "natural" and "healthy," neither film mentions steroids, though male bodybuilders in particular often use them. At one point in *Pumping Iron* Lou Ferrigno takes handfuls of pills, but they are probably vitamins. Except for an oblique—and catty—suggestion by Rachel McLish that Bev Francis may have used steroids ("the question is not how she did it [i.e. how she got so big], but where she's at right now") *Pumping Iron II: The Women* also shies away from the question of drugs. Alteration of the female body through costume (Rachel's bikini top is judged illegal because padded) and breast implants (an issue the judges say they ignore because implants are too hard to detect) are the only artificial interventions the film acknowledges.

6. The effacement of production is typical of documentary film and classic narrative cinema. Following Edward Buscombe and Roy Peters, Garry Whannel describes how these cinematic conventions have been adapted to television sports coverage in order to "minimi[ze] audience awareness of the mediating effect of television." The visual style of television sports coverage has in turn influenced the *Pumping Iron* films as sports documentaries. See Garry Whannel, "Fields in Vision: Sport and Representation," *Screen* 25, no. 3 (May-June 1984): 101. See also Edward Buscombe, ed., *Football on Television* (British Film Institute Television Monograph, London, 1974); and Roy Peters, *Television Coverage of Sport* (Stenciled paper, Centre for Contemporary Cultural Studies, Birmingham, 1976).

7. As Kate Millet points out, however, "the heavier musculature of the male, a secondary sexual characteristic and common among mammals, is biological in origin but is also culturally encouraged through breeding, diet and exercise." Moreover, physical strength has little to do with gender roles and power. On the contrary: "At present, as in the past, physical exertion is very generally a class factor, those at the bottom performing the most strenuous tasks, whether they be strong or not." Kate Millet, *Sexual Politics* (Garden City, N.Y.: Doubleday, 1970), 27.

8. Richard Dyer, "Don't Look Now," *Screen* 23, no. 3-4 (September-October 1982): 67-68.

9. Steve Neale, "Masculinity as Spectacle," *Screen* 24, no. 6 (November-December 1983): 15-16.

10. Sigmund Freud, "The 'Uncanny,' " in *On Creativity and the Unconscious* (New York: Harper and Row, 1958), 122-61.

11. Freud's analyses encompass both perspectives, but the second is the more basic. Susan Lurie critiques Freud's assumption that men and boys are the norm: "In psychoanalysis the meaning of woman is fixed not as difference, but as 'mutation' in the context of a desired sameness." Susan Lurie, "The Construction of the 'Castrated Woman' in Psychoanalysis and Cinema," *Discourse*, no. 4 (Winter 1981-82): 54. For similar critiques, see also Stephen Heath, "Difference," *Screen* 19, no. 3 (Autumn 1978): 51-112, and Karen Horney, "The Dread of Woman," in *Feminine Psychology* (New York: W.W. Norton, 1967), 133-46.

12. The first of the three choices Freud discusses is homosexuality. Homosexuals, he argues, openly acknowledge the primacy of the phallus: men are taken as sexual objects because they possess the penis, which the child imagines the mother he loved also had. Yet this solution is unacceptable to society. Fetishism is preferable because "it endow[s] women with the attribute which makes them acceptable as sexual objects." Unlike homosexuality, fetishes are not prohibited by society; on the contrary, as Freud remarks, "they are easily obtainable and sexual gratification by their means is thus very convenient." For these reasons, "the fetishist has no trouble in getting what other men have to woo and exert themselves to obtain." Sigmund Freud,

"Fetishism," in *Sexuality and the Psychology of Love* (New York: Macmillan, 1963), 216.

13. Laurie Jane Schulze, "*Getting Physical*: Text/Context/Reading and the Made-for-TV Movie," *Cinema Journal* 25, no. 2 (Winter 1986): 43.

14. Joan Nestle, "The Fem Question," in *Pleasure and Danger: Exploring Female Sexuality*, ed. Carole S. Vance (London: Routledge and Kegan Paul, 1984), 233.

15. Sigmund Freud, "Anxiety and Instinctual Life," in *New Introductory Lectures on Psychoanalysis* (New York: W.W. Norton, 1965), 77-78.

16. Ibid., 76-77. Karen Horney would agree, though as usual her evaluation of this phenomenon is critical both of the phenomenon and of Freud's position. See, for example, Karen Horney, "The Overvaluation of Love," in *Feminine Psychology*, 182-213, and "The Neurotic Need for Love," *Feminine Psychology*, 245-58.

17. Adrienne Rich, "Compulsory Heterosexuality and Lesbian Existence," *Signs* 5, no. 4 (Summer 1980): 187.

18. No doubt Freud would argue that those women in the film (Bev, Carla) or in the audience (feminists, lesbians) who do not fear the loss of love by men do so only because they covet the phallus/penis directly. They have not made the requisite substitution of baby for penis.

19. See Rich, "Compulsory Heterosexuality and Lesbian Existence," 631-60.

20. Marcia Pally, "Women of 'Iron'," *Film Comment* 21, no. 4 (July-august 1985): 62.

21. Ibid., 60.

22. Dyer, "Don't Look Now," 71.

23. The confusion of these three categories, as Gayle Rubin convincingly argues, is all the more easily accomplished because in English "sex" refers both to gender and gender identity and to sexual activity. See Rubin, "Thinking Sex: Notes for a Radical Theory of the Politics of Sexuality," in *Pleasure and Danger*, 307. In sharp contrast to many feminists, Rubin refuses to see women's experience of sexuality as engendering. For her "sexual oppression cuts across other modes of social inequality, sorting out individuals and groups according to its own intrinsic dynamics. It is not reducible to, or understandable in terms of, class, race, ethnicity, or gender." Ibid., 293.

24. A notable exception is *The Cosby Show*. Writing in *TV Guide*, Mary Helen Washington describes the show's portrayal of race as follows: "[Cosby] has chosen to handle the family's blackness [as] simply a given—neither ignored nor flaunted but written into the show as though blackness were normal—not exotic, not stupid, not shameful, not polemical." Mary Helen Washington, "Please, Mr. Cosby, Build on Your Success," *TV Guide* (22 March 1986): 8.

25. See Homi K. Bhabha, "The Other Question. . . . ," *Screen 24*, no. 6 (November-December 1983): 18-36.

26. According to Nik Cohn in *Women of Iron: The World of Female Bodybuilders* (n.p.: Wideview Books, 1981), 59, Carla's own experiences agree with the film's privileging of sexual difference over racial difference. As an adult,

Carla has found sexual discrimination to pose more problems than racial discrimination. As a child, she was sheltered from racial prejudice by class privilege:

> Of all the top women bodybuilders, she was the only black. A lot of brothers and sisters had asked her if that was a dilemma. She always told them *No*, and that was the truth. She had never been taught that color was a limitation. Those were not the kind of roots she'd grown from.
> Her childhood had been wonderful. Her father was a chemist in Newark, and his children were provided with everything they needed. Carla had four sisters and a brother. They lived in a huge house. There were horses and boats, and lots of space to breathe in. *A typical American middle class background*, she called it. They summered on a yacht.

27. Gloria I. Joseph, "The Media and Blacks—Selling It Like It Isn't," *Common Differences*, ed., Gloria I. Joseph and Jill Lewis (Garden City, NY: Doubleday, 1981), 163.
28. Sander L. Gilman, "Black Bodies, White Bodies," *Critical Inquiry* 12, no. 1 (Autumn 1985): 238.
29. See Foucault, "The Confession of the Flesh," in *Power/Knowledge*, 194-95.
30. Bhabha, "The Other Question," 27. Bhabha goes on to suggest that blacks themselves participate in the creation and perpetuation of the stereotype, much as women desire to be seen as different and consent to be fetishized out of a fear of loss of love.
31. Edward Said, *Orientalism* (London: Routledge and Kegan Paul, 1978), 58-59.
32. Charles Gaines, *Pumping Iron: The Art and Sport of Bodybuilding* (New York: Simon and Schuster, 1981), 220-22.
33. Whannel, "Fields in Vision," 99.
34. Pally, "Women of 'Iron'," 60.
35. While in the history of Western art men have traditionally been portrayed as muscular, "the shape to which the female body tends to return . . . is one which emphasizes its biological functions . . . most often suggested by a softly curved cello shape. . . ." Charles Gaines, *Pumping Iron II: The Unprecedented Woman* (New York: Simon and Schuster, 1984), 20.
36. There is a clear racial as well as a sexist bias in the advertising business surrounding women's bodybuilding. Gloria Steinem writes: "Though she has great beauty and the speech skills of a first-class actress, Carla Dunlap has been offered no television commercials. Even the dozens of bodybuilding magazines have declined to put this first black woman champion on the cover." Gloria Steinem, "Coming Up: The Unprecedented Women," *Ms.* 14, no. 1 (July 1985): 109.

Chapter 20

Personal Best:
Women in Love

Linda Williams
University of California–Irvine

Robert Towne's *Personal Best* is a film about two women pentathletes who meet at the 1976 Olympic trials, become friends and lovers, then separate and meet again at the 1980 Olympic trials as competitors. Basically a sports movie, it differs from the genre's male pattern of individualist competition in its representation of female athletes who not only perform their "personal best" but also support one another in doing so.

The film has been much praised for its realistic representation of athletic female bodies at the moment of concentrated performance, for picturing the "wild beauty of young women with the mystic gusto usually reserved for young men" (Michael Sragow, *Rolling Stone*), for "presenting fresh images of women on screen . . . a special treat" (Gene Siskel, *Chicago Tribune*), and for daring "with great delicacy and insight, to show a loving sexual relationship between two young women, not as a statement about homosexuality, but as a paradigm of authentic human intimacy" (Jack Kroll, *Newsweek*).[1]

Just about everyone found *something* to like in the film. Straight women like the "positive" portrayal of (literally) strong female protagonists committed to excellence in their field. Men like the sports subject and the fact that it provides the occasion for the relatively unclothed spectacle of female bodies in competitive contexts that excuse the usual voyeuristic pleasure of the way men look at them. Many (though certainly not all) lesbians like the guilt-free portrayal of a lesbian relationship. Runners of both sexes like the celebration of running itself.

Like most Hollywood films, *Personal Best* broadly appeals to a wide variety of contemporary social attitudes and tastes. Although the film presents itself as ''daring'' in its depiction of a sexual relationship between two women, it is not daring enough to delve very far into the emotional details of that relationship or to suggest that such a relationship could endure. As a result there are many lacunae and motivational puzzlements in the basic narrative. Not the least of these occurs at a point two-thirds of the way through the film when a line of dialogue indicates, much to the audience's surprise, that what has seemed to be a relatively short-term affair has been going on for three years. What may at first appear to be the ineptness of a first-time director is in fact a confusion arising from the strain of juggling so many diverging social attitudes into a package that would titillate, but not offend, most viewers. In what follows I would like to examine the qualities for which the film has been most praised—its iconography of physically active, powerful women and its lesbian love theme—in order to discover the ways in which they are contradicted or undercut by predominantly patriarchal attitudes and points of view.

FEMALE ICONOGRAPHY

Many of the discussions of *Personal Best* have centered on the photography of the track and field sequences. What is somewhat surprising in this discussion is that very often, among the film's relatively few negative reviews, male critics have attacked what they consider to be a voyeuristic presentation of female bodies.[2] Female critics, however, have tended to defend the film against these very charges. Robert Hatch, for example, writes in *The Nation*:

> During track and field events, the cameras focus obsessively on the women's crotches—most outrageously during a slow-motion passage when six or eight of them practice the high jump by turning back-somersaults over the bar. This is cheesecake; it demeans women, and the lubricious chuckles in the audience suggest that it does so successfully.[3]

Veronika Geng, however, writing for the *New York Review of Books*, defends these very same shots:

> The idea that (cinematographer) Michael Chapman and Towne are using the camera voyeuristically; and that women must be protected from them by several manly, heroic film critics, is preposterous. Visually, *Personal Best* is designed around the autonomous movements of the women. When they are still, the camera never prowls their bodies. When they move, they make their own trajectories through the frame. If the camera moves with them, it goes from the general to the specific—from the sources of athletic power, the legs and pelvis, to a particular face.

(Pornography looks at a specific woman and then debases her into generalized body parts; with Towne, looking at the body parts makes him fall in love with the whole woman.) In the high jump, the hinge of the movement is the crotch (and too bad if you can't stand seeing it), but each character pushes her entire body into the frame, and the payoff is the unique reaction on her face. Every photographic choice— the distance of the camera, a change from slow-motion to normal speed— is attuned to the women's feelings and picks out the individuality in physical movement.[4]

What Hatch sees as the cheesecake of the unindividuated and fragmented body, Geng sees as the autonomous expression of individuality through movement. Who is right? Or do men and women simply respond differently to the same images?

This issue is a complicated one and I do not pretend to have all the answers. It would be tempting to reply that where men see cheesecake women see autonomous beings. We could thus relegate the entire issue to the "eye of the beholder" who sees what he/she is sexually programmed to see. But if we look closely at Geng's defense of Towne, we will see that she is not at all describing what *her* eye beholds but creating a rather elaborate defense of the male director's point of view—as both creator and consumer of these images. The defense is telling. For I strongly suspect that such images invite women to consume them from a temporarily assumed male point of view. If women could not learn to at least partially assume the male viewpoint in consuming such images, they would experience constant visual displeasure in the bombardment of female body parts provided by the media. Geng reveals the extent to which women have become complicit in the objectification of female bodies.

The assertion that the various fragments of the female body add up to a whole that is attuned to the subjective expression of the woman's feelings might be possible in an innocent world that had not already appropriated female bodies to the measure of male desire. But in the context of our already fallen patriarchal world, Eve's body is no longer innocent, no longer her own.

Nor can activity alone constitute the autonomy of the female image. Even the briefest glance at television ads and magazine covers—from *Runner's World* to the *Playboy* issue that features *Personal Best* star Mariel Hemingway on the cover and interviews Towne within—reveals the sleek active bodies of an increasingly androgynous feminine ideal displaying the "new cleaveage" of ass to leg. From the breast fetishes of the fifties we move to the ass, crotch and muscle fetishes of the eighties. At this point in time, when commercials have already fetishized the fragmented female body to sell the most mundane commodities, analytic slow motion montages of athletic bodies in motion merely confirm the current style of fashionably fetishized female bodies constructed to the measure of male desire. Where the desire once consigned women to a passive voluptuousness, it now represents them as so many trained seals flexing their muscles to male awe and approval. Thus even Jane Fonda finds herself, in *On Golden Pond*, obliged to perform a muscle-flexing backflip to resolve the father-daughter differences of that film, thereby proving to her father Henry—in one of the least satisfying plot resolutions ever concocted—that she is really just as good as the son he always wanted her to be.

The point, however, is not to berate Geng for an "unliberated" enjoyment of female bodies. Women viewers, traditionally deprived of active women characters with whom they can identify, are naturally inclined to celebrate *any* female images that break out—however slightly—of the traditional molds of passive and decorous objects. (I recently found myself applauding Lauren Bacall's graceful ability to catch the match box Humphry Bogart tosses her in *To Have and Have Not*, even though the vast majority of her movements are self-consciously and narcissistically calculated to please both Bogart and the male viewer.)

The question then arises: what would a nonpatriarchal representation of the athletic female body be? There is no answer that works for all time. In 1982 a slow-motion analysis of female athletes will be read in the context of the patriarchy's commercial and sexual appropriation of those very same images. It could very well be that what we need at this point in time is to restore the integrity of the whole body in real time and space.[5] Even the *Wide World of Sports* allows all athletes this much integrity before launching into the slow-motion replay.

WOMEN IN LOVE

Personal Best's other claim to originality is the lesbian relationship between its two female characters. Here the film makes more explicit a female love relationship that was hinted at in *Julia*, the last decade's enormously popular epic of female friendship and love. In *Personal Best* the track and field sports context of the narrative permits an emphasis on the physical and sensual that renders the women's erotic relationship a "natural" by-product of their highly physical existence. This, I think, is the source of the almost overwhelming acceptance of the film's treatment of the normally taboo subject of homosexual love.

In box office terms, the combination of sports and sex was a stroke of genius. Those who would normally be shocked or at least irritated by a lesbian relationship in any other context find it quite "natural" among female athletes who, it is presumed, are simply more physical than other people. The film thus capitalizes on public awareness of, and curiosity about, lesbian athletes like Billie Jean King while evading any real presentation of lesbian identity. Thus Kroll, in the statement quoted above, can take Chris and Tory's relationship not as a "statement about homosexuality but as a paradigm of authentic human intimacy." Authenticity for Kroll seems to consist of avoiding the very issues of sexual identity that the lesbian relationship raises. My own criticism of *Personal Best* is not that it should have made a "statement about homosexuality," but that in studiously avoiding even mentioning the *word* lesbian—let alone the word love—the film's notion of "authentic human intimacy" tends to reduce this relationship to a kind of pre-verbal and pre-oedipal regression to narcissism.

The first lovemaking scene between the two athletes, Chris and Tory (Mariel Hemingway and Patrice Donnelly), occurs early in the film. It is presented as the outgrowth of a prolonged and herculean arm-wrestling contest whose ups and downs prefigure the various ups and downs of the women's competitive careers. Only the physicality of the arm-wrestling and the proximity of the two remarkably fit and beautiful bodies prepares us for their sudden passion. In the very next scene they celebrate their love in an ecstatic work-out run along the beach. A three-year love affair follows.

What we see of this affair is somewhat confusing. At times it is presented as an idyll of sensuality; at other times it seems tense and troubled. The two women both live and train together. Under Tory's guidance Chris at first gains confidence and skill. But as Chris improves, Tory begins to decline. A key moment in their relationship occurs at the Pan Am Games in Columbia. When Chris becomes ill with stomach cramps, Tory spends the night nursing her, cradling her in her arms on the floor of a dressing room shower in a pose that recalls that of a madonna and child. The next day Chris is well and performs magnificently while Tory is tired and does poorly. Although Chris clings desperately to the maternal care and support that Tory gives her, it becomes increasingly obvious that she performs best under adverse conditions and needs not to depend on Tory. As Chris's skills improve, she reluctantly begins to challenge Tory in the pentathlon. Tory seems able to accept this challenge and still love Chris, but her concern for Chris's well-being tends to hurt her own performance.

The real problem, however, is not that they must compete with one another but that they must do so within the context of a personal relationship of unequals. For Tory's relationship to Chris, as the madonna and child scene in the shower clearly suggests, is that of a mother. This mothering is the real impediment to the growth and endurance of their relationship. Yet this mothering also renders the relationship safe in the eyes of the film's ultimately patriarchal system of values. The film can afford to celebrate nostalgically the sensual lost eden of a female-to-female bond precisely because it chooses to depict this bond as the non-viable pre-oedipal dependence and narcissistic identification of mother and daughter.

Chris and Tory's love affair is doomed not because they are lesbians, the film seems to say, but because of the regressive nature of their narcissistic relation. The failure to define the lesbian nature of their relationship as anything other than a regression to mother-daughter narcissism is one of the major disappointments of the film. The remarkable fact that the film goes to great lengths to avoid giving a name to the lesbian nature of Chris and Tory's relationship indicates the extent of the evasion.

The closest the film comes to defining their relationship is Tory's statement: "We may be friends but every once in a while we fuck each other." This definition of a three-year love affair as friendship plus occasional sex seems hopelessly inadequate. The very language of the formulation "fuck each other" assumes an oppressively phallic model for its sexual content. If ever two people had a chance *not* to "fuck each other" (with all the manipulation and abuse the term implies), it would be these two women.

In other words, we find in *Personal Best* what we have so often found in the action films of male bonding: a gratuitous and decorative love interest with no organic relation to the real concerns of the film. Chris and Tory's love remains an emotional and sexual interlude in a larger configuration that cannot deal with its implications. Thus, having put the two women together, the film must then find a way to drive them apart.

If Chris and Tory were driven apart by the pressures of competing in a patriarchal system of ruthless competition, then we could clearly blame this system and celebrate the women's triumph over it in the end. But what actually drives them apart is a blatantly contrived scene in which Tory accidentally moves a marker that causes Chris an injury. Because neither of the women can account for the accident, the coach can drive a wedge of suspicion between them. Although we deplore the evil suspicions of the macho coach, the melodramatic contrivance of the unlikely accident actually effects the separation. The coach is ultimately proven wrong in his suspicions and in his ruthless handling of the two women, but nothing in the film proves wrong their contrived separation. Quite the contrary. From this point on the film shifts focus (from Chris and Tory to Chris alone) and tone (from serious melodrama to comic relief) as it recounts Chris's initiation into the joys of adult heterosexuality.

Another evasion of the lesbian theme occurs in the contradictory presentation of Tory, played by the novice actress and former hurdler Patrice Donnelly. Although Tory looks and acts a good ten years older than Chris, she appears in a role that would make her roughly Chris's contemporary. Similarly, although provided with an ex-boyfriend (mentioned briefly) and no previous experience with other women, she is visually coded—short hair, square features, tailored jackets—to look the part of the "dyke" in opposition to Mariel Hemingway's more feminine long hair, unassertive presence, and general girlishness. Tory takes the initiative in their first sexual encounter, appears jealous of Chris when she in the company of men, and, after they separate, seems to lurk in the background of Chris's life, a frustrated lesbian.

The film thus delivers a double message: on the one hand it presents two heterosexual women who "simply" fall into an affair without examining the meaning of their relationship; on the other hand, it indirectly implies that one of them is older, more experienced and a "real" lesbian. The fact that Tory is almost completely dropped as a character after she and Chris separate suggests that Hollywood has not entirely given up the old policy of punishing the homosexuals in its stories. Instead of death or suicide, the punishment has simply been reduced to narrative banishment.

The repression of the lesbian woman-identified content of Chris and Tory's relationship is all the more remarkable given the film's ostensible moral that women athletes can be both tough and compassionate, that the "killer instinct" that motivates male competition, and which is advocated by their coach, can be tempered with a female ethic of support and cooperation that is not only good for the soul but can also win in the end. In other words, the film asserts on the level of its sports theme what it is afraid to assert on the level of its sexual theme.

By the end of the film Chris, who began as a whiny little girl in terror first of her father then of her male coach, finds the strength to oppose her coach's order not to associate with Tory. At the climactic meet she helps Tory win a crucial event by taking out the competition too fast. The plan works, cooperation in competition prevails, and both women qualify for the Olympic team, which never went to Moscow, with the satisfaction that they have performed their "personal best." But the personal best of competitive sports has here clearly supplanted the personal best of relationship. Again, what the film offers on the level of its sports theme—that women can be competitors with a positive difference—it takes away on the level of its sexual theme—that they can also be lovers with a positive difference.

The shift in tone is quite remarkable. Chris achieves her rite of passage under the tutelage of Denny, an ex-swimmer whose ingratiating buffoonery comes as a literal relief to the emotional intensity of the Chris/Tory relationship. Denny functions as a modified and reasonable substitute for the excessive and unreasonable patriarchal authority of Chris's father and coach. It is Denny who delivers the final moral of the film's title, "The only ass you need to whip is your own." And it is Denny whose (full frontal but briefly spied) penis becomes the final symbol of Chris's delighted reconciliation with patriarchy: a comic scene in which Denny goes to the toilet accompanied by a curious and enthusiastic Chris who stands behind him to "hold it."

In this scene, what appears on the surface to be a clever role-reversal—woman objectifying and fetishizing a male body part—is really a not-very-subtle comic expression of Chris's embrace of a newly-found adult heterosexuality. Chris's maturity is then proven in the very next scene when she defies her coach to befriend the now weakened and child-like Tory. Although Chris's support of Tory prepares the "happy end" of both women's mutual triumph in the final meet, the moral is clear: Chris's strength and maturity derive not from Tory, who mothered her, but from Denny whose laid-back fathering has finally made her a woman.

And so, what began as a promising depiction of women in love and competition becomes a series of dirty phallic jokes whose function is to dispel the seriousness and tension of the original woman-to-woman relation: "What's gotten into you?" says one of Chris's friends, and Chris, in dreamy reply, simply looks at Denny.

If the phallus has become a running joke throughout the film, first for its absence and then later (with a vengeance) for its presence, it never really becomes the butt of the joke; everything is ultimately envisioned from its point of view. Denny's function in the film makes this painfully clear. If we have had any early doubts about the voyeuristic presentation of women's bodies in the first half of the film, Denny's bugged-eyed appreciation of Chris's body must dispel them. His comic, knee-jerk reactions to Chris's athletic beauty stand for the pleasures of the male viewer who is "wowed" by the power and beauty of the newly streamlined feminine ideal. Scenes in which he bumps his head on the side of the pool as punishment for too much underwater looking, or does bench presses while blowing air up Chris's crotch are pure burlesque, and like all burlesque render the involuntary male sexual response comically forgivable.

The women in *Personal Best* do not define for themselves the challenge their relationship poses to patriarchy. This allows the film to recuperate their (unnamed) sensual pleasure into its own regime of voyeurism. Ultimately, the many nude scenes and crotch-shots can be enjoyed much the way the lesbian turn-ons of traditional heterosexual pornography are enjoyed—as so much titillation before the penis makes its grand entrance. For all its lyrically natural and guiltless sensuality, for all its celebration of women athletes as possessed of both excellence and integrity, *Personal Best* fails to provide a genuinely feminist depiction of women in love or competition.

ACKNOWLEDGMENTS

I would like to thank Judy Gardiner, Richard Gardiner, Meg Halsey, Kathy Minogue, Michelle Citron, Julia Lesage and Chuck Kleinhans for either contributing their own valuable ideas on this film or for helping me to clarify my own ideas.

NOTES

1. These statements are gleaned from the current newspaper ad for the film.
2. Male critics who deplore the film's voyeurism include: Vincent Canby in the *New York Times*, Carlos Clarens in *The Soho News*, Robert Hatch in *The Nation*, and Dave Kerr in *The Chicago Reader*. Female critics who defend the film's presentation of the female body include: Barbara Presley Nobel in *In These Times*, Pauline Kael in *The New Yorker*, and Veronika Geng in the *New York Review of Books*. Of course, many male critics have also praised the film extravagantly, as demonstrated by the excerpts quoted above. But it does seem significant, that among the male critics who dislike the film, so many of them isolate the issue of voyeurism as an important element of their criticism and that, similarly, female critics feel obligated to defend the film on this very issue. I have not conducted a survey of the gay and lesbian and feminist press; opinion on the film appears to be somewhat divided in it.
3. *The Nation*. February 27, 1982, pp. 251-252.
4. March 18, 1982, p. 45.
5. This is, in fact, what a great many current feminist filmmakers have chosen to do. See, for example, the films of Chantal Akerman, Marguerite Duras, Yvonne Rainer, Michelle Citron, Helke Sander and Ulrike Ottinger.

PART V

SPORT AND THE POLITICS OF SEXUALITY

lthough the relation between sexuality and sport serves as a central structure for body/identity/gender meanings, sexuality remains one of the most neglected areas of inquiry in sport studies. For over a decade, feminism and the newly emerging sociology of sexuality have figured prominently in the critique of biological and physiological drive theories of sexuality and have indicated the need to consider political issues embedded in and raised by historical and cultural forms of sexuality. To a great extent, theories of sexuality and specifically lesbian identity and marginalization remain absent in sport studies and, as Susan Cahn might suggest, represent the heterosexualization of sport-related forms.

The essays included in this section are by no means the only essays in this volume that examine the interstices of sexualities, bodies, sport, and culture; but, in this section, we highlight essays that specifically work toward an understanding of heterosexism and homophobia and their relationship to sport. That is, the essays in this section ask, although in quite different ways, how sport has been used to construct and police sexualities and to both reproduce and struggle against heterosexism.

The articles in this section join the debates, which address sport as a site for the reproduction of difference and emphasize and problematize the naturalization of sexual differences through which females are positioned as naturally subordinate. The articles argue against constructions of a biologically determined body and problematize characterizations of a fixed, stable body; they raise questions about the complex relationship between sport, the body, and femininity; they consider the role of media representations of particular images of the body; and they address the controversy over the regulation of the body.

In "Crushes, Competition, and Closets: The Emergence of Homophobia in Women's Physical Education," Susan Cahn traces and relates the historical shifts in dominant ideologies of sexuality, images of the female athlete, and those practices instituted by white, middle-class physical educators. Cahn argues that the institutionalization of homophobia in physical education was initiated in response to economic changes, the commodification of sexuality, and the entrance of sexological discourses into popular consciousness during the 1930s. Although the turn-of-the-century images associated with the female athlete were primarily positive and constructions of deviance were unquestionably heterosexual, Cahn suggests that the popularization of sexological theories during the 1930s made women-only environments suspicious. This assertion combined with a "common-sense" equation between masculinity and lesbianism, and masculinity and sport (in white, middle-class America), marked women's physical education as simultaneously homosexual and homophobic. Cahn argues that physical educators responded by instituting practices that attempted to actively heterosexualize women's physical education by cultivating beauty, appearance, and the prospect of male companionship and approval and by endorsing policies that reproduced and institutionalized heterosexism and homophobia in physical education.

In "Feminist Bodybuilding," Anne Balsamo examines how the media gaze recuperates the female athlete's body through "dominant codes of femininity and racial identity.'' She discusses the codings of the female athlete's body through biological and medical discourse, the historical equation of the female body—including that of the female athlete—with reproduction, and the pathologization that regulates women's participation in physical activity. Next, she concentrates on popular images of female athletes, specifically Florence Griffith-Joyner, to suggest how potentially transgressive female bodies have been appropriated and represented through terms of femininity, race, and positioned as objects of male pleasure. Finally, she considers the implications of female bodybuilding by examining *Pumping Iron II: The Women* to show how the tension between femininity and muscularity is managed through filmic grammar. She argues that the positioning of Carla Dunlap, the only African-American contestant and the ''surprise'' winner in a contest staged between two white women representing the poles of a continuum of musculature-femininity, not only sidesteps the question of femininity as it has been articulated in the film, but also reinscribes traditional racial codes of black women's bodies.

In ''The Embodiment of Gender,'' David Whitson is concerned with the relation between the body (understood to be a key ideological resource for the production and maintenance of gender relations), power, and resistance. Drawing on the work of R.W. Connell, Iris Young, and Catherine MacKinnon, Whitson discusses how the historical complex of practices and processes in sport produces masculine and feminine modes of embodiment through an unequal, gendered distribution of bodily knowledges. Whitson suggests that this economy of opportunity normalizes the gender order and its corresponding hegemonic masculinity through the embodiment of force and domination over others and the production and normalization of feminine bodies that are sexualized and constrained in terms of skill, movements through space, and expectations. Whitson also examines alternative sport forms and the possibilities they provide for bodily experiences and different forms of empowerment both for women and men. Although alternative physical practices have been incorporated through consumer culture and inserted into bourgeois, liberal ideology, Whitson argues that to simply dismiss such practices would be a mistake. The contradictions and potential embedded in alternative practices should remain a site of struggle, because they challenge the historical constraints of feminine embodiment and subjectivity.

In ''Double Fault: Renee Richards and the Construction and Naturalization of Difference,'' Birrell and Cole argue that the media negotiate the problems posed by the Renee Richards case by working to legitimate both the possibility of transsexualism and the status quo. This legitimation is accomplished by obscuring the historical relationship between women and sport and by positioning the debate around Richards in a frame embedded in sexual essentialism and liberal assumptions of individualism and equality. These at times correspondent and at times contradictory liberal and essentialist claims together form a frame in which women are constructed and represented through their appearance as suitable objects of masculine pleasure, and in which athletic performance and strength are depicted in terms of sexual difference (thereby inscribing women's bodies—including that of Richards—as naturally physically inferior).

Chapter 21

Crushes, Competition, and Closets:
The Emergence of Homophobia in Women's Physical Education

Susan Cahn
State University of New York at Buffalo

In the early decades of this century, the figure of the "athletic girl" stood as a positive symbol of the emancipated "New Woman." A 1911 advocate for girls' field hockey proudly proclaimed that "today the athletic girl has prominence, not the loud, masculinely dressed, man-apeing individual, but the whole-hearted, rosy-cheeked, healthy girl who exercises because she loves it and who plays for the joy of playing" (MacLaughlin, 1911, p. 41). But by midcentury, the young athletic woman—in the figure of the physical education major—evoked a different response. A Texas student newspaper described players in a 1955 women's football game, contrasting the "demure sorority girl" and debutante fashion model types with

> the physical education major who gruffly gives out pre-game instructions to her team. Heavy set and bold mannered, she approaches the football as if it were a greased pig, pounces upon it readily, and is soon lost in the crowd of players as she bellows out words of caution and firmly slaps fellow players on the back. ("Powder Puffs," 1955)

Within the profession, educators and PE majors were fully aware of this portrait and did their best to eradicate it. One student spoke for many when she said, "People outside our profession have us generally stereotyped, and I feel that it is important to show evidence through our appearance and actions that we are not what they think we are'' (University of Wisconsin Physical Education Club, Unpublished file paper, n.d.).

What explains this drastic shift? And why were physical educators so concerned, yet in the end unable to alter their tarnished image? In this paper, I will trace the roots of the change to the 1930s, arguing that from the '30s through the '50s the familiar notion of the mannish athlete took on an added meaning, becoming a coded message about lesbianism. I will first describe the early 20th-century notion of mannishness, when it had no particular lesbian connotation. Then I will explore a transition that began in the 1930s, in which physical educators began to orient their programs around a new feminine heterosexual ideal. Finally, I will argue that though they acted out of a defensive response to changes in the larger culture, women educators responded to homophobic criticisms by devising policies and philosophies that institutionalized heterosexism in the profession.

This analysis will focus on the dominant ideology within physical education. During these decades the field consisted primarily of white, middle-class educators. Though those on the margins of the profession—women in black colleges, rural school districts, or city recreation departments—did not necessarily accept the ideas of the leadership, the dominant perspective went unchallenged in professional journals and organizations. The leadership's views shaped the curriculum, policies, and philosophy of physical education programs responsible for training successive generations of PE majors. With their control of professional publications and organizational resources, women leaders wielded their resources to repair the public image of physical educators. By tracing the roots of these developments, we can learn something of the specifics of homophobia in our society—how with the word *lesbian* never spoken, fear and hatred of lesbianism entered the fabric of our culture.[1]

EARLY 20TH-CENTURY NOTIONS OF "MANNISHNESS"

The notion of sport as masculine had deep roots in American society, especially among the white middle class. It stemmed from a history of sport as a male activity and from a gender ideology that labeled aggression, physical and sexual expression, competitive spirit, and athletic skill as masculine. Through the 1920s, critics of PE leveled three charges: (1) too much exercise would damage female reproductive capacity; (2) the excitement of sport would cause women to lose control, conjuring up images of frenzied, distraught coeds on the verge of sexual, physical, and emotional breakdown; and (3) women athletes would adopt masculine styles of dress, talk, haircuts, and mannerisms.

Observers collapsed these dangers into a more general notion of mannishness. The mannish athlete crossed boundaries of gender, not of sex. To the extent that the image implied sexual deviance, it was heterosexual deviance. Early 20th-century experts warned that competition could induce ''powerful impulses'' leading girls into a "temptation to excess" and the "pitfall of over-indulgence" (Inglis, 1910, p. 183; Paret, 1900, p. 1567; Sargent, 1913, pp. 71-73). These dangers presumed a heterosexual context, conveying the impression that loss of physical control would lead to aggressive heterosexual activity outside the norms of feminine respectability.

The negative concept of mannishness existed alongside a positive association between the athlete and the modern woman. On many campuses, women's athletic associations held center stage in college life. Students joined eagerly in spirited class rivalries, annual "Big Games" with ritual mascots and banners, and spring field days and pageants. At public events, spectators packed the stands and cheered wildly, applauding the energy and freedom of the modern athletic girl, judging from college yearbooks and women's athletic association scrapbooks of the times (e.g., those in Smith, Radcliffe, and Universities of Wisconsin, Minnesota, and Texas archives). One disgruntled student complained that the close association between sport and the modern woman actually caused excessive and dangerous athletic play. In an effort to prove that she was a "good sport," the image-conscious student often played past the point of exhaustion. Those who more wisely limited their play were tagged "no sport" and "old maid" ("A Plea to Women," 1915, p. 449).

The derogatory notion of the old maid described the nonathlete and was not associated with early notions of mannishness. In part, this was because same-sex activity and friendship remained acceptable into the 1920s. For a few decades, the New Woman, distinguished by her bold sexuality and her familiarity with men, overlapped with an older pattern of female community, passion, and intimacy. Women's athletic associations promoted membership with claims of "generous, democratic good fellowship." They championed the "vitalizing force" of an athletic community populated by the "all-round girl" of "womanly attributes" and "charming wholesomeness" (*Sportsgirl*, 1924-1925; University of Minnesota, 1909-1910).

The idea of the mannish lesbian, which linked women's sexual love with masculine behavior, did not permeate popular culture until at least the 1920s. Before this, some women spoke without shame of feeling "like a boy." Abby Parsons Macduffie, a Radcliffe student in the 1880s, wrote joyfully in her first letter home, "I have got some gymnasium slippers now and I feel very nice in my suit. I wish I could wear it all the time. I feel just like a boy in it, strut around and cross my feet delightfully." In 1911, a literary quote appeared under the yearbook photo of Theoda Bush, known for her athletic skill and boyish appearance: "A girl who was so like a boy was his ideal of a woman" (Radcliffe athletics materials, n.d.). Theoda's boyishness was remarkable to her classmates, but in no sense pushed her outside the bounds of assumed heterosexuality.

Passionate same-sex love also formed part of the tradition of female community. Physical educators at first saw nothing unusual about crushes. Mabel Lee, looking back on her early career, spoke with familiarity of the "occasional girl's" passionate crush, adding with homophobic hindsight that she had "no idea . . . I was encountering an extreme problem" (Lee, 1977, p. 231). As late as 1932, the PE staff at the University of Wisconsin discussed "the 'crush' situation" at a staff meeting. They did not seem particularly alarmed, noting that "the tendency the last few years has been to exaggerate these things. Any attachment which excludes other people is not good" (University of Wisconsin Department of Women's Physical Education, 1927-1954).

Staff comments about students in the late 1920s reveal an increasingly punitive stance toward mannishness paired with a remarkably open discussion of students' personal appearance. Wisconsin faculty described students variously as "dirty looking," "too boyish," and having "mannish habits and clothes." Positive evaluations of students included "exceedingly attractive," ". . . good material. Nice body," and a wonderful nonsequitur, "hysterical since she was in a sleigh that turned over. Is cute" (University of Wisconsin Department of Women's Physical Education, 1927-1954). Such uncensored comments reveal not only the intimate, intrusive nature of faculty supervision of female students, but also a kind of unself-conscious appreciation of women's bodies that because of emerging lesbian taboos would soon be unspeakable.

TRANSITION TO A MODERN HETEROSEXUAL IMPERATIVE

The 1930s mark an important turning point in physical education, years in which the positive image of the PE major as a modern athlete receded before a negative portrait of physical educators as mannish, social misfits. The fundamental explanation for this change lies outside of the profession in sweeping cultural changes in sexuality, at the center of which lay a new construction of womanhood. Middle-class Victorians had defined femininity and masculinity around polarized gender prescriptions in dress, activity, and demeanor—what historians refer to as an ideology of separate spheres. But as modern women found jobs, entered colleges, danced at cafes and nightclubs, and threw away their corsets, they challenged gender ideals based on separation and difference. Similarly, declining birth rates, public advocacy of birth control, and medical affirmation of female eroticism undermined the icon of sexually pure, maternal womanhood. Finally, because films, songs, advertisements, and advice literature celebrated male-female companionship, the intimacy, passion, and community women found in each other's company seemed old-fashioned and sexually suspect. In the dominant culture, femininity became increasingly identified with heterosexual attractiveness and "success."

Three other arenas of sexual change contributed to the new emphasis on heterosexuality. By the 1920s, the economic structure of the United States depended increasingly on consumer goods rather than primary manufacturing. Industries like cosmetics, mass-produced clothing, and hair products linked consumer goods to enhanced sex appeal. Advertisers also used sexual ploys to sell nonsexual consumer goods like cars and washing machines. This sexualized economy brought the power of corporate America to bear on the new link between heterosexual appeal and feminine ideals. As one advertisement announced, "The first duty of woman is to attract" (D'Emilio & Freedman, 1988, p. 278).

Modern youth culture operated in a heterosexual milieu as well. Movies, dance halls, and amusement parks offered young men and women a social arena free from the restrictive gaze of parents and neighbors. By the 1920s, middle-class and small-town youth incorporated these previously urban, working-class activities into an adolescent high school culture. Girls and boys socialized in classes, after-school activities, and evening get-togethers, using the automobile for both transportation and privacy (D'Emilio & Freedman, 1988, p. 240). As youth of the 1920s and '30s attended college in greater numbers, women students found physical educators' emphasis on hygiene, posture, and single-sex activity alien and dull.

Complementing the centrality of sex in economics and leisure, scientific professions also began to view sex as profoundly significant to an individual's identity. Since the late 19th century, theorists like Havelock Ellis and Sigmund Freud had propounded the importance of sexuality to social and psychic life. By the '20s and '30s these views had filtered into mainstream awareness, losing much of their sophistication and radical content along the way. Estelle Freedman and John D'Emilio have argued that modern sexual theories contributed to a new understanding of sex as critical to self-definition. Sexuality became "a marker of identity, the wellspring of an individual's true nature" (D'Emilio & Freedman, p. 226). Specifically, the sense of sexuality as self helps account for the emergence of self-defined gay and lesbian people. Same-sex attraction constituted the basis of alternative sexual identities and emerging homosexual subcultures (D'Emilio & Freedman, Chapter 10).

As doctors and psychologists incorporated this new meaning of sexuality into categories of illness, social deviance, and sexual perversity, they provided an intellectual framework for the modern lesbian taboo. Scientific theories linked deviant sexual identities to gender dysfunction. In the 1930s, psychologists developed masculinity and femininity tests using perceived lesbian characteristics to define the masculine end of the women's scale. Moreover, early test results found that the only women who rated "more masculine" than lesbians were a group of 37 superior women college athletes (Lewin, 1984; Minton, 1986). As the figure of the "mannish lesbian" entered popular awareness, within women's sports pre-existing notions of mannishness and sexual release converged, providing a host culture for popular homophobic images.

Women in physical education were especially vulnerable to the homophobic atmosphere created by the reorientation of sexuality around heterosexual norms. During the Great Depression, the autonomy of educated, single, professional women left a bad taste in the mouths of jobless men and poor families struggling to survive in hard times. Moreover, PE teachers worked in a profession already publicly associated with masculinity. And ironically, the strategies physical educators had devised to defend against earlier criticisms backfired in the 1930s.

Physical educators had doggedly pursued a separatist course, arguing that only women could properly supervise girls' physical development and that only an all-female setting could protect women's freedom to exercise without embarrassment. Yet by the late 1930s, women together seemed unnatural. The 1937 student yearbook at Minnesota titled its women's athletics section, "Over in No Man's Land." Fifteen years later the yearbook explained that, "Believe it or not, members of the Women's Athletic Association are normal . . ." finding proof in the fact that "at least one . . . of WAA's 300 members is engaged" (University of Minnesota, 1937; 1952, p. 257).

The policy of separatism went hand in hand with the profession's attempts to distance women's sport from sexual connotations it held in the popular arena. To white, middle-class professionals, the sexual tone of commercial sport, which utilized beauty contests and tight-fitting uniforms to attract crowds, stood in direct opposition to the standards of propriety they believed would legitimize women's sport. Educators reacted by condemning popular athletics and instituting stringent bans on competition. They also devised methods to expunge sexual connotations from in-school athletics: modifying the rules of women's games to reduce stress-induced lapses of control, designing loose-fitting gym uniforms to preserve modesty, and monitoring student habits of dress, diet, sleep, and socializing.

Strategies of separatism and sexual denial were inseparable from physical educators' efforts to control women's sports. In the 1920s women leaders went head to head with the male-controlled Amateur Athletic Union in a battle for control of women's sports, especially basketball and track athletics. They leveled scathing attacks on male-controlled sport, criticizing the win-at-all-cost competitiveness, elitism, and commercial exploitation they saw. Again, this initially effective strategy failed in the atmosphere of the 1930s. Women's criticism of men struck the public as divisive, while their critique of sexual exploitation in sport appeared old-fashioned and narrow-minded.

THE INSTITUTIONALIZATION OF HETEROSEXISM

Finding that traditional approaches only added to their problems, physical educators buckled under external homophobic pressure. In the 1930s they embraced an activist approach toward heterosexuality. Coursework emphasized beauty and social charm over rigorous health and fitness. At Radcliffe, for example, faculty redesigned health classes to include "advice on dress, carriage, hair, skin, voice, or any factor that would tend to improve personal appearance and thus contribute to social and economic success" (Radcliffe athletics materials, n.d.). They defined this Depression-era objective as one of seeking "social security."

Intramural programs now advertised with promises of heterosexual popularity instead of female companionship. Women's Athletic Associations minimized team sports, instead recommending tennis, golf, bowling, horseback riding, and archery as "life-time sports" with "carry-over value" (Athletic Federation of College Women, 1933). These claims assumed that graduates would never again be in a position to play women's team sports, nor would they want to. Programs highlighted corecreational activities for men and women. Corec bowling, volleyball, and swimming along with coed "fun nights" of Ping-Pong and shuffleboard replaced interclass basketball tournaments and weekend campouts for women. Team sports continued to draw the majority of participants. However, organizers exchanged the old rationales of fitness and fun for promises of trimmer waistlines, slimmer hips, and prettier complexions. The 1941 University of Minnesota yearbook explained that "sorority girls get in trim for the posture contest through their competition in basketball teams" (University of Minnesota, 1941, p. 294).

Though the emphasis on beauty does not necessarily denote concern with heterosexuality, explicit references to sexual adjustment and beauty as the path to male approval support this interpretation. Alice Sefton articulated the connection when she protested a sportswriter's charge that women looked too ugly when they played hard. She admitted that the athlete might momentarily display a strained face and bulging muscles, but with the fitness, suppleness, and grace achieved in sport, "she may be more beautiful on the dance floor that evening" (Sefton, 1937, p. 481).

Physical educators also revised their philosophies, placing heterosexual adjustment at the center of their objectives. In a 1938 meeting of the National Amateur Athletic Federation Women's Division, comprised primarily of physical educators, Margaret Birdsong "gave a scholarly presentation in which she described the different types of people who are unadjusted to heterosexual cooperative activity." Her list included "the arrested development type," and "the domineering type." Another guest speaker, Dr. Pritchard, "bade us to 'sense the enriching values in a democracy and develop cultural prejudice *against* segregation of the sexes' " (National Amateur Athletic Federation Women's Division, 1938). The two messages linked failed heterosexual development to exclusive female environments. "Experts" (Birdsong and Pritchard) attributed sexual maladjustment to the "lack of ability to mix" and warned physical educators that "recreation can either contribute to these negative attitudes or, if wisely handled, form the most usable instrument for more constructive social cooperation" (National Amateur Athletic Federation Women's Division, 1938). Physical educators, who had long advocated female separatism in sport, were thus pressed to actively promote heterosexuality or risk implicit indictment for encouraging undemocratic same-sex association.

The profession responded with positive claims for the role of physical education in heterosexual development. In a paper on post-war objectives, Mildred Schaeffer explained that coursework must offer all students the means "for meeting the social life of modern times." Specifically, physical education should help women "make social adaptations," "be recognized socially," and "develop an interest in school dances and mixers and a desire to voluntarily attend them" (Schaeffer, 1945, pp. 446, 447). While women's classes emphasized lifelong sport and daily life skills, including instruction in dodging automobiles and lifting luggage, departments also added some coeducational classes to foster "broader, keener, more sympathetic understanding of the opposite sex" ("Coeducational classes,"

1955, p. 18). At Texas, Director Anna Hiss explained the new philosophy as one of "building muscle tone rather than muscle," thus appealing to "the 'glamor' girl rather than the 'muscle-bound' strictly athletic type of yesteryear" (University of Texas, 1946, n.p.).

Professional leaders showed great concern over the poor reputation of PE majors on campus, caused by their low standing in both academic and social settings. Student athletic associations noticed the intimidating effect skilled majors had on nonmajor students, labeling it "majoritis" (Athletic Federation of College Women, 1931; University of Minnesota Department of Women's Physical Education, 1925). One study argued that to overcome the profession's disrepute, students must demonstrate a neat and pleasing appearance, good taste in dress, charm, social intelligence, and an "average cultural background." In addition they "should have or possess the possibilities of an attractive personal appearance" (Rugen, 1933).

To nourish such qualities, departments implemented dress codes forbidding shorts, slacks, and men's shirts and socks, adding as well a ban on "boyish hair cuts."[2] The Ohio PE Association's brochure for prospective majors left no doubt about the impression it sought to project, stating flat out that "the mannish concept of a physical educator is no longer acceptable." The pamphlet's cover showed a man in a suit and a woman in highheels and a skirt walking joyfully hand in hand *away* from a background of athletic fields (Ohio Association for Health, Physical Education and Recreation, 1946).

Already well-schooled in patrolling student behavior, the profession began to focus on self-regulation in the post-war era. Facing a shortage of physical educators in the 1950s, leaders laid heavy stress on creating an appealing, nonthreatening appearance to outsiders. Staff dress codes forbade teachers to appear outside the athletic complex in shorts or sweat suits, with Texas policy dictating that "legs should be kept shaved" (University of Texas, 1949-50, p. 16). And professional journals cautioned against "casual styles" that might "lead us back into some dangerous channels" (Ashton, 1957, p. 49). Worried that their former separatist stance had created an anti-male impression, women students and teachers supported joint conferences and social events with men's groups.

The pressure to establish impeccably feminine and heterosexual credentials continued unabated throughout the 1950s. The emphases on dress and physical appearance were cornerstones of most programs, complemented by coed intramurals, individual sports instruction, and only minimal opportunities for intercollegiate competition. Leaders increasingly looked to professionals outside their field for advice on sexual matters, inviting psychologists and sexologists to give workshops on guidance techniques, psychosexual development, and sex education. Concerns about femininity reached their logical if absurd conclusion in a mid-50s article that advised teachers to "feminize your facilities." The author of this article suggested pastel locker rooms, abundant mirrors with purse shelves and tissue holders for lipstick blotting, decorated wastebaskets, deodorizers, and ruffled bulletin boards, arguing that with such improvements "so-called 'muscle girls' attain a more acceptable status in the eyes of the non-athletically inclined" (Lumpkin, 1955, p. 28).

By emphasizing beauty, coed recreation, individual sport, and modest athletic achievement, physical educators hoped to attract the nonathletic type, the girl who was more interested in boys than sports. And by suppressing competition and imposing stringent dress and behavioral codes, they hoped to stamp out any distasteful signs of mannishness that might actually exist among the students to whom physical education did appeal.

Unfortunately for physical educators, the damage had already been done. Portrayals of PE majors and teachers as amazons, social misfits, prudes, or lesbians gained rather than lost power in the middle decades of the century. While a *Boston Herald* article applauded an exhibit of Smith College synchronized swimmers, it reminded readers of "the priggishness, the repression, and the false values of the old regime" (Boston Herald, 1939, n.p.). In their efforts to blot out such portrayals, even physical educators lent some credence to the notion that the unsuccessful heterosexual girl might turn to sport. Gertrude Mooney reassured anxious parents that "the mannish, shoulder swinging, shirt-and-tie type of athlete" had no place in the educational curriculum. However, she did acknowledge that in some cases "a girl who feels herself socially inadequate in feminine charms finds her outlet in losing herself in such an engaging pastime as athletics," thus creating the wrong impression in others (Mooney, 1937).

By incorporating homophobic images from the culture at large, physical educators may even have heightened the association between sport and lesbianism. A newspaper account of a 1956 awards banquet for women given by the University of Texas Sports Association (UTSA) led off with the headline, "UTSA Gives Awards," followed by the subhead "Gayness Necessary." The second headline referred to a guestspeaker's talk on good attitudes, entitled "The Importance of Being Debonair," but the lesbian allusion was unmistakable, and I believe fully intentional (University of Texas, 1956).

CONCLUDING REMARKS

Why had 30 years of concerted effort to dispel an image of mannishness failed so miserably? The charge of mannishness had originated in popular associations between masculinity and athletics. In the 1920s and '30s, a fundamental reorientation of sexual meanings and practices fused female eroticism to heterosexual pleasure and individual sexual identity. As a result, notions of femininity and heterosexual attractiveness formed a single ideal. Mannishness, once primarily a sign of gender crossing, assumed a specifically lesbian-sexual connotation; and the strong cultural association between sport and masculinity made women's athletics ripe for emerging lesbian stereotypes.

In this context, physical educators found themselves in a particularly vulnerable position and encountered heavy pressure to prove their heterosexuality. They failed in part because the initial strategies physical educators had used to promote their professional interests backfired in the altered sexual environment of the

1930s. Formerly effective commitments to separatism and sexual respectability contributed to a picture of PE teachers as prudish old maids, whereas the legacy of gender antagonism and criticism of male athletics fed directly into stereotypes of ball-busting career women and man-hating lesbians. Another part of the explanation lies in the pervasiveness of homophobia in the larger culture, a general fear and hatred of gay people that peaked in the 1950s Cold War atmosphere.

It is also possible that the association between lesbianism and physical education was not only a homophobic stereotype, but a lesbian reality. Besides the obvious fact that the requirement of self-support meant that lesbians worked in every sort of job, evidence from oral histories leads me to believe that there may have been a stronger lesbian presence in physical education than in many other occupations.[3] The fear of exposure limits open discussion of the issue among physical educators and makes verifiable proof difficult to obtain. My conclusion is therefore tentative, but I want to put forth this idea for consideration: The homophobic atmosphere, which is the historical legacy of physical education, functioned as a sort of sexual field-of-force. It repelled many heterosexual women who were uncomfortable with the PE image at the same time it attracted sports-minded lesbians. They surely also worried about the profession's "queer" aura, but may have been drawn by the sense of difference, the physical focus, and the female culture of physical education.

Whether lesbian or not, physical educators responded to homophobic pressures by formulating programs and philosophies that institutionalized heterosexism in PE. The word *lesbian* almost never appeared in professional literature or department records. However, one can read the changes in policy and philosophy as a concerted attempt to remove the taint of lesbiansim and to achieve heterosexual legitimacy. Educators institutionalized heterosexism in a variety of ways, ranging from the most mundane details to the loftiest ideals of the profession. Uniform and locker room design, the rules of sports, and student and staff dress codes constituted material elements of a homophobic culture. Philosophical commitment to coed classes, intramural sport, and coed recreational games over intercollegiate competition, along with educational objectives of social acceptability and sexual adjustment formed the ideological axis of institutionalized heterosexism.

None of these elements in and of themselves *necessarily* signify homophobia. In fact, some of what I am calling homophobia had roots in other strongly held beliefs; for instance, the emphasis on noncompetitive sport also grew from a genuine commitment to expand athletic opportunity for all women. But, in the context of a larger system of sexual meanings, one that since the 1930s has associated female sport with mannishness and lesbianism, the shifts in physical education helped institutionalize the fear and hatred of lesbians in educational and athletic realms. Efforts to dispel the lesbian aura surrounding PE and sport had a paradoxical outcome. They served only to increase public and professional sensitivity to the "mannish lesbian" in sport, while professional policies strengthened the institutional bulwark that still maintains heterosexuality as the privileged sexual mode, thus deepening lesbian oppression.

REFERENCES

A plea to women for the use of common sense in physical training. (1915). *American Physical Education Review*, **20**, 449.

Ashton, D. (1957). Recruiting future teachers. *Journal of Health, Physical Education and Recreation*, **28**, 49.

Athletic Federation of College Women (AFCW). (1931). [Minutes of 1931 sectional conferences of the Department of Women's Physical Education] AFCW general subject file, University of Wisconsin Archives, Madison, unpublished raw data.

Athletic Federation of College Women (AFCW). (1933). [1933 convention report of the Department of Women's Physical Education] AFCW conference file, University of Wisconsin Archives, Madison, unpublished data.

Boston Herald. (1939, Feb. 25). (From Smith College archives, student Athletic Association files.)

Coeducational classes. (1955). *Journal of Health, Physical Education and Recreation*, **26**, 18.

D'Emilio, J., & Freedman, E. (1988). *Intimate matters: A history of sexuality in America*. New York: Harper & Row.

Inglis, W. (1910, March). Exercise for girls. *Harpers Bazaar*, **44**, 183.

Lee, M. (1977). *Memories of a bloomer girl*. Washington, DC: American Alliance for Health, Physical Education and Recreation.

Lewin, M. (1984). Rather worse than folly? Psychology measures femininity and masculinity. In M. Lewin (Ed.), *In the shadow of the past* (Part I, pp. 155-178; Part II, pp. 179-204). New York: Columbia University Press.

Lumpkin, M.C. (1955). Feminize your facilities. *Journal of Health and Physical Education*, **26**, 28.

MacLaughlin, H.S. (1911). Field hockey—Girls. *American Physical Education Review*, **16**, 41.

Minton, H.L. (1986). Femininity in men and masculinity in women: American psychiatry and psychology portray homosexuality in the 1930's. *Journal of Homosexuality*, **13**, 1-22.

Mooney, G. (1937). *The benefits and dangers of athletics for the high school girl*. (University of Texas Physical Training for Women Records, Box 3R251, Health Education folder, Barker Texas History Center, University of Texas, Austin)

National Amateur Athletic Federation—Women's Division. (1938, June 1). [Newsletter #79]. (Papers of the Department of Women's Physical Education, University of Wisconsin Archives, Madison)

Ohio Association for Health, Physical Education and Recreation. (1946). *Physical education as a career* [Brochure]. (*Blanche Trilling* subject files, ''PE as a profession,'' Department of Women's Physical Education, University of Minnesota Archives, Minneapolis)

Paret, J.P. (1900, Oct. 20). Basket-ball for young women. *Harpers Bazaar,* **33**, 1567.

Powder puffs in the huddle. (1955, October 26). *Texan.* (*Texan* scrapbook 1955-56, Box 3R212, University of Texas Physical Training for Women, Barker Texas History Center, University of Texas, Austin)

Radcliffe athletics materials. (1880s to 1950s). Collected by K. Powell. (Accession No. R87, Radcliffe College Archives, Cambridge, MA)

Rugen, M.E. (1933). Standards for judging, selecting and retaining professional physical education students. Papers presented at 1933 Midwestern Association of Physical Educators of College Women (MAPECW). (Misc. Research Folder #8, Box 7 of EAPECW Records, Sophia Smith Collection, Smith College, Northampton, MA)

Sargent, D.A. (1913, March). Are athletics making girls masculine? *Ladies Home Journal,* **29**, 71-73.

Schaeffer, M.A. (1945). Desirable objectives in post-war physical education. *Journal of Health and Physical Education,* **16**, 446-447.

Sefton, A.A. (1937). Must women in sports look beautiful? *Journal of Health and Physical Education,* **8**, 481.

Sportsgirl. (1924-1925). (Copy in records of University of Texas Physical Training for Women, Box 3R247, Barker Texas History Center, University of Texas, Austin)

University of Minnesota. (1937). *Gopher* [yearbook]. (University of Minnesota Archives, Minneapolis)

University of Minnesota. (1941). *Gopher* [yearbook]. (University of Minnesota Archives, Minneapolis)

University of Minnesota. (1952). *Gopher* [yearbook]. (University of Minnesota Archives, Minneapolis)

University of Minnesota Department of Physical Education. (1909-1910). [Pamphlet]. (Miscellaneous file, University of Minnesota Archives, Minneapolis)

University of Minnesota Department of Women's Physical Education. (1925). [Alumnae bulletin, **1**(2)]. (Misc. file, Department of Women's Physical Education, University of Minnesota Archives, Minneapolis)

University of Texas. (1946, November 21). *Texan.* (*Texan* Scrapbook, Box 3R212, records of University of Texas Physical Training for Women, Barker Texas History Center, University of Texas, Austin)

University of Texas. (1949-50). [Physical training staff handbook]. (Records of University of Texas Physical Training for Women, Box 3R213, Barker Texas History Center, University of Texas, Austin)

University of Texas. (1956, May 10). *Texan.* (*Texan* Scrapbook, Box 3R212, records of University of Texas Physical Training for Women, Barker Texas History Center, University of Texas, Austin)

University of Wisconsin Department of Women's Physical Education. (1927-1954). [Minutes of staff meetings]. (University of Wisconsin Archives, Madison)

University of Wisconsin Physical Education Club. [Student-faculty committee file]. (Papers of the Department of Women's Physical Education, University of Wisconsin Archives, Madison)

NOTES

1. I am using *homophobia* to mean the fear and hatred of lesbian/gay people, love, or sex. Heterosexism is the institutional privileging of heterosexual love and sex and institutionalized oppression of gay and lesbian people in the dominant structures and ideologies of society. In this paper, I am arguing that the relationship between homophobia and heterosexism is dialectical. Homophobia in the surrounding culture pressed physical educators into defensive actions that institutionalized heterosexual ideals and power in sport and education. This process in turn further entrenched heterosexuality as the unchallenged norm, fueling homophobic reactions to physical educators who appeared to violate sex and gender norms.

2. These restrictions are spelled out explicitly in the staff minutes and PE handbooks for majors found in the records of women's physical education departments at the Universities of Minnesota, Wisconsin, and Texas.

3. I draw this conclusion from confidential interviews I conducted with physical educators who were trained in and began working as early as the 1930s but primarily in the 1940s and 1950s. Some are retired and some are still active in the field today. Of the 13 narrators, 12 never married and 1 married and divorced. Two are admitted heterosexuals, five identified themselves as lesbians, and six preferred to keep their sexual identity private but did discuss the lesbian presence in sport and physical education.

Chapter 22

Feminist Bodybuilding

Anne Balsamo
Georgia Institute of Technology

The broad objective of this essay is to contribute to the development of a thick perception of the gendered body in contemporary culture. For Michel Feher, editor of a three-volume collection of essays that describe an array of historical regimes of the body (*Zone #3, 4, 5: Fragments for a History of the Human Body*), this process involves an analysis of the "different modes of construction of the human body."[1] I borrow Feher's conceptionalization of the modes of body construction as a framework for understanding the ways through which the body is conceptualized in feminist discourse. The female body has been "built" within feminist discourse in several different ways; in the course of this essay I draw on three domains of feminist body work:

- Scholarship that investigates the *ideological* construction of the female body in the history of women's sport,
- *Semiotic* analyses of media representations of female athletes,
- A *cultural* interpretation of a filmic narrative about technologically reconstructed female bodies.

More specifically, the first section reviews historical studies of women and sport to illustrate how the physiological body is culturally redefined according to dominant beliefs about women's proper and moral responsibilities for human reproduction. The second section focuses on media representations of prominent female athletes to examine how ideals about feminine beauty are revised to include signs of muscularity and vigorous health. Although these representations

Note. An earlier version of this essay was presented to the Women's Studies Forum at the University of Illinois at Urbana-Champaign, in April 1988. I would like to thank Paula Treichler, Susan Greendorfer, and John Loy for their comments on earlier drafts. A substantial revision of this material will appear in my forthcoming book, *Technologies of the Gendered Body* (Duke University Press).

highlight the athletic capabilities and power of the female body, they also show the ways that power is symbolically recuperated to a dominant cultural order through the sexualization of the bodies of athletic "stars." The final section offers a reading of *Pumping Iron II: The Women* that examines how the film stages a symbolic contest about the proper definition of femininity; as a winner of the bodybuilding contest is announced, so too is the preferred form of female embodiment. Each section addresses one form of feminist bodybuilding; they all illuminate the way in which the "naturally" female body is culturally reconstructed according to dominant codes of femininity and racial identity.

THE IDEOLOGICAL TREATMENT
OF THE SPORTING BODY

Lynda Birke and Gail Vines (1987), feminist sport sociologists, identify both science and sport as cults of masculinity marked by a belief in the superiority of the male body. Indeed, historical research on the cultural construction of the female body illuminates how sport experts continued the quest to locate woman's inferiority in her "physiological body" after the "science" of craniology failed to prove that her inferiority resided in her brain. In a similar line of analysis, Helen Lenskyj (1986) explains how reproduction became a defining characteristic of female athletes, regardless of whether an individual woman in fact menstruated or became pregnant. Her research documents how the female athlete's gender identity became intimately tied to her reproductive physiology. The physiological "facts" of her reproductive system establish the biologically sexed female body as the "natural" emblem or guarantor of female identity. Quoting from medical textbooks of the early 19th century, Lenskyj describes how the medical profession emphasized the fact of "reproduction" when prescribing safe and appropriate sporting activities for women.

> Both women's unique anatomy and physiology and their special moral obligations disqualif[y] them from vigorous physical activity. Women have a moral duty to preserve their vital energy for childbearing and to cultivate personality traits suited to the wife-and-mother role. Sport wastes vital forces, strains female bodies and fosters traits unbecoming to "true womanhood." (p. 18)

Encumbered as they were with the burdens of menstruation, pregnancy, lactation, and menopause, women were thus instructed to forego athletic activity in favor of less strenuous pursuits. According to this passage, both women's physiology and their moral obligations tied to that physiology combine to disqualify women from vigorous sporting activity.

Patricia Vertinsky (1987) describes yet another way in which women were discouraged from participating in sport through what we now understand to be culturally defined "facts" of the female body. These facts asserted that women were "eternally wounded" because they bled during part of their reproductive (menstrual) cycle. This popular myth—again supported by medical knowledge of the time—defined women as chronically weak and as victims of a pathological physiology. Two things happen here: Not only is the female body irrevocably tied to a culturally constructed obligation of reproduction, but also, through the association between femininity and "the wound," the female body is coded as inherently pathological. Limiting women's participation in sport and exercise functioned both to control women's unruly physiology and to protect them for the important job of species reproduction.

These historical studies illuminate the process whereby one set of beliefs (about female physiological inferiority) is articulated with another discursive system (concerning women's athletic practices). Through their feminist analyses of the historical discourse on women and sport, both Lenskyj and Vertinsky show how physiological characteristics come to count as definitive emblems of female identity. Their body scholarship involves "rereading" the female body as it is inscribed in one discourse from within another textual/sexual system. The textual system they use to read the female body "against the grain" is informed by feminist cultural theory; as such it provides a perspective from which to document the process of cultural recoding of the female body, as first a "gendered" body and second one in need of special protection from the rigors of physical exertion. In this sense, their analyses provide a way of understanding the process of transcoding whereby the "natural" female body was taken up as a cultural emblem of the reproductive body, with the consequence that women were often discouraged from participating in athletic activities.

THE SEXUALIZATION OF THE TRANSGRESSIVE BODY

Lenskyj's and Vertinsky's analyses suggest that, historically, the properly feminine body was considered to be constitutionally weak and pathological. To be both female and strong explicitly violates traditional codes of feminine identity. Thus women who use bodybuilding technology to sculpt their bodies are doubly transgressive: First, because femininity and nature are so closely allied, any attempt to *reconstruct* the body is transgressive against the "natural" identity of the female body. Second, when female athletes use technology to achieve physical muscularity—a male body prerogative—they transgress the "natural" order of gender identity. What we discover through an analysis of media images of female athletes is that representations of their bodies often highlight their transgressive nature.

For example, a recent *National Enquirer* article ("Prizewinning Bodybuilder," 1987) featured a photo of bodybuilder Tina Plackinger accompanied by the headline "Prizewinning Bodybuilder Quits Taking Steroids Because . . . Drugs Were Turning Me Into a Man." Here the juxtaposition of physical strength, represented in the photograph by Plackinger's well-defined "ripped" biceps, triceps, and chest muscles, with the markers of her female body (breasts, long curly hair) creates a gender "hybrid" that invokes corporeal codes of femininity as well as of masculinity. The reference to Plackinger's steroid use as part of her body reconstruction program further establishes the transgressive nature of her body. Plackinger's use of steroids to produce a grotesquely muscular body violates the "natural" order not only of health and fitness but also of femininity and weakness. Of course, the specter of a transgressed gender boundary visually enhances the "spectacular" rhetoric of the article.

But this also happens in the media treatment of professionally trained amateur athletes. A close analysis of the newspaper accounts of Florence Griffith-Joyner's performances at the 1988 Olympic Games reveals the process of sexualization at work. The week before the Seoul Olympics, glossy photographs of Griffith-Joyner graced the covers of *U.S. News and World Report*, *Time*, and *Newsweek*. Most stories found a way to mention her body, not only in reference to its athletic capacity, but more obviously as it served as a mannequin for her flamboyant track outfits. One sportswriter (Hersch, 1988a) began his account of her record-breaking performance by ironically calling attention to her running outfit:

> Okay, let's get the important stuff out of the way first. Florence Griffith-Joyner wore a shocking pink one-legger with a white bikini bottom in the first round of the 200 meters in the U.S. Olympic trials Friday morning. She wore a fluorescent gold body suit with an orange print string bikini bottom in the quarterfinals Friday night. For both races, the fingernails on her left hand were painted cobalt blue and decorated with Hawaiian scenes, including palm trees, birds and the moon. The fingernails on her right hand were multicolored with a variety of rhinestone designs, including a cross. It took her three to five minutes to do each nail. By the way, it took her nowhere near that long to run the 200 meters Friday night. In fact, it took her less time than any American woman in history, (21.77 seconds, .04 sec. faster than the American record). (p. 1)

The problem with such an account is not that her flamboyant outfits discredit her athletic ability—she is widely recognized as a talented athlete—but rather that her appearance invokes the production of stereotypical comments about her sexual attractiveness. Given that female athletes cannot easily escape the cultural fascination that objectifies the female body, and in light of her own penchant for highly stylized athletic outfits, "Flo-Jo" was recognized as much for her sexual desirability as for her athletic ability, perhaps more so. Tony Duffy (Hersch, 1988b), a sports photographer, had this to say about Griffith-Joyner's media popularity:

> She was one of the sexiest girls at the 1984 Olympics. . . . She has this Polynesian look and an exotic feeling about her. I did a photo shoot of

Florence eight weeks ago, in body suits and bathing suits on the beach, and I couldn't give the pictures away. In the past two days (after her Olympic trials record), my phone has been ringing off the hook. *Playboy, Sports Illustrated, People, Life*—everyone wants pictures of her.[2]

This quotation describes the construction of Flo-Jo as cultural icon of exotic otherness. Accompanying newspaper images of Flo-Jo foreground corporeal markers of erotic identity: long, thick, curly hair; lean arms and torso; thick, muscular legs; dark skin. Without much coaching, we read in such newspaper images the construction of Flo-Jo as an idealized female body. But she is more than simply a body, she is identified as an attractive, *exotic* female body; her transgressive identity is as much a product of the color of her skin, her "Polynesian look," as of her athletic accomplishments. As such, these physical transgressions contribute to her construction as an object of desire. In contemporary U.S. culture, racial and ethnic identities function as signs of cultural difference; skin color, hair texture, and facial features are among the more familiar physiological markers of the cultural construction of "otherness." Much in the way that the biological "facts" of a woman's reproductive system are used to define her as a gendered body, so too are certain body "facts" invoked to construct Griffith-Joyner as an eroticized other. In this way we see how the athletic female body is also inscribed within other ideological systems of meaning, including race, ethnicity, and physical ability. This analysis describes how the black female body is constructed as a sign of transgressive cultural difference and as a "natural" sexual object.[3]

THE TECHNOLOGICAL CONSTRUCTION
OF THE IDEAL FEMININE BODY

The analysis of media representations of the female body shows quite clearly how that body symbolizes cultural ideals of "natural" femininity and erotic beauty. But the symbolic transformation of the female body is only part of the story. Through the practices of bodybuilding, weight training, and powerlifting, many female bodies are technologically transformed into material embodiments of such ideals. Because the form and quality of the bodies of women bodybuilders directly contradict received beliefs about the inherent pathology of femininity, female bodybuilding appears to be one arena in which the culturally constructed "natural" attributes of femininity could be redesigned in a more empowering fashion. But on closer examination, we see how technologically recrafted female bodies are delegitimated as cultural markers of proper femininity.

During the decade of the 1980s, an entire subculture grew up around female bodybuilding. The annual Miss Olympia contest was first staged in 1980 (Kennedy & Mason, 1984). By 1989 there were dozens of annual competitions, ranging from the World Professional Women's Bodybuilding Championships to amateur contests sponsored by local fitness centers. In 1989, estimates of the number of female amateur competitors put that figure at 16,000, compared to 40 to 150 in 1980. The *Hardcore Bodybuilder's Source Book* (Kennedy & Mason) lists several products specifically designed for female readers: training courses and routines, cookbooks, foods, jewelry, posing-wear, posters, skin and hair care products, and bodybuilding horoscopes. This subculture includes glossy magazines, such as *Muscle & Fitness*, as well as special workout books, such as Rachel McLish's *Flex Appeal*.

The film *Pumping Iron II: The Women* gained wide acclaim as a cult classic among female bodybuilders and gym participants. The film unfolds a cultural narrative about the "natural" definition of femininity as it applies to the technologically reconstructed female body.[4] In an early scene, the head judge instructs other judges about the rules of competition and describes the ultimate purpose of the contest:

> We hope that this evening we can clear up the definite meaning—the analysis of the word femininity [by] determining what to look for [in these women competitors]. This is an official IFBB analysis of the meaning of that word.[5]

In an unambiguous address, the audience is told that the (film's) contest will determine with perfect clarity the "definite meaning" of the word *femininity*. Apparently, the quality of feminine muscle definition is an ongoing concern for the judges of female bodybuilding contests. As reported in the *The Hardcore Bodybuilder's Source Book* (Kennedy & Mason, 1984), judges are given the following instructions about judging female competitors:

> First and foremost, the judge must bear in mind that he or she is judging a woman's bodybuilding competition and is looking for an ideal feminine physique. Therefore, the most important aspect is shape, a feminine shape. Other aspects are similar to those described for assessing men, but in regard to muscular development, it must not be carried to excess where it resembles the *massive muscularity of the male physique* [emphasis added]. (p. 181)

In fact, judges are instructed to look for certain faults in women that are not usually seen in men: stretch marks, surgical scars, and cellulite; they are also directed to observe whether female competitors walk and move gracefully, which seemingly is not a concern with male competitors.[6]

The film stages a contest between competing forms of female embodiment personified by two well-known female bodybuilders: Bev Francis, a muscular powerlifter, and Rachel McLish, a beauty-girl bodybuilder.[7] But viewers of the film audience know that it is not a documentary at all; it is really a fictional account of a staged competition, the Caesar's Palace World Cup Championship. The film relies on several techniques and genre conventions to establish its documentary look: The camera records spontaneous (nonscripted) interactions between characters, contestants are interviewed by an off-screen voice, and conversations are filmed at close range. And although the film uses "real" bodybuilders, this pseudodocumentary lists them in "starring roles" to compete in a contest that had been elaborately scripted.

The film records the reaction of judges and other women contestants to the embodied differences between the two stars. Symbolically, Bev represents the negative image of female bodybuilding: women who look like men. Rachel symbolizes the positive image: women with muscles who still look feminine (soft, curvy, and sexy when dressed in a bikini). Beginning with the sequences that introduce Bev and Rachel, the film visually constructs a system of differences between these two types of female bodies. Their differences concern not only the muscularity of their bodies, but their clothes, their local gyms, and their countries, cities, and families of origin. Narratively, the contest between Bev and Rachel structures the film's plot, so that at one level the film is about the competition between these two female bodies. But at another level, it is a film about ideologies of femininity.

The first shots of Rachel show her dressed in a zebra-print bikini wearing a feather headdress and gold chains around her neck and belly. She is posing for a photo session for *Muscle & Fitness*. Back in her home gym in Los Angeles, Rachel's posing coach wonders if her nonbodybuilding activities (commercials, posters, a beauty book project) diminish her status as a world-class bodybuilding champion. "Don't you think all this has made you a little soft, a little powderpuffish?" her coach inquires. "I've always considered myself a powderpuff," drawls Rachel, "a really strong powderpuff."

In contrast, Bev's introductory sequence opens with a shot of the rocky, rugged gray landscape of Melbourne, Australia. We meet Bev as she walks sideways up the walls of a hotel corridor. The next scene shows her competing in a powerlifting contest; she has just been introduced as a former ballet dancer who is now the strongest woman in the world. Bev, shown wearing a powerlifting suit and sleeveless T-shirt, successfully dead-lifts 510 pounds. Relaxing after the contest, Bev talks with her family (and presumably the film's interviewer) about the upcoming competition in Las Vegas. She ponders the reaction she will receive from an American audience who until now have only seen one type of female bodybuilder: the skinny woman with little muscles.

As the drama of the film unfolds, these two female bodies face off. Side by side on stage, Bev and Rachel are the first pair of competitors judged in the opening round of compulsory poses. While the other competitors pose, the audience is visually treated to several titillating shots of Rachel; for example, the camera caresses her with a long, slow take that moves from her ankles to her thighs to her face. Bev is not treated so kindly by the camera; rather we witness her in the dressing room sitting hunched over, elbows on knees, talking with her trainer. "Did I look like a girl?" she asks sarcastically. "How was my feminine quality?"

At the end of the contest, Bev's name is announced first: She finishes last of eight finalists. Her last-place finish symbolizes the significance of her body transgressions when a judge explains that women with "big grotesque muscles" violate the natural difference between men and women. But Rachel's physique is not simply elevated as the ideal female form. Portrayed throughout the film as a petulant "bad girl," Rachel finishes third. When Carla Dunlap is announced as the winner, the film abruptly jags away from its narrative predictability. Carla, a former Miss Olympia, is clearly the best candidate in overall athletic ability and bodybuilding sophistication. In terms of the film, however, her victory comes as a surprise because she is never constructed as a featured competitor in the way that Bev and Rachel are.[8] In fact, we learn very little about her personal body history or her philosophy about bodybuilding. Several times in the film she functions simply as a narrator, first to introduce Bev and the significance of Bev's participation in the contest, and later to interpret for the audience the meaning of the judges' struggle over competing definitions of femininity.

Yet Carla is an interesting selection as the winner. She is the only featured competitor who is not associated with a male trainer, husband, or father. Instead, her "real life" companions are a sister and mother who serve as surrogate audience for her explanations about the significance of Bev's and Rachel's participation in the contest. She is the only contestant to be shown doing physical activities other than bodybuilding (synchronized swimming and dancing). In choosing Carla, the film works hard to achieve a compromise position on the issue of femininity versus muscularity. Carla has neither the massive muscle-bound physique of Bev Francis nor the powderpuff figure of Rachel McLish.

But is Carla's winning a compromise or a cop-out? Carla is the only black contestant. Although her racial identity is not discussed explicitly, by promoting her as the compromise between two technologically reconstructed forms of female embodiment the film implicitly engages a host of body issues that invoke different forms of body transgression. Carla's victory signals a transgressive body posture through her identification as a black woman in a film world populated by white women. The meaning of Carla's victory is subversively significant, with respect not to the issue of muscularity versus femininity but to her racial identity. If this was indeed a contest to determine the proper meaning of the word "femininity," then how do we interpret the answer we've been given? What can it mean that a black female body is offered as a compromise between ideologies of muscularity and femininity?

For Annette Kuhn (1988), "Pumping Iron II" raises several issues regarding visual representation and feminist politics. Kuhn argues that Carla's victory merely sidesteps the film's central question:

> The issue of the appropriate body for a female bodybuilder is not actually resolved: rather it is displaced on to a set of discourses centering on—but also skirting—race, femininity and the body, a complex of discourses which the film cannot acknowledge, let alone handle. Carla's body can be "read" only as a compromise: other major issues are left dangling.
> (p. 18)

On the one hand, Carla's success as a bodybuilder is only one of many athletic achievements of black women. She and Florence Griffith-Joyner are only the two most recent black female athletes to achieve media popularity in U.S. culture. The reading that the film promotes suggests that it is not unusual (or noteworthy) for a black woman to succeed as an accomplished athlete in U.S. sports; such a reading purports to be "color-blind" by purposefully foregoing any mention of race. Yet on the other hand, Carla's victory suggests that racial distinctions are somehow less disturbing to a natural order than are the gender transgressions that Bev's body symbolizes.

But according to bell hooks (1984), such an interpretation is constructed within a discourse of white racism.

> Racist stereotypes of the strong, superhuman black woman are operative myths in the minds of many white women, allowing them to ignore the extent to which black women are likely to be victimized in this society and the role white women play in the maintenance and perpetration of that victimization. (p. 13)

Informed by hooks's analysis, we can look again at Carla's role. Although she is never portrayed as a victim per se, she is constrained in many ways. We see her constructed as an interpreter and guide to help the audience make sense of the meaning of the contest between two white women's bodies. Carla herself is not featured as a competent, accomplished professional bodybuilder. She is not empowered to elaborate her own identity as a bodybuilder. In this sense, Carla's narrative, repressed throughout the film, emerges as an emblem of the film's sexist and racist agenda. In the end, the film sidesteps the issue of technologically constructed gender differences and opens onto the issue of racial difference, only to end without addressing either issue or the interaction between them. By denying Carla her own story, the film teaches us that the only stories that count are those about white bodies. Scripted in this way, Carla's victory enables the racist fiction that asserts that white bodies are the bodies that matter, even if black bodies win from time to time. But it also points out that when white female bodybuilders engage in transgressive body practices, they enjoy a greater range of possibilities for reconstructing their corporeal identities in opposition to a traditional notion of white femininity defined as weak, pathological, and passive. Black transgressive bodies cannot as easily escape a "naturalized" race identity that codes the black body as "naturally" powerful. The efficacy of this power is recuperated, though, as Carla is also shown to be "naturally" subservient to the white bodies she competes against.

Thus, in sidelining Carla's story, the film sidesteps a much more potent challenge to the ideological contest playing out on the fictional stage of Caesar's Palace. What is much more interesting about Carla's story is that it is populated by supportive women and female relatives; men simply do not figure in Carla's narrative. In failing to offer a fuller account of her "woman-centered" athletic life, the film reveals how the debate about proper femininity and improper female masculinity that preoccupies most of the contestants, judges, and audience is constructed within a dualistic logic that privileges the ideal-type distinctions between masculinity and femininity as the most significant markers of cultural difference. The repressed elements of the film, Carla's racial identity and her connections to other women, suggest some of the other submerged discourses that structure the organization of technological body practices but are rarely acknowledged in media accounts of technologically transgressive female bodies. In this case, we can begin to sense other factors that influence the meaning of transgressive bodily practices, namely those of racial identity and of homo-social relationships.

CONCLUSION

What I discover, not surprisingly, is that despite their appearance as forms of resistance, these technological body transgressions rearticulate the power relations of a dominant social order. When female bodies participate in bodybuilding activities or other athletic events that are traditionally understood to be the domain of male bodies, the meanings of the female bodies are not simply recoded according to an oppositional or empowered set of gendered connotations. Although these bodies transgress gender boundaries, they are not reconstructed according to an opposite gender identity. They reveal instead how culture processes transgressive bodies in such a way as to keep each body in its place; that is, subjected to its "other": For white women, this other is the idealized "strong" male body; for black women it is the white female body. A closer study of the popular culture of female bodybuilding reveals the artificiality of attributes of "natural" gender identity and the changeability of cultural ideals of gender identity, yet it also announces quite loudly the persistence with which gender and race hierarchies structure technological practices and limit the disruptive possibilities of technological transgressions.

REFERENCES

Birke, L.I.A., & Vines, G. (1987). A sporting chance: The anatomy of destiny? *Women's Studies International Forum, 10*, 337-347.

Cohn, N., & Laffont, J-P. (1981). *Women of iron: The world of female body-builders.* U.S.A.: Wideview Books.

Feher, M. (Ed.) (1989). *Zone #3, 4, 5: Fragments for a History of the Human Body.* New York: Urzone.

Hersch, P. (1988a, July 23). Griffith-Joyner sets U.S. record in style. *Chicago Tribune* sec. 4: 1.

Hersch, P. (1988b, July 22). Running style. *Chicago Tribune* sec. 2: 1, 2.

hooks, b. (1984). *Feminist theory: From margin to center.* Boston: South End Press.

Kennedy, R., & Mason, V. (1984). *The hardcore bodybuilder's source book.* New York: Sterling.

Kuhn, A. (1988). The body and cinema: Some problems for feminism. In S. Sheridan (Ed.), *Grafts: Feminist Cultural Criticism* (pp. 11-23). London: Verso.

Lenskyj, H. (1986). *Out of bounds: Women, sport and sexuality.* Toronto: Women's Press.

Prizewinning Bodybuilder Quits Taking Steroids Because . . . Drugs were Turning Me Into a Man. (1987, September 22). *National Enquirer,* p. 4.

Vertinsky, P. (1987). Exercise, physical capability, and the eternally wounded woman in late nineteenth century North America. *Journal of Sport History* [Special issue: *Sport, Exercise, and American Medicine*], **14,** 7-27.

Williamson, J. (1978). *Decoding advertisements: Ideology and meaning in advertising.* London: Marion Boyars.

NOTES

1. Michel Feher, "Introduction," *Zone 3: Fragments for a History of the Human Body* (New York: Urzone, 1989), 11-17.

2. The quotation from Duffy is from an article by Phil Hersch, sportswriter for the *Chicago Tribune.* This article appeared in the Tempo section of the newspaper rather than in the Sports section. (Tempo is a light news section focusing on current social issues and the arts; it includes the "Dear Abby" and Bob Greene columns.) The explicit focus of the article was Griffith-Joyner's track outfits and her running history. The article included a comment by rival runner Gwen Torrence, who said that she would not be interested in the one-legged outfit that Griffith-Joyner wears: "We're out there to run like Superwoman, not look like Superwoman." "Running Style," *Chicago Tribune* July 22, 1988, sec. 2:1,2.

3. Jennifer A. Hargreaves analyzes the ideology of masculinity that is prominent in sport in "Where's the Virtue? Where's the Grace? A Discussion of the Social Production of Gender Relations in and Through Sport," *Theory, Culture and Society* 3.1 (1986): 56-78. Another excellent study of the ideological system of the body is Sander L. Gilman's "Black Bodies, White Bodies: Toward an Iconography of Female Sexuality in Late Nineteenth-Century Art, Medicine, and Literature," *Critical Inquiry* 12 (Autumn 1985): 96-117.

4. Laurie Jane Schulze analyzes a made-for-TV movie, *Getting Physical,* in terms of the economic conditions of television production and the narrative form of television movies. In her reading, the movie presents several iconographic strategies to disrupt a hegemonic recuperation of a potentially problematic figure: a female bodybuilder. Laurie Jane Schulze, "'Getting physical:

text/context/reading and the made-for-television movie," *Cinema Journal* 25.2 (Winter 1986): 16-30.

5. "Pumping Iron II: The Women," dir. George Butler with Carla Dunlap, Bev Francis, and Rachel McLish, 1985.

6. Physiologically, being "ripped" is a matter of fat content and water retention. Stripping off fat allows the muscle to bulge, producing the "ripped" look that many men popularize. Being "ripped" means that every sinew, tendon, and vein stands out under the skin, demonstrating very little fat content. The softer, rounder, smoother muscle definition of women occurs because there is more fat between the skin's outer layer and the muscle. Because women also battle a physiological sensitivity to fluid retention, they are advised to achieve better muscularity by minimizing sodium intake during "peaking cycles" (the final 4 days before a competition). Given women's physiological predisposition to higher body fat, the decision to remove fat is more than an appearance question: It is a matter of altering the biological composition of the female body. Fat removal is accomplished primarily through diet and a strenuous workout regimen with machines and weights that work to burn off all unnecessary body fat through calorie expenditure.

7. The film was created by Charles Gaines and George Butler based on their book, *Pumping Iron II: The Unprecedented Woman* (1984).

8. The film includes a sequence that shows Carla performing a synchronized swimming routine. Her biography in the book *Women of Iron: The World of Female Bodybuilders* (1981) describes Carla as a compulsive athlete who is expert in floor gymnastics, yoga, speed swimming, and dance. One of the few black women in bodybuilding (for most of the early 1980s), she was often asked if her race caused any problems. The reply: "No. She had never been taught that color was a limitation. . . . Her father was a chemist in Newark, and his children were provided with everything they needed. Carla had four sisters and a brother. They lived in a huge house. There were horses and boats, and lots of space to breathe in. A typical American middle-class background, she called it" (p. 59). Carla reports being plagued early in her bodybuilding career, by a physical structure that was deemed "too muscular" by various judges.

Chapter 23

The Embodiment of Gender: Discipline, Domination, and Empowerment

David Whitson
University of Alberta

I watch my daughter. From morning to night her body is her home. She lives in it and with it. When she runs around the kitchen she uses all of her self. She feels pleasure and expresses it without hesitation. . . . I sometimes feel she is more a model for me than I am for her. (A mother, quoted in Boston Women's Health Book Collective, 1976, p. 40)

When we were kids there was release in playing, the sweetness of being able to move and control your body. . . . I felt released because I could move around anybody. I was free. (Hockey player Eric Nesterenko, quoted in Terkel, 1974, p. 383)

These reflections remind us of the virtual identity of body and self that we mostly take for granted in childhood. We ran, climbed, skipped, and threw, and in these activities of early childhood we discovered things about ourselves and what we could do in the world. We took an innocent pleasure in learning to move and control our bodies and experienced a growing sense of self that was intimately connected with our experience of our bodies, both what we could do and what we looked like. Yet the two recollections, one by a woman and the other by a man, serve not only to remind us how most of us become alienated from our bodies in adult life; they also point out how differently the childhoods of girls and boys come to be structured: by discourses of femininity and masculinity and by gendered practices of play that teach us to inhabit and experience our bodies in profoundly different ways.

In the first section of this chapter, I briefly review these practices and the ideologies that have justified and, for many, naturalized such differences. The encouragement and the institutional support that boys generally enjoy in any efforts they make to develop physical strength and sports skills are contrasted with the historical construction of femininity as prettiness and vulnerability and the ambiguous messages that are encountered even today by strong, active females. In the second section, I examine the challenges associated with the broadening of opportunities for physical empowerment and ask what "the embodyment of power" (Gilroy, 1989) means—for women and for men. Feminist and masculinist discourses of sport pose the question of how and indeed whether empowerment, the confident sense of self that comes from being skilled in the use of one's body, can be detached from an emphasis on force and domination, which are integral to the body contact sports that comprise the "major games" of male popular culture. Finally, I examine the current popularity of newer sports and other forms of noncombative physical practice, activities ranging from dance and yoga to aerobics and various forms of exercise in natural environments (Bloch, 1987). For although critics are correct to point out the commodification, the sexual imagery, and the individualism that are all present in the marketing of fitness (and the social marketing of wellness), it is still important to distinguish between marketing discourse and the expanded experiences of their bodies and themselves that many women and men—of different ages, body types, and social locations—enjoy and explore in these new activities.

EMBODY-ING POWER: MASCULINIZING AND FEMINIZING PRACTICES

> Through football I learned . . . how my body could be used as a force, how my shoulders, back, hips and legs, driven in a straight line against a ball carrier's thighs, could topple him easily. As early as nine years old, I began to know my own body in ways that only an athlete or a dancer know[s] it. (Oriard, 1982, pp. 18-19)

This recollection by Michael Oriard, a former Kansas City Chief-turned-English professor, illustrates what Bob Connell's essay "Men's Bodies" (1983) has articulated in a more general way, namely how childhood sports teach boys to use their bodies in skilled, forceful ways while providing them a detailed and accurate knowledge of their physical capacities and limits. Boys learn how to develop force (through leverage, coordination, and follow-through) and to transmit this power through their limbs or through extensions, like ball bats and golf clubs. In contrast, Iris Young (1980) has suggested that the movement patterns of most girls are characterized by their partiality, by their failure to take the sort of advantage described by Oriard of the torque that is generated when the entire body is mobilized into a throw, a swing, or a tackle:

Not only is there a typical style of throwing like a girl, but there is a more or less typical style of running like a girl, climbing like a girl, swinging like a girl, hitting like a girl. They have in common, first, that the whole body is not put into fluid and directed motion, but rather, in swinging and hitting, for example, the motion is concentrated in one body part; and second, that the woman's motion tends not to reach, extend, lean, stretch, and follow through in the direction of her intention. (p. 143)

What is meant by the phrase "throwing like a girl," Young suggests, is precisely the tendency of many girls not to put their whole bodies into the motion, unlike most boys. Likewise, she suggests that when women who are not used to physical work are faced with physical tasks, they frequently fail to use the strength they do have to the fullest. She argues, drawing on de Beauvoir and Merleau-Ponty, that these partial and half-hearted movement patterns derive ultimately from discourses and practices that have encouraged the woman to experience her body as an object-for-others, whereas men have learned to experience themselves in the active, forceful ways depicted so clearly by Oriard: to act, instead of being looked at and acted upon. She begins from Merleau-Ponty's proposition that human subjectivity, one's fundamental experience of one's self in the world and one's basic orientation to the external world (to other people as well as the object world) is rooted in the lived body and in how one learns to live one's body. For Merleau-Ponty (1962; also see Young, 1980, pp. 140-142, 146-148), *I, I can,* and *I cannot* are all embodied experiences, and one's sense of oneself as an active person is developed precisely through experiences of mastering one's body and realizing one's intentions in physical movements in and through space.

Young proceeds to argue, following de Beauvoir (1974), that women historically have been taught to embody what she calls "inhibited intentionality," in which feminine body comportment, feminine movement patterns, and tentative uses of space all say *I cannot* in the very act of trying. In such movement habits, says de Beauvoir, women embody the contradictory nature of their experience in patriarchal societies, a contradiction between their phenomenal experience of themselves as active subjects and their social construction as objects for others. "Femininity" here is not an essence that all women have naturally or even that some have more than others. It is, rather, a product of discourses, practices, and social relations that construct the situation of women in patriarchal societies in ways that typically dis-able women in relation to men.

If, as Merleau-Ponty argues, the basic structures of human existence— consciousness, intentionality, purposiveness, etc.—have their foundation in the body as active and expressing subject, then the inhibition on women's development of our body subjectivity implies a profound inhibition of our humanity. (Young, 1979, p. 49)

For Young, this is neither natural nor inevitable; indeed she makes the point that there have always been women whose exceptional experiences have enabled them to transcend these inhibitions. Nonetheless the "typical" effect of the feminizing practices that construct the female body as object is to inhibit women, at the same time that many kinds of masculinizing practice teach boys to live their bodies and to experience themselves in active and powerful ways. Sport is only one of these masculinizing practices; but Connell (1983) underlines how important sport is in the formative experience of boys, and histories of "athleticism" in the English boys' schools remind us that organized sport has always been about teaching boys to be power-full people, through experiences of physical discipline and accomplishment. In contrast, Sheila Fletcher (1984) has described how, while the private schools of the Victorian period were using sport to teach "manliness" to upper-class boys, upper-class girls were learning to be "ladies." The Victorian ideal of the lady, of feminine weakness as the object of male desire and protection, required of girls a learned helplessness that alienated them from whatever physical competence and confidence they might have acquired as children. While Fletcher depicts the unhappiness and the lived contradiction that this caused for many girls, Young argues that, despite considerable historical change in some aspects of gender relations, the *legacy* of "femininity" is still a constraint on women's experience of their bodies. Despite the recent expansion of organized sport for girls, *their* sports are often kept less "physical" than boys', and girls are not encouraged as readily as boys are to push themselves and to really develop their physical skills. Swimming and gymnastics constitute obvious and sometimes controversial exceptions to this. However, Young contrasts the parental and peer encouragement that normally reinforces boys in their sporting endeavors, as well as the wide range of sports and programs that are normally available to boys, with the more ambiguous messages and the more restricted range of opportunities that girls must negotiate.

Here it may be worth referring to what developmental psychologist John Shotter (1984) has called a "political economy of developmental opportunities" in which some people, because of their social location, have access to more and different kinds of developmental opportunities than others. Despite the economic language, moreover, Shotter is clear that it is not simply a matter of class or financial resources. The development of "personal powers" and the sense of self that results involves other people (initially parents, and subsequently "society") recognizing what is skilled and valuable in what a child does spontaneously, and holding it up for the child's own recognition and pleasure. Out of the latter, Shotter suggests, comes a boy's or girl's desire to develop natural capacities into personal skills; but within the prevailing discourses and engendering practices outlined above, boys and girls are typically (though not always) offered very different kinds of developmental opportunities, and often with the "best" of intentions.

Indeed, even when parental support is strong and training and competitive opportunities are available, Young (1979) suggests that as the girl athlete enters adolescence, "she increasingly experiences the sexually objectifying gaze of men" (p. 47). She cannot help becoming aware that many people, women as well as men, are assessing her more in terms of her looks than her accomplishments, and that according to the standards that are applied to her and to other women, ''femininity'' and power are incompatible. Blye Frank's work (1991) reminds us that adolescent males are also very much concerned with their looks and with projecting a masculine body image; but the important difference is that ''masculinity'' equates precisely with appearing physically powerful and strong (see Connell, 1983). This is why teenaged boys often spend much time in body-building and martial arts. However for girls, it becomes difficult not to want to develop ''habits of feminine body comportment—walking like a girl, standing and sitting like a girl, gesturing like a girl, and so on'' (Young, 1980, p. 153), habits in which women learn to embody male expectations of weakness and incompetence. There are differences, of course, in the extent to which individual women want to, or indeed can, conform their body comportment to these male-defined images of femininity. However, the discourse of masculine strength and feminine weakness continues to constitute both expectations and self-expectations, and Young's point is that to whatever extent a female is induced into pursuing a feminine persona, the more likely it is that she will feel ambivalent about her own strength and will actually *become* more inhibited and tentative in her movement patterns. ''To the degree that we choose ourselves as body-objects, we find it difficult to become enthusiastic body subjects and frequently do not desire to challenge our bodies in sport'' (1979, p. 48).

Young's analysis is extended by that of Sheila Scraton (1987). Her work on the subcultures of high school women in England suggests that for many young women, femininity is actively embraced as a way of rejecting parental and school control over their sexuality. Young women, like young men, are staking public claims to adult sexual identities; and given the generally sexist character of youth cultures, they often feel considerable pressure to look ''sexy.'' In the context of these pressures, young women understandably resist the school's attempts (e.g., in physical education) to make them wear asexual clothing and otherwise comport themselves in public in ways that go against the personae they are trying to embody. Moreover, ''gym'' is often disciplined and regimented and as such is not easily compatible with expectations of enthusiastic fun and sexual self-expression among modern young women (Matthews, 1987). In Scraton's view, this way of understanding young women's resistance, in which gender intersects with age (and sometimes class and ethnicity, too), can offer more insight than do the standard biological explanations of why so many young women, even ones who have been active as girls, drop out of physical activity in their adolescent years.[1] Yet the end result, to return to Young, is that girls are disabled, both in absolute terms and in relation to boys, who are actively empowered by a host of formative experiences that teach them how to use their bodies in powerful ways. Following Shotter (1984), ''texts of identity'' create a variety of different possibilities for individual development, and although these are not determining in individual cases, one's social location has a powerful effect on the texts that are readily available.

Discourses of masculine strength and feminine weakness and the ways of being that they help to normalize have also been addressed by Catherine

MacKinnon (1987), who suggests (like Young) that male ideas and images of femininity have been all too commonly embodied in women who become weak and vulnerable. In her view, it is not only that many women choose to live their bodies as vulnerable and in doing so actually render themselves more vulnerable, although this is clearly important. It is also that received ideas that say women cannot do certain physical things or push themselves in certain kinds of physical training without harm (e.g., in weight training or distance running) become self-fulfilling prophecies. "The notion that women cannot do certain things, cannot break certain records, cannot engage in certain physical pursuits has been part of preventing women from doing these things" (p. 119). This is one way of understanding the power of ideology. Today, of course, women have dramatically surpassed what were once thought their limits both in strength and aerobic events; and the women who have done so have created new kinds of role models, new images of possibility that open the imagination to still greater levels of accomplishment. MacKinnon goes on to suggest, though, that the women who have embodied these accomplishments have done more than challenge received notions about women in sport. In living their bodies as skilled and forceful subjects rather than as objects of the male gaze, and especially in embodying power themselves, they challenge one of the fundamental sources of male power, the ideological equation of physical power itself with masculinity.

EMPOWERMENT: DOMINATION AND PLEASURE

MacKinnon goes on to propose, however, that the meanings and practices that have been naturalized in much of men's sport may not be what women want and that a closer analysis of just what is empowering and pleasurable in physical activity is called for. The strategic questions surrounding whether women's interests are best served by equalizing access to "malestream" sports, or whether it is more important to develop both a critique of these and an alternative model of what sport could be like, are not ones I can presume to answer. However, MacKinnon's discussion, along with those of some other feminist writers,[2] throws into relief some perspectives on power and pleasure, as lived in physical performance, that have implications for women and men alike.

A useful starting point is MacKinnon's observation that from a feminist's perspective, sport for men looks like a form of combat. Even in sports that don't involve direct personal confrontation, many men are intensely competitive; and in those that do involve body contact, sport is a narrative of pitting oneself against an individual on the other side and prevailing in the contest, dominating and subduing one's opponent. MacKinnon's comments here articulate directly with the observations of Bob Connell and his colleagues on why football (and other body contact sports) remain important masculinizing practices in Western societies. "It's confrontative in a way that other competitive sports are not. In the course of play you are constantly running up against someone, and have to overcome him in a test of personal superiority'' (Connell, Ashenden, Kessler, & Dowsett, 1982, p. 94). This is indeed the reality of line play in football, and of ''battles along the boards'' in hockey. It is dominate or lose, and men who acquire reputations as indomitable in these struggles, the Ronnie Lotts and Mark Messiers, become icons of a dominating masculinity that is widely celebrated among men (Messner, 1990).

What we are talking about here is a traditionally masculine way of embodying power, where this means the capacity to achieve one's ends, by force if necessary, even in the face of opposition. At its best, this model of masculinity defines the ''real'' man as a person of few words, but with a powerful sense of his own abilities and the toughness and physical competence to handle any difficulties or challenges. Male sports heroes were long presented as embodiments of this kind of masculinity, as indeed movies and television have often presented an older kind of Western hero or police detective.[3] Sometimes sports stars have fit this bill reasonably closely, though often enough the lines between a ''necessary'' toughness and an active enjoyment of aggression and intimidation are difficult to discern. Ideally, though, the dominating athlete has been represented as the kind of man people respect, but don't cross; a man who normally respects the rules of social institutions but is capable of using personal force to achieve his ends if necessary. However, Joyce Carol Oates (1987) has suggested that the atavistic pleasure one observes among many sports fans when brawling erupts out of more rule-bound athletic contests manifests the extent to which sectors of society still celebrate those who can turn physical power into social power.

Here we can begin to see why combative sports and aggressive players have been celebrated among many men. The devaluation of physical work and the ascendancy of intellectual and interpersonal skills in a service and information society, the entry of women into many workplaces and the increasing economic independence of women, and the gradual willingness of the law to intervene in domestic violence: All of these contribute to the erosion of a world in which a powerful male body could translate into social power. Body contact sports are now one of the few areas of public life in which force and intimidation are still allowed to triumph, where men who love to hit can still enjoy doing so, and others will celebrate their toughness and their willingness to pay the price. Messner (1990) has suggested that these kinds of heroes continue to ''prove'' (for those who want to read it in this way) that men are superior to women and that aggression is not only effective but admirable. The prominence of these kinds of activities and heroes in popular culture thus rehearses a widely followed narrative in which masculine violence is legitimated and a force-full way of being male is honoured (see Miedzian, 1991; Kidd, 1987).

However, MacKinnon proposes, and of course she is not alone, that there is more to sport than combat and more to empowerment through physical activity than learning to hit effectively. If the constitutive structure and the basic story line of our major team games involve the domination of opponents and the control of territory through force, MacKinnon suggests that this vision of sport leaves out ''some rather major elements'' of the sporting experience. These include the pleasures that can be taken in smooth, powerful motion (e.g., in running or swimming), in coordination and fine motor skills, in self-awareness and self-possession, in partnership and shared fun (see Nelson, 1991). These are experiences that both men and women can and do enjoy, MacKinnon suggests, *but they are seldom allowed to be the central purpose of male sport* (1987, p. 121).

Empowerment, in this alternative discourse, means learning how to move in coordinated and increasingly skillful ways and often how to coordinate your own movements with those of others. It may mean learning how to use equipment, like sticks, racquets, or skis, as extensions of your limbs, for example, in the well-struck golf or tennis shot or in the grace and skill or different skiing disciplines. It may even mean learning how to generate force and power and to take advantage of these in competitive games. But the pleasure and the sense of accomplishment are in the skills and a competent, confident sense of self, rather than in the domination of others. It may even be that for many women today, a confident, less vulnerable sense of self will require knowledge of how to mobilize force in self-defense. However, even this typically involves learning how to use one's body skillfully, just as it has for generations of smaller men. This is consistent with Young's discussion, and it is not inconsistent with a definition of "personal power" as self-discovery: that is, experimenting with, then developing through skilled practice, and finally enjoying what we can do with our bodies. This is what developmental psychologists describe as mastery play, or the development of natural talents into skills that we can draw on, when necessary, and can enjoy the feel of, whenever we care to use them (see Shotter, 1973, 1974).

Certainly there are numerous accounts in which men describe enjoying particular moments of embodied skill in this way. Eric Nesterenko, in the comments quoted at the beginning of this chapter, goes on to talk about the pleasure he still took in skating, in leaning into turns, defying the forces of gravity with his sense of balance and his "feel" for just what his body would allow him to do (Terkel, 1974). Some of my favorite accounts, because they recall experiences I can recognize, are by runners who describe the pleasures of fast runs and the pleasures of partnership with other runners, who are part of these experiences and help to make them happen.[4] However, accounts of "flow" and the enjoyment of skill and of moments of embodied self-awareness are familiar in the literature of skiing, tennis, surfing, swimming, and, doubtless, of other sports as well. Even in games like football and hockey, former athletes Oriard and Nesterenko convey clearly the pleasures they took in the skills of these games. However, their overall experiences amply confirm MacKinnon's point that this kind of enjoyment was seldom allowed to be their central purpose. Normally, it was subordinated to the quest for victory, a quest that demanded an emphasis on force—and a capacity to absorb force and play through pain—in pursuit of domination. Both the personal and academic literatures underline that this becomes the norm in organized male sport at an early age.

There are also many accounts in which women talk of the pleasures they have found in skilled physical performance and of the sense of empowerment they have experienced when doing so. Helen Lenskyj (quoted in Scraton, 1987) captures the import of this when she suggests that even though many women have grown up alienated from their bodies, not knowing the extent of their strength and endurance and not daring to find out,

> those of us who have dared have found a new avenue for self-realisation as women and as feminists—joyful at the discovery that our bodies are strong and resilient, capable of hard work and hard play. (p. 181)

Just as is true for men, there is a range of activities in which women speak of enjoying the feelings that come with skill, of taking pleasure in movement and in partnership, and of discovering new aspects of themselves in the process. Indeed, it may be worth remarking that for some women, martial arts have provided a context in which they have learned to express force and to overcome the sort of partial, tentative movement habits described by Young (1980). At the other end of a kind of continuum, dance and yoga have also become popular disciplines through which women (and increasing numbers of men) have learned to know their bodies and to live them as subjects. Here, the emphasis is very much on skill and on body awareness, on the integration of mind and body as self. Charlotte Bloch (1987) suggests that over the last 10 to 15 years, some remarkable shifts have occurred in what she calls the dominant body culture, not the least of which has been the emergence of new sports and the popularity of modes of exercise (some old and some new) that are alternatives to sport's traditional emphasis on competition and combat. Included here might be yoga and other body-consciousness movements (e.g., t'ai chi, Feldenkrais), aerobics and other dance-based activities, bodybuilding, skateboarding and rollerskating, jogging and cycling, as well as a variety of wilderness and outdoor activities. None of these are combative activities, and those that do lend themselves to competitions can also be enjoyed either as modes of wilderness travel or simply as pastimes in which to enjoy the athleticism of one's body, of playing with one's own skills. All of these activities are enjoyed by women and men, both separately and together. Granskog's discussion of triathlon (1991) serves to illustrate these things, as well as the potential of these activities to afford the experiences of mastery, self-discipline, and discovery alluded to by Lenskyj. Granskog describes how the training, the support given and received within the triathlon subculture, and the challenge of qualifying for and completing the Ironman triathlon all provide opportunities for discoveries that can be especially important for women. One comment that "it gave me a dose of self-confidence like I've never experienced before, and my self-respect is at an all-time high" (p. 28) is indicative of the empowerment that women triathletes have reported to result from their involvement in the sport.

However, Birrell and Richter's discussion (1987) of feminist transformations of baseball—not a body contact sport but in other ways very representative of the culture of male team sports—can make some points about competition and skill, and about their place in the pleasures of sport and physical activity. First, Birrell and Richter show that a competitive game can be played without the single-minded quest for victory that has spoiled many women's experiences of the "male model" of sport. They do not devalue competition; indeed, several women speak of enjoying the challenge of a good game, adding that the experience is less satisfying when players fool around or don't try. Still, they argue that the emphasis on winning that informs the standard discourse of male sport produces a variety of practices that override any sense of good opponents as partners, who bring out the best in us, and that often blot out the pleasure that might be felt when using physical skills. Here, their analysis recalls MacKinnon's point that the quest for domination produces a structure of meanings and practices (Birrell and Richter call it "a rationalist structure") in which partnership and having fun together, and pleasure in skill and self-exploration, are not allowed to be the primary purposes of sporting participation (see Nelson, 1991).

Secondly, there is the issue of skill. Feminist baseball teams as a matter of principle do not wish to reproduce the hierarchies based on skill that characterize the social relations of so many teams. They want to actively support less skilled and less experienced players, that is, to provide a supportive atmosphere in which less confident women can make mistakes while learning to feel more at home with their bodies and with the game. Nonetheless, few would go so far as to agree with the antiskill slogan worn by one team: "Every error helps another woman." Women who are skilled (or who want to develop skills) are bothered by this objection to skill. They have been empowered themselves precisely through learning *how* to do confidently and well things that they were once very tentative and apprehensive about, and their skills are an important source of the pleasures they derive from the game. Yet we need to recognize that the hegemony of the rational, instrumental approach to skill development has often meant authoritarian regimens of pratice in which "no pain, no gain" has been the guiding principle. These take the fun, and the sense of playing with our bodies, out of sport. In reaction against this, it is not surprising that the notion that "anything worth doing is worth doing badly" (George Bernard Shaw) has some appeal. Yet on balance, the observations of Birrell and Richter (1987) as well as those of other women who have written about empowerment through physical activity (Gilroy, 1989; Theberge, 1987), suggest that the development of some level of skill and fitness are necessary foundations of any enjoyment of physical practices. The experiences of self-realization and empowerment described by Lenskyj and by Granskog remind us that self-discipline and practice are necessary conditions of finding that we can do things we never thought we could do and do them well.

Finally, there is the issue of physical domination. The experiences of self-discipline and strength and endurance celebrated by Lenskyj and Granskog, and likewise the pride in skill and in competitive achievement described by Birrell and Richter, do not necessarily (and typically don't) involve the physical domination of another person. Neither does the language of empowerment they use have much in common with that often used by football or hockey people when talking about the demands of their sports and what power means in the context of a body contact sport.[5] This raises the issue of the relative place of experiences of skill and strength (both physical and mental, and the integration of the two), as opposed to the physical domination of other people, in experiences of personal power or empowerment, as well as the further issue of how and why the capacity to dominate has been ideologically constructed as a cornerstone of masculine identities. Beyond this, we must reflect on the relative balance of force and skill in the constitutive structure of sports and physical activities, especially those that are widely followed in our popular culture. We must ask ourselves about the cultural meanings of these textual activites and their effects on discourses of masculinity and femininity and on the gender order. Adapting Connell's observation (1983) that the demands of every sport involve a particular balance between force and skill, it can be suggested that the more it is force that is decisive, the more a physically dominating, hegemonic masculinity can be publicly celebrated and the more likely that the culture of sport will be part of the defense of the existing gender order.

These are not new issues, of course, but they remain important ones, if only because changes in sport and body culture are uneven and difficult to read with confidence. One of the points made both by Birrell and Richter and by MacKinnon is that for feminist reconstructions of sporting and physical practices to have a broader effect (among women and men alike), popular understandings of empowerment and the powerful body must move away from the traditional masculine preoccupation with force and domination toward a new emphasis on personal experiences of skill and of pleasure in motion, and on sharing these experiences with others. On the surface, the burgeoning interest in noncontact sports and other modes of competitive exercise suggest that this is actually happening. Women are much better represented in all of these activities than they are in the traditional team games (in some, of course, they are the major participants); and if Young (1979) is correct, the physical empowerment of more women and the entry into sport of greater numbers of women will steadily contribute toward breaking down the masculinist connotations of sport itself. Yet there remains the distinct possibility that the traditional male games will retain their privileged place in popular culture, and some critics have raised important questions about aspects of the growth of aerobics and other "participation sports."

NEW ACTIVITIES, OLD PROBLEMS?

To bring the questions into focus, consider the running and jogging boom that has swept the western world over the last quarter century. It may be hard to realize today that it all began in the 1960s in the desire of disparate and anonymous individuals to enjoy a simple form of exercise without the disciplines and expectations of organized track and field. People honked and pointed at runners on the streets; there were a few "fun runs"; *Runners World* was a mimeographed cult sheet in California. But in less than 10 years, the running industry boomed, replete with fashions, mass marathons, and its own "promotional culture".[6] A proliferation of multinational sport shoe companies now bring out more "new and improved" models each year than does the automotive industry, as well as accessories that were undreamt of 10 years ago. Individuals market themselves as experts in everything from the psychology of running to race organization services. *Runners World* is now only one of several glossy vehicles for the promotion of all these wares, as well as the personalities and training programs of a new elite. It's important to recognize that running has been reconstructed so that it attracts many participants who were and are excluded from high-performance track athletics, especially men and women who are past their physical prime. Yet as Mike Featherstone (1982) has noted, the growth of running cannot be disconnected from the growth of a promotional discourse in which a series of themes—progress, mobility, self-realization, and self-control—were articulated with running in ways that spoke to the circumstances and aspirations of many young adults formed in the affluent postwar years.

Not dissimilar phenomena can be observed in the growth of activities like mountain biking, triathlon, and cross-country skiing. In terms of skill and endurance, all of these "lifestyle sports" offer pleasure in physicality. They typically also offer real pleasure in their environment and often in companionship and in subcultural solidarity. They offer these pleasures to women and men alike, and importantly to older women and men who can pursue "personal bests" at their own pace, with the personal meanings and the sense of empowerment depicted in Granskog's (1991) discussion of the Ironman Triathlon:

> The Ironman represents for many the opportunity to express the reality that ordinary people from all walks of life can indeed achieve extraordinary athletic accomplishments. In many ways one might argue that the entire process is a . . . quest to test one's limits and beyond. (p. 13)

At the same time, all of these sports have also become quickly commodified, both fashion conscious and fashion-able; the equipment and the typical venues themselves often require considerable disposable income. Jeremy Howell (1991) echoes Featherstone, suggesting that the promotional discourse that has associated lifestyle sports with upwardly mobile, self-actualizing individuals has helped to insert the fit body into our images of "success" in ways that are not unproblematic. Robert Crawford (1985) has suggested that this equation of fitness and health with success and conspicuous consumption does indeed create self-expectations and obsessions—"healthism"—that become the source of health problems such as eating disorders and injuries, which in the former case affect women in particular.

Arguably of greatest significance, though, is the growth of aerobics. This is because, even more so than running and cross-country skiing, this activity has been part of the legitimation of physical activity for women. Indeed, in its constitutive links with dance and music, its potential for popularizing a radical break with the hegemony of competitive physical activities is perhaps unique. Yet although it has been the context for much that is positive—new opportunities for adult women to experience physical empowerment, as well as opportunities for support and friendship like those that have always been available to men— aerobics, too, has proved easy to incorporate, to commodify, and in some distinctive ways. There has been the familiar commercialization of the activity, particularly the fashionable clothing and the fitness club itself. Beyond this, the marketing of fitness as an aid to sex appeal articulates easily with the objectification of the female body. Marg MacNeill's (1988) discussion of the sexual imagery and the commodification of the fit female body underlines this all too clearly.

However, focusing entirely on the incorporative capacities of the system downplays the extent to which there have been real gains associated with these changes in the dominant body culture. If anything of what Young (1979, 1980) and MacKinnon (1987) have said is correct (about the empowering potential of women learning to use their bodies actively), surely it is important that millions of women who, in the sporting culture of earlier periods, would not have taken part in vigorous and challenging physical activities, now want to do so. It also seems an advance that they can choose from a much broader range of activities and social environments—from baseball to yoga—to find a way of being physical that is enjoyable and wholly their own. It further seems important that the increasing range of wilderness and aerobic activities, and the increasing legitimacy of dance and yoga for men, has opened up many spaces in which men, too, can experience different kinds of physicality and ways of being strong other than through use of force. The cumulative effect of these changes can only contribute to reinforcing the legitimacy of other ways of being male, despite predictable innuendo and resistance from males who would defend hegemonic masculinity. Moreover, the new availability of noncombative forms of exercise has also clearly spoken to the needs of millions of middle-aged men, for whom the body used to be little more than a briefcase for other, more serious kinds of ambitions, something we attended to only if it broke down before the book got written or the deal closed.

With regard to aerobics, although the critiques of the commodification and sexualization of these activities are important, it is also important to note the very real pleasure that so many women clearly find in these kinds of classes, and not only in the commercial ones, but in the thousands of much less visible classes in schools and community centers, where the atmosphere is usually quite different from that of ''20-Minute Workout.'' Bruce and Markula (1989) suggest that women's pleasure in these classes is both real and widespread, and they reiterate both the empowerment issue and the sense of partnership in doing physical things with other women, which was cited by Birrell and Richter. Both of these issues are reinforced in Susan Willis's discussion of ''working out'' (1990); and though she revisits the critical question raised by MacNeill and Featherstone, she considers that the remarkable success of *Our Bodies, Ourselves* highlights just how important the body and physicality are to women today. The new availability of appropriate and enjoyable forms of exercise has been especially important, she suggests, to middle-aged and older women, who were completely neglected in the exercise discourses and practices of earlier periods.

It is worthwhile, indeed, following Jill Julius Matthews (1987), to briefly consider some of the early discourses of women's exercise. For in the emergence and eclipse of different languages of advocacy, we can see precursors of some of the same tensions and commercial forces that have been alluded to here. Matthews describes a natural health movement in Britain in the early 1900s very much involved with women's health issues; it promoted dress and dietary reform and vigorous open-air exercise, especially hiking, for women. In the process, the movement articulated a case against the medical profession's management of women's bodies that foreshadowed later developments. However, Matthews also notes that in the movement's moral strictures against any articulation of exercise with fashion or sexuality, and in its opposition to dieting for appearance rather than health, it lost credibility among younger women who, for their part, took for granted the freedoms to exercise and express themselves physically for which the movement had fought.

> The natural health movement had prepared the way over decades, but could not recognize itself in the fashionable pleasures of the fit, slim, tanned body, in the fads of the young moderns. . . . To become relevant to women's desire for modern bodies, the movement would have had to release some of its old certainties and its earnestness, make itself more flexible and more fun. (pp. 21-22)

Drawing extensively on Sheila Fletcher (1984), Matthews goes on to point to similar tensions in the history of women's physical education, where again, the intimate links that the founding generations had articulated between the establishment of skilled movement disciplines for women and the broader project of women's liberation became submerged in other issues. Like the natural health movement, the pioneers of women's physical education helped to establish the legitimacy of women transforming their bodies, and they legitimized distinctive exercise practices that offered ways of experiencing the body different than those of the combative games that were the whole of male physical training. However, although they did much to establish viable practices of bodily self-transformation for women, women's physical education largely refused to identify itself with modern young women's desires for attractive bodies. In part because of an appreciation of how this fed into the discourse of compulsory heterosexuality, "the very desire for physical beauty was itself suspect" (p. 25). Such a position could not be sustained in the face of other kinds of articulations in the media and in popular culture, and Matthews indicates that by the 1930s, those discourses of women's exercise that found an audience began to emphasize "attractiveness, fun, and pleasure" (p. 29). These are the beginnings of the articulation of exercise with the desire and fashion that is familiar today and the beginnings of the commodification of exercise itself.

Matthews, like MacNeill, reminds us that the incorporation of exercise into mass culture has served to establish popular standards for the female body—young, slender, tanned, fit—that for many women are impossible and even oppressive. "The modern female body was not just different from the old, it was different in the same way for everyone." (p. 31). However it *was* different from older images of embodied constraint and helplessness, and it spoke to many women's aspirations to transform themselves. Anticipating Rick Gruneau's point (1993) that the discourse of modernity legitimates the systematic and purposeful transformation of the person just as it advocates the rational remaking of society, Matthews argues that since the development of modern mass culture, for the many women who have seen themselves as "modern," the fun and fashion associated with fitness and the experiences of self-transformation associated with changing one's body have made exercise an obvious site for participating in the experience of modernity. It has remained for subsequent generations of women (ranging from the authors of *Our Bodies, Ourselves* to more recent feminist academics) to critique the effects of the imagery of the modern female body, to legitimize different bodily shapes and practices, and to situate these issues within a larger debate about the place of the body in the gender order (see Haug, 1987).

CONCLUDING REMARKS

In this chapter I have sought to explicate how gendered identities are both social and historical constructs and how gendered subjectivities are embodied by individuals as they grow from childhood into adult sexual identities. Masculinity and femininity become personally embodied in the ways described previously; yet this always occurs in specific social contexts that historically have privileged masculinity over femininity and particular ways of being male or female over other ways. Sports and other texts of physical competence have been important in this, insofar as they have naturalized norms of male strength and female weakness and have actively reproduced these through developmental practices that have taught males and females to live their bodies in active or passive ways. Body contact games, in particular, have historically naturalized an aggressive way of "doing masculinity" (Frank, 1991) in which physical domination is legitimated; over time, these confrontative sports have become important masculinizing practices that initiate young males into a hierarchy of gendered identities in which the capacity to dominate is honored and physical power confers social power.

I have tried to make a case for the importance of a variety of other physical practices, some new (or at least newly popular, e.g., some of the aerobic and wilderness sports) and others of a longer history (e.g., dance and other non-competitive movement forms, aerobics, and other exercise practices). In all of these activities, the challenges and the pleasures are in skill and self-possession rather than confrontation and offer empowering experiences to women and men alike. They have also constituted cultural texts in which different ways of being female and male, different ways of "doing" femininity and masculinity, are modelled and legitimized, and texts in which the embodiment of strength, skill, and discipline and the subjective empowerment described by Granskog and others are equated neither with gender nor with the domination of others.

We must acknowledge that, in commercial culture, many of these activities have been promoted in part by articulating them with other, less progressive themes (with fashion, individuation, consumption), and that in this process, the experience of personal transformation is typically detached from the socially transformative dimension of modernism suggested by Gruneau. However, I want to close by recalling that Stuart Hall (1984) suggests that it has been an all too common mistake on the left to see the commodification of leisure (I would add "fitness") as entirely manipulative, as if the consumers of leisure goods and experiences were passive dupes. In Hall's view, this position, like that of earlier critics of mass culture, overlooks the extent to which new forms of leisure consumption have opened up for many people—and especially women and young people—opportunities and lives that are somewhat less limited and constrained than were those of their counterparts only a few generations ago. Hall considers that the left cannot simply decry the commercialism that surrounds leisure products and experiences that people patently want, even though market segmentation now means that alternative and subcultural practices and styles are quickly articulated with other, more ambiguous social identities. Indeed, Mariana Valverde (1991), following Hall, has proposed that subjectivity "ought not to be seen either as constructed by ideology or as flowing from some inner source of coherent meaning" (p. 182). Subject positions, she suggests, are multidimensional, and they are constructed out of our responses to a number of distinct and often competing cultural discourses (e.g., feminism and traditional texts of feminine sexuality; Julia Roberts vs. *Thelma and Louise*) that converge upon us with greater or lesser effectiveness. Thus, the degrees of enthusiasm with which the texts of identity made available through the marketplace (e.g., the slim and fit woman, the mountain biker, the skateboarder or surfer) are taken up by individuals will depend on the other subject positions that are already part of our identities and the variety of alternative subject positions available to us in our particular time and social location. This underlines the importance of those sports and other physical practices that encourage femininity and masculinity to be embodied in a variety of shapes and ways and that allow power to be embodied in ways not tied to domination or gender. In any event, the texts and images of physical being that succeed in making an effective place for themselves in popular culture—and today, this means commercial culture—are likely to be more important than ever in the formation of gendered identities.

REFERENCES

Birrell, S., & Richter, D. (1987). Is a diamond forever? Feminist transformations of sport. *Women's Studies International Forum, 10*(4), 395-409.

Bloch, C. (1987). Everyday life, sensuality, and body culture. *Women's Studies International Forum,* **10**(4), 433-442.

Boston Women's Health Book Collective. (1976). *Our Bodies, Ourselves.* New York: Simon & Schuster.

Bruce, T., & Markula, P. (1989, November). Female pleasure: The enjoyment of aerobics. Paper presented at North American Society for the Sociology of Sport, Washington, DC.

Connell, R.W. (1983). Men's bodies. In R.W. Connell, *Which way is up?* (pp. 17-32). Sydney: Allen & Unwin.

Connell, R.W., Ashenden, D.J., Kessler, S., & Dowsett, G.W. (1982). *Making the difference.* Sydney: Allen & Unwin.

Crawford, R. (1985). A cultural account of ''health'': Control, release, and the social body. In P. McKinlay (Ed.), *Issues in the political economy of health care* (pp. 60-103). New York: Tavistock.

de Beauvoir, S. (1974). *The second sex.* New York: Vintage Books.

Featherstone, M. (1982). The body in consumer culture. *Theory, Culture & Society,* **1**(2), 18-33.

Fletcher, S. (1984). *Women first: The female tradition in English physical education.* London: Athlone.

Frank, B. (1991, November). Sports, looks, and a woman: What every guy needs to be masculine. Paper presented at North American Society for the Sociology of Sport, Milwaukee, WI.

Gilroy, S. (1989). The embody-ment of power: Gender and physical activity. *Leisure Studies,* **8**(2), 163-172.

Granskog, J. (1991, November). In search of the ultimate: Ritual aspects of the Hawaiian Ironman Triathlon. Paper presented at North American Society for the Sociology of Sport, Milwaukee, WI.

Gruneau, R. (1993). The critique of sport in modernity: Theorizing power, culture, and the politics of the body. In E. Dunning & J. Maguire (Eds.), *The sports process* (pp. 85-109). Champaign, IL: Human Kinetics.

Hall, S. (1984, January). The culture gap. *Marxism Today,* pp. 18-22.

Haug, F. (Ed.) (1987). *Female sexualization: A collective work of memory.* London: Verso.

Howell, J. (1991). ''A Revolution in Motion'': Advertising and the politics of nostalgia. *Sociology of Sport Journal,* **8**(3), 258-271.

Kidd, B. (1987). Sports and masculinity. In M. Kaufman (Ed.), *Beyond patriarchy* (pp. 250-265). Toronto: Oxford University Press.

MacNeill, M. (1988). Active women, media representations, and ideology. In J. Harvey & H. Cantelon (Eds.), *Not just a game* (pp. 195-211). Ottawa: University of Ottawa Press.

MacKinnon, C. (1987). Women, self-possession, and sport. In *Feminism unmodified: Discourses on life and law* (pp. 117-124). Cambridge, MA: Harvard University Press.

Matthews, J.J. (1987). Building the body beautiful. *Australian Feminist Studies,* **5** (Summer), 17-34.

Merleau-Ponty, M. (1962). *Phenomenology of perception.* New York: Humanities Press.

Messner, M. (1990). Masculinities and athletic careers: Bonding and status differences. In M.A. Messner & D.F. Sabo (Eds.), *Sport, men, and the gender order* (pp. 97-108). Champaign, IL: Human Kinetics.

Miedzian, M. (1991). *Boys will be boys: Breaking the links between masculinity and violence.* New York: Doubleday.

Nelson, M.B. (1991). *Are we winning yet?* New York: Random House.

Oates, J.C. (1987). *On boxing.* Garden City, NJ: Doubleday.

Oriard, M. (1982). *The end of autumn.* Garden City, NJ: Doubleday.

Scraton, S. (1987). Boys muscle in where angels fear to tread: Girls' subcultures and physical activity. In J. Horne, D. Jary, & A. Tomlinson (Eds.), *Sport, leisure and social relations* (pp. 160-186). London: Routledge.

Shotter, J. (1973). Prolegomena to an understanding of play. *Journal for Theory of Social Behaviour,* **3**(1), 47-89.

Shotter, J. (1974). The development of personal powers. In M. Richards (Ed.), *The integration of a child into a social world* (pp. 215-244). Cambridge: Cambridge University Press.

Shotter, J. (1984). *Social accountability and selfhood.* London: Blackwell.

Theberge, N. (1987). Sport and women's empowerment. *Women's Studies International Forum,* **10**(4), 387-393.

Terkel, S. (1974). *Working.* New York: Avon Books.

Valverde, M. (1991). As if subjects existed: Analyzing social discourses. *Canadian Review of Sociology and Anthropology,* **28**(2), 173-187.

Wernick, A. (1991). Global promo: The cultural triumph of exchange. *Theory, Culture & Society,* **8**, 89-109.

Willis, S. (1990). Work(ing) out. *Cultural Studies,* **4**(1), 1-18.

Young, I. (1979). The exclusion of women from sport: Conceptual and existential dimensions. *Philosophy in Context,* **9**, 44-53.

Young, I. (1980). Throwing like a girl: A phenomenology of feminine body comportment, motility, and spatiality. *Human Studies,* **3**, 137-156.

NOTES

1. Rob Beamish has also pointed, in a review of Scraton, to the catch-22 that this resistance sets up for young women, because their rejection of physical activity ultimately serves to immerse them more deeply in a culture of femininity that will oppress them as adult women (*Canadian Review of Sociology and Anthropology,* **27**(2), p. 278).

2. See Birrell and Richter (1987), Theberge (1987), and Gilroy (1989).

3. I am indebted to Rick Gruneau for this idea.

4. See Joe Henderson's *Thoughts on the Run* (1972) and Ian Jackson's *Yoga and the Athlete* (1975), both published by Runner's World Publications,

Mountain View, CA. See also Mike Spino's classic "Running: A Spiritual Experience" in J. Scott (Ed.), *The athletic revolution*, New York: Free Press, 1972, pp. 222-225.

5. Oriard offers a self-critical reflection on the physical combat of line play in football, but there are numerous football accounts that reflect straightforward pride in the capacity to dominate. For hockey, see Robert Faulkner's "Making violence by doing work: Selves, situations, and the world of professional hockey" in D. Landers (Ed.), *Social problems in athletics*, Champaign, IL: University of Illinois Press, 1976, pp. 93-112.

6. The term comes from Andy Wernick (1991), though he does not discuss this particular example.

Chapter 24

Double Fault:
Renee Richards and
the Construction and Naturalization
of Difference

Susan Birrell
The University of Iowa

Cheryl L. Cole
University of Illinois at Urbana-Champaign

In July of 1976, a reporter covering a local tennis tournament in La Jolla, California, became suspicious when the defending champion in the women's division was soundly thrashed by a 6-ft 2-in. newcomer by the name of Renee Clarke. Searching further, the reporter discovered that Renee Clarke was actually Renee Richards, a constructed-female transsexual[1] who less than a year before had been Richard Raskind, a man ranked highly by the United States Tennis Association in the 35-and-over men's division. The media clamor that ensued might have died down had Richards not accepted an invitation to play in a national tournament in South Orange, New Jersey, that his/her[2] old friend Eugene Scott was organizing as a warm-up to the U.S. Open. The United States Tennis Association (USTA) and the Women's Tennis Association (WTA) promptly withdrew their sanctions from the South Orange tournament. In protest of Richards' participation, 25 of the 32 women originally scheduled to play in South Orange withdrew to enter an alternative tournament hastily arranged and sanctioned by the USTA and the WTA. Undaunted, the 41-year-old Richards advanced through three rounds before losing in the semifinals to 17-year-old Lea Antonopolis. Thus begins one of the more sensational and most illuminating incidents in contemporary sport.

A few days later, Richards announced his/her intention to play women's singles in the 1976 U.S. Open at Forest Hills, and the antagonism between Renee Richards and the women's tennis world was formalized. The USTA, the WTA, and the U.S. Open Committee responded by requiring that all women competitors take a sex chromatin test known as the Barr body test. Richards refused, and the U.S. Open went on without him/her. One year later s/he took the case to the New York Supreme Court, which ruled that "this person is now female" and that requiring Richards to pass the Barr body test was "grossly unfair, discriminatory and inequitable, and violative of her rights" (*Richards v. USTA*, 1977, p. 272). The court's decision cleared the way for Richards to play in the women's singles at the 1977 U.S. Open where s/he lost in the first round to Virginia Wade, 6-1, 6-4. Richards' modest professional career continued until 1981 when s/he retired from competition at age 47. After a successful year as Martina Navratilova's coach, s/he left professional tennis and returned to his/her ophthalmology practice.

The entrance of Renee Richards into women's professional tennis created confusion and controversy for the players, the fans, organized tennis, and the public. Adding drama to the general controversy over the sexual status of transsexuals was Richards' decision to participate as a women in a cultural activity still accepted as legitimately divided into two sex categories. The confusion that followed Richards' action illuminates sport as an important element in a political field that produces and reproduces two apparently natural, mutually exclusive, "opposite" sexes.

The controversy over Richards' contested entrance into women's sport was addressed at length in the press and later reexamined in Richards' autobiography, *Second Serve* (1983), and the television movie, *Second Serve*. These sources framed the Renee Richards story within traditional liberal rhetoric as a story about fairness and human rights focused around the problematic status of the transsexual. By focusing on the question of individual sex legitimacy, that is, whether Renee Richards is a man or a woman, the media obscured the broader political and social issues.

The purpose of our analysis is to show how our culture constructs woman and produces particular notions of gender, sex, the body, and difference by examining a case where these ideological processes are literally enacted: the construction of a "woman," Renee Richards, from a "man." In Richards' rather spectacular case, the construction can be examined on two dimensions: the relatively private technical construction of Richards accomplished by an array of medical and legal experts, and the more public construction of Richards accomplished through the discursive practices of the print media and the autobiographical construction offered by Richards in the book and television movie, *Second Serve*.

In this paper we examine the media's construction of the controversy surrounding Renee Richards; we offer a critical reading of discursive practices that construct and control transsexualism, sexuality, sex, and gender; and we explore the particular problematic posed by Richards' entrance into the highly gendered world of professional sport. Moreover, by asking how it is possible to "change" sexes, what it means to want to change, and what it means to be able to change, we argue that transsexualism simultaneously illuminates and mystifies the cultural constructions of woman and man by positioning a seemingly anomalous case within hegemonic discourses of sex difference, sex and gender identity, and the gendering of bodies.

Although initially Renee Richards appears to be newsworthy because s/he is a sexual anomaly who challenges taken-for-granted assumptions about sex and gender, our critical reading suggests how the media frames invoked to explain the meaning of Renee Richards reproduce rather than challenge dominant gender arrangements and ideologies, specifically the assumption that there are two and only two, obviously universal, natural, bipolar, mutually exclusive sexes that necessarily correspond to stable gender identity and gendered behavior. And while the media coverage of the controversy surrounding Richards' desire to play women's professional tennis is seemingly confined to the immediate event, we will suggest that the media enter into and depend upon a broader discourse produced by a constellation of institutions empowered to enforce boundaries between woman and man based on essential conceptualizations of gender, sex, and difference.

TRANSSEXUALISM AND THE TECHNOLOGICAL CONSTRUCTION OF WOMAN

Within the dominant discourse of sex research, the category of transsexual is assigned to a person who believes he or she was born into the wrong body, a belief Jan Morris describes as "a passionate, lifelong, ineradicable conviction" (1974, p. 8). The anatomical structure of the body that indexes sex, particularly the genitals, is in direct conflict with the preoperative transsexual's sense of self as a gendered individual. In contrast to transvestites, who habitually cross-dress, "true transsexuals feel that they *belong* to the other sex, they want to *be* and *function* as members of the opposite sex, not only to appear as such" (Benjamin, 1966, p. 13). Such an identity depends on the belief that there are two neatly distinct and absolute categories of sex/gender. As Jan Morris understands it, "I was born into the wrong body, being feminine by gender but male by sex, and I could achieve completeness only when the one was adjusted to the other" (1974, p. 26).

Anxieties constructed through sex, gender, and sexuality in our culture reside ultimately in the body and our attitudes toward our own body as well as the bodies of others. Foucault (1979) suggests, "The body is directly involved in a political field; power relations have an intimate hold upon it: they invest it, train it, and torture it, force it to carry out its tasks, to perform ceremonies and emit signs" (pp. 25-26).

The gender dysphoria that transsexuals suffer often drives them to seek "sex reassignment," a lengthy process that requires the services of a number of experts in normalizing disciplines: surgeons, gynecologists, endocrinologists, plastic surgeons, psychiatrists, speech therapists, and lawyers. These experts enact a discourse that legitimates sex reassignment by working together to alter what is presented as the unalterable. In this sense, gender dysphoria and transsexualism are not neutral categories but elements in a social system that controls and regulates the body, sex, and gender relations.

For the constructed-female transsexual—estimated as comprising about 80 to 90% of the 10,000 transsexuals in the United States (Grimm, 1987)—the sex reassignment process begins with extensive psychotherapy to ensure that surgery is advisable. This is followed by a lengthy period during which the preoperative transsexual must live as a member of the opposite sex as proof of his or her ability to accomplish appropriately gendered behavior. Finally a series of operations is performed during which the sex signifiers are exchanged: male sex organs are removed and an artificial vagina is constructed and implanted. Massive doses of female sex hormones, breast implants, cosmetic plastic surgery on the face and Adam's apple, and speech therapy further sustain the apparent change.

The knowledge that organizes our understanding of transsexualism has been divided into two major approaches (Bolin, 1987): clinical approaches that characterize the psychiatric and psychological research and are based on a medical model in which transsexualism is constituted as an individual problem, "a syndrome subject to treatment" (p. 41); and sociocultural approaches taken by ethnomethodologists and anthropologists, which focus on "the relationship of . . . transsexualism to the culture at large" (p. 47).

Clinical approaches (e.g., Benjamin, 1966; Money & Ehrhardt, 1972; Money & Tucker, 1975; Stoller, 1975), are concerned with transsexual etiology or the biological and/or psychological variables that have caused transsexualism.[3] They subscribe to some form of sexual essentialism while locating the problem within the individual and the dysfunctional family, "with the family as the largest unit of external etiological influence" (Bolin, 1987, p. 59). However, by focusing on the individual as the pathological victim of a disconcerting sexual syndrome, the body and transsexualism are removed from the technologies of gender[4] and the broader network of social relations in which we experience and understand our lives. In this view, the transsexual is blamed for failing to adjust to a rigid system of gender stereotypes. Therapeutic management programs designed to create gender reversal and surgical treatment, though an object of some dispute, are viewed as legitimate treatments to cure transsexuals. Gender dysphoria is represented as a state that can be most effectively corrected through the combination of biomedical and legal authorization of the exchange of the material signifiers that reconstitute sex status.

Sociocultural approaches view transsexualism not as an individual malady but as an epiphenomenon that can be understood only within the context of a particular culture. Sociocultural researchers (e.g., Bolin, 1988; Garfinkel & Stoller, 1967; Kando, 1973; Kessler & McKenna, 1978; Williams, 1986) are interested in "what transsexualism reveals about the cultural construction of gender and the sex/gender system" (Bolin, 1987, p. 47). For example, while the disproportionate number of transsexuals are male to female, historically the reverse was true (Bullough, 1975), testimony to the cultural and historical specificity of transsexual emergence.[5] And the ethnocentricity of our two-sex/two-gender paradigm is revealed through ethnographic descriptions of different sex/gender arrangements in other cultures such as the Berdasch and the Amazonia (Williams, 1986).[6]

The existence of transsexualism is discomforting because it simultaneously disrupts and confirms our commonsense about the nature of sex, gender, and the relationships between them. Transsexualism unravels and rebinds our cultural notion that there are two and only two, mutually exclusive, naturally occurring, immutable, *opposite* sexes. The acute gender dysphoria that impels a transsexual to consider surgical remedy suggests that radically reconfiguring the body through the removal and construction of sex signifiers is easier than living in a culture in which rigid gender ideologies do not permit men to act in stereotypically feminine ways.

The transsexual's solution to gender dysphoria is to change sexes: an individual solution to a systemic problem. Gender dysphoria is the personal manifestation of a larger cultural problem, in this case the institutionalization of a system that reduces sex to two mutually exclusive, natural categories. By seeking surgical remedy, the transsexual acquiesces to a system that locates individuals as either male or female subjects. Ironically the transsexual's personal relief reinforces the very system that produces transsexualism.

CONTESTING SEX:
THE LEGAL CONSTRUCTION OF WOMAN

In her critique, *The Transsexual Empire*, Jan Raymond (1979) raises important critical issues: Who is empowered to legitimate transsexual surgery as a valid medical procedure and treatment? Who is authorized to decide who qualifies for sex reassignment and what will the proof of qualification be? Who will determine the legal status of the postoperative transsexual? Raymond bases her argument on the cultural construction of gender identity and transsexualism.[7] The successful male candidate for sex reassignment surgery, for example, must demonstrate stereotypical female behavior patterns and attitudes to those "authorities" who hold the power to reconstruct his body.

By conceptualizing transsexualism within a scientific/clinical discourse as an exceptional pathological condition traceable to early childhood abnormalities, and by dealing with it on a case by case basis, those who have power through and within the technologies of gender, especially the transsexual empire, give themselves license to offer a technological solution to the cultural problem of inflexible gender role prescriptions. For a culture organized around rigid gender roles and for the individuals most discomfitted by those demands, the transsexual empire prescribes the small but expensive Band-Aid of reconstructive surgery.

The Renee Richards case offered a particularly public opportunity to examine Raymond's thesis, but the power of the transsexual empire is one of the major issues obscured by the news media in that case. The coverage of Richards' entrance into women's tennis fails to acknowledge the existence of the male-dominated transsexual empire of surgeons, lawyers, and psychologists whose technological and discursive practices make it legally and, Raymond would argue, morally possible to change one's body/sex. Although medical technology makes sex reassignment possible, the legal system insists upon and is the final arbiter of sex identity.[8] Renee Richards was positioned as a woman through legal discourses and was granted the legal right to play tennis as a woman because the New York Supreme Court accepted as its criterion of womanhood a female-appearing phenotype brought about by cosmetic surgery and sustained by massive amounts of female hormones.

In formulating their decision, the court was persuaded by the argument of the expert witnesses Richards called upon in his/her behalf: the surgeon who performed the sex reassignment operation, his/her gynecologist, and John Money, a psychologist from Johns Hopkins—considered the most prominent sex reassignment expert in the U.S. and a major architect of the transsexual empire. In effect, the court accepted as voices of legitimation those very people responsible for producing Richards as a postoperative transsexual in the first place.

Opposing Richards in court were the defendants—the USTA, the WTA, and the U.S. Open Committee, who argued that "there is a competitive advantage for a male who has undergone 'sex-change' surgery as a result of physical training and development as a male" (*Richards v. USTA*, 1977, p. 269). To support their case, they submitted affidavits from an expert witness defending the validity of the Barr body test; from three women professional tennis players: Francoise Durr, Janet Newberry, and Kristien Shaw; and from the Director of Women's Tennis for the USTA, Vicki Berner. Those who would articulate oppositional discourses, however, lacked access to both the institutions and the means of challenging them directly. Thus the Renee Richards case offers literal and dramatic evidence that when an individual's sex is contested, and when the discourses of womanhood are contested, male-dominated institutions have disproportionate power to decide what is and is not a woman. Acting in concert, the medical and legal institutions have the power to authorize, regulate, and control the body and sex.

MEDIA CONVENTIONS AND FRAMES, AND THE CONSTRUCTION OF WOMAN

The construction of Renee Richards began with the transformation of Richard Raskind to Renee Richards through extensive psychological and medical procedures. Thus Renee Richards exists as Renee Richards at least in part because it is technologically possible. The construction continues more publicly in the news media's coverage of the controversy and in Richards' autobiography, *Second Serve* (1983), and the television movie adaptation of the autobiography in 1985. By drawing upon examples from both the news media and the autobiographies, we argue that dominant liberal conventions shape the narrative and thus public understandings of Renee Richards and transsexualism.[9]

The media produce news, not truth. While the media appear simply to report what happened, they actively construct news through frames, values, and conventions. Having made the initial decision that an incident is worthy of treatment as news, reporters and editors make choices that foreground some elements of the potential narrative and obscure others, and they define and delineate issues through a series of choices including headlines, descriptive word choices, photographs, who to authorize with an interview, and what to report (Hartley, 1982). Gitlin (1980) suggests that the hegemonic frames, codes, and conventions in U.S. news include an emphasis on elements of drama and personality; conventions of balance, brevity, and stereotyping in which the complexity of an event is collapsed into two opposing positions and authorities representing each side are offered the opportunity to comment; temporality; and suspicion of difference and disorder as threat. In the production of news, the frame constructed and choices made offer a preferred reading of the events. As Hall (1977) summarizes the effect,

> It is masked, frequently by the intervention of the professional ideologies—those practical-technical routinizations of practices (news values, news sense, lively presentation, "exciting pictures," good stories, hot news, etc.) which, at the phenomenal level, structure the everyday practices of encoding and set the encoder within the bracket of a professional-technical neutrality which, in any case distances him [sic] effectively from the ideological content of the material he is handling and the ideological inflections of codes he is employing. Hence, though events will not be systematically encoded in a single way, they will tend, systematically, to draw on a very limited repertoire: and that repertoire . . . will have the overall tendency of making things "mean" within the sphere of the dominant ideology. (p. 344)

Following convention, the newspapers recognized the tennis controversy as news because its immediacy and finiteness mark it as newsworthy within the media's ideological code. The coverage of the Renee Richards story began in the national news media on July 24, 1976, the first news mention of Richards during the South Orange tournament, and it ended on August 18, 1977, the date the papers reported the court decision that granted Richards the right to participate as a woman in the 1977 U.S. Open. By using the official proclamation of the law to provide closure for the story, the newspapers implied that the end of the tennis controversy marked the logical resolution to the issue of transsexualism itself.

To the newspapers, the threshold of newsworthiness had passed. Indeed only Richards' intentions to enter women's sport had qualified the story as news in the first place: The mere existence of a transsexual in society has not been news since Christine Jorgensen (1967). Thus the newspapers focus on what seems to be a concrete event: the controversy surrounding Renee Richards' decision to enter women's tennis. But by isolating the event in the present, the historical and cultural context and significance are excluded from the frame. In other words, the ideological codes that journalists follow in their apparent impartiality actively mystify the ideological determinants of the story.

The media identified two issues that guided their coverage: Is it fair to allow Renee Richards to play women's professional tennis? And is Renee Richards a man or a woman? Both issues are clearly embedded in ideological frames of liberalism and sexual essentialism. The central narrative was constructed around liberal notions of human rights, and fairness clearly was defined in terms of Richards, not in terms of the women players who had to accommodate him/her as one of them. Richards was represented as the central character within a drama of heroic confrontation between an individual and the tennis bureaucracy. Richards was thus positioned within a familiar cultural discourse of heroic narrative, a story worthy of Frank Capra, about an individual's struggle to prevail against the tyranny of the system.

Generally obscured in the newspapers' construction of this drama of human rights were any serious consideration of the women players' case, particularly the social and historical context within which sport in North America has developed as an activity that privileges males; the meaning of the sex test ordered by the USTA; the meaning of the antifeminist sentiment that was packaged as pro-Richards rhetoric; and the wider implications of the Richards controversy, including the cultural meaning of transsexualism, sex, and gender, and the power of the male-dominated medical and legal professions to construct and legitimate the female.

The news coverage and the autobiographies differ in the relationship between the issues of whether Richards should be allowed to play women's tennis and whether Richards is a man or a woman. The news media focused on the former and implicated the latter, while the autobiography and film used the former as an occasion to focus on the latter. The news media clearly defined the issues in terms of tennis, and the Renee Richards story unfolded as news almost entirely on the sport pages of newspapers and the sport sections of magazines. In contrast, the autobiographies rely on the familiar autobiographical convention of exposing personal truths to address broader issues of transsexualism. In the entire book of 373 pages, tennis comprises only 46 pages, a proportion that is matched in the film as well. Tennis, it is clear, is merely the occasion for the unfolding of a deeper personal narrative.

Yet even taken together, the news media's exposition of the tennis controversy and the autobiographies' analyses of transsexualism as personal history do not offer a critical understanding of transsexualism. Both accounts work within the constraints of a dominant discourse that constructs two essential, universal, and opposite sexes. By maintaining a tight frame around Richards and by presenting Richards as an isolated case, they endorse an individualistic, clinical model and neglect the larger cultural context of gender arrangements. Beneath the surface of their narratives, the ideology of gender relations lies undisturbed and important questions go unasked: What is a woman? On what basis should we make our decision? Who shall be empowered to decide? How have women been con-structed? What is the connection between sex and gender, since transsexual gender identity makes it clear that one cannot necessarily be mapped from the other? These issues are not centralized in the narrative; they are too controversial and complex to be treated within the media conventions of balance, immediacy, objectivity, and appeals to authority.

The Gendering of Renee Richards

The news media focused primarily on whether Richards should be allowed to play women's tennis, but the issue of whether Richards is a man or a woman formed an implicit frame for their narratives. Indeed, the most significant framing device the papers used in their construction of the story was the gendering of Richards as a female. The framing of Richards as female was accomplished through their choice of personal pronouns and through the descriptions of Richards they drew for their readers.

While there was some doubt in their minds about which sex category Richards belonged in and whether Richards was a transvestite or a transsexual (*The New York Times*, July 24, 1976), in fact they resolved the problem for themselves and their readers by referring to Richards as "she" from the very first day of coverage. This choice of personal pronoun was made a full year before a legal decision was made,[10] and it is one of the primary ways that the public came to know Richards. By framing Richards as "she," the press resolved the very issue it was purporting to cover: the contest over his/her sex. In a similar manner, the casting of Vanessa Redgrave to portray Richards in the television movie tells viewers from the very first minute that Renee Richards is truly and naturally a female.

An individual contesting his or her sex creates a linguistic dilemma in cultures in which pronouns and adjectives denote gender. The dilemma is reflected in the quotes from women protesting Richards. Glynnis Coles was quite consistent: "I don't think he should be playing . . . As far as I'm concerned he's just a man who's had an operation" (*The Washington Post*, January 1, 1978). But Diane Fromholtz' complaint captured the ambiguity most protesters could not work through: "People are laughing at us, at the way she walks on and acts like a female" (*The Washington Post*, January 1, 1978). With the very act of refuting Richards' claims to be female, Fromholtz genders Richards female. The most telling statement was Roz Reid's protest on behalf of his wife, Kerry Melville Reid: "We don't believe Renee is a woman. Kerry will never play her again" (*The Washington Post*, January 1, 1978).

Officials also had difficulty with the ambiguity. Early in the controversy W.E. Hester, vice-president of the USTA, stated, "I don't know on what grounds we could admit her and on what grounds we can refuse to admit him" (*Los Angeles Times*, August 12, 1976). The USTA first described Richards as "a man [who had] won a woman's tournament" (*The New York Times*, July 24, 1976) and "a biological male" (*The New York Times*, August 14, 1976), then, as more sophisticated discourses developed, as a "person not genetically female" (*The New York Times*, August 15, 1976). Phillippe Chatrier of the International Tennis Federation, determined to bar Richards from international competition, said "Mr.-Miss Richards should not be allowed to play" (*Winston-Salem Journal*, October 22, 1977).

Richards was also gendered by the press in terms of the descriptions they offered of him/her, many of which captured the ambiguity that the press and the public were trying to resolve. *The New York Times* noted, "Dr. Richards displays traits associated with both sexes. The soft husky voice is mostly male but the high cheekbones, shapely legs, graceful gold pierced earrings and peach nail polish . . . are distinctly female" (August 19, 1976). And Neil Amdur reported Richards' declaration that "I'm as much a woman as anyone on the U.S. tour" and added,

> At 6 feet 2 inches, Dr. Richards who weighs 147 pounds is considerably taller than most women, even women athletes. She has tight muscles in her calves, the kind you might expect to see on a male sprinter or a halfback in football. Yet her facial features, the high cheekbones, the brown eyes and the sharply defined eyebrows—are distinctly feminine. She carries herself considerably smoother than many female athletes . . . Her voice is soft, somewhat raspy but firm in the manner of a confident professional. (*The New York Times*, August 21, 1976)

Elsewhere the press followed their convention of mentioning details of physical appearance of women athletes they generally ignore in male athletes. By reporting on physical appearance, the press legitimates physicality as a valid means for assessing one's sex status, thus confusing the issue of the sex/gender relationship and obscuring the cultural production of such relationships.

Richards' autobiography makes even more explicit the cultural confusion about sex, gender, and sexuality. Throughout the book Richards dwells on his/her appearance and the confirmation of his/her true female self, his/her "success as a girl" that is reflected in male attention to his/her female-appearing body: "Renee fed on [the attention] because [it] represented a casual and ready acceptance of her femaleness. Men held doors open for me, young boys and sometimes older men looked me over appreciatively" (p. 31). On a trip to Casablanca, Richards was mistaken for a woman and picked up for the first time. His/her suitor had "eyes that appraised me with obvious interest. This was the first time I had ever been openly, unreservedly ogled by a man. I quite liked it . . . The more he appreciated me the more I felt like a girl" (p. 220).

Elsewhere in the autobiography Richards enacts male-defined conceptions of feminine behavior. These include the almost total objectification of his/her new body, an exhibitionism evident throughout the book and symbolized by sitting naked for an hour in the locker room while being interviewed by reporters after the South Orange tournament (*The Washington Post*, August 22, 1976), and his/her desire to relate to men in submissive ways. Of one male friend who had known him/her only as Renee, s/he says, "He'd always treated me with overtones of male superiority, and I loved it, considering this treatment a compliment of my validity as a woman" (p. 321).

His/her submission to men is most marked in the accounts of intimacy in which s/he clearly equates sexuality, specifically sexual passivity and submission, with being a woman. In his/her adolescent years, for example, s/he enacted mock rapes with a male high school friend under the guise of wrestling naked on his bed.

> Eventually I would have to surrender to his compelling strength. There was something about this situation that pleased me . . . I struggled like hell because that was crucial to my feeling. I had to know that his dominance was real . . . It was very sensual to surrender like that. (p. 45)

His/her trip to Europe was full of sexual encounters with strange men: a truck driver who helped by scraping ice off the windshield of his/her Maserati, then made sexual advances ("After all, he had done me a favor and deserved something for his trouble . . . It's not every day that a truck driver gets to make out with a classy dame in a Maserati" p. 237); a dangerous episode with a stranger in Marrakech; and a *ménage à trois* in Majorca. Finally, after the reconstructive surgery, Richards "waited three months, resigning myself to a lengthy virginity" (p. 287) before being "deflowered" by a former homosexual lover:

> I got a real sense of satisfaction out of being the object of his desire . . . Tremendously exciting also were his encompassing size, the smell of him, his hairiness, and his weight pressing down on me . . . [H]e finished quickly, and I loved that as well. I was warmed by his sense of urgency and the forceful thrusts that accompanied his climax. I didn't have an orgasm myself . . . Nonetheless, I loved it. I was at last fully capable of the woman's role. (pp. 294-296)

By offering his/her body as a source of sexual pleasure for men, Richards apparently believes s/he has been re-sexed as a woman. S/he has clearly incorporated the dominant cultural discourse on femininity, gendered bodies, and femaleness into his/her consciousness.

Constructing the Oppositions

Since conventions limit journalists' abilities to deal with the complexity of the issues posed by controversy, and since reporters are required to cover and present only two sides of a story, the controversy over Renee Richards' entrance into women's professional tennis was reduced and assembled into two mutually exclusive and opposing positions. Support for Richards came from his/her old male tennis friends such as Gene Scott and Bobby Riggs, and from two prominent women, Gladys Heldman, who provide several opportunities for Richards to play on a women's tour she was promoting, and Billie Jean King, who invited Richards to play women's doubles with her on that tour.

Opposition came from the rank and file of the women's tour, some of whom refused to play Richards. Their position was represented by Beth Norton in a letter to the WTA quoted in the *Winston-Salem Journal* in which she protested

> the unfairness of forcing young girls to compete with a middle-aged transsexual who previously has been a nationally ranked men's player . . . [and who had] 30 years experience playing men's and boy's tennis . . . It is only fair that her rights should not impose upon the rights of girls earning a professional living in the women's tour. The rights of all of us as individuals should be taken into consideration. (February 14, 1978)

However, the voices of the individual women tennis players who opposed Richards were generally silenced by the media,[11] who represented opposition to Richards as "the tennis establishment," "organized tennis," or most often by the impersonal device of initials: the WTA, the USTA, the USOC. The use of initials and the fact that most spokespersons for these groups were men not only depersonalized the opposition but obscured sex and gender in a situation that is in fact *about* sex and gender. Richards' sex status was constantly foregrounded while the sex of his/her opposition was obscured.

The autobiographies obscure the opposition even more, never acknowledging adverse reaction from anyone other than the USTA and the WTA. Richards claims "most of the women . . . were on my side" (1984, p. 346). S/he reports receiving 40,000 letters after the La Jolla tournament, of which "nine-tenths was positive" (p. 324), and s/he notes a pattern of support from the fans: "I was treated respectfully and if there were hecklers I never heard them" (p. 350). The newspapers confirmed this impression (*The New York Times*, August 28, 1976).

Thus opposition to Richards was framed as organizational impulses to protect the carefully nurtured image of women's tennis by protecting the women players from unfair competition.[12] What might have been reported as a series of individual dramas that paralleled the structure of the sport itself—Richards vs. Antonopolis, Richards vs. Smith, Richards vs. Evert—was instead packaged as Richards vs. The Establishment. The controversy was framed within the classic American liberal tradition of the heroic struggle of one individual against the bureaucracy. Given such a plot, the American tradition is to root for the beleaguered underdog.

Richards solidified his/her role as an underdog by being positioned and by positioning him/herself as a spokesperson for a minority group. S/he first discovered this possibility at the La Jolla tournament when a woman of color said,

Renee . . . I don't want you to withdraw. I am a member of a minority myself . . . I've found that when people don't know what pigeonhole to put you in, your only alternative is to show them what you are and act as if you have the right to be that. You won't be doing yourself a favor if you run away from this tournament. You'll be giving in to stupidity. Hold your head up and play. (Richards, 1983, p. 317)

Richards noted, "This was the first time anybody had ever put the issues in broader perspective," and s/he began to consider him/herself "a kind of standard bearer" (p. 317). S/he was deluged with letters of support from "people who were members of minorities. Among others, I heard from blacks, convicts, Chicanos, hippies, homosexuals, people with physical handicaps and, of course, trans-sexuals" (p. 325). Notably absent from his/her list of oppressed groups is women. The support surprised Richards, who admitted,

I've never even been political [but] . . . I was susceptible to this flood of sentiment. Until you have pawed through thirty thousand letters pleading with you to stand up for your rights and, in so doing, stand up for the rights of the world's downtrodden, you don't know what pressure is. Left to my own devices, I probably would have resolved my personal pique at being summarily barred from competition—but, my god, the whole world seemed to be looking for me to be their Joan of Arc. (p. 325)

The broadened support an identity as Joan of Arc could provide him/her was not lost on Richards, who returned to that theme throughout the book and regularly spoke to it during interviews with the press. In a story headlined, "Renee Richards Pursuing Tennis Career for a Cause" (August 19, 1976), *The New York Times* positioned Richards as a champion for all transsexuals, and later they broadened Richards' underdog status by quoting him/her: "[The USTA] have done the same thing with me that they've done with every other minority" (September 1, 1976).

However, Richards' inability to recognize *women* as an historically oppressed group whose interests should be protected, or whose interests might, indeed *do*, interfere with his/her own, contradicts his/her stance as a spokesperson for human rights. Richards acknowledged in the autobiography that much as s/he desired to live life as a woman, s/he had little sensitivity to the political implications of that life: "My idea of how a lady is treated was formed prior to women's liberation" (p. 291). Like many transsexuals, s/he displays an exaggerated, stereotypical notion of feminine behavior drawn from masculine hegemonic notions of gender. This attitude was exacerbated by the requirement that s/he prove to psychiatric and medical authorities that s/he was ready for the drastic surgical step of sex reassignment by demonstrating almost hyperfeminine behavior.

Moreover, Richards is clearly unaware of the advantages of Raskind's life of white male privilege, including attendance at a boys' prep school, graduation from Yale, completion of medical school, a successful surgical practice, the thrill of being approached by a scout from the New York Yankees, and access to highly competitive tennis which s/he took as his/her natural right as a male. His/her own sister, who so longed for such opportunities, was summarily denied them. Yet Richards never acknowledges the implications for women of his/her entrance into their world. As one colleague has suggested to us, "Renee Richards should have had his consciousness raised before he had his sex changed."

Support for Richards as Suspicion of Women

Richards' apparent inability to recognize the political position of women problematizes the media's construction of him/her as a symbol for human rights. But while Richards was positioned by the press as a symbol of human rights, support for him/her can be read for meanings overlooked by the media: Indeed it is difficult to read the support for Richards as anything other than opposition to women. Richards' entrance into women's professional sport occasioned an outburst of antifeminist sentiment that was unexamined by the press.

The vehemence of this opposition to the women players can be read within a Foucauldian (1979) context of anxiety, suspicion, and surveillance. Terry (1989) has argued that "we witness daily technological developments designed to keep a watchful eye on those entities considered suspicious . . . in an effort to contain 'danger' and restore 'security' " (p. 14). Given the challenges transsexuals pose to the dominant gender system, medical and legal surveillance systems work together to contain what they consider to be dangerous. In a similar manner, growing anxiety about changes in women's social positions and participation in traditional masculine practices such as sport have intensified suspicion of women.

The historical struggles of women and sport are particularly important in locating the sources of the tension around the women players, since Richards entered women's sport in the wake of the women's liberation movement and dramatic gains for women, and for women in sport, throughout the 1960s and 1970s. Billie Jean King's defeat of Bobby Riggs in 1974 in "the battle of the sexes" and the success of Gladys Heldman and King in organizing resistance to male control of the women's tennis circuit in the early 1970s marked the end of men's complete dominance in tennis. Ironically, Richards' desire to play on the women's tour depended upon the recent struggles of women players and organizers whose successes gave the tour increased economic viability. Thus Richards stood to benefit directly from the hard-won opportunities for women in sport at the very moment s/he was challenging them.

While the media's narratives make general references to the history of sex discrimination in tennis and to past confrontations, in effect they provided space for male voices to frame women's successes within an atmosphere of suspicion, and readers were not given a context in which to understand these challenges to the women's integrity. By directing attention to the event's immediacy and presenting the controversy apart from its historical context, the origins of opposition are obscured. Jameson (1983) notes,

> the disappearance of a sense of history, the way in which our entire contemporary social system has little by little begun to lose its capacity to retain its own past, has begun to live in a perpetual present and in a perpetual change which obliterates traditions of the kind which all earlier social formations have had in one way or another to preserve . . . One is tempted to say that the very function of the news media would thus be to help us forget, to serve as the very agents and mechanisms for our historical amnesia. (p. 125)

The support for Richards can be read within a context of anxiety and suspicion of women's recent gains in sport. Gene Scott's support of Richards was particularly revealing of this suspicion: "The women players are always talking about sex discrimination but when it comes to a real issue they run and hide. If we followed them we'd still be reading by candlelight" (quoted in Kennedy, 1976, p. 19).

Although Scott's comments allude to a history of struggle around women and sport, to him the "real" issue is not the hard-won rights of the women players but the rights of constructed-female transsexuals. Equally telling was Scott's comment to *The Washington Post*:

> I think the women players today are basically sheep followers. They have worked hard and gotten a terrific recognition factor and lots of spectators. The prize money has escalated out of all proportion. But they did all this by cultivating a reputation of being in a mood of change and imagination. [Their reaction to Renee Richards] shows this is all bunk. They're actually afraid of new ideas. (August 21, 1976)

This quote betrays Scott's feelings about women's equality when he complains that "the prize money has escalated out of all proportion." He dismisses the women players' opposition to Richards as childish whimpering: "I've heard the women whine for years about Chris Evert's dominating on clay" (*The Washington Post*, August 21, 1976).

Ilie Nastase's comment also reveals more disdain for the women players than support for Richards: "If she wears a dress, why not? Now you see how strong the women players are. She could be their mother, yet they complain. They're afraid" (quoted in Kennedy, 1976, p. 18).

Richards was proud to report that Nastase "was one of my earliest supporters; he once made a remark that I was more feminine than some of the women already on the tour" (p. 332). Such comments represent the women players as imperfect women by casting suspicion on their femininity and sexuality and belittling women's historical struggles. Through similar homophobic comments about the women players, Richards attempted to establish his/her own claim to female status. Explaining why s/he refused to take the sex chromosome test, for example, Richards argued "in my case such tests were irrelevant. Of all the potential competitors my sex was the least in doubt. It was a matter of public record based on legal documentation" (p. 343). Admitting that at 6-ft 1-in. "I looked so damn fearsome," Richards continued, "Still Betty Stove was six feet tall and hefty besides. So were some lesser known pros, yet their *sexuality* had never been questioned" (our emphasis, p. 344). Throughout the autobiography, Richards used the concepts sex status and sexuality interchangeably. That confusion suggests the homophobia that also forms the basis for the men's anxieties. Elsewhere the confusion can be understood as a central feature in Richards' construction of him/herself as a gendered being.

In all the coverage of the Renee Richards controversy, not one mention was made of a male player who did *not* support Richards, a rather extraordinary detail that may indicate either the press' reluctance to report opposition among male players or the depths of antiwoman sentiment on the tour. As one woman player who opposed Richards complained, "They want to see anybody beat us, even a transsexual" (quoted in Steinem, 1977, p. 85). Thus "support" for Richards came in a form that simultaneously cast suspicion on or discredited the women players. Steinem pointed out the tactic as well:

> When the women players themselves questioned the fairness of their facing someone trained physically and culturally for 40 years as a man, they were ridiculed as poor sports, anti-civil libertarians, or cowards who feared they couldn't win. (p. 85)

The press sometimes joined in the trivialization of the women's opposition. *The Washington Post* acknowledged "Few on Tour Support Richards" and that 80% of the women opposed Richards: "some of it friendly, some impersonal, some viciously hostile." Yet in one of the few stories dealing with the reactions of individual women players, *The Post* chose to report instances of "downright cruel" behavior, including two British players who appeared at a tournament wearing T-shirts with the message, "I am a real woman."

A final example of producing sympathy for Richards by casting suspicion on or blaming women can be found in Richards' autobiography. The book is an extended narrative of personal etiology in which Richards recounts in detail the anguish of gender dysphoria, his/her analysis of the causes, and his/her 41-year search for remedies, including the mutilation of his/her penis in a denial of the signifier of manhood, vivid accounts of sexual adventures into hyperheterosexuality, transvestism, homosexuality, and quasi-lesbianism, and the cruel series of promises and rejections from the medical establishment, the psychiatric community, and family and friends as s/he finally sought sex reassignment.

In the book and movie, a major focus of blame and suspicion was Richards' mother. The book begins, for example, with the words, "My mother was a headstrong woman" (p. 1), and within two pages the reader has been acquainted with the sex role reversals traditionally believed to be the root of transsexualism and male homosexuality: the domineering mother, the submissive father. Richards paints a picture of a childhood full of gender confusion—an older sister named Michael who wanted to be a boy, and his mother and sister's habit of dressing him in girl's clothes, including a traumatic incident at age 4 when he was humiliated by being made to appear in public dressed as a girl. Richards argues that "my early life is strewn with unsubtle touches that beg to be seen as reasons for my sexual confusion. If they aren't the true cause they ought to be" (p. 5).

Most of these incidents are depicted in the film as well, and a rather foreshortened analysis is offered by his/her psychiatrist mother (Louise Fletcher in a tight performance reminiscent of her portrayal of Nurse Ratched in *One Flew Over the Cuckoo's Nest*). When confronted by her son's admission of deep sexual confusion, she prescribes psychiatric therapy and states simply, "Maybe it's my fault . . . You probably identified with me instead of your father. Quite *natural* really. I was so strong" (our emphasis). To underscore her strength, she is portrayed in her first scene as a feminist, and her first line, delivered to someone on the phone while her son awaits her attention, is "But women have *always* had to fight." In both the book and the film, strong women come in for more than their share of blame for Richards' condition while cultural constructions of rigid gender and sex ideologies go unaddressed.

Competitive Equality and the "Natural Inferiority" of Women

Opposition to Richards was framed in terms of the issues of competitive equality and the domino effect. As the USTA saw it, "The entry into women's events . . . of persons not genetically female would introduce an element of inequality and unfairness into the championships" (*The New York Times*, August 15, 1976). USTA counsel Peter Leisure argued in court, "It would be unfair to have women who have worked hard and prepared for this tournament beaten by a person who is *more than woman* (our emphasis, *The New York Times*, August 11, 1977). Added to the fear that Richards' formerly male body provided an insurmountable natural advantage over the women players was the fear that Richards would "open the way to problems in the future from young male players with transsexual tendencies" (*The New York Times*, December 31, 1976). As Richards viewed the issue,

> If I was allowed to play, then the floodgates would be opened and through them would come tumbling an endless stream of made-over Neanderthals who would brutalize Chris Evert and Evonne Goolagong. . . . Some player who was not quite good enough in men's tennis might decide to change only in order to overpower the women players. (p. 345)

These debates over fairness were translated into issues related to the body and power. The body, one of the most seemingly natural elements of social life, was foregrounded by the press. Descriptions emphasizing Richards'/women's physical appearance and women's physical inferiority were presented uncritically and circulated by the media. The logic they employed seemed to say that if Richards is weaker than s/he was or if s/he adorns his/her body in stereotypical feminine ways, then Richards is weak enough and feminine enough to be allowed to play.

Because the media focused on men's "natural" ability rather than the years of privileged access to sport that Richard Raskind had enjoyed, they foregrounded physical definitions of sex and gender and obscured cultural ones. Richards also constructed the argument in physiological and biomechanical terms. S/he noted with characteristic humor, "they think of me as a bionic woman" (*The New York Times*, August 18, 1976), but s/he refuted this view. Noting the changes in his/her body as the result of hormonal treatments, s/he said "The tone of the muscles . . . seemed to be softer now" (p. 172). Of his/her tennis game s/he remarked "I didn't notice much decrease in my general abilities though I was definitely less strong. After six months of hormone therapy I estimate that I had about four-fifths of my previous strength" (p. 178). In fact Richards argued that his/her heavier male bone structure and hormonally reduced muscle mass actually meant "I was playing with a handicap" (p. 344). S/he argued that his/her losses proved a point: "they served to inform the public that I was not an unbeatable behemoth out to prey on helpless little girls" (p. 350).

The discourse on bodies within the Richards controversy demonstrates the cultural significance of constructing women's bodies as different from and representing them as physically inferior to men's bodies. The challenge of Richards' presence in women's sport works to naturalize women as physically inferior, and that assumption of the natural inferiority of women is evident in Richards' thinking throughout the autobiography. Playing social tennis in Europe while undergoing hormonal treatment prior to his/her operation, Richards was pleased at his/her partners' reaction to his/her superior skill but "when I missed a ball, they were quick to blame it on my being a woman. I didn't mind these jibes because they affirmed my womanliness" (p. 238).

Richards' mediocre performances on court were also used by the press to suggest his/her acceptability as a woman. After Richards lost to Antonopolis in South Orange (August 28, 1976), *The New York Times* asked, "So what was all the fuss about?" Billie Jean King argued in Richards' defense, "she does not enjoy physical superiority or strength so as to have an advantage over women competitors in the sport of tennis" (*Richards v. USTA*, 1977, p. 272). And the USTA eventually decided against an appeal because Richards "did not represent the physical threat that officials and players once feared" (*The New York Times*, August 18, 1977). Richards him/herself noted that "none of the fears that drove them to ban me ever proved warranted. I certainly haven't dominated the world of women's tennis" (p. 365).[13]

Richards' inability to dominate women's tennis is offered as proof of his/her status as a woman. Radically reconfiguring his/her body through the exchange of material sex-signifiers has apparently cost Richards his/her natural superiority as a (former) male. Through reference to his/her weakened condition, the news media and Richards construct Richards as less-than-male and thus an acceptable challenge for women players.

Representation and Constraint

In this paper we have tried to show how meanings of sex, gender, difference, and power are literally inscribed onto the body and then how that body is represented through the discourse of news and the autobiographical constructions of individual subjectivity. The ambiguity of Richards' constructed-female transsexual body triggered a crisis in representation in terms of sport and the gendered body. However, the media not only ignored the contradictions posed by Richards but positioned him/her as a hero and a signifier of resistance while women as a group became targets for the exercise of power through criticism. Homophobic and sexist discourses were constructed to contain women as suspicious. Dyer (1982) reminds us that,

> A major legacy of the social and political movements of the Sixties and Seventies has been the realization of the importance of representation. The political chances of different groups in society—powerful or weak, central or marginal—are crucially affected by how they are represented, whether in legal and parliamentary discourse, in educational practices, or in the arts. The mass media in particular have a crucial role to play, because they are a centralised source of definitions of what people are like in any given society. How a particular group is represented determines in a very real sense what it can do in society. (p. 43)

The Renee Richards case provides a dramatic moment for examining these issues.

Our examination of the media's representation of the controversy around Renee Richards is an attempt to illuminate the everyday practices of the media and the processes through which representations define femininity. In this case, the media accepted as unproblematic the assumptions of liberalism, dominant images of femininity, and ideologies of sport. While the contradictions embedded in and through the processes of transsexualism potentially trigger a crisis in representations of sex and gender, the conventions of the media make it difficult to articulate and interpret the controversy outside of dominant discourses.

This is not to suggest that all readings are symmetrical with encodings or preferred readings. The varied and complex lived experience of social actors no doubt produce readings that depart from the frame constructed by the commercial media. But the tight frame and the narrative constructed around the controversy, combined with a neglect of the historical position of women and sport, the meaning of the possibility of transsexualism, and the technologies of gender, work to constrain the possibility of alternative readings. These conventions produce what Hall (1977) has suggested is the endemic tendency of the media: support of the status quo.

RENEE RICHARDS, SPORT,
AND THE PRODUCTION OF DIFFERENCE

Renee Richards' determination to enter women's sport, the support and opposition to that move, and the representation of the controversy that the media constructed provide fascinating insight into our cultural understandings of sex difference, gender behavior, and the role that sport plays in their production and reproduction.

The entrance of a transsexual into women's sport posed an interesting dilemma that was symbolized by the fact that Richards had to sue to gain the legal right to enter sport as a woman. After all, Jan Morris did not have to sue to be allowed to be a writer, Christine Jorgensen did not have to sue to become an entertainer, and Richards continued his/her career as an ophthalmologist. The particular difficulty of this dilemma reveals sport not only as a gender producing, gender affirming system but as a difference and power producing system. For sport works to differentiate winners from losers, the men from the boys, the men from the women. As a significant gendering activity, sport not only reproduces gender and sex differences but it produces a logic of differentiation.

Because sport celebrates physicality within a competitive frame, working to determine winners based on physical superiority, it is a major site for the naturalization of sex and gender differences. Moreover, sport's logic continually reproduces men as naturally superior to women (Connell, 1983; Willis, 1982). The sex test instituted for the 1968 Olympic Games is a clear example of the manner in which sex categories are vigilantly maintained in sport. The sex test arose from the suspicion that superior female athletic performances, such as those of Ewa Klobukowska, were actually accomplished by women who were not truly women or by craftily disguised men. The implication is that superior athletic prowess is the natural domain of males.

The prestige of athletic victory, the "natural" inferiority of women constructed through sport's power as metaphor, and thus the easier competition assumed in the women's division all lead to the logical conclusion that enterprising men might try to pass as women. Renee Richards represented one form that challenge might take. Although Richards asked, "How hungry for tennis success must you be to have your penis chopped off in pursuit of it? How many men would do it for a million dollars?" (p. 345). In fact the U.S. obsession with sport makes it not at all unlikely that some man would willingly sacrifice his penis for victory; drug abuse, steroid use, blood doping, urine transplants, overtraining, and risking life-threatening or severe injuries are all a part of the modern sport scene.

A critical reading of the Renee Richards incident illuminates the part sport plays in the reproduction of an ideology of sex difference/power, gender and sex identity, and the regulation of the body. As Willis (1982) and others argue, sport is a central site for the naturalization of sex and gender difference, that is, sport produces a narrative structured around physical superiority in which sex differences are understood as, and thus reproduced as, real and meaningful. Transsexualism appears to challenge the neatness and logic—indeed the "reality"—of a sex/gender system marked by biological difference. This reveals not only the social construction of gender but the social construction of the sex-gender connection. Moreover, transsexualism demonstrates that it is not only the categories of difference that are culturally produced but the notion of difference itself.

It would seem as though the re-sexing of an individual such as Richards deconstructs notions of natural sex identity, but in fact by remaining gendered, Richards reaffirms the concept of sexual difference. By apparently changing sex, Renee Richards appears to upset our dominant ideology of gender relations, but in fact s/he stabilizes that ideology by merely shifting categories, by demonstrating dramatically the cultural necessity of a gendered home and that the "mistakes of nature" can be technologically regulated by humankind.

As Joan Scott and other poststructuralists point out, "meaning is made through implicit and explicit contrast" (1988, p. 36), through antithesis and difference. Primary among these binary oppositions that structure our discourses and thus our consciousness, indeed the archetype of that ideological practice, is sexual difference. When sex difference is contested, the entire ideological enterprise of meaning through difference is shaken. While Renee Richards demonstrates the disproportionate power that male-dominated institutions have in the construction and legitimation of woman, even more profound is the illumination that the Renee Richards incident casts on our cultural mandate to maintain sexual difference. There are no alternative categories for Richards or other nonconforming subjects to inhabit in the law, medical science, language, or sport. Their order depends upon the maintenance of the familiar binary opposition of male/female. The Renee Richards case is not only about tennis and transsexualism, not only about the construction of woman, but about the construction of difference itself.

REFERENCES

Benjamin, H. (1966). *The transsexual phenomenon*. New York: Julian.

Bolin, A. (1987). Transsexualism and the limits of traditional analysis. *American Behavioral Scientist*, **31**, 41-65.

Bolin, A. (1988). *In search of Eve: Transsexual rites of passage*. South Hadley, MA: Bergen & Garvey.

Brod, H. (1987). Cross-culture, cross-gender: cultural marginality and gender transcendence. *American Behavioral Scientist*, **31**, 5-11.

Bullough, V.L. (1975). Transsexualism in history. *Archives of Sexual Behavior*, **4**, 561-571.

Connell, R. (1983). *Which way is up?* Sydney: Allen & Unwin.

de Lauretis, T. (1987). *Technologies of gender: Essays on theory, film, and fiction*. Bloomington: Indiana University Press.

Devor, H. (1987). Gender blending females: Women and sometimes men. *American Behavioral Scientist*, **31**, 12-39.

Dunlap, M.C. (1979). The constitutional rights of sexual minorities: A crisis of the male/female dichotomy. *Hastings Law Journal, 30,* 1131-1149.

Dyer, R. (1982). The celluloid closet. *Birmingham Arts Lab Bulletin, 1,* 43.

Foucault, M. (1979). *Discipline and punish: The birth of the prison.* New York: Vintage.

Garfinkel, H., & Stoller, R.J. (1967). Passing and the managed achievement of sex status in an "intersexed" person. In H. Garfinkel (Ed.), *Studies in ethnomethodology* (pp. 116-135). Englewood Cliffs, NJ: Prentice-Hall.

Gitlin, T. (1980). *The whole world is watching.* Berkeley: University of California Press.

Grimm, D.E. (1987). Toward a theory of gender. *American Behavioral Scientist, 31,* 66-85.

Hall, S. (1977). Culture, the media and "ideological effect." In J. Curran, M. Gurevich, & J. Woollocott (Eds.), *Mass communication and society* (pp. 315-348). London: Edward Arnold.

Hartley, J. (1982). *Understanding news.* New York: Methuen.

Jameson, F. (1983). Postmodernism and consumer society. In H. Foster (Ed.), *The antiaesthetic: Essays on postmodern cultures* (pp. 111-125). Post Townsend, WA: Bay Press.

Jorgensen, C. (1967). *Christine Jorgensen: A personal autobiography.* New York: Bantam.

Kando, T. (1973). *Sex change: The achievement of gender identity among feminized transsexuals.* Springfield, IL: C.C. Thomas.

Kennedy, R. (1976, Sept. 6). She'd rather switch—And fight. *Sports Illustrated,* pp. 16-19.

Kessler, S.J., & McKenna, W. (1978). *Gender: An ethnomethodological approach.* New York: Wiley.

Los Angeles Times. (Selected articles.) August 12, 1976-January 1, 1978.

Martino, M. (1977). *Emergence: A transsexual autobiography.* New York: Signet.

Money, J., & Ehrhardt, A. (1972). *Man and woman, boy and girl.* Baltimore: Johns Hopkins University Press.

Money, J., & Tucker, P. (1975). *Sexual signatures: On being a man or a woman.* Boston: Little, Brown.

Morris, J. (1974). *Conundrum.* New York: Henry Holt.

New York Times, The. (Selected articles.) July 24, 1976-August 18, 1977.

Raymond, J. (1979). *The transsexual empire.* Boston: Beacon Press.

Richards, R., with Ames, J. (1983). *Second serve.* New York: Stein & Day.

Richards v. United States Tennis Association, 400 N.Y.S. 2nd 267 (1977).

Scott, J.W. (1988). Deconstructing equality-versus-difference: Or, the use of post-structuralist theory for feminism. *Feminist Studies, 14,* 33-50.

Seligson, M. (1977, Feb.). The packaging of Renee Richards. *Ms.,* pp. 74-76, 85.

Steinem, G. (1977, Feb.). If the shoe doesn't fit, change the foot. *Ms.,* pp. 76, 85, 86.

Stoller, R. (1975). *Sex and gender, Vol. 2: The transsexual experiment.* New York: Jason Aronson.

Terry, J. (1989). The body invaded: Medical surveillance of women as reproducers. *Socialist Review*, **19**, 13-45.

Washington Post, The. (Selected articles.) August 12, 1976-January 1, 1978.

Williams, W.L. (1986). *The spirit and the flesh: Sexual diversity of American
Indian culture.* Boston: Beacon.

Williams, W.L. (1987). Women, men, and others. *American Behavioral Scientist*,
31, 135-141.

Willis, P. (1982). Women in sport in ideology. In J. Hargreaves (Ed.), *Sport,
culture and ideology* (pp. 117-135). London: Routledge & Kegan Paul.

Winston-Salem Journal. (Selected articles.) August 5, 1977-February 14, 1978.

NOTES

1. A major purpose of this paper is to problematize one fiction of science, the discourse of transsexualism, including the assumptions about the ontological status of sex and femininity, and to ask how sex reassignment or sex change is possible. We problematize some terms through the use of quotation marks at first mention. We use the phrase "constructed-female transsexual" because it reflects the constructedness of sex and gender.

2. The pronoun used to describe Richards is a significant political move. We have opted to refer to Renee Richards as s/he to denote Richards' bisexed lived experience and his/her difference from those who have lived only one sexual identity. Had we countered the mainstream positioning of Richards as female by repositioning him as male, the choice of a singular pronoun would deny either Richards' past or present positioning.

3. This is true as well of the autobiographies of transsexuals (e.g., Jorgensen, 1967; Martino, 1977; Morris, 1974; Richards, 1983) which struggle to comprehend their own personal etiology, which dwell on the personal anguish of gender dysphoria, and which end on a note of personal triumph.

4. According to de Lauretis (1987), the concept of technologies of gender "takes . . . its conceptual premise from Foucault's theory of sexuality as a 'technology of sex' and proposes that gender, too, both as a representation and self-representation, is the product of various social technologies, such as cinema, as well as by institutional discourses, epistemologies, and critical practices; [meaning] not only academic criticism, but more broadly social and cultural practices" (p. ix).

5. According to Bullough (1975), strict religious sanctions and "a kind of mystic view of the inferiority of the female" made it almost impossible for men to assume the female role without harsh reprisals. Thus the majority of preoperative transsexuals, or transvestites, prior to the 19th century were women.

6. We persist in our two-sexes/two-gender paradigm despite the counter-examples in our own culture: tomboys, sissies, transvestites, female impersonators, drag queens, gay men, lesbians, gender blending women (Devor, 1987). These anomalies are repositioned within dominant discourse through a variety of cultural practices: labeling homosexuals as queers, refusing to take transvestites and drag queens seriously, waiting for tomboys to grow out of their inappropriate behavior, and completely misunderstanding the meaning of the Berdasch by imposing an ethnocentric model on them (Williams, 1987).

7. Raymond's book clearly illuminates the relationship between sex stereotypes and the medical empire's understanding and treatment of transsexuals. But although her argument is based on an understanding of the cultural constructedness of gender, she contradicts her explanation of the cultural construction of gender identity and transsexualism when she argues that female-transsexuals can never be real women because women's biology makes females unique.

8. While a number of criteria traditionally have been available to distinguish between the sexes—including chromosomes, anatomy or morphological structure, genital or gonadal evidence, endocrine or hormonal balances, and psychological factors (Money & Ehrhardt, 1972)—the law accepts genital anatomy as its means of "official sex designation" (Dunlap, 1979, p. 1132).

9. Our analysis is of three metropolitan newspapers of national reputation: *The New York Times*, *The Washington Post*, and the *Los Angeles Times*. We analyzed all news stories, editorials, photographs, and cartoons featuring Renee Richards that appeared between July 24, 1976, the first news mention of Richards during the South Orange tournament, and August 12, 1982, when Richards returned to his/her medical practice. We also included articles in popular magazines such as *Sports Illustrated*, *Ms.*, *Time*, and *Newsweek*.

10. The legal system also accomplished gendering through language. In the very case which was to determine Richards' legal sex status, the court referred to Richards as "she" in the very first sentence: "A professional tennis player who had undergone sex reassignment surgery which allegedly changed her sex from male to female" (*Richards v. USTA*, 1977, p. 267).

11. Reactions of feminists outside of tennis were not covered by the news media. Writing in *Ms.* magazine, Gloria Steinem (1977) noted the deeper cultural meaning of transsexualism underlying the Richards story and she decried the diversionary effect that attention to Richards had on women's issues. Marcia Seligson (1977), by focusing upon the promotional efforts launched in Richards' behalf and the opportunism s/he displayed, expressed serious doubts about his/her sincerity and commitment.

12. The USTA's opposition to Richards represented male protectionism not of women's rights but of commercial profit. The economic rationality of the tour depends upon a clear division of competitors by sex because one tenet of profit maximization is to provide a product that clearly differentiates

itself from the competition. Richards had to be challenged because s/he problematized the division of sport into two separate markets.

13. Richards' *dominance* of the tour is not the point. None of the top players ever lost to Richards but many of the less experienced players did. Allowing Richards to play in the U.S. Open in 1977 did not displace King or Evert but some lower ranked professional woman player whose interests were equally worthy of protection. The USTA's action makes it clear that it was not the rank and file players they sought to protect but the top stars, and thus the economic vitality of the tour.

ACKNOWLEDGMENTS

An earlier version of this paper was presented at the 1987 meetings of the North American Society for the Sociology of Sport. The paper was substantially revised during a developmental leave provided by The University of Iowa and generously supported by the staff and colleagues at University House. The senior author gratefully acknowledges this collegial support. We would also like to thank Nancy Theberge, Linda Yanney, Nancy Romalov, and the reviewers for *SSJ* for bringing important sources to our attention and for useful critical feedback.

Index

Page numbers in italics refer to tables.

About the Editors

Susan Birrell   **Cheryl L. Cole**

Susan Birrell is a professor in the department of Sport, Health, Leisure and Physical Studies at the University of Iowa. She is also a former chairperson of the school's Women's Studies Program.

Birrell holds a PhD in human movement with a concentration in sociology of sport from the University of Massachusetts at Amherst. She is co-editor of the book *Sport in the Sociocultural Process* and a former editorial board member for the *Sociology of Sport Journal*. She is also a frequent and noted speaker who has given the keynote address at the 1990 North American Society for the Sociology of Sport conference and the 1992 Western Society of Women Physical Educators (WSWPE) conference.

In 1981, Dr. Birrell received the Fourth Annual Research on Women Award, presented by WSWPE. She is a member of the National Women's Studies Association and an executive board member of the North American Society for the Sociology of Sport.

Cheryl L. Cole is an assistant professor at the University of Illinois at Urbana-Champaign (UIUC). Before coming to UIUC, she was an assistant professor in the Department of Sociology at the University of Colorado at Colorado Springs, where she taught courses in feminist cultural studies, social theory, gender/sexuality/the body, and popular culture.

Cole holds an interdisciplinary PhD in the sociology of culture and women's studies from the University of Iowa and a PhD in sport studies from the University of Southern California. She was a keynote speaker at the 1992 conference for the Humanities and Technology Association; she was the recipient of a 1992 Regional Rockefeller Scholar Award from the University of Arizona; and she has received research grants from the University of Illinois Research Board and the University of Colorado's Committee on Research and Creative Writing. Dr. Cole is a member of the American Sociological Association, the North American Society for the Sociology of Sport, and the Society for Literature and Science.